BOAZ YAKIN & JOE INFURNARI

MARATHON

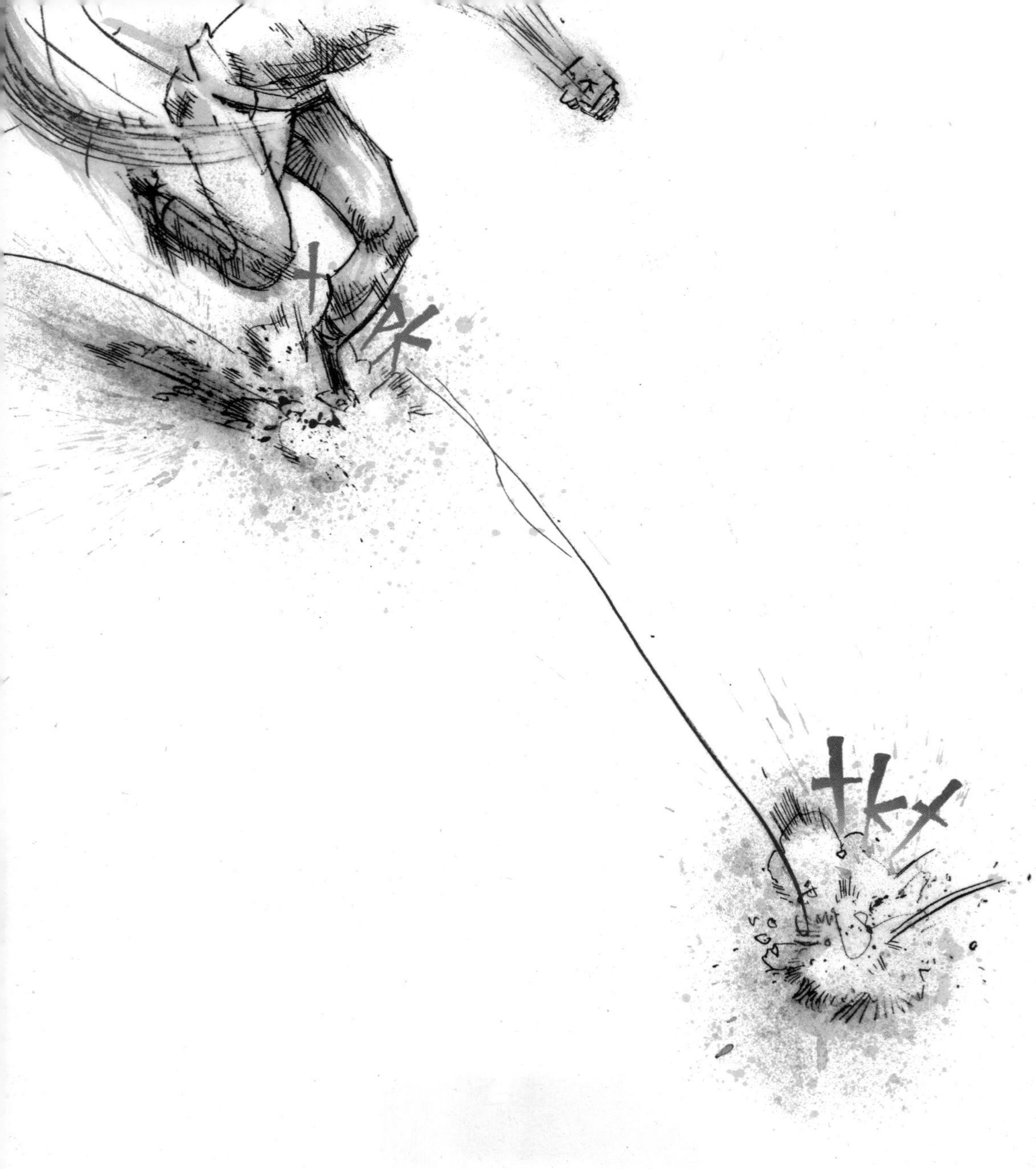
TPK
TKX

BOAZ YAKIN & JOE INFURNARI

MARATHON

:01
First Second
New York & London

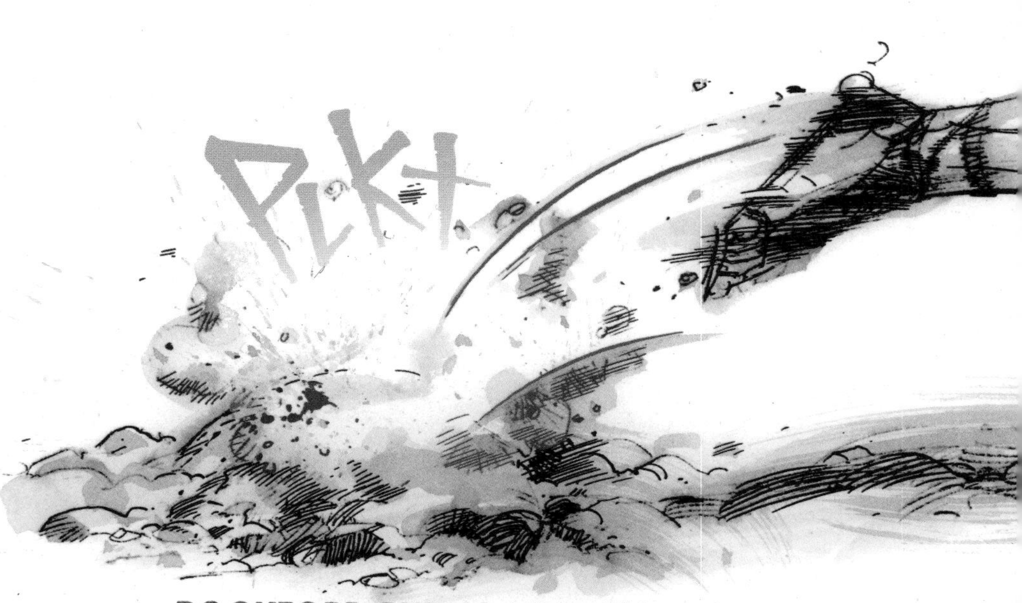
PLKT

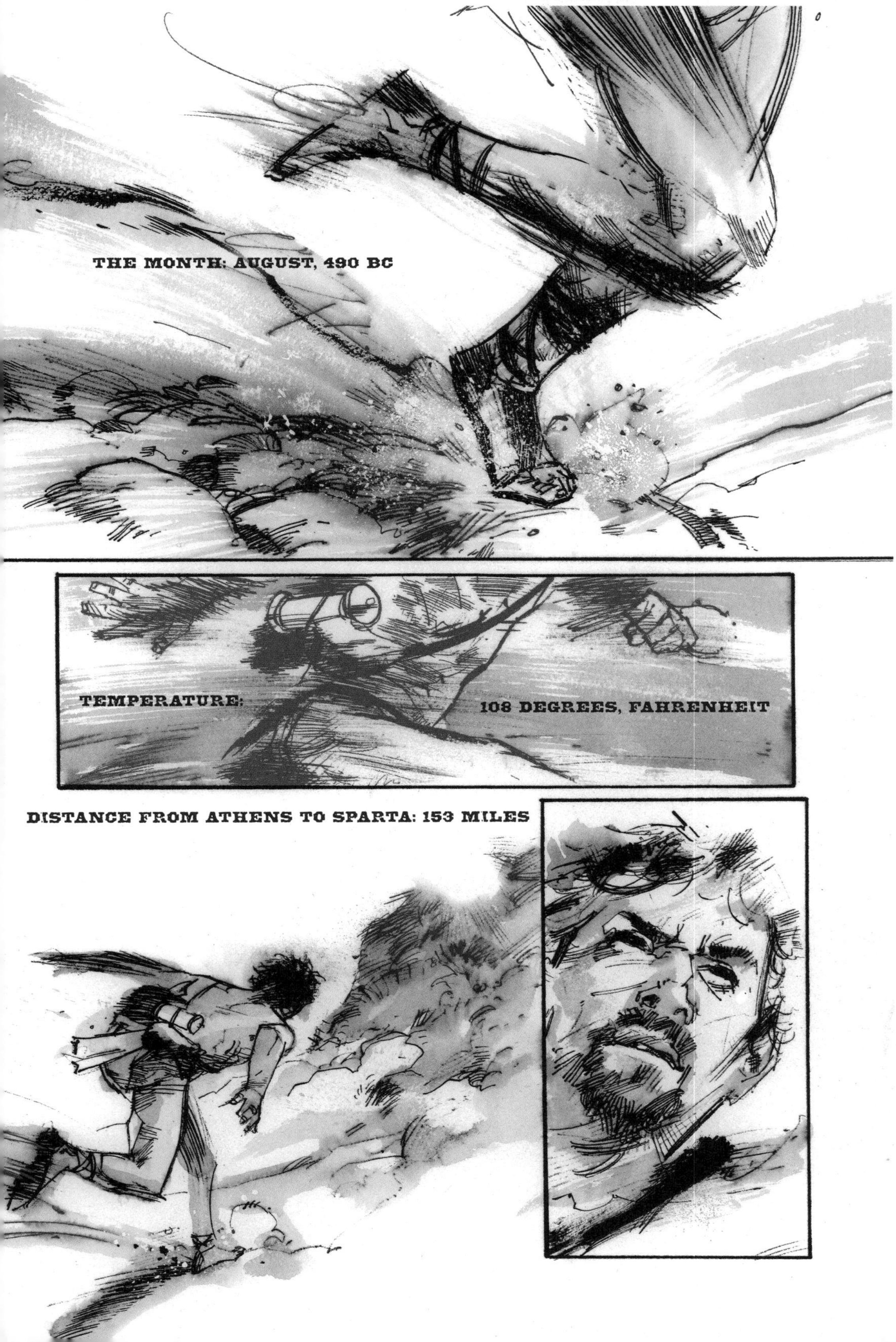
THE MONTH: AUGUST, 490 BC
TEMPERATURE:
108 DEGREES, FAHRENHEIT
DISTANCE FROM ATHENS TO SPARTA: 153 MILES

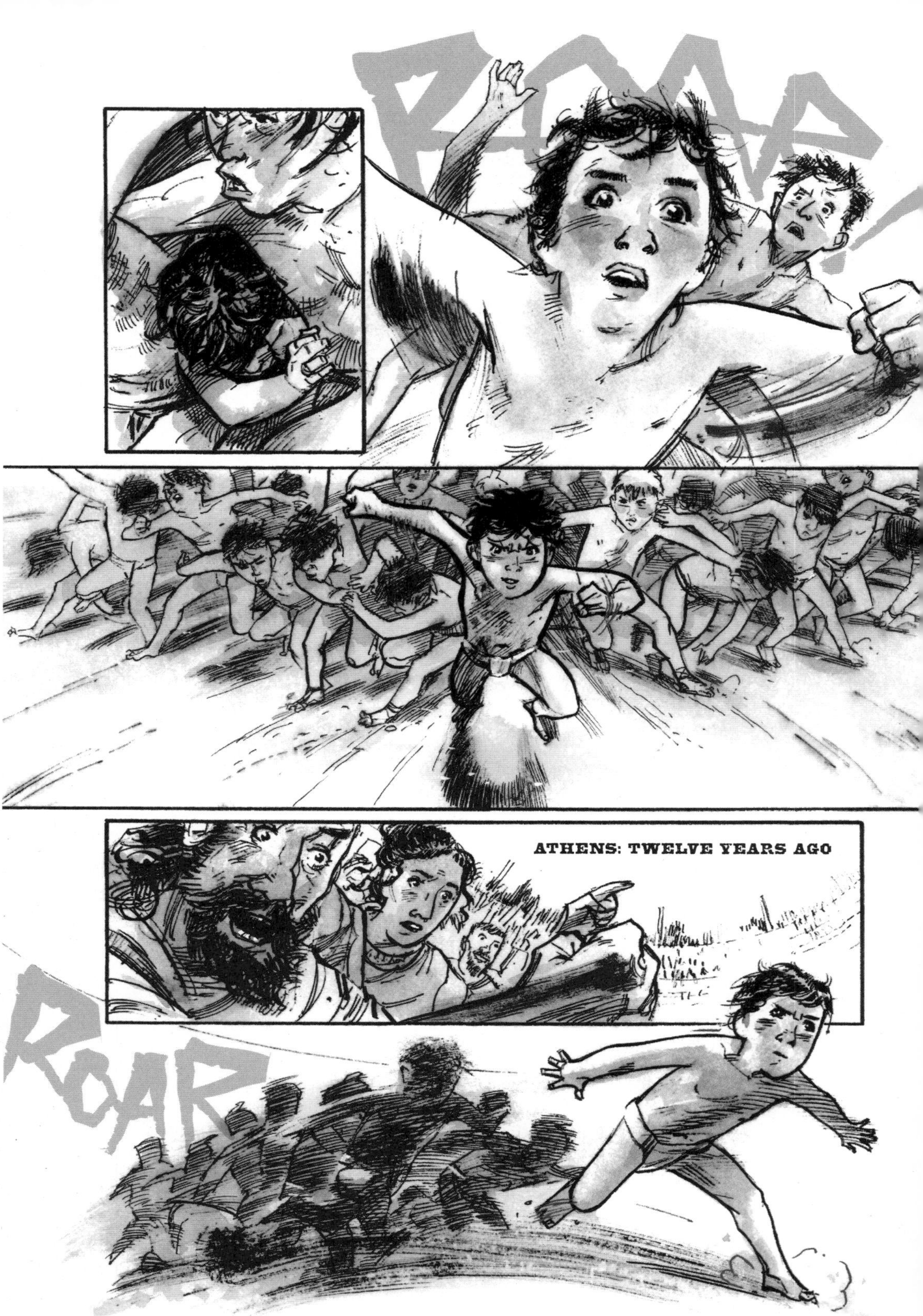
ATHENS: TWELVE YEARS AGO
ROAR

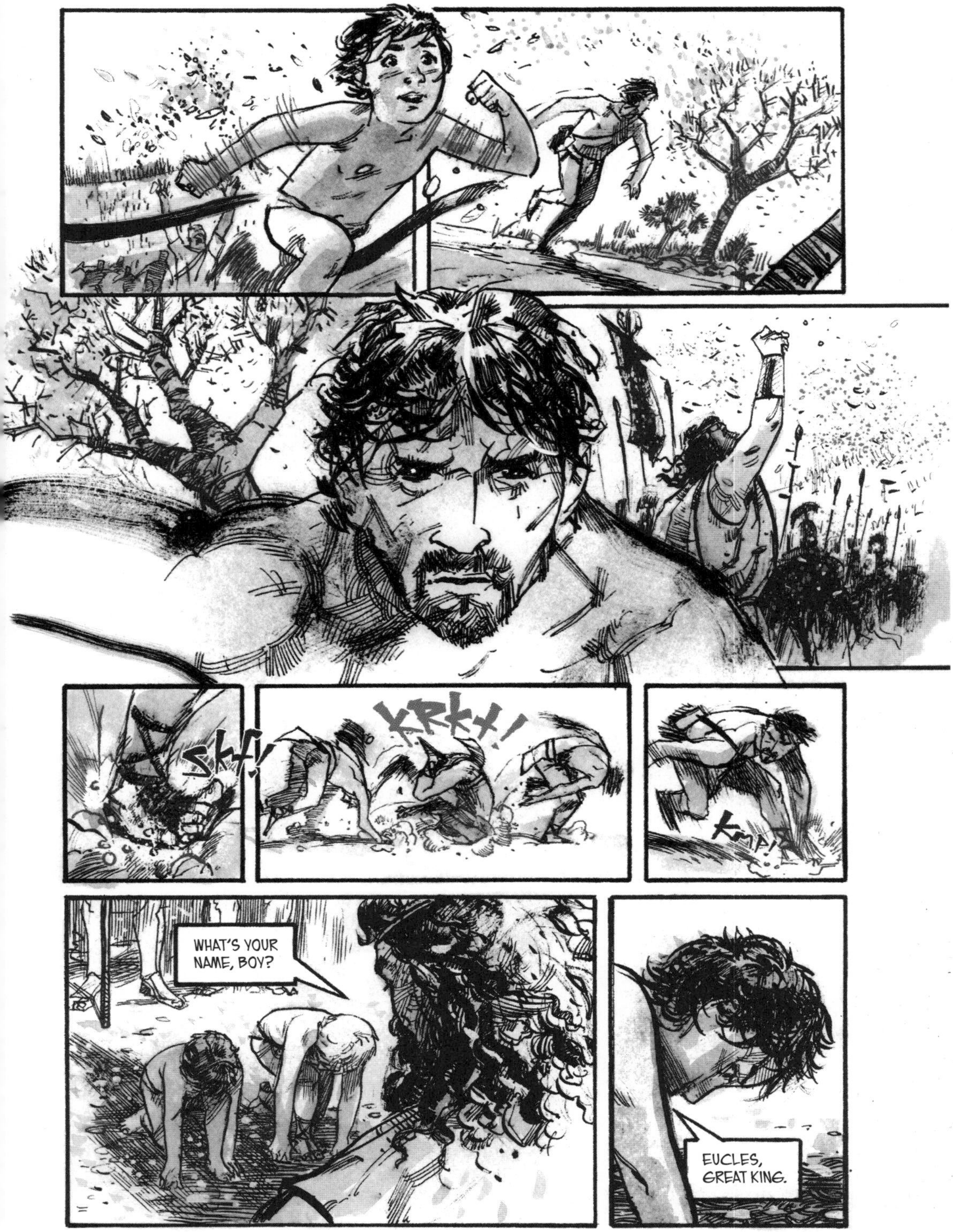
SKF!
KRKK!
KMP!
WHAT'S YOUR NAME, BOY?
EUCLES, GREAT KING.

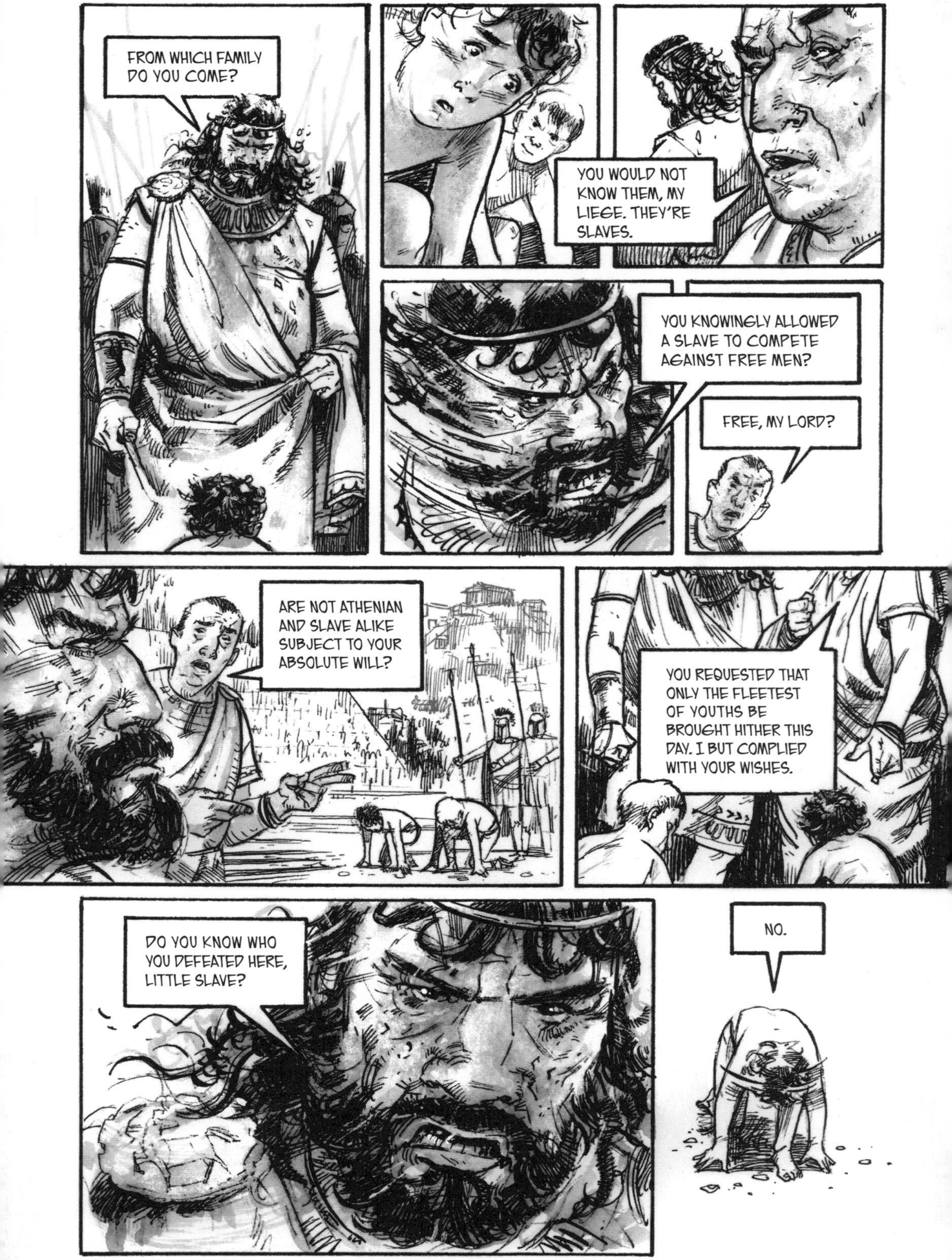
FROM WHICH FAMILY DO YOU COME?
YOU WOULD NOT KNOW THEM, MY LIEGE. THEY'RE SLAVES.
YOU KNOWINGLY ALLOWED A SLAVE TO COMPETE AGAINST FREE MEN?
FREE, MY LORD?
ARE NOT ATHENIAN AND SLAVE ALIKE SUBJECT TO YOUR ABSOLUTE WILL?
YOU REQUESTED THAT ONLY THE FLEETEST OF YOUTHS BE BROUGHT HITHER THIS DAY. I BUT COMPLIED WITH YOUR WISHES.
DO YOU KNOW WHO YOU DEFEATED HERE, LITTLE SLAVE?
NO.

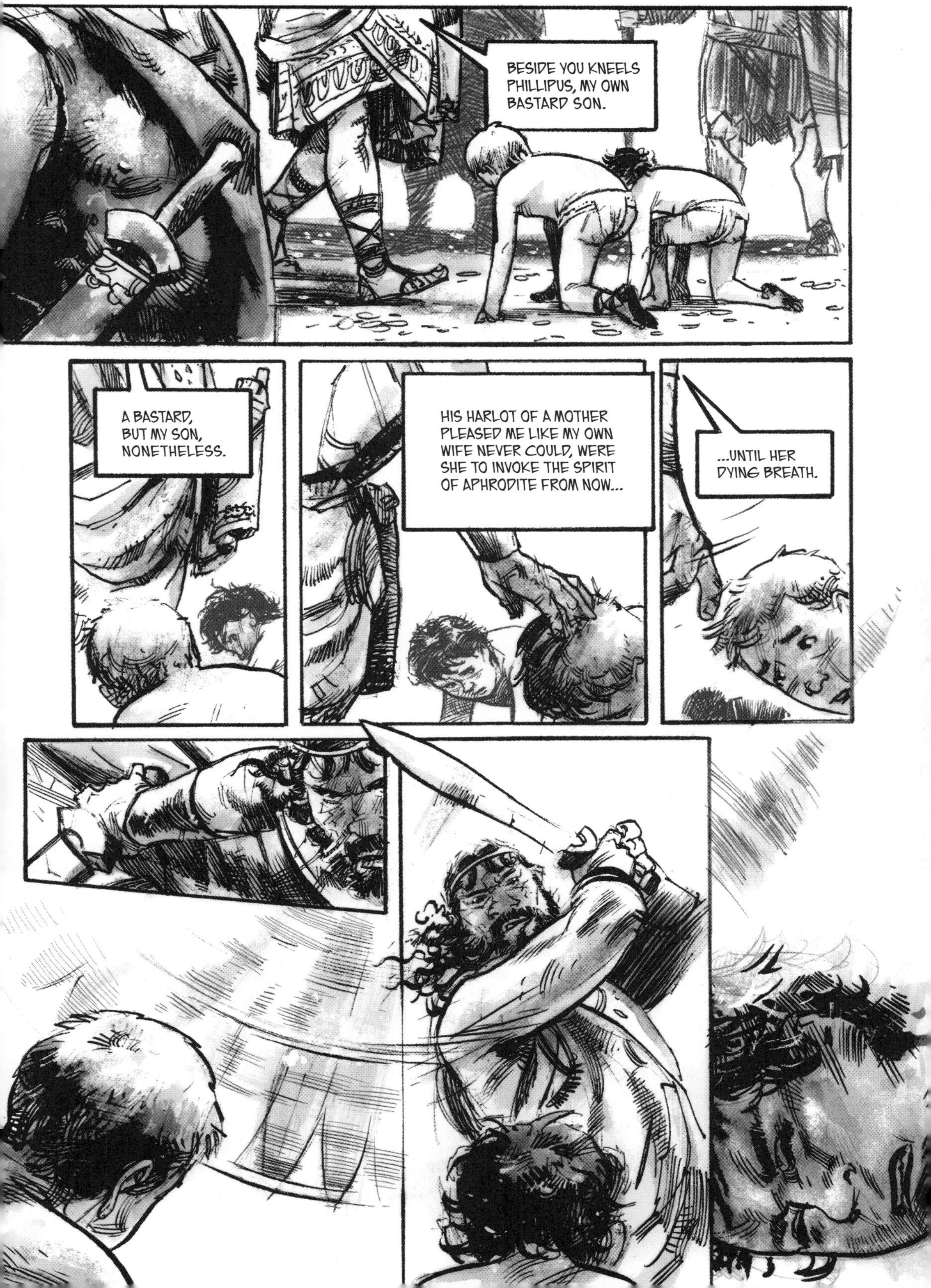
BESIDE YOU KNEELS PHILLIPUS, MY OWN BASTARD SON.
A BASTARD, BUT MY SON, NONETHELESS.
HIS HARLOT OF A MOTHER PLEASED ME LIKE MY OWN WIFE NEVER COULD, WERE SHE TO INVOKE THE SPIRIT OF APHRODITE FROM NOW...
...UNTIL HER DYING BREATH.

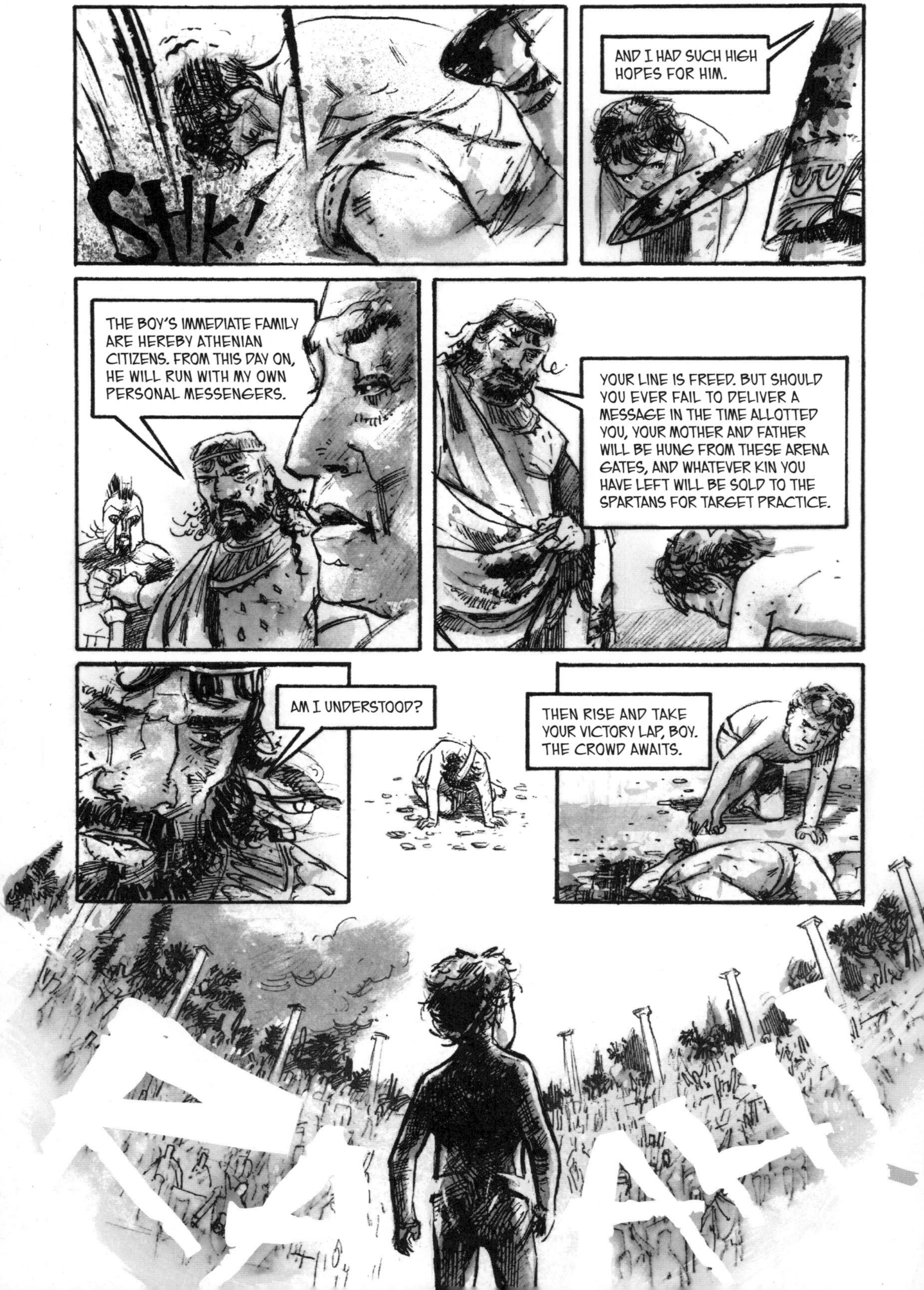
SHK!
AND I HAD SUCH HIGH HOPES FOR HIM.
THE BOY'S IMMEDIATE FAMILY ARE HEREBY ATHENIAN CITIZENS. FROM THIS DAY ON, HE WILL RUN WITH MY OWN PERSONAL MESSENGERS.
YOUR LINE IS FREED. BUT SHOULD YOU EVER FAIL TO DELIVER A MESSAGE IN THE TIME ALLOTTED YOU, YOUR MOTHER AND FATHER WILL BE HUNG FROM THESE ARENA GATES, AND WHATEVER KIN YOU HAVE LEFT WILL BE SOLD TO THE SPARTANS FOR TARGET PRACTICE.
AM I UNDERSTOOD?
THEN RISE AND TAKE YOUR VICTORY LAP, BOY. THE CROWD AWAITS.
AAAH!

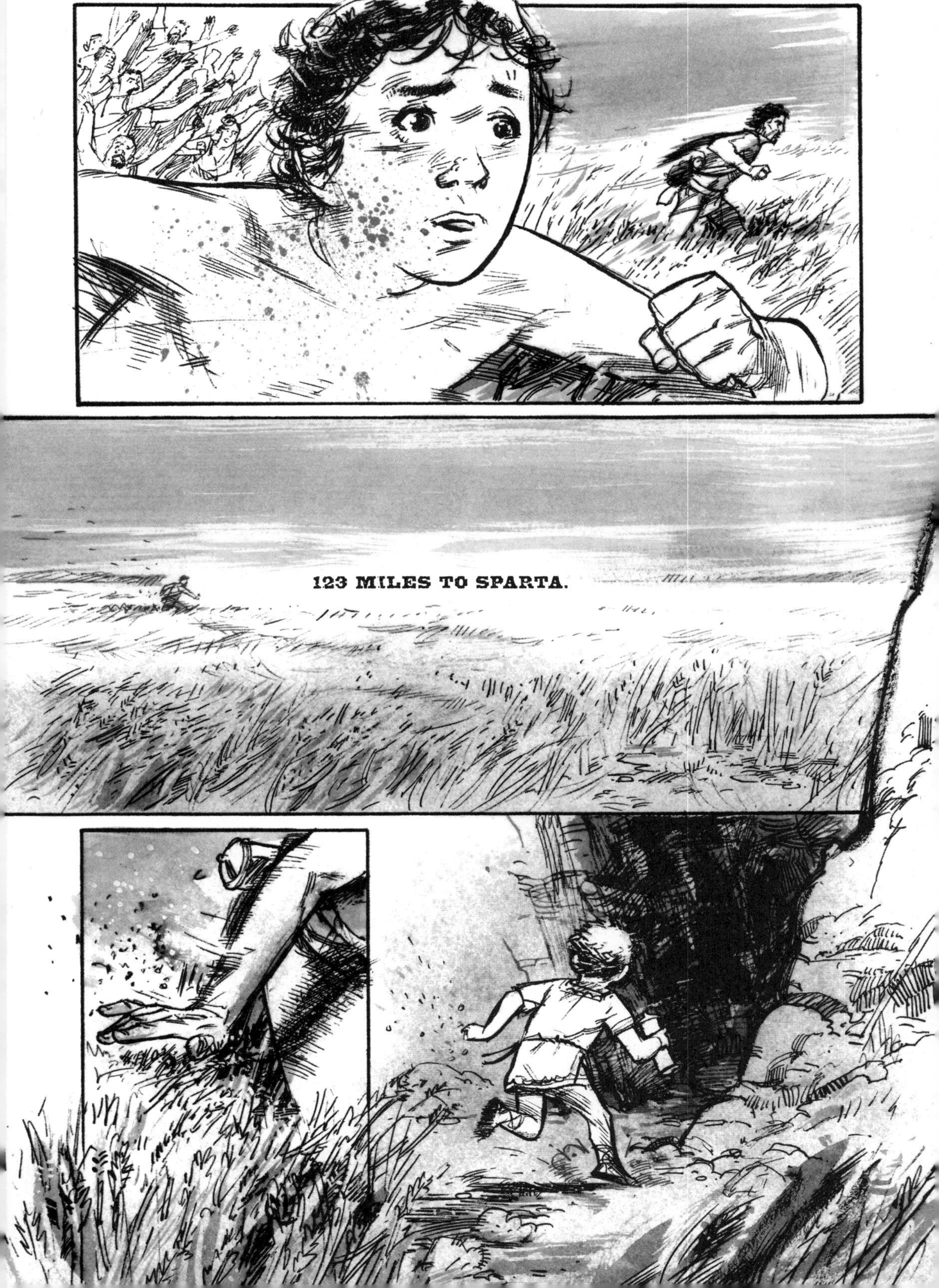
123 MILES TO SPARTA.

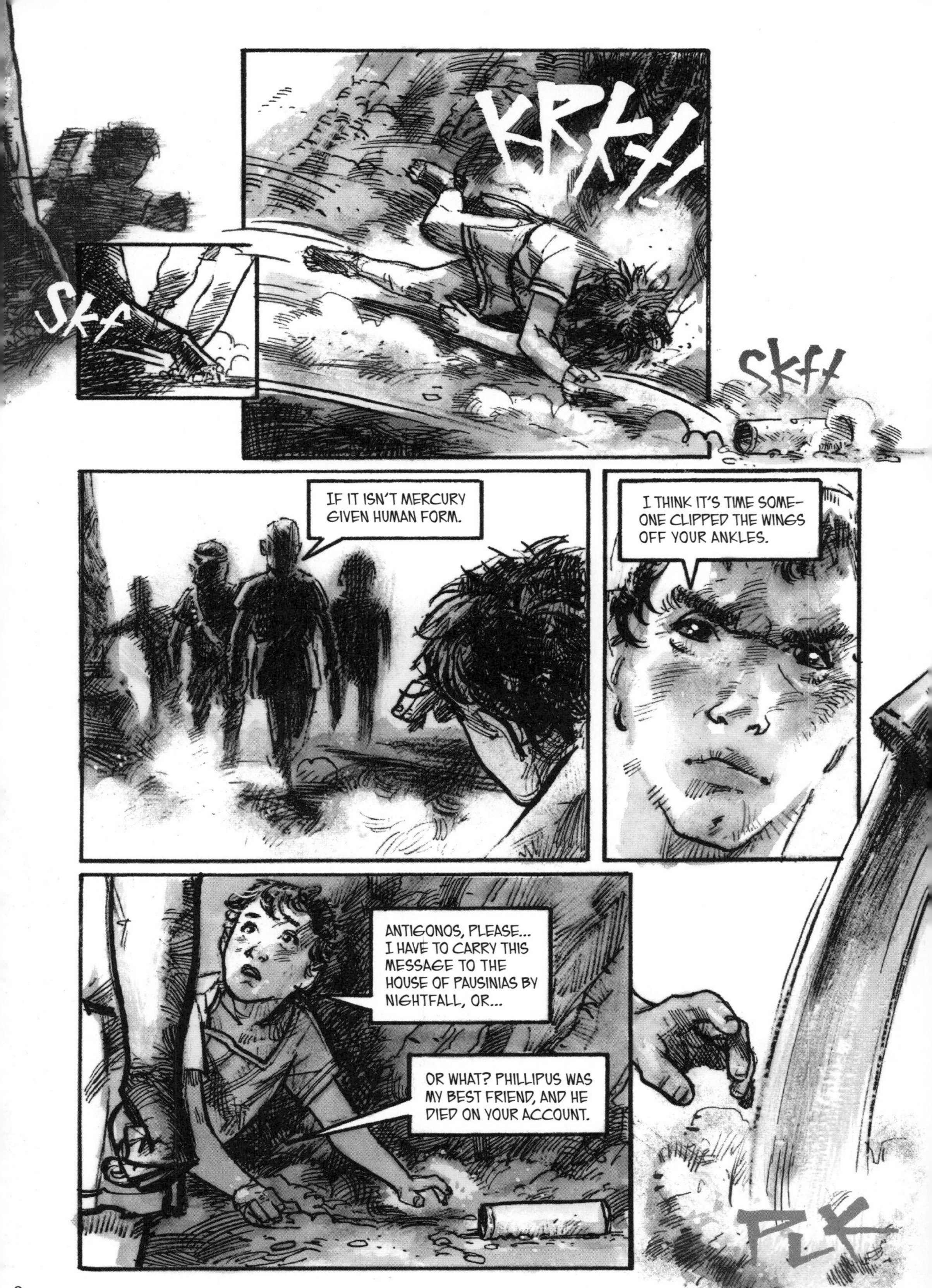
KRKH!
SKF
SKFT
IF IT ISN'T MERCURY GIVEN HUMAN FORM.
I THINK IT'S TIME SOME-ONE CLIPPED THE WINGS OFF YOUR ANKLES.
ANTIGONOS, PLEASE... I HAVE TO CARRY THIS MESSAGE TO THE HOUSE OF PAUSINIAS BY NIGHTFALL, OR...
OR WHAT? PHILLIPUS WAS MY BEST FRIEND, AND HE DIED ON YOUR ACCOUNT.
PLK

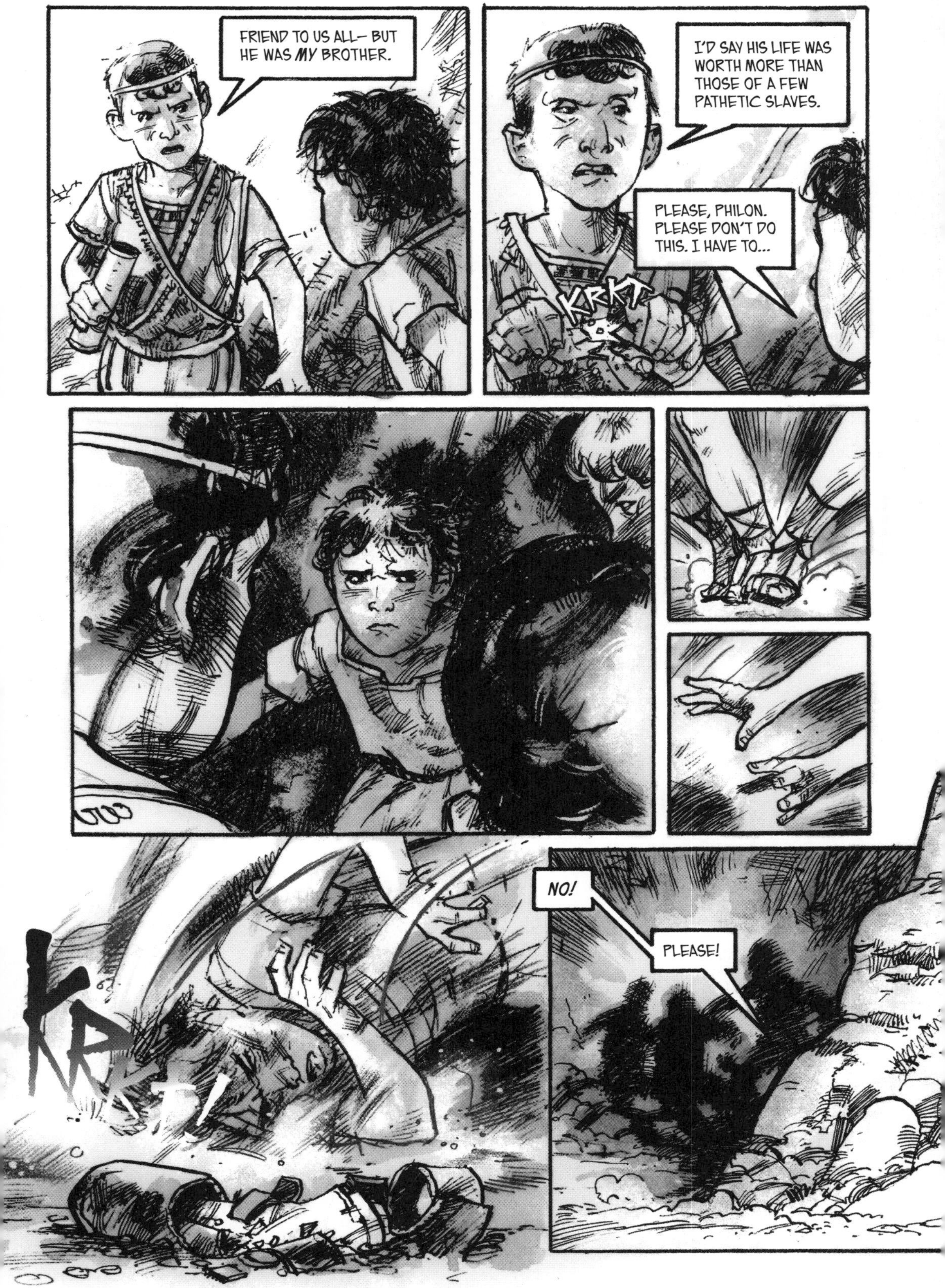
FRIEND TO US ALL— BUT HE WAS *MY* BROTHER.
I'D SAY HIS LIFE WAS WORTH MORE THAN THOSE OF A FEW PATHETIC SLAVES.
PLEASE, PHILON. PLEASE DON'T DO THIS. I HAVE TO...
KRKT
NO!
PLEASE!
KRKT!

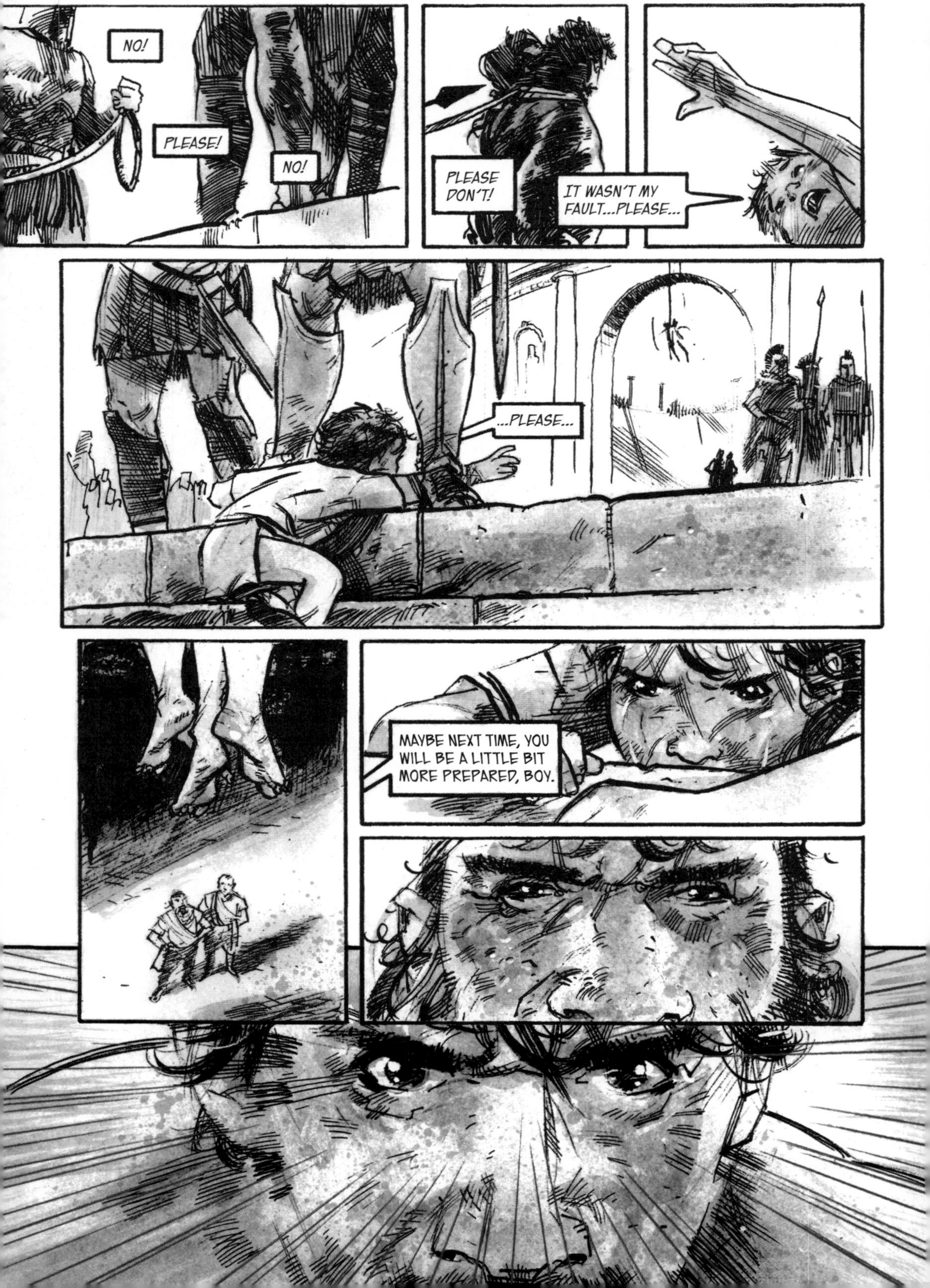
NO!
PLEASE!
NO!
PLEASE DON'T!
IT WASN'T MY FAULT...PLEASE...
...PLEASE...
MAYBE NEXT TIME, YOU WILL BE A LITTLE BIT MORE PREPARED, BOY.

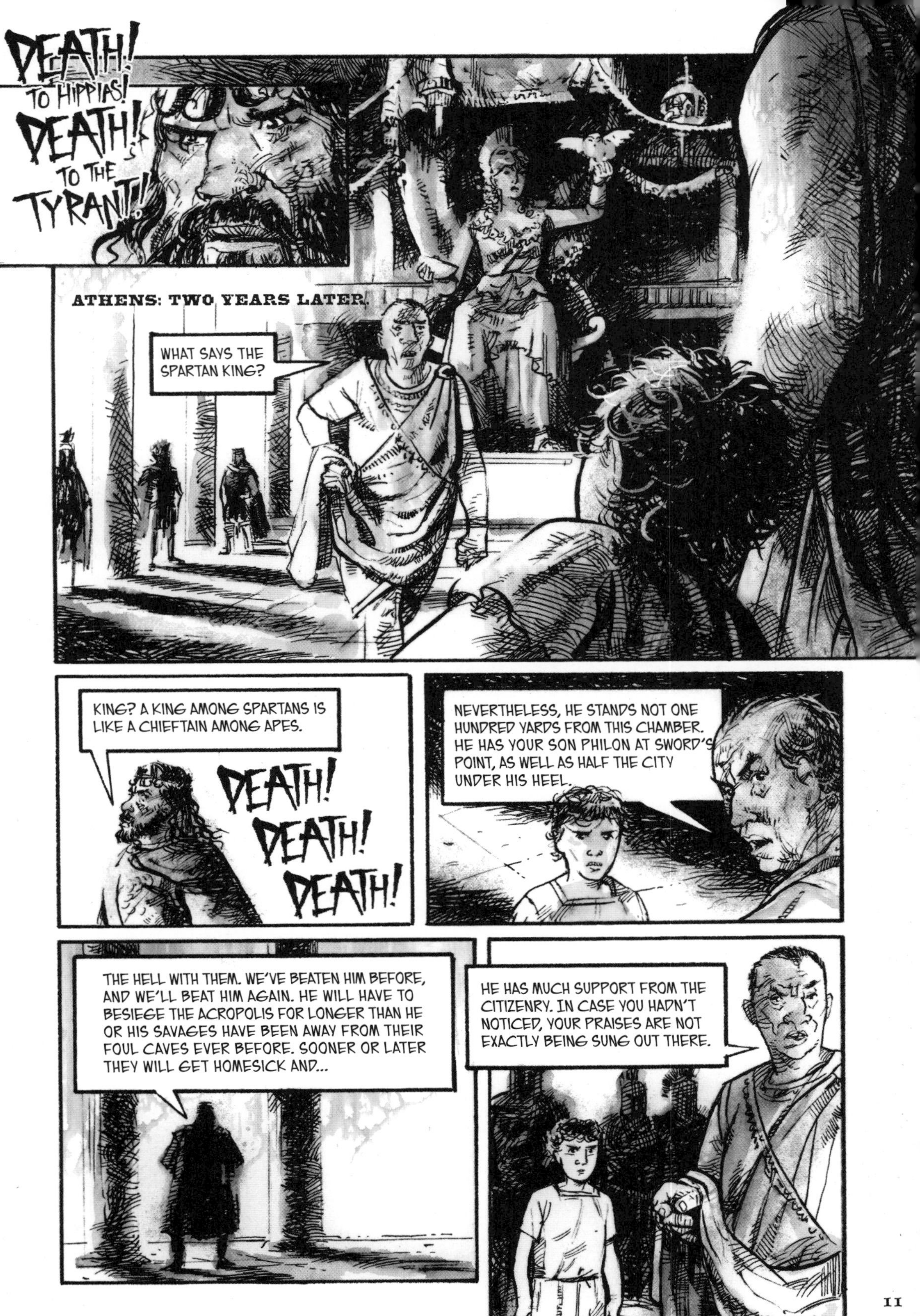
DEATH! TO HIPPIAS! DEATH! TO THE TYRANT!
ATHENS: TWO YEARS LATER.
WHAT SAYS THE SPARTAN KING?
KING? A KING AMONG SPARTANS IS LIKE A CHIEFTAIN AMONG APES.
DEATH! DEATH! DEATH!
NEVERTHELESS, HE STANDS NOT ONE HUNDRED YARDS FROM THIS CHAMBER. HE HAS YOUR SON PHILON AT SWORD'S POINT, AS WELL AS HALF THE CITY UNDER HIS HEEL.
THE HELL WITH THEM. WE'VE BEATEN HIM BEFORE, AND WE'LL BEAT HIM AGAIN. HE WILL HAVE TO BESIEGE THE ACROPOLIS FOR LONGER THAN HE OR HIS SAVAGES HAVE BEEN AWAY FROM THEIR FOUL CAVES EVER BEFORE. SOONER OR LATER THEY WILL GET HOMESICK AND...
HE HAS MUCH SUPPORT FROM THE CITIZENRY. IN CASE YOU HADN'T NOTICED, YOUR PRAISES ARE NOT EXACTLY BEING SUNG OUT THERE.

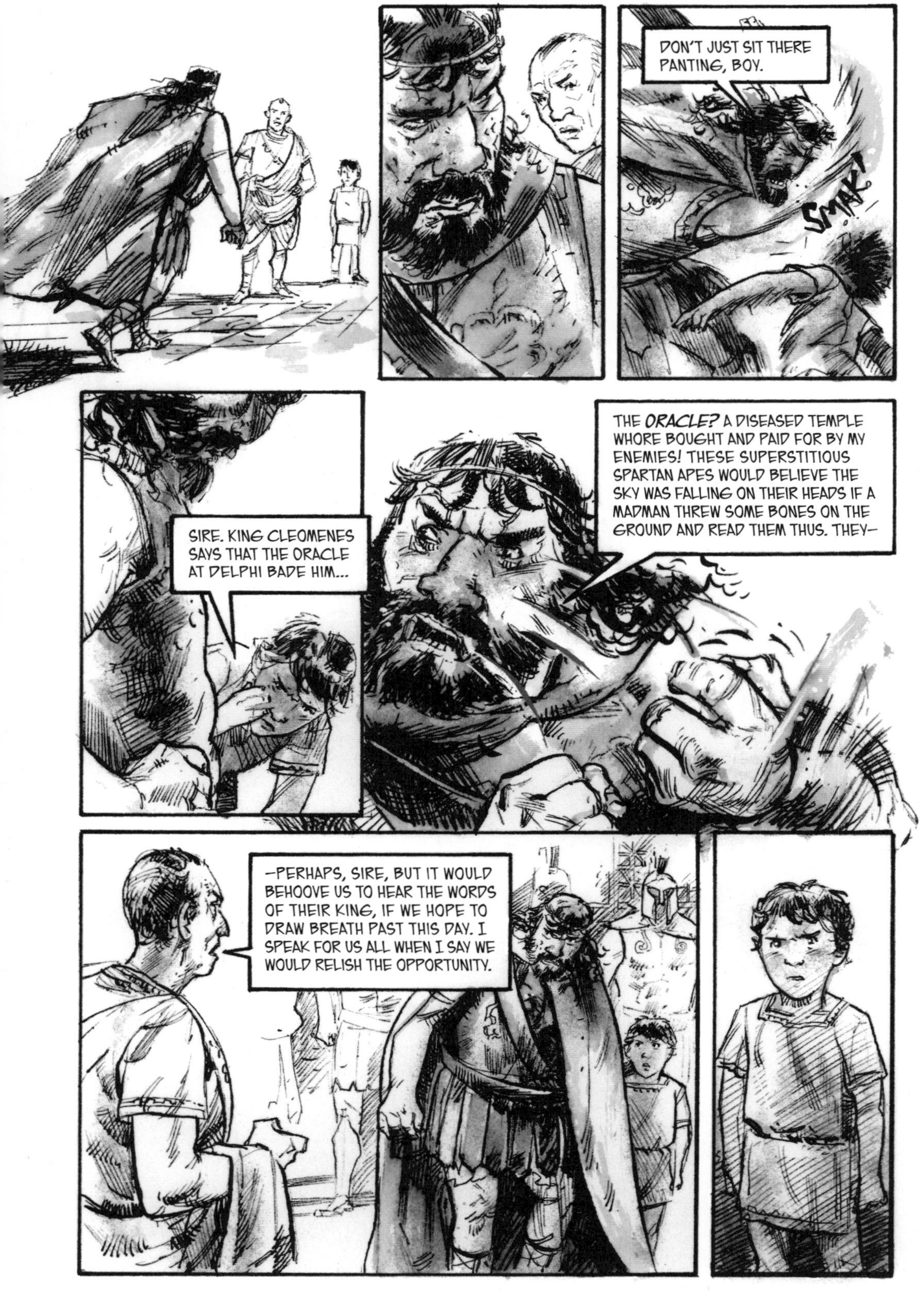
DON'T JUST SIT THERE PANTING, BOY.
SMAK!
SIRE. KING CLEOMENES SAYS THAT THE ORACLE AT DELPHI BADE HIM...
THE ORACLE? A DISEASED TEMPLE WHORE BOUGHT AND PAID FOR BY MY ENEMIES! THESE SUPERSTITIOUS SPARTAN APES WOULD BELIEVE THE SKY WAS FALLING ON THEIR HEADS IF A MADMAN THREW SOME BONES ON THE GROUND AND READ THEM THUS. THEY—
—PERHAPS, SIRE, BUT IT WOULD BEHOOVE US TO HEAR THE WORDS OF THEIR KING, IF WE HOPE TO DRAW BREATH PAST THIS DAY. I SPEAK FOR US ALL WHEN I SAY WE WOULD RELISH THE OPPORTUNITY.

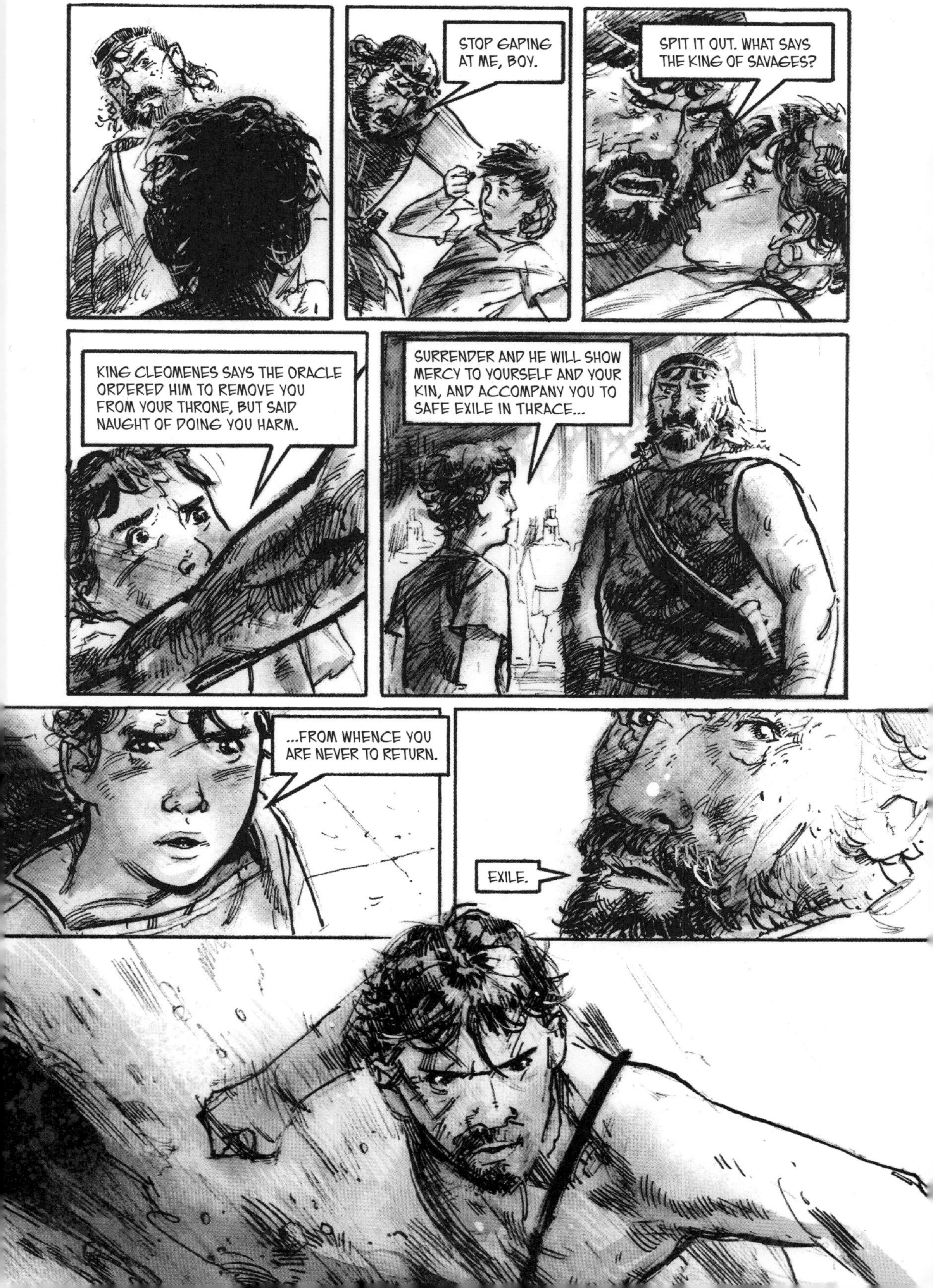
STOP GAPING AT ME, BOY.
SPIT IT OUT. WHAT SAYS THE KING OF SAVAGES?
KING CLEOMENES SAYS THE ORACLE ORDERED HIM TO REMOVE YOU FROM YOUR THRONE, BUT SAID NAUGHT OF DOING YOU HARM.
SURRENDER AND HE WILL SHOW MERCY TO YOURSELF AND YOUR KIN, AND ACCOMPANY YOU TO SAFE EXILE IN THRACE...
...FROM WHENCE YOU ARE NEVER TO RETURN.
EXILE.

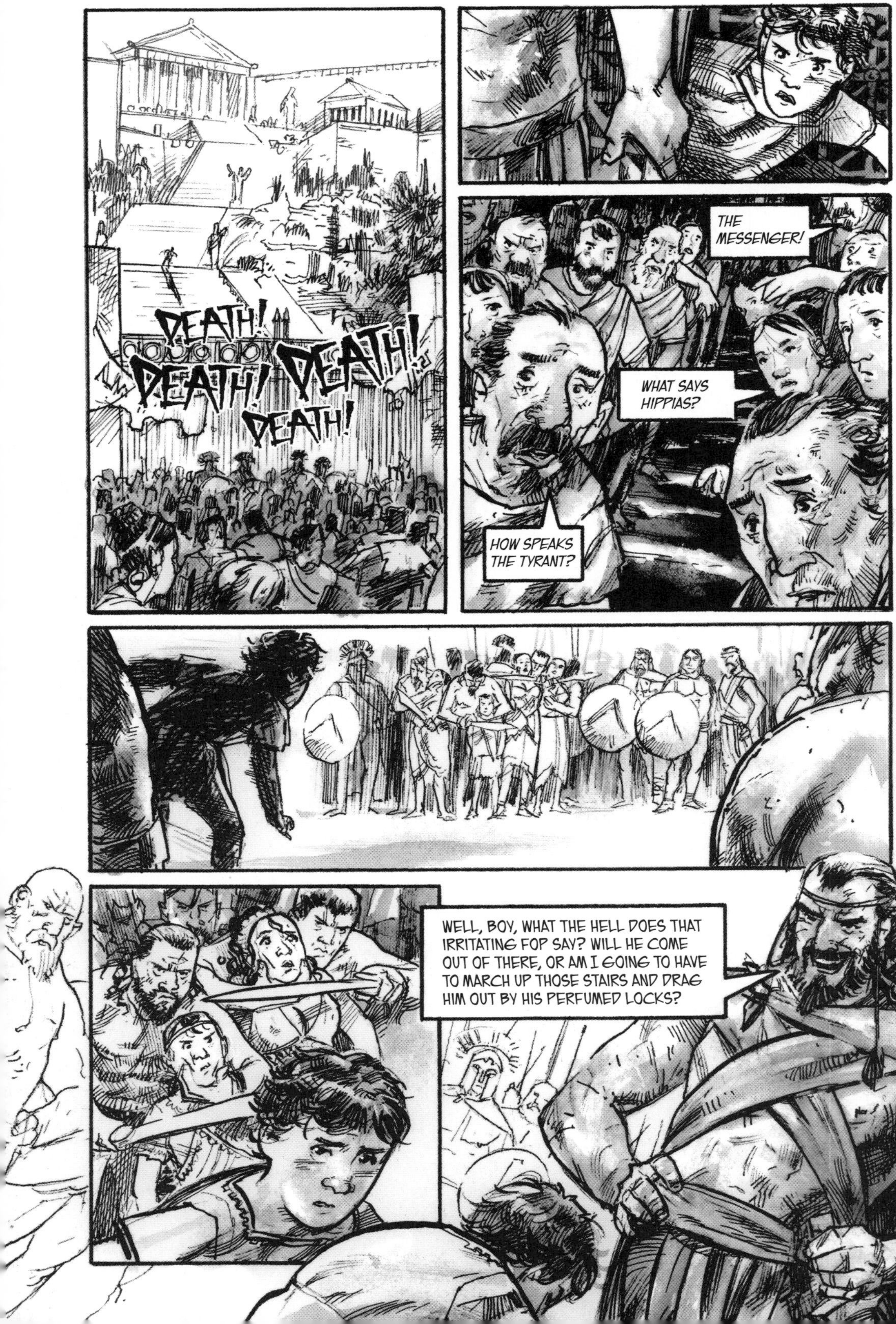
DEATH! DEATH! DEATH! DEATH!
THE MESSENGER!
WHAT SAYS HIPPIAS?
HOW SPEAKS THE TYRANT?
WELL, BOY, WHAT THE HELL DOES THAT IRRITATING FOP SAY? WILL HE COME OUT OF THERE, OR AM I GOING TO HAVE TO MARCH UP THOSE STAIRS AND DRAG HIM OUT BY HIS PERFUMED LOCKS?

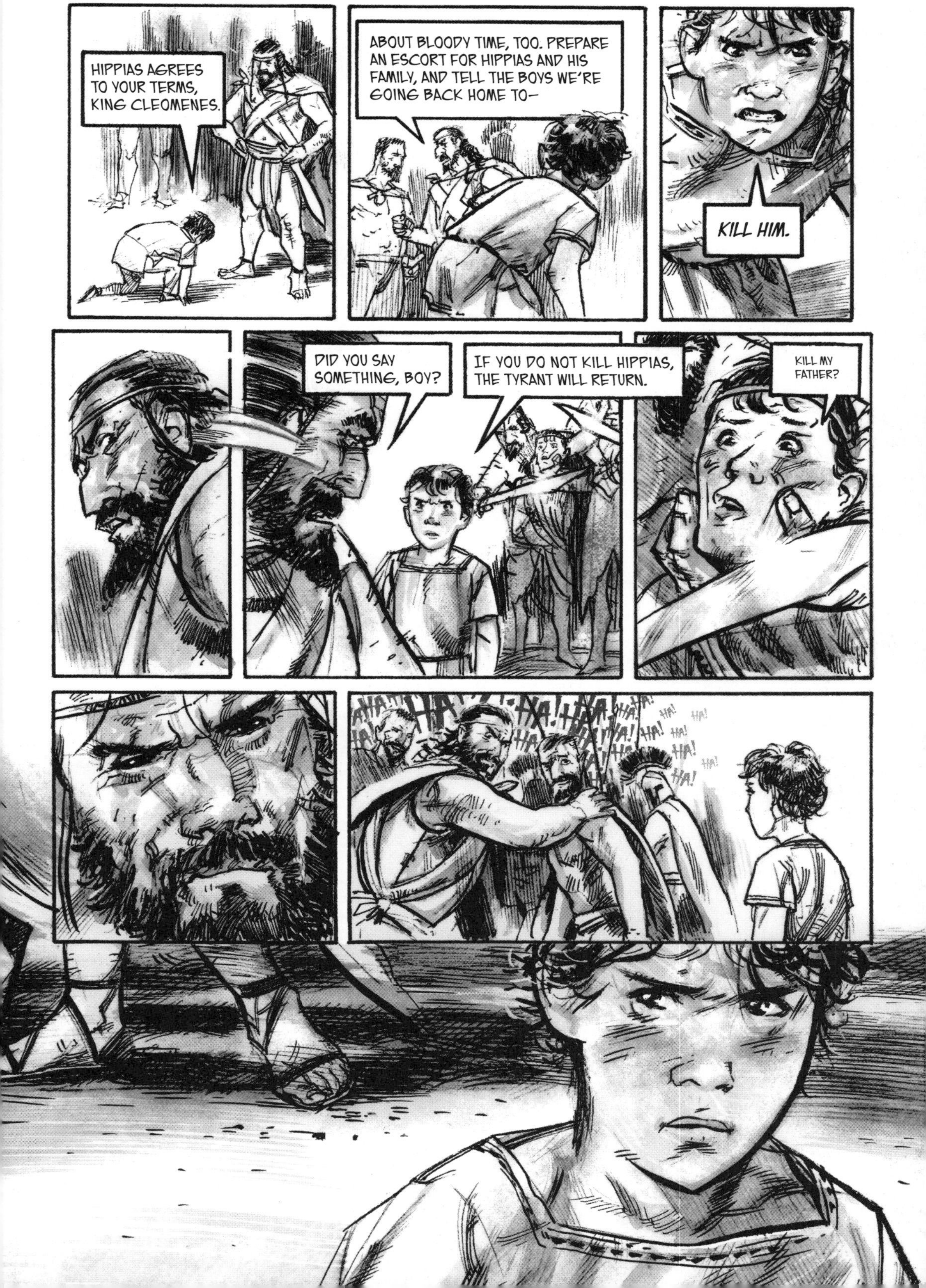
HIPPIAS AGREES TO YOUR TERMS, KING CLEOMENES.
ABOUT BLOODY TIME, TOO. PREPARE AN ESCORT FOR HIPPIAS AND HIS FAMILY, AND TELL THE BOYS WE'RE GOING BACK HOME TO–
KILL HIM.
DID YOU SAY SOMETHING, BOY?
IF YOU DO NOT KILL HIPPIAS, THE TYRANT WILL RETURN.
KILL MY FATHER?
HA! HA! HA! HA! HA! HA! HA! HA! HA!

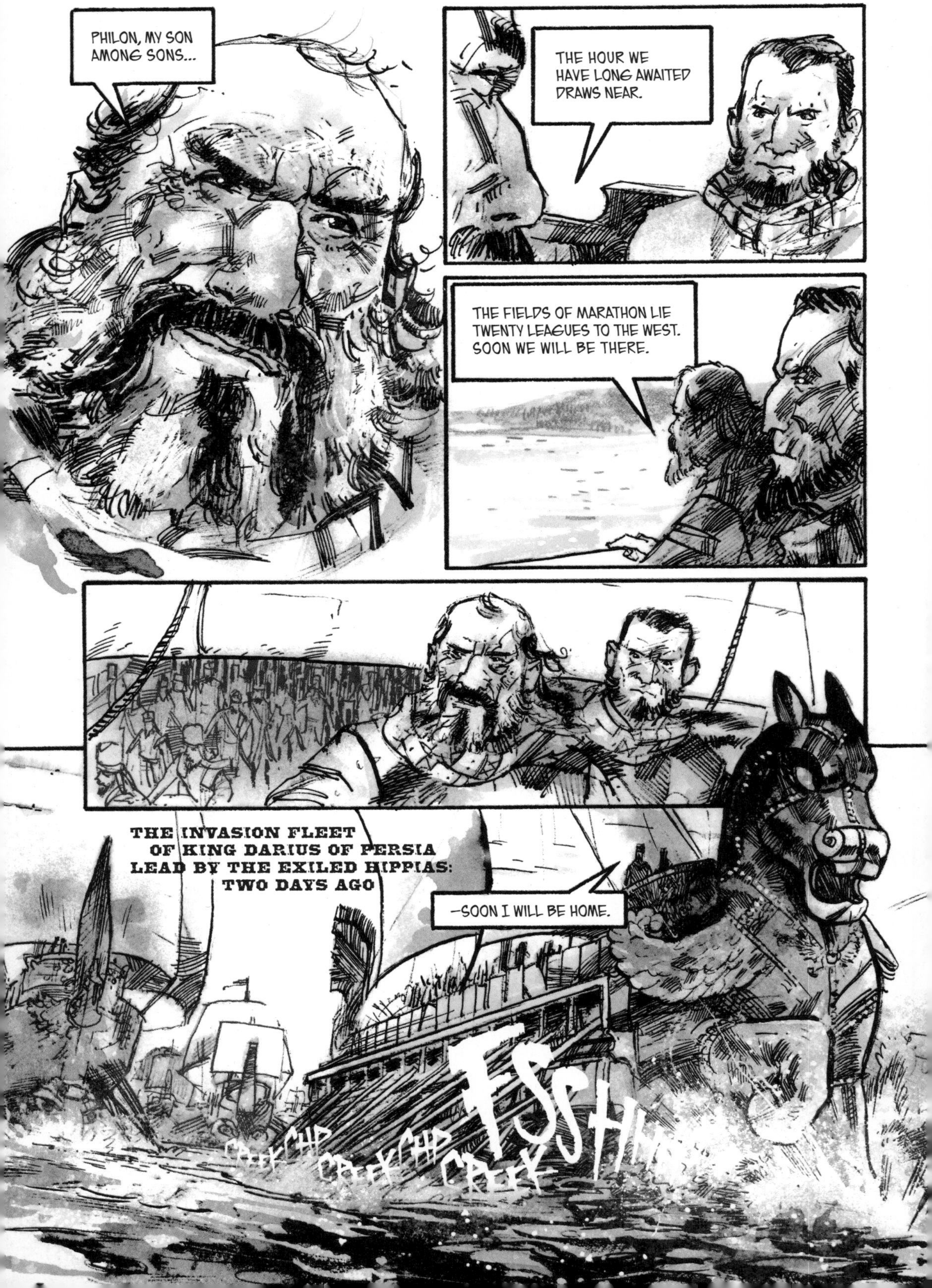
PHILON, MY SON AMONG SONS...
THE HOUR WE HAVE LONG AWAITED DRAWS NEAR.
THE FIELDS OF MARATHON LIE TWENTY LEAGUES TO THE WEST. SOON WE WILL BE THERE.
THE INVASION FLEET OF KING DARIUS OF PERSIA LEAD BY THE EXILED HIPPIAS: TWO DAYS AGO
—SOON I WILL BE HOME.
CREEK CHP CREEK CHP CREEK FSSHH

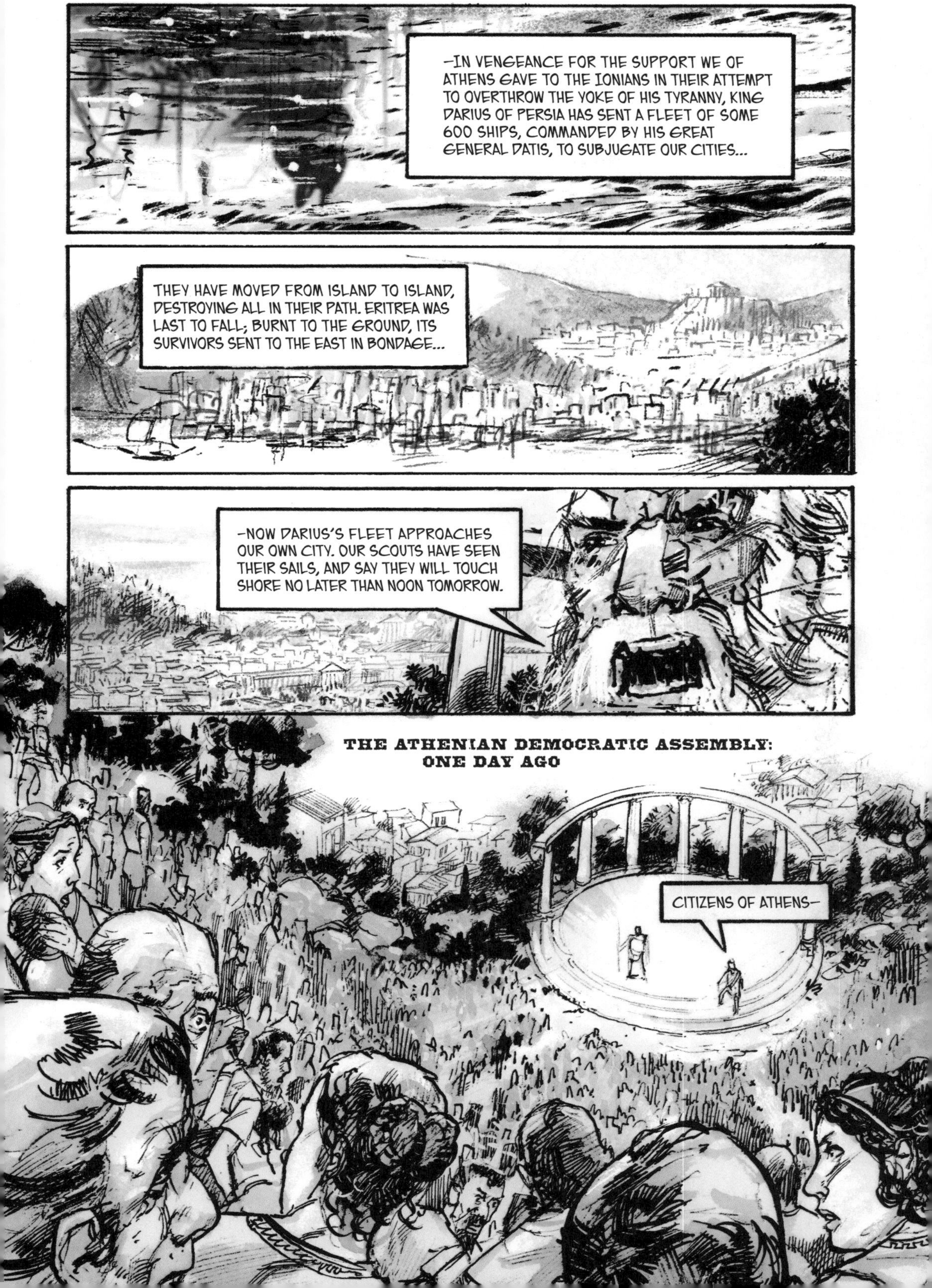
–IN VENGEANCE FOR THE SUPPORT WE OF ATHENS GAVE TO THE IONIANS IN THEIR ATTEMPT TO OVERTHROW THE YOKE OF HIS TYRANNY, KING DARIUS OF PERSIA HAS SENT A FLEET OF SOME 600 SHIPS, COMMANDED BY HIS GREAT GENERAL DATIS, TO SUBJUGATE OUR CITIES...
THEY HAVE MOVED FROM ISLAND TO ISLAND, DESTROYING ALL IN THEIR PATH. ERITREA WAS LAST TO FALL; BURNT TO THE GROUND, ITS SURVIVORS SENT TO THE EAST IN BONDAGE...
–NOW DARIUS'S FLEET APPROACHES OUR OWN CITY. OUR SCOUTS HAVE SEEN THEIR SAILS, AND SAY THEY WILL TOUCH SHORE NO LATER THAN NOON TOMORROW.
THE ATHENIAN DEMOCRATIC ASSEMBLY: ONE DAY AGO
CITIZENS OF ATHENS–

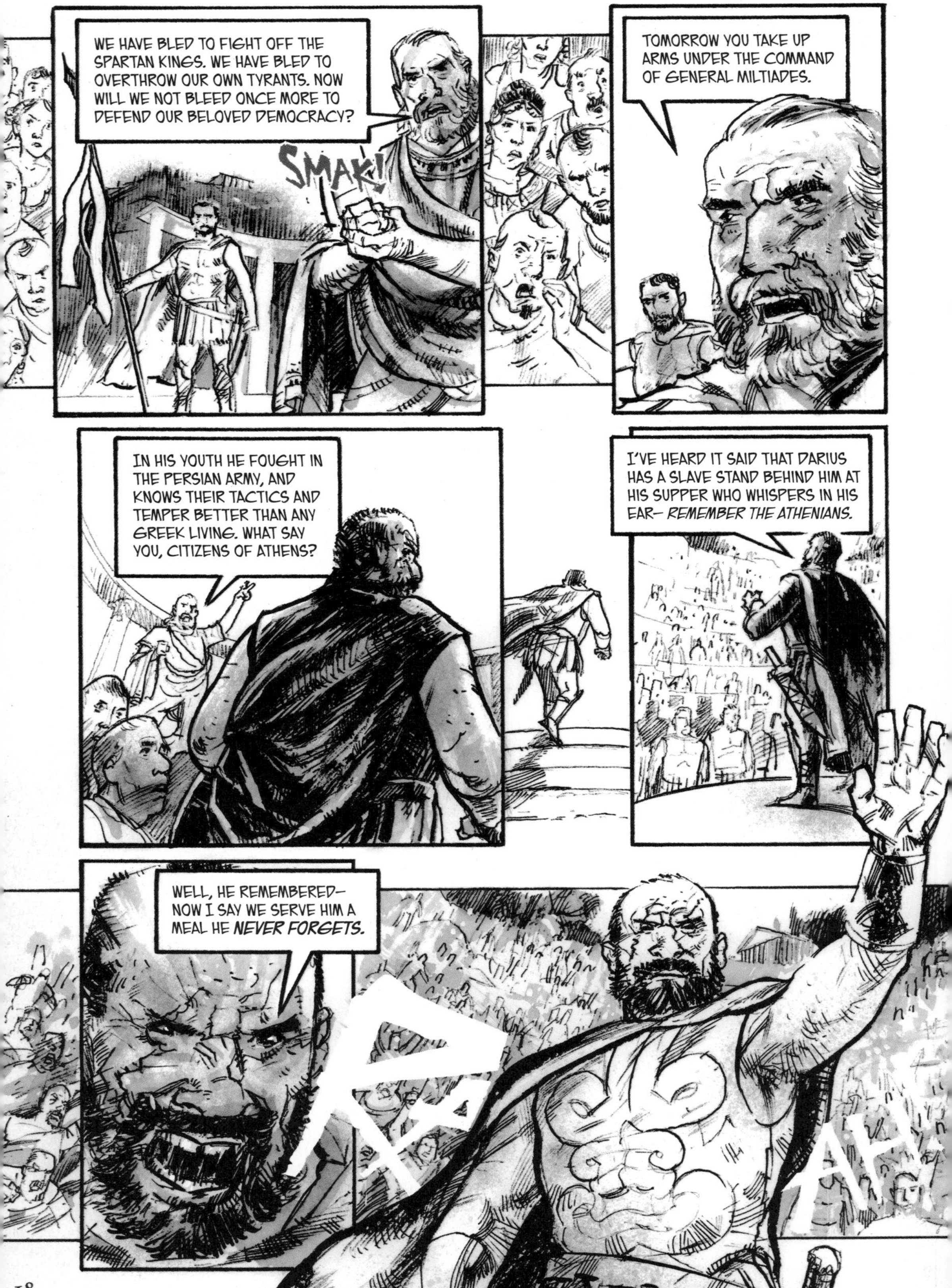
WE HAVE BLED TO FIGHT OFF THE SPARTAN KINGS. WE HAVE BLED TO OVERTHROW OUR OWN TYRANTS. NOW WILL WE NOT BLEED ONCE MORE TO DEFEND OUR BELOVED DEMOCRACY?
SMAK!
TOMORROW YOU TAKE UP ARMS UNDER THE COMMAND OF GENERAL MILTIADES.
IN HIS YOUTH HE FOUGHT IN THE PERSIAN ARMY, AND KNOWS THEIR TACTICS AND TEMPER BETTER THAN ANY GREEK LIVING. WHAT SAY YOU, CITIZENS OF ATHENS?
I'VE HEARD IT SAID THAT DARIUS HAS A SLAVE STAND BEHIND HIM AT HIS SUPPER WHO WHISPERS IN HIS EAR— *REMEMBER THE ATHENIANS.*
WELL, HE REMEMBERED— NOW I SAY WE SERVE HIM A MEAL HE *NEVER FORGETS.*
AH!

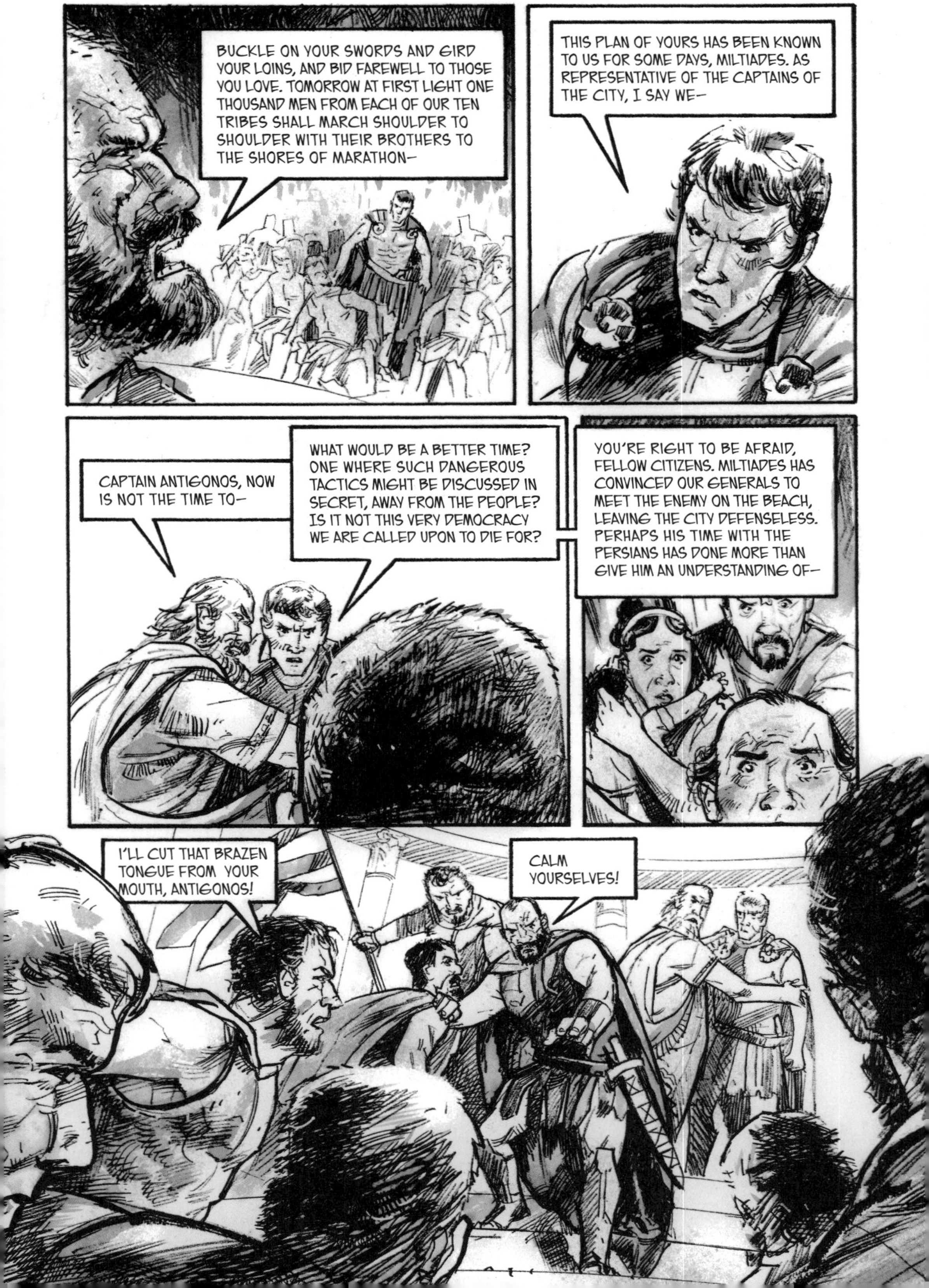
BUCKLE ON YOUR SWORDS AND GIRD YOUR LOINS, AND BID FAREWELL TO THOSE YOU LOVE. TOMORROW AT FIRST LIGHT ONE THOUSAND MEN FROM EACH OF OUR TEN TRIBES SHALL MARCH SHOULDER TO SHOULDER WITH THEIR BROTHERS TO THE SHORES OF MARATHON–
THIS PLAN OF YOURS HAS BEEN KNOWN TO US FOR SOME DAYS, MILTIADES. AS REPRESENTATIVE OF THE CAPTAINS OF THE CITY, I SAY WE–
CAPTAIN ANTIGONOS, NOW IS NOT THE TIME TO–
WHAT WOULD BE A BETTER TIME? ONE WHERE SUCH DANGEROUS TACTICS MIGHT BE DISCUSSED IN SECRET, AWAY FROM THE PEOPLE? IS IT NOT THIS VERY DEMOCRACY WE ARE CALLED UPON TO DIE FOR?
YOU'RE RIGHT TO BE AFRAID, FELLOW CITIZENS. MILTIADES HAS CONVINCED OUR GENERALS TO MEET THE ENEMY ON THE BEACH, LEAVING THE CITY DEFENSELESS. PERHAPS HIS TIME WITH THE PERSIANS HAS DONE MORE THAN GIVE HIM AN UNDERSTANDING OF–
I'LL CUT THAT BRAZEN TONGUE FROM YOUR MOUTH, ANTIGONOS!
CALM YOURSELVES!

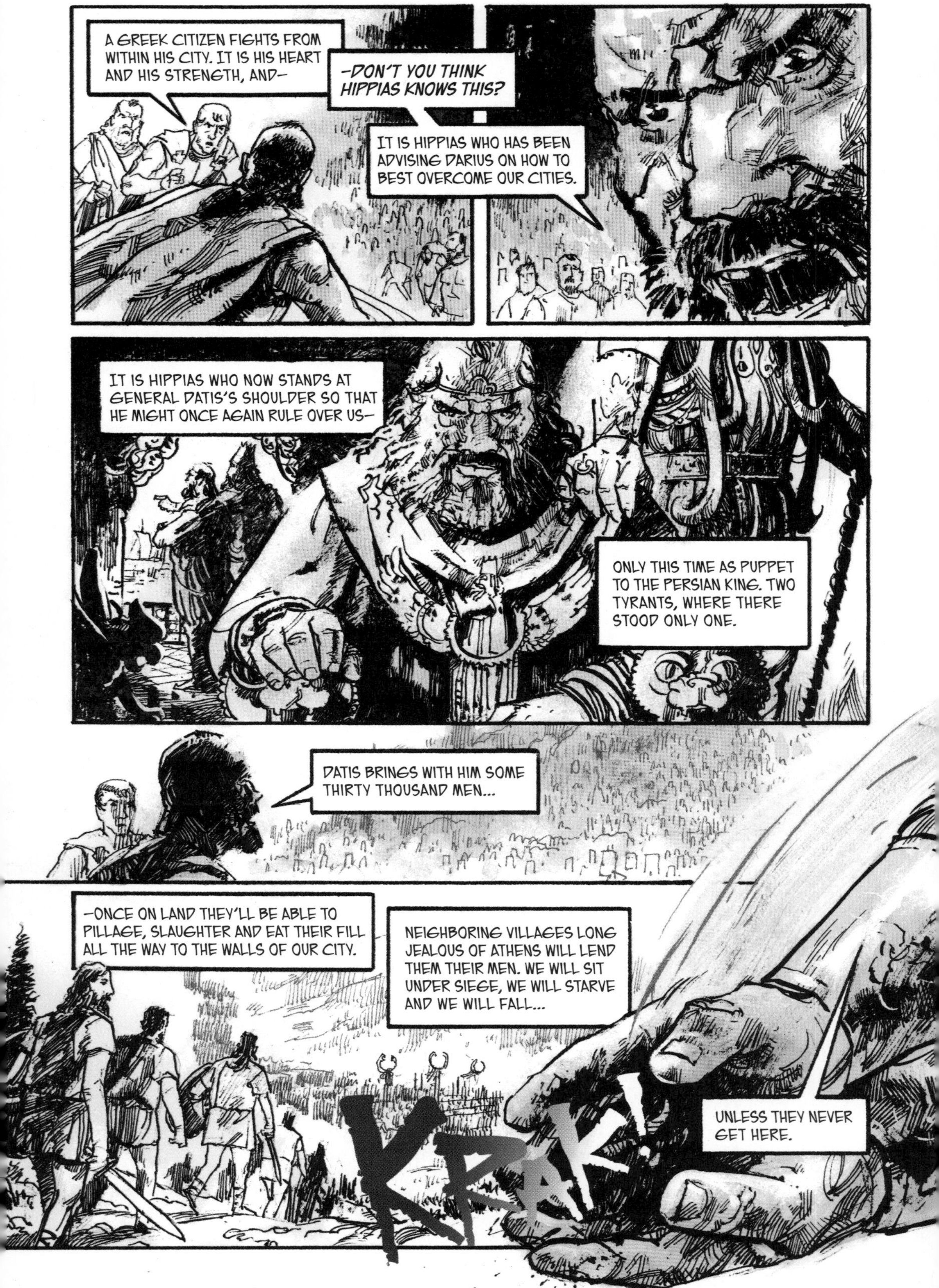
A GREEK CITIZEN FIGHTS FROM WITHIN HIS CITY. IT IS HIS HEART AND HIS STRENGTH, AND–
–DON'T YOU THINK HIPPIAS KNOWS THIS?
IT IS HIPPIAS WHO HAS BEEN ADVISING DARIUS ON HOW TO BEST OVERCOME OUR CITIES.
IT IS HIPPIAS WHO NOW STANDS AT GENERAL DATIS'S SHOULDER SO THAT HE MIGHT ONCE AGAIN RULE OVER US–
ONLY THIS TIME AS PUPPET TO THE PERSIAN KING. TWO TYRANTS, WHERE THERE STOOD ONLY ONE.
DATIS BRINGS WITH HIM SOME THIRTY THOUSAND MEN...
–ONCE ON LAND THEY'LL BE ABLE TO PILLAGE, SLAUGHTER AND EAT THEIR FILL ALL THE WAY TO THE WALLS OF OUR CITY.
NEIGHBORING VILLAGES LONG JEALOUS OF ATHENS WILL LEND THEM THEIR MEN. WE WILL SIT UNDER SIEGE, WE WILL STARVE AND WE WILL FALL...
KRAK!
UNLESS THEY NEVER GET HERE.

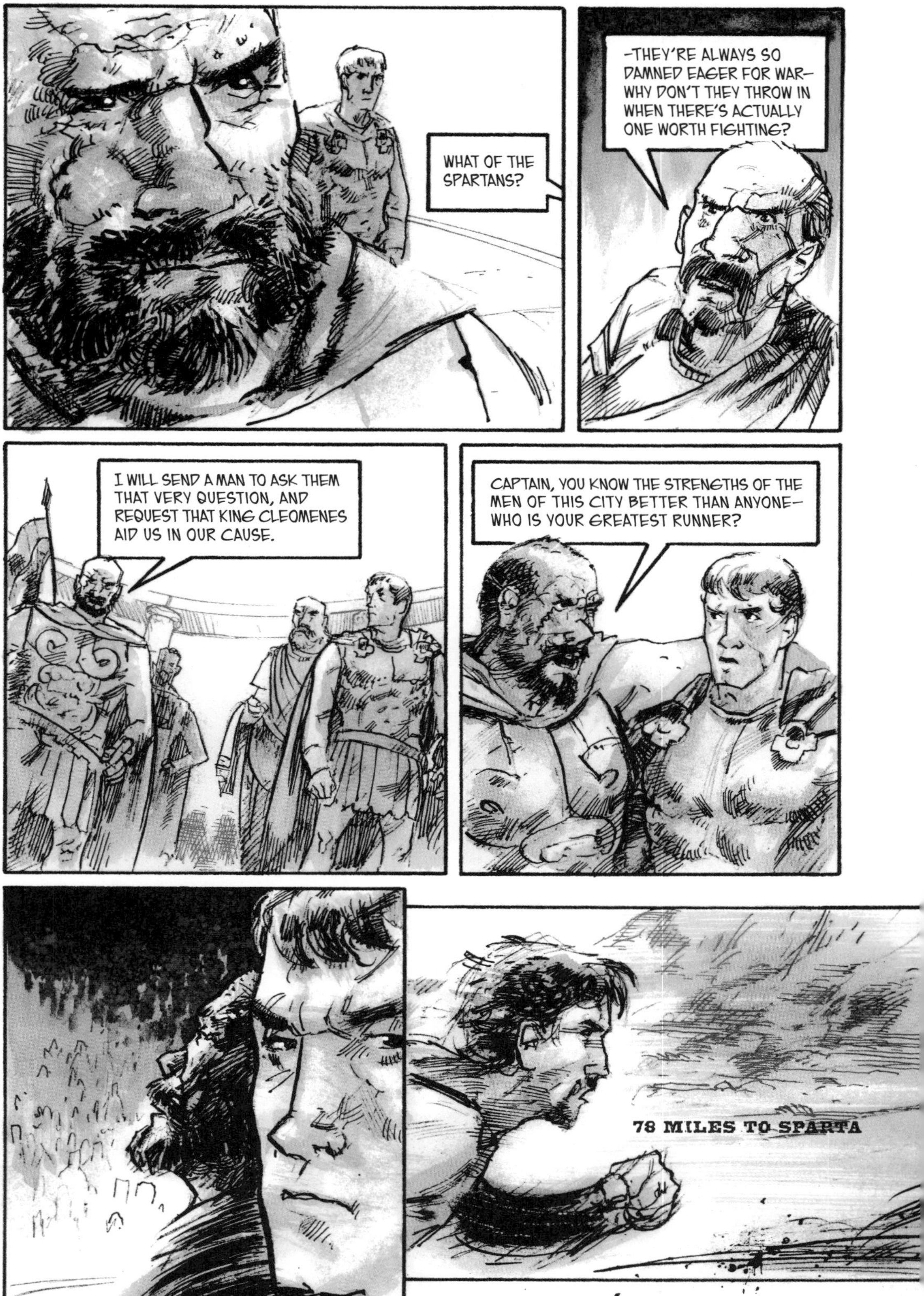
WHAT OF THE SPARTANS?
-THEY'RE ALWAYS SO DAMNED EAGER FOR WAR- WHY DON'T THEY THROW IN WHEN THERE'S ACTUALLY ONE WORTH FIGHTING?
I WILL SEND A MAN TO ASK THEM THAT VERY QUESTION, AND REQUEST THAT KING CLEOMENES AID US IN OUR CAUSE.
CAPTAIN, YOU KNOW THE STRENGTHS OF THE MEN OF THIS CITY BETTER THAN ANYONE- WHO IS YOUR GREATEST RUNNER?
78 MILES TO SPARTA

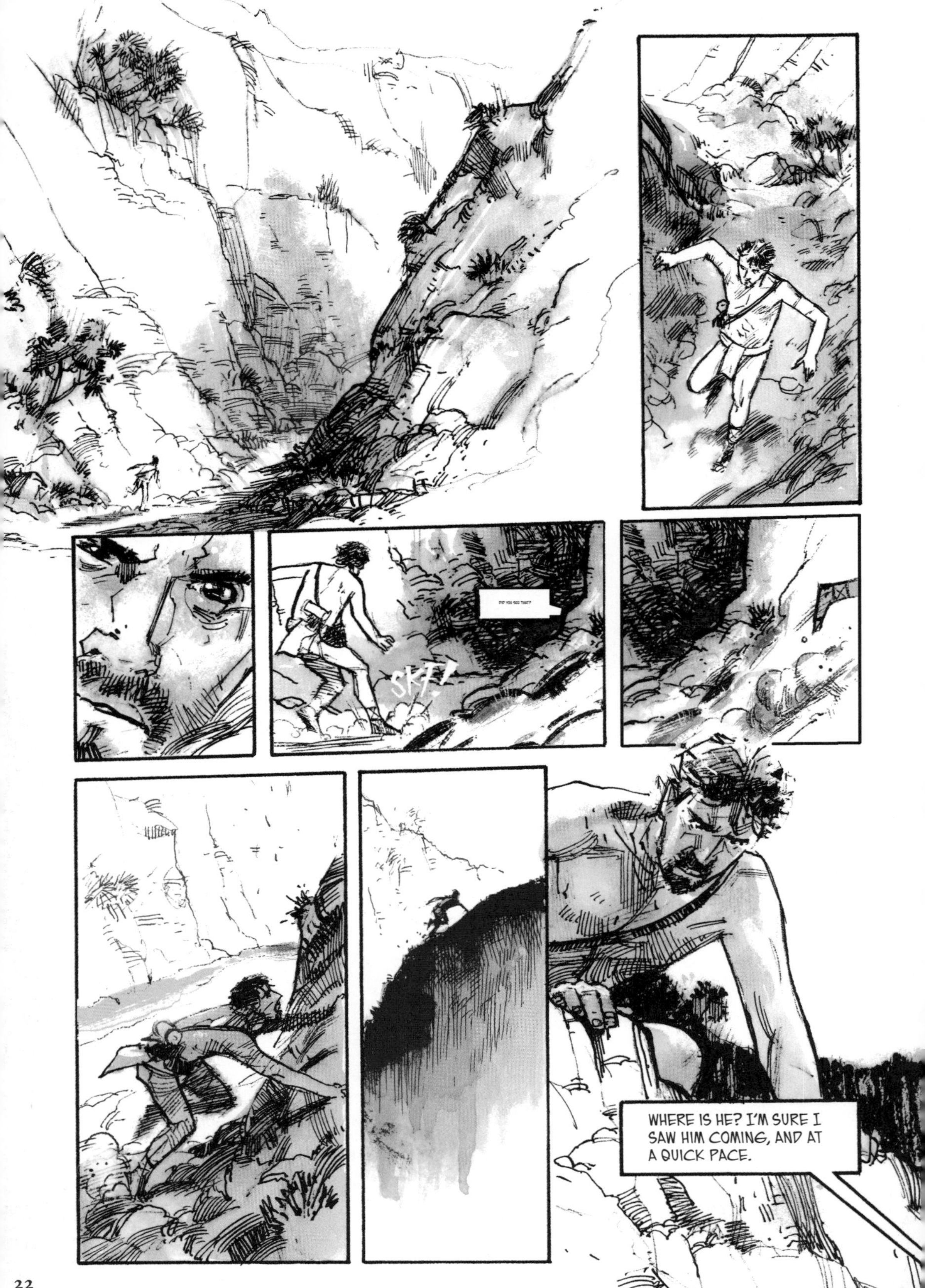
DID YOU SEE THAT?
SKT!
WHERE IS HE? I'M SURE I SAW HIM COMING, AND AT A QUICK PACE.

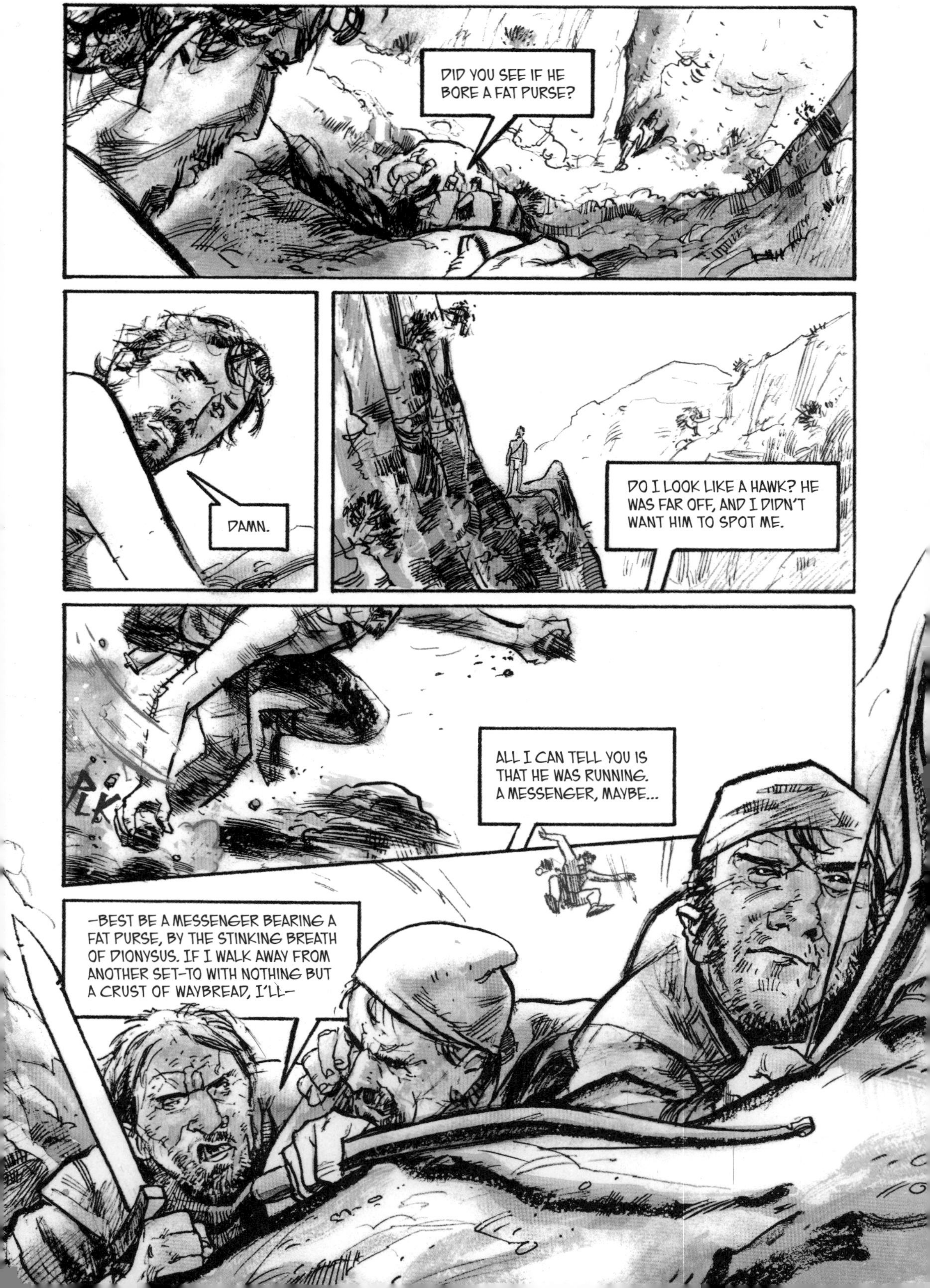
DID YOU SEE IF HE BORE A FAT PURSE?
DAMN.
DO I LOOK LIKE A HAWK? HE WAS FAR OFF, AND I DIDN'T WANT HIM TO SPOT ME.
PLK
ALL I CAN TELL YOU IS THAT HE WAS RUNNING. A MESSENGER, MAYBE...
—BEST BE A MESSENGER BEARING A FAT PURSE, BY THE STINKING BREATH OF DIONYSUS. IF I WALK AWAY FROM ANOTHER SET-TO WITH NOTHING BUT A CRUST OF WAYBREAD, I'LL—

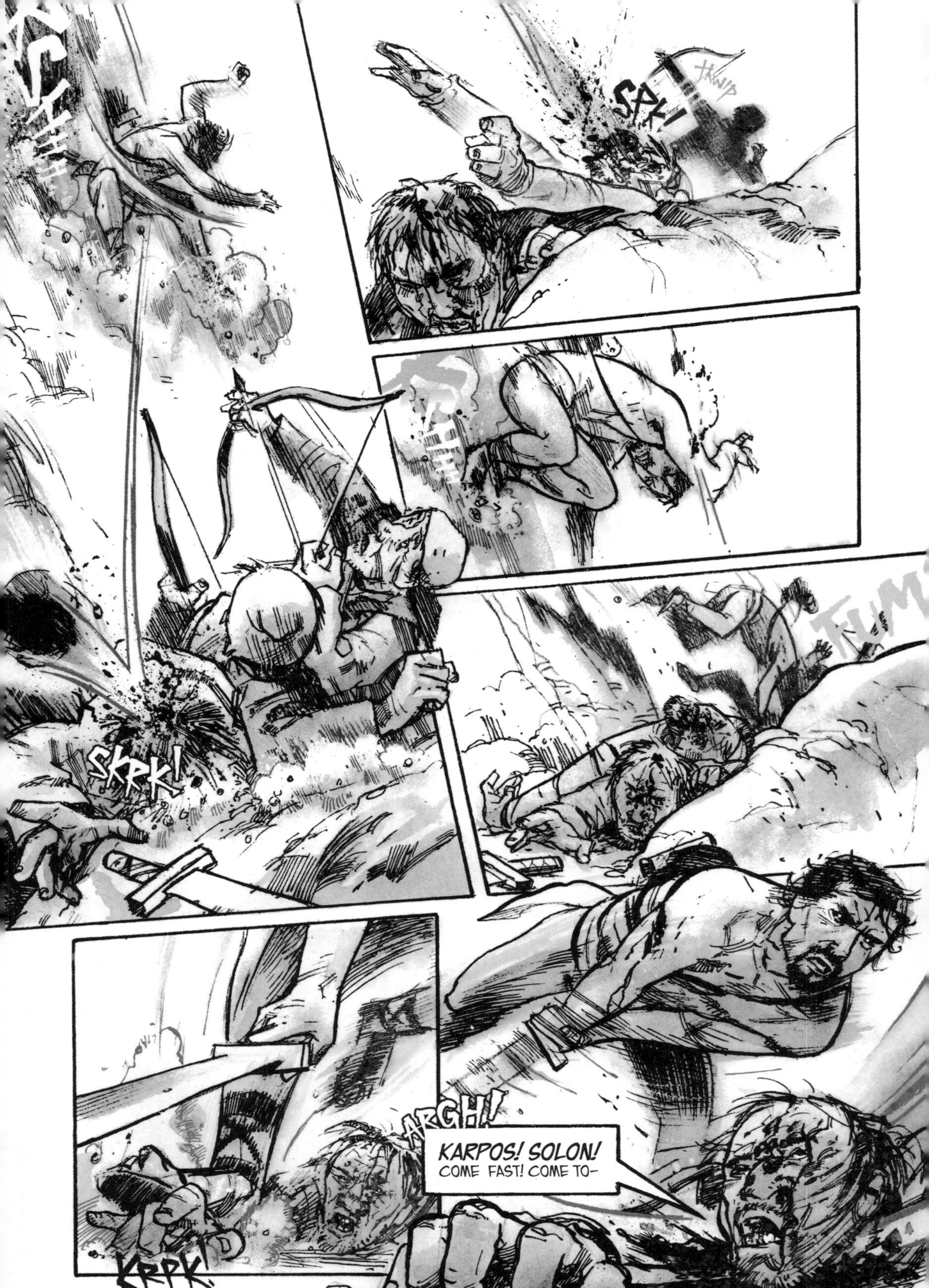
KSHHH
SPK!
THWIP
KSHHH
SKRK!
TUMP
ARGH!
KARPOS! SOLON!
COME FAST! COME TO–
KRPK!

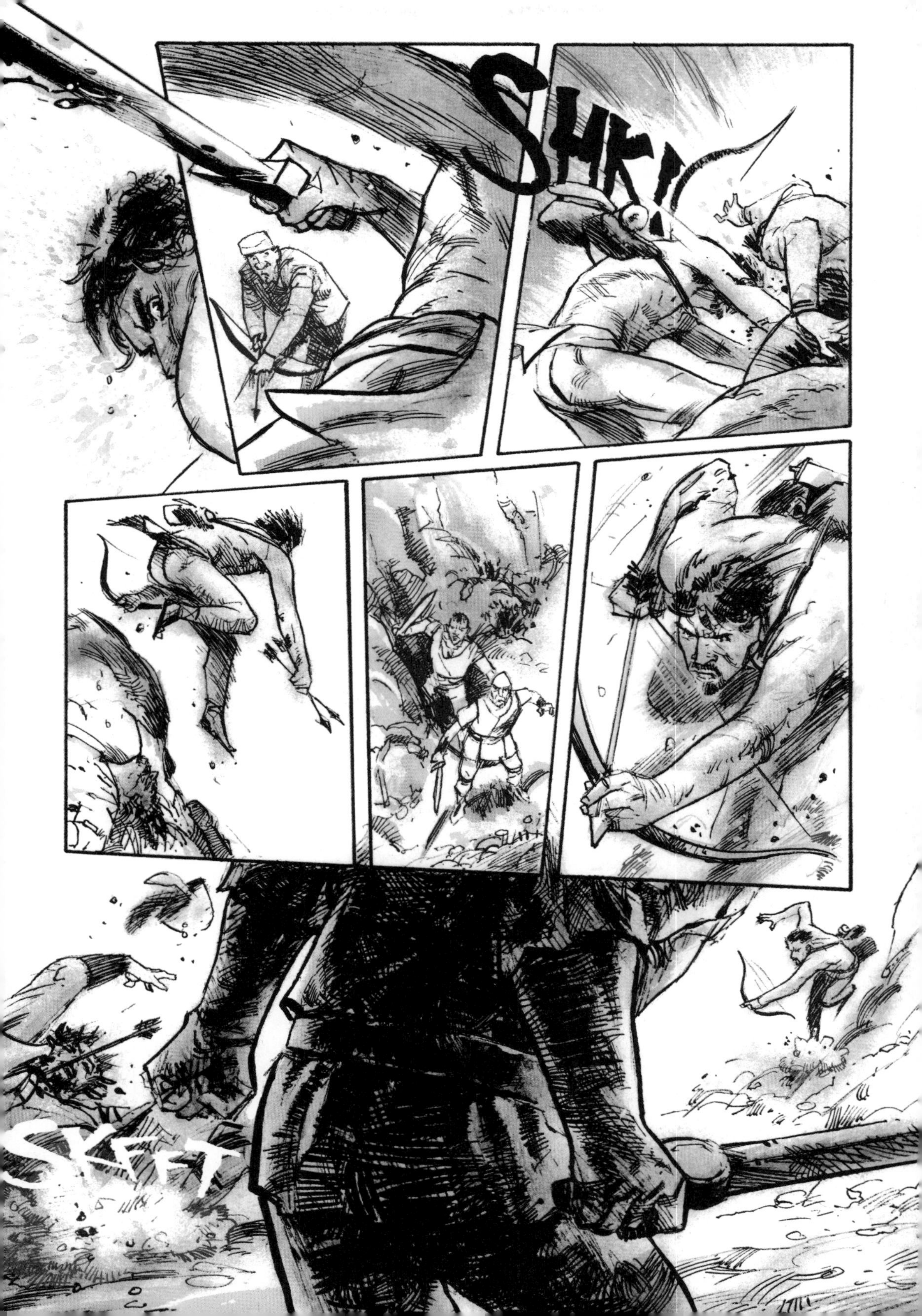
SHK!
SKFT

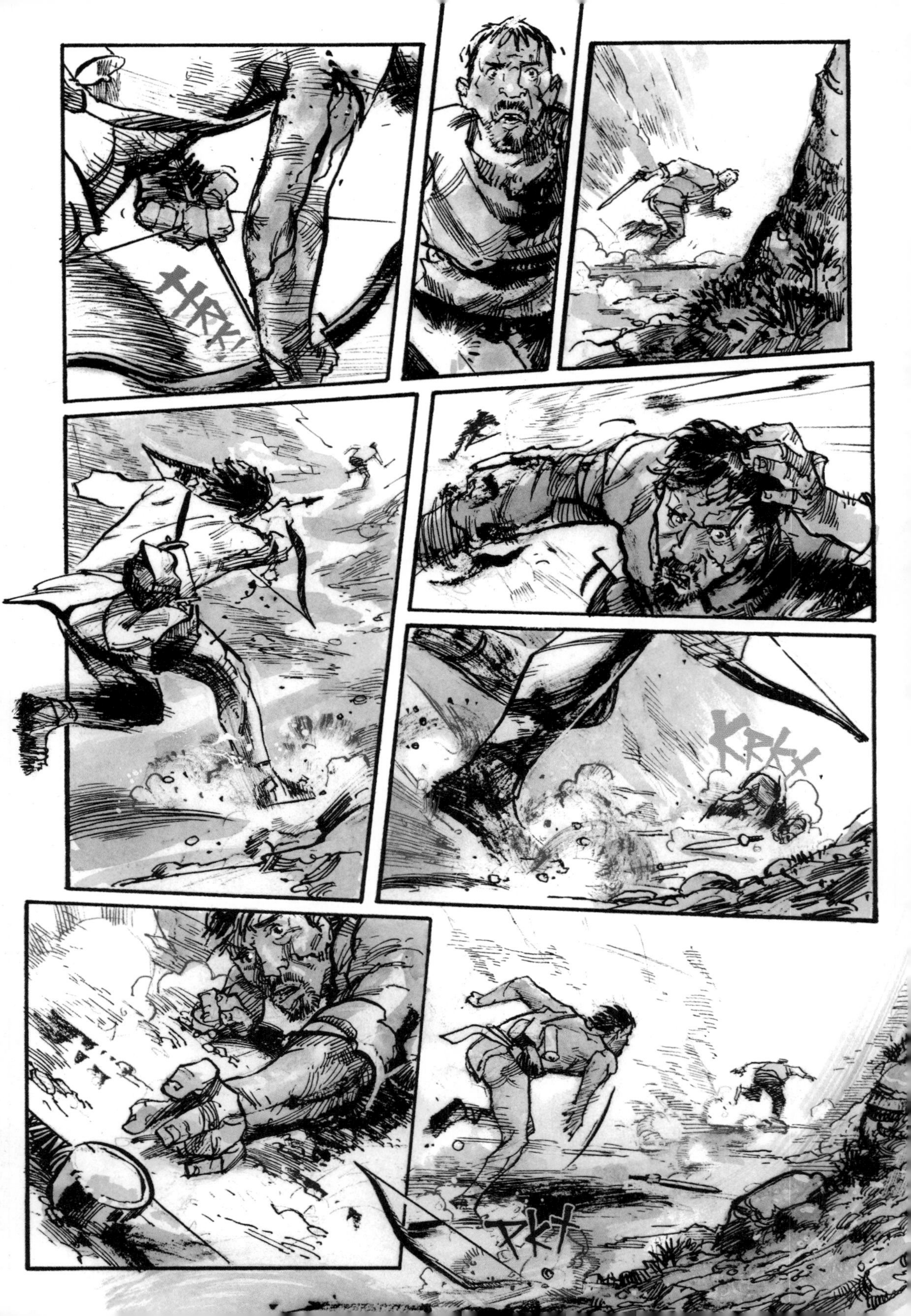
HRK!
KRKX
PKH

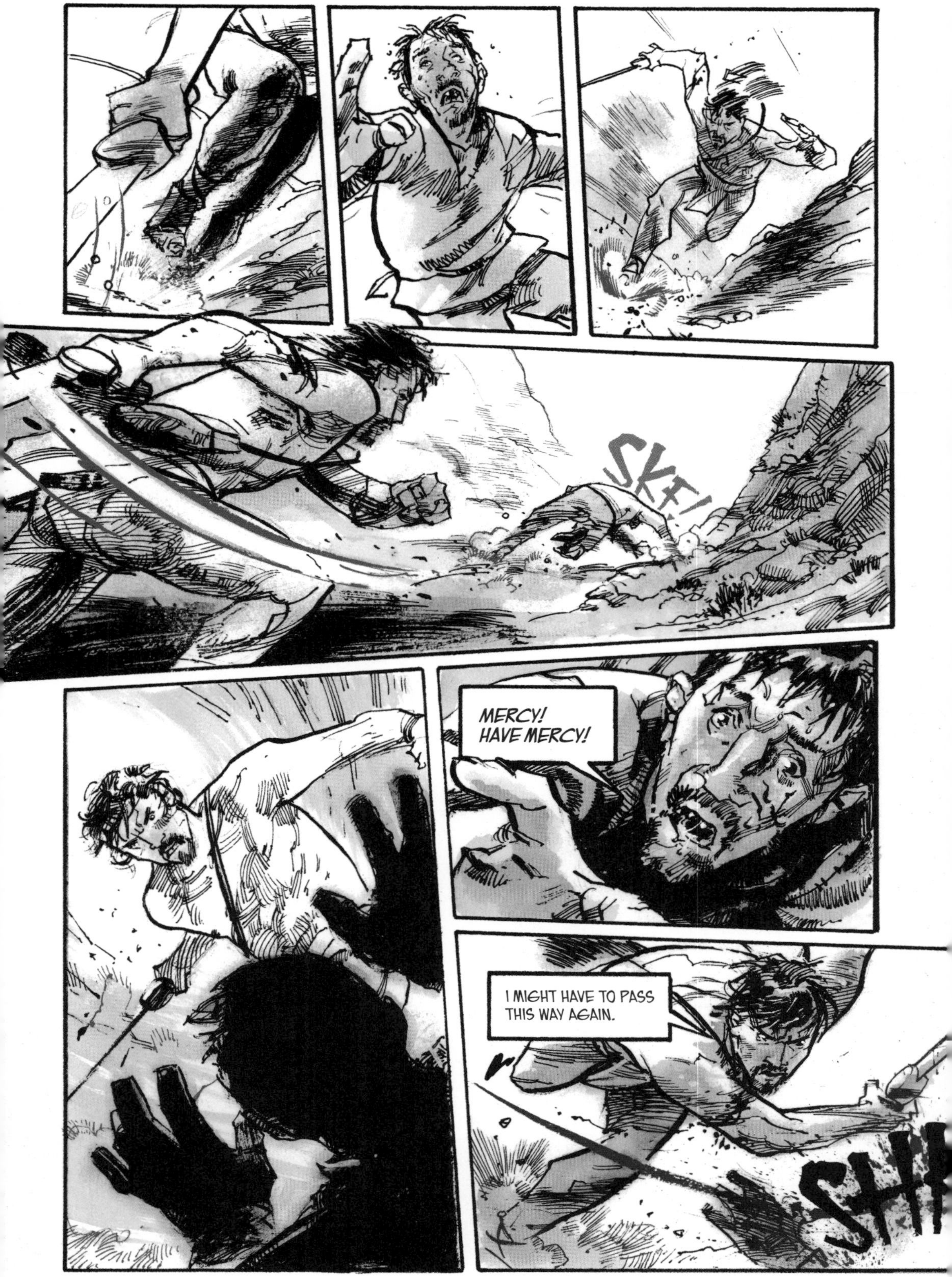
SKE!
MERCY!
HAVE MERCY!
I MIGHT HAVE TO PASS
THIS WAY AGAIN.
SHH

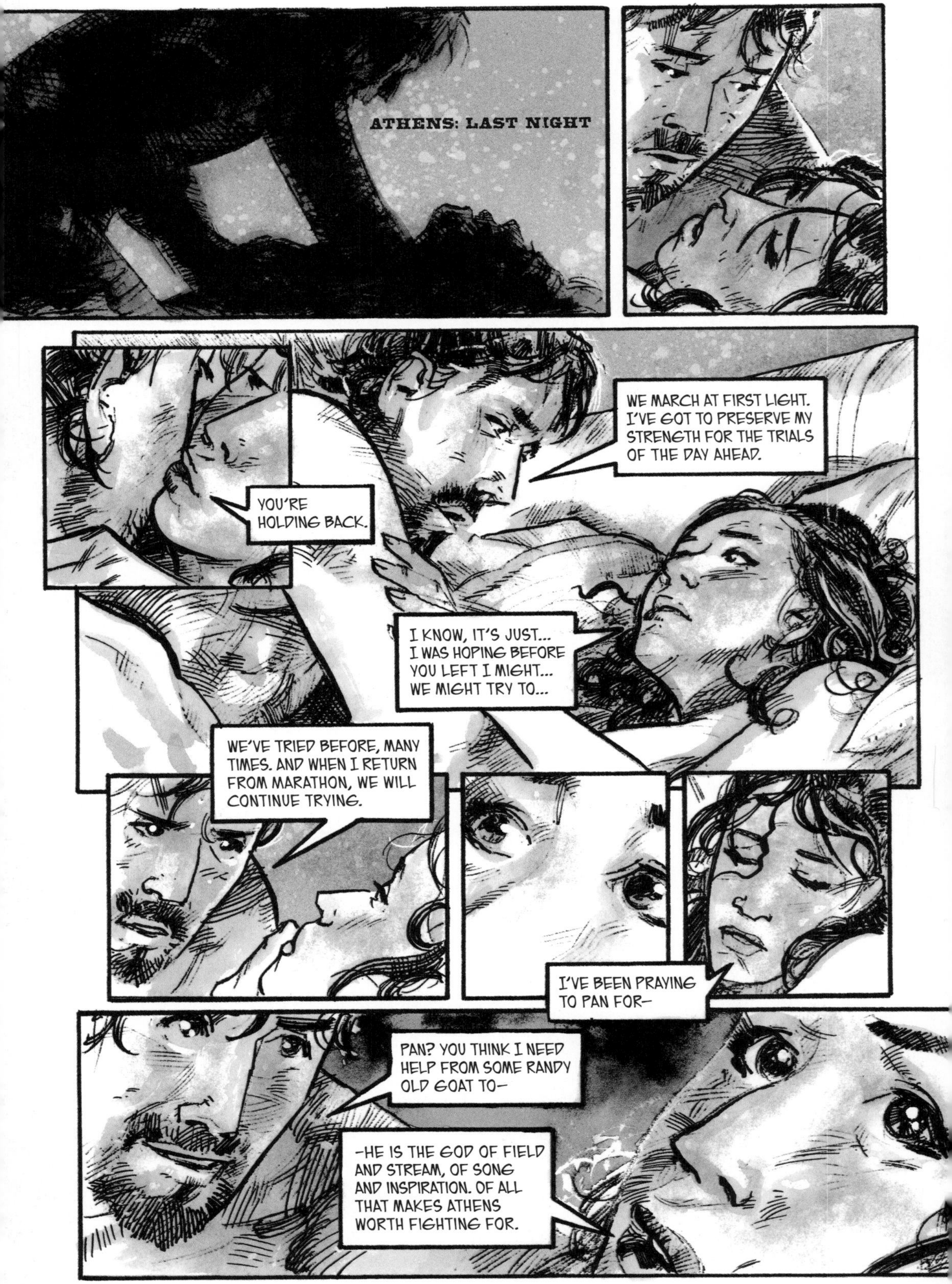
ATHENS: LAST NIGHT
WE MARCH AT FIRST LIGHT. I'VE GOT TO PRESERVE MY STRENGTH FOR THE TRIALS OF THE DAY AHEAD.
YOU'RE HOLDING BACK.
I KNOW, IT'S JUST... I WAS HOPING BEFORE YOU LEFT I MIGHT... WE MIGHT TRY TO...
WE'VE TRIED BEFORE, MANY TIMES. AND WHEN I RETURN FROM MARATHON, WE WILL CONTINUE TRYING.
I'VE BEEN PRAYING TO PAN FOR–
PAN? YOU THINK I NEED HELP FROM SOME RANDY OLD GOAT TO–
–HE IS THE GOD OF FIELD AND STREAM, OF SONG AND INSPIRATION. OF ALL THAT MAKES ATHENS WORTH FIGHTING FOR.

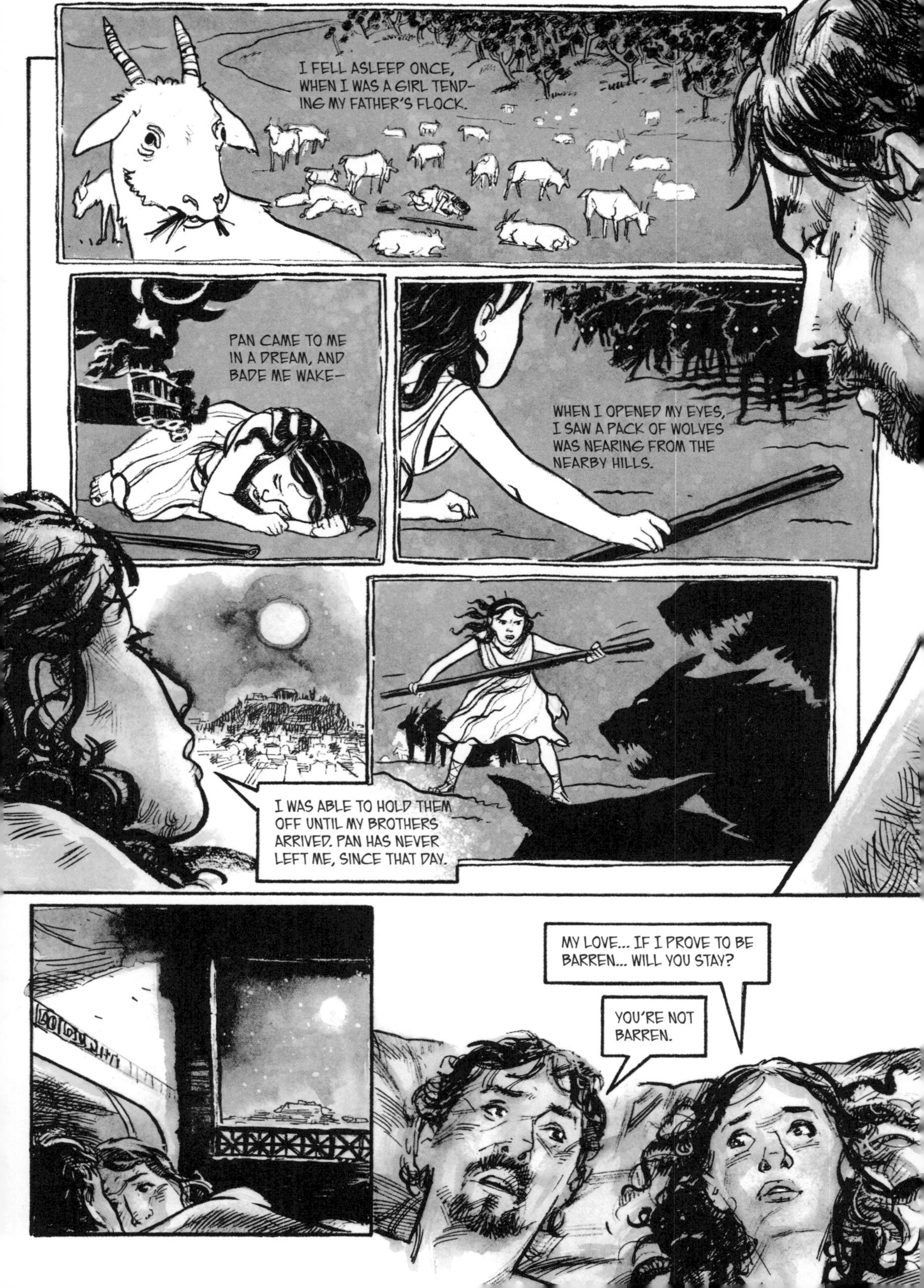
I FELL ASLEEP ONCE, WHEN I WAS A GIRL TEND-ING MY FATHER'S FLOCK.
PAN CAME TO ME IN A DREAM, AND BADE ME WAKE—
WHEN I OPENED MY EYES, I SAW A PACK OF WOLVES WAS NEARING FROM THE NEARBY HILLS.
I WAS ABLE TO HOLD THEM OFF UNTIL MY BROTHERS ARRIVED. PAN HAS NEVER LEFT ME, SINCE THAT DAY.
MY LOVE... IF I PROVE TO BE BARREN... WILL YOU STAY?
YOU'RE NOT BARREN.

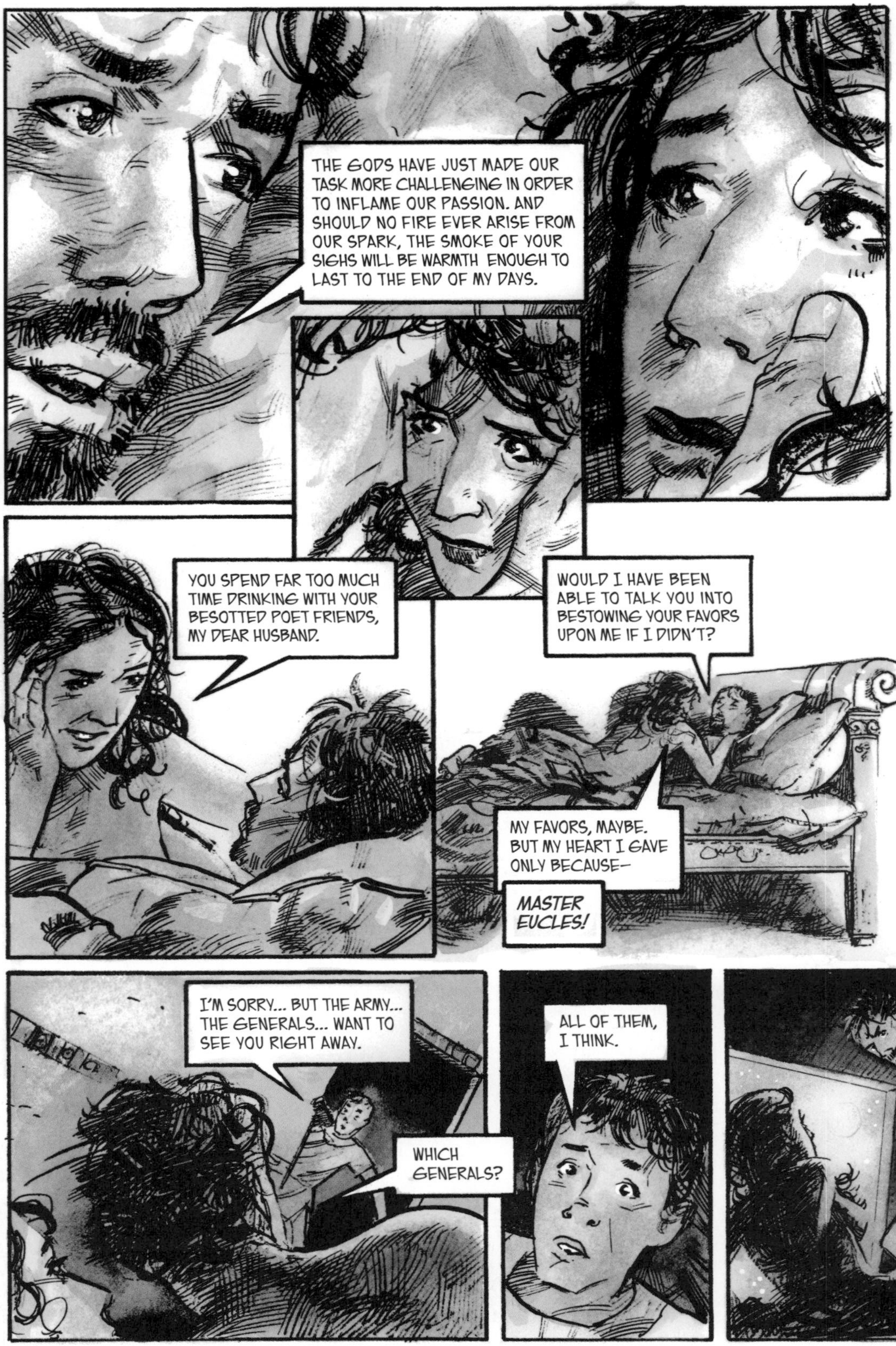
THE GODS HAVE JUST MADE OUR TASK MORE CHALLENGING IN ORDER TO INFLAME OUR PASSION. AND SHOULD NO FIRE EVER ARISE FROM OUR SPARK, THE SMOKE OF YOUR SIGHS WILL BE WARMTH ENOUGH TO LAST TO THE END OF MY DAYS.
YOU SPEND FAR TOO MUCH TIME DRINKING WITH YOUR BESOTTED POET FRIENDS, MY DEAR HUSBAND.
WOULD I HAVE BEEN ABLE TO TALK YOU INTO BESTOWING YOUR FAVORS UPON ME IF I DIDN'T?
MY FAVORS, MAYBE. BUT MY HEART I GAVE ONLY BECAUSE–
MASTER EUCLES!
I'M SORRY... BUT THE ARMY... THE GENERALS... WANT TO SEE YOU RIGHT AWAY.
WHICH GENERALS?
ALL OF THEM, I THINK.

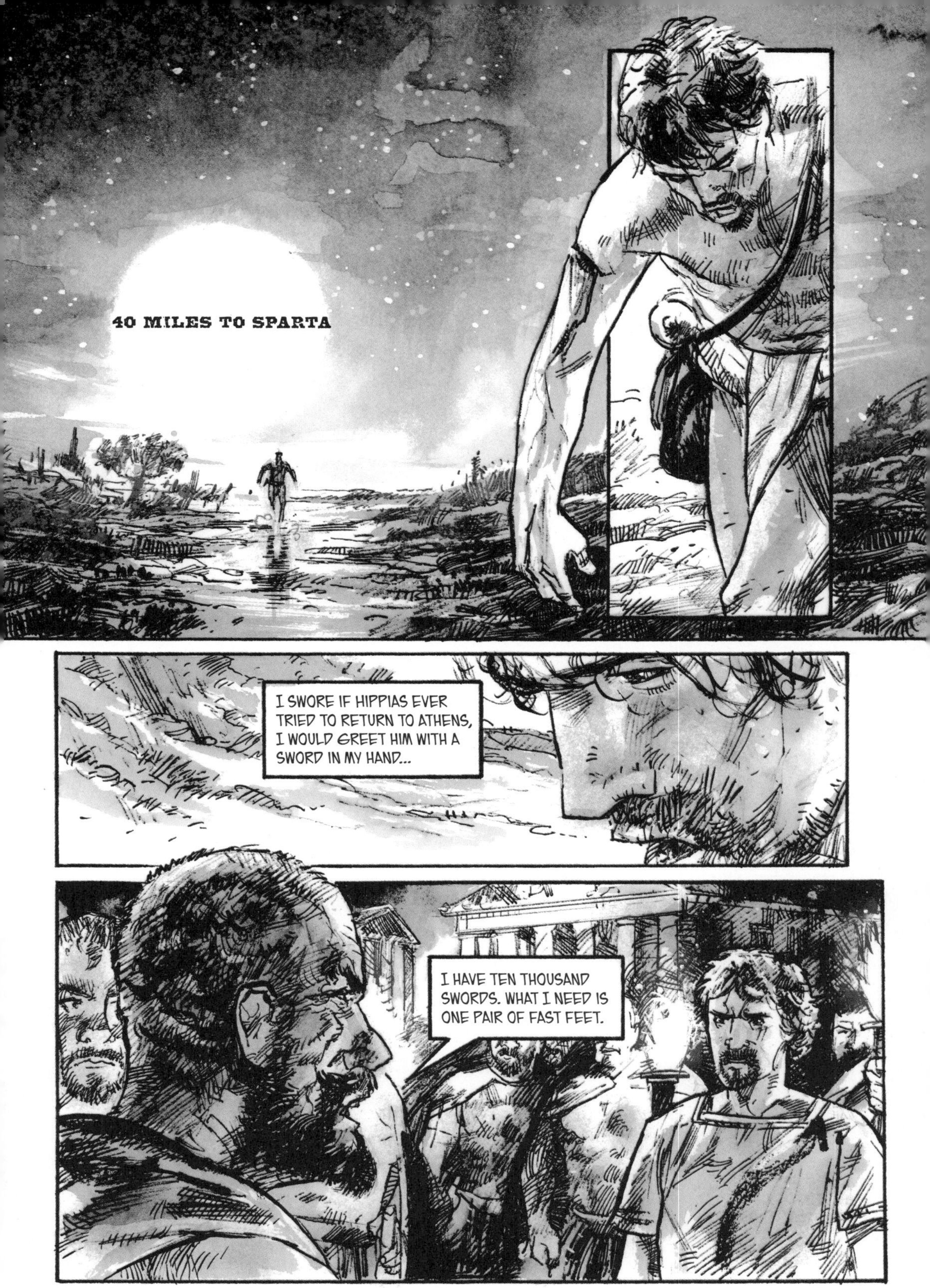
40 MILES TO SPARTA
I SWORE IF HIPPIAS EVER TRIED TO RETURN TO ATHENS, I WOULD GREET HIM WITH A SWORD IN MY HAND...
I HAVE TEN THOUSAND SWORDS. WHAT I NEED IS ONE PAIR OF FAST FEET.

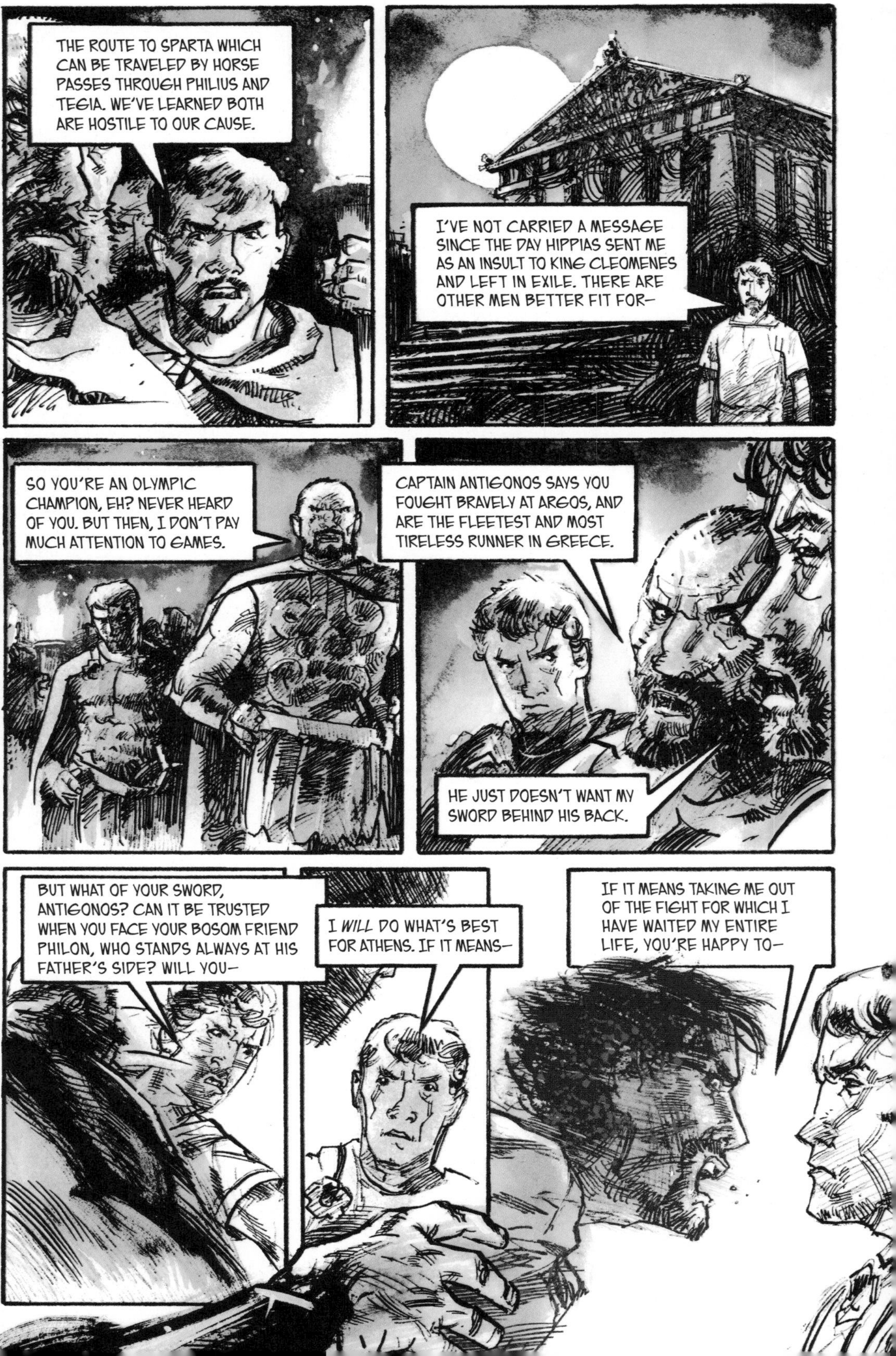
THE ROUTE TO SPARTA WHICH CAN BE TRAVELED BY HORSE PASSES THROUGH PHILIUS AND TEGIA. WE'VE LEARNED BOTH ARE HOSTILE TO OUR CAUSE.
I'VE NOT CARRIED A MESSAGE SINCE THE DAY HIPPIAS SENT ME AS AN INSULT TO KING CLEOMENES AND LEFT IN EXILE. THERE ARE OTHER MEN BETTER FIT FOR—
SO YOU'RE AN OLYMPIC CHAMPION, EH? NEVER HEARD OF YOU. BUT THEN, I DON'T PAY MUCH ATTENTION TO GAMES.
CAPTAIN ANTIGONOS SAYS YOU FOUGHT BRAVELY AT ARGOS, AND ARE THE FLEETEST AND MOST TIRELESS RUNNER IN GREECE.
HE JUST DOESN'T WANT MY SWORD BEHIND HIS BACK.
BUT WHAT OF YOUR SWORD, ANTIGONOS? CAN IT BE TRUSTED WHEN YOU FACE YOUR BOSOM FRIEND PHILON, WHO STANDS ALWAYS AT HIS FATHER'S SIDE? WILL YOU—
I *WILL* DO WHAT'S BEST FOR ATHENS. IF IT MEANS—
IF IT MEANS TAKING ME OUT OF THE FIGHT FOR WHICH I HAVE WAITED MY ENTIRE LIFE, YOU'RE HAPPY TO—

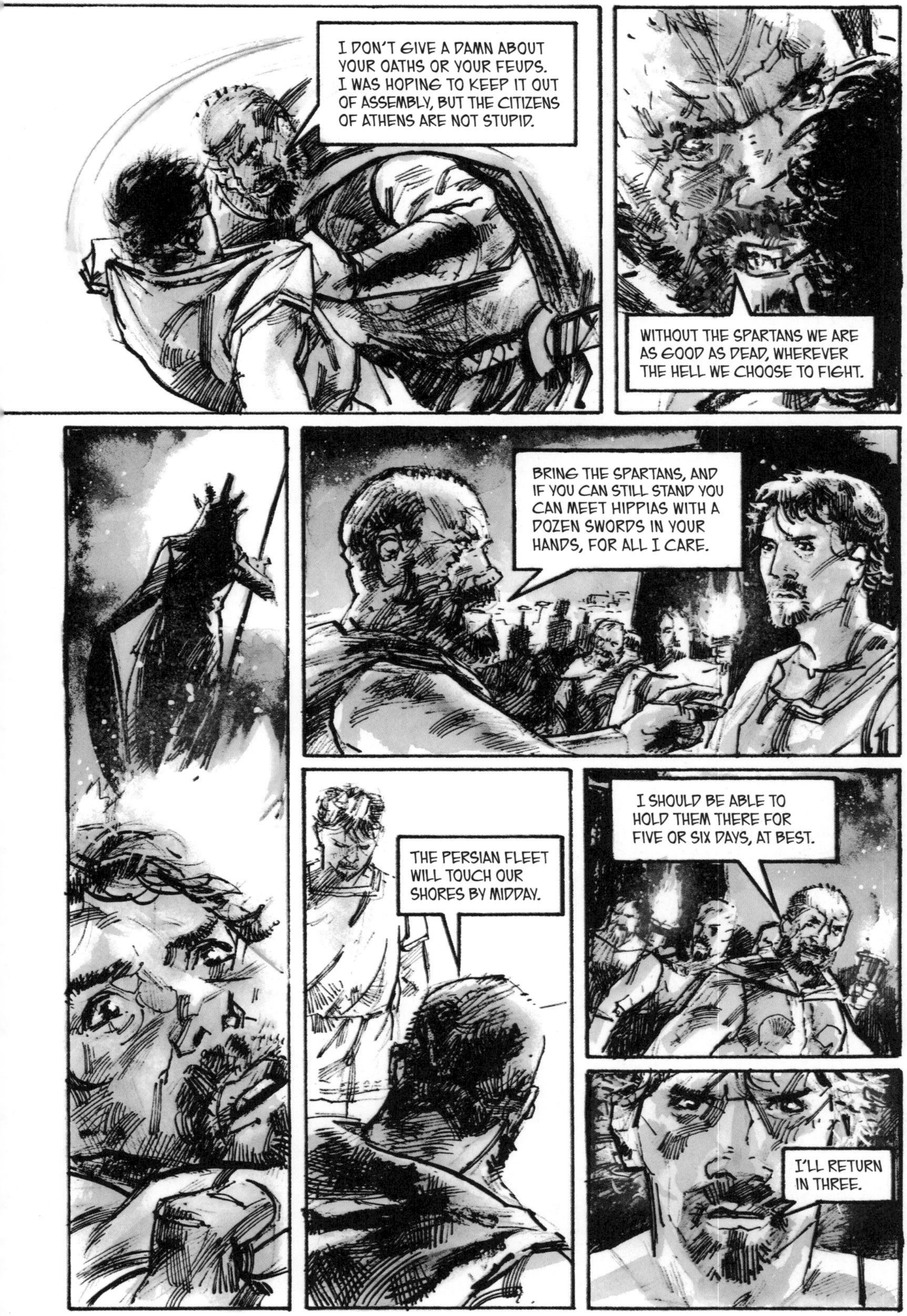
I DON'T GIVE A DAMN ABOUT YOUR OATHS OR YOUR FEUDS. I WAS HOPING TO KEEP IT OUT OF ASSEMBLY, BUT THE CITIZENS OF ATHENS ARE NOT STUPID.
WITHOUT THE SPARTANS WE ARE AS GOOD AS DEAD, WHEREVER THE HELL WE CHOOSE TO FIGHT.
BRING THE SPARTANS, AND IF YOU CAN STILL STAND YOU CAN MEET HIPPIAS WITH A DOZEN SWORDS IN YOUR HANDS, FOR ALL I CARE.
THE PERSIAN FLEET WILL TOUCH OUR SHORES BY MIDDAY.
I SHOULD BE ABLE TO HOLD THEM THERE FOR FIVE OR SIX DAYS, AT BEST.
I'LL RETURN IN THREE.

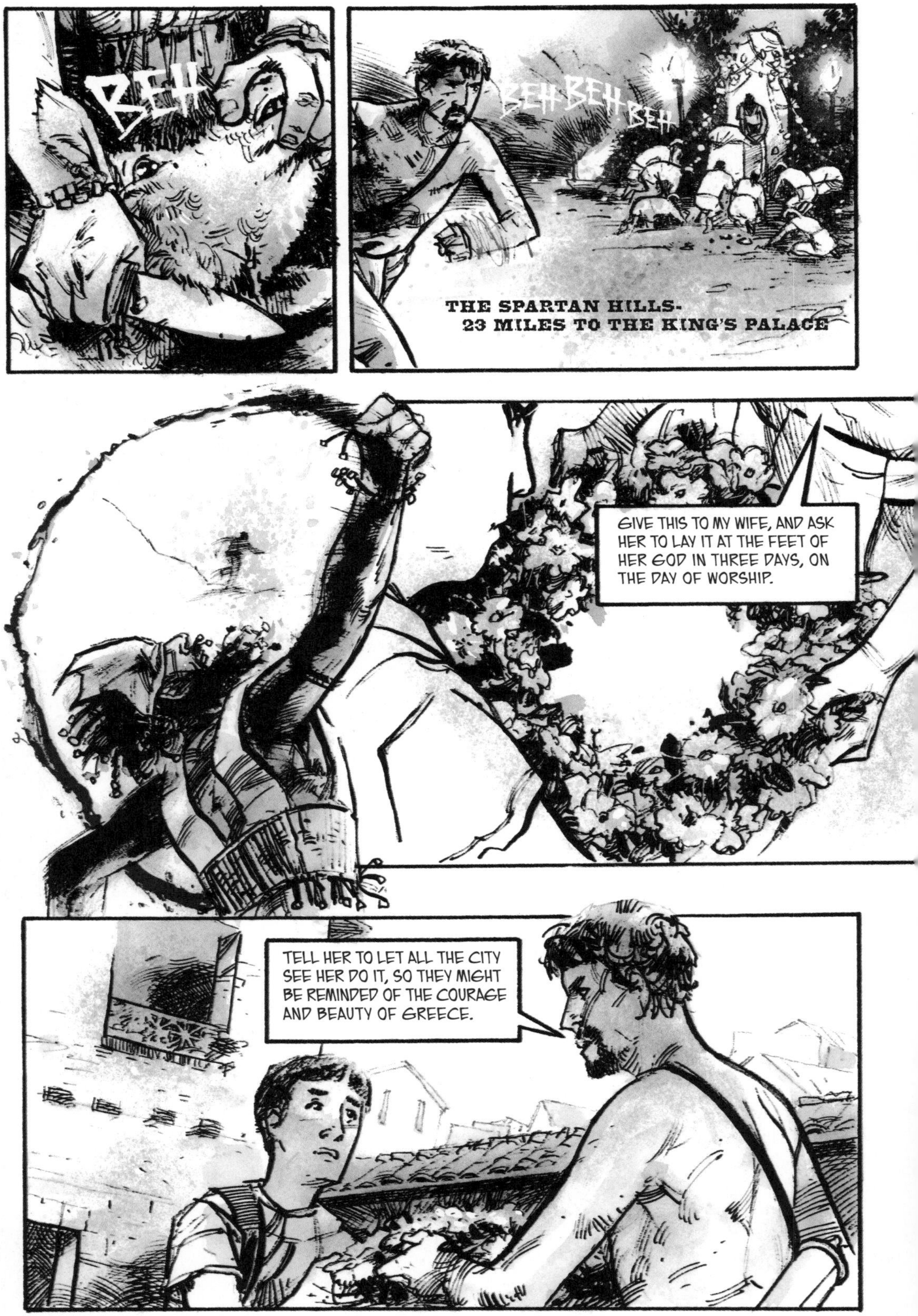
BEH
BEH BEH BEH BEH
THE SPARTAN HILLS-
23 MILES TO THE KING'S PALACE
GIVE THIS TO MY WIFE, AND ASK HER TO LAY IT AT THE FEET OF HER GOD IN THREE DAYS, ON THE DAY OF WORSHIP.
TELL HER TO LET ALL THE CITY SEE HER DO IT, SO THEY MIGHT BE REMINDED OF THE COURAGE AND BEAUTY OF GREECE.

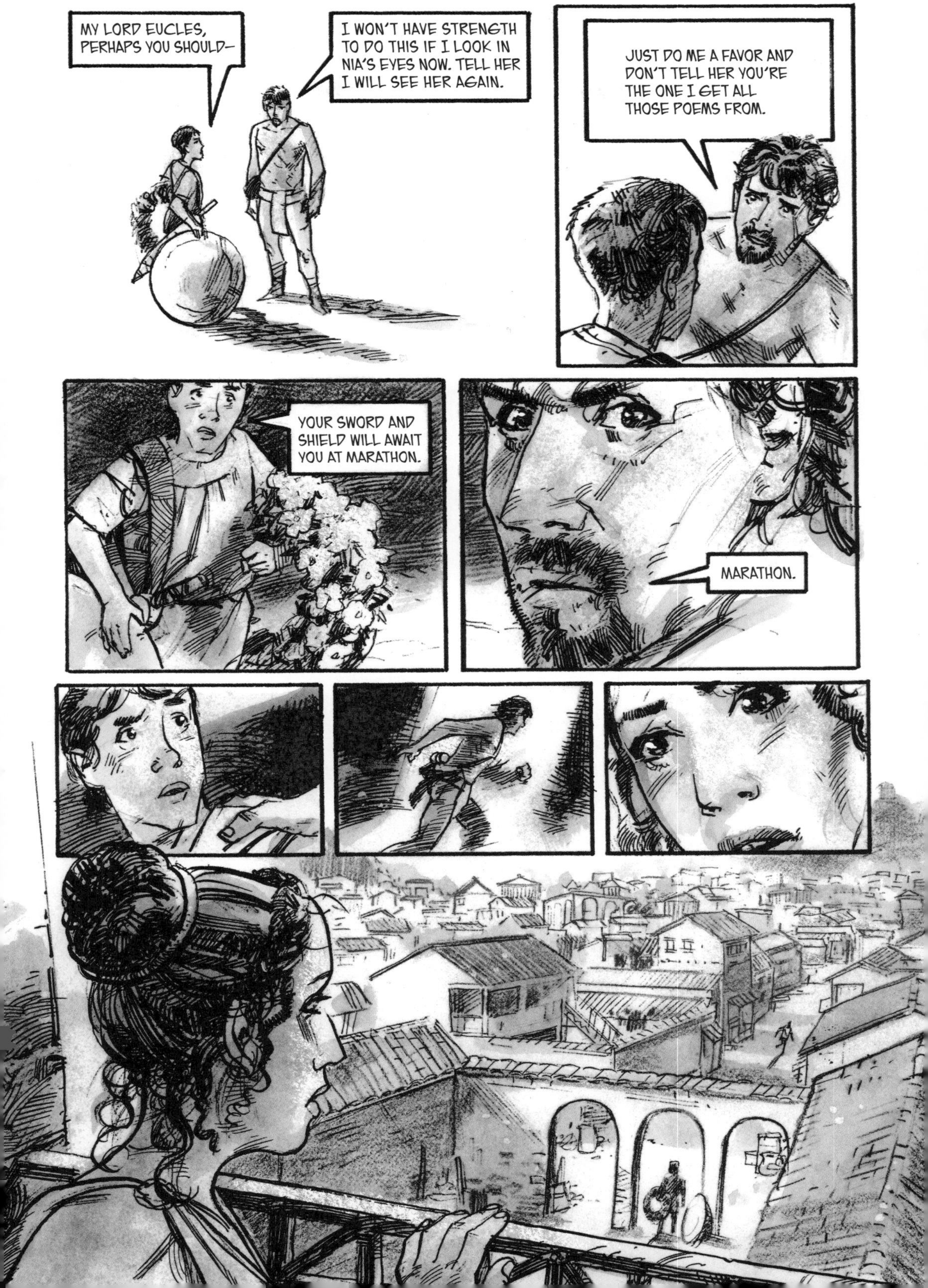
MY LORD EUCLES, PERHAPS YOU SHOULD–
I WON'T HAVE STRENGTH TO DO THIS IF I LOOK IN NIA'S EYES NOW. TELL HER I WILL SEE HER AGAIN.
JUST DO ME A FAVOR AND DON'T TELL HER YOU'RE THE ONE I GET ALL THOSE POEMS FROM.
YOUR SWORD AND SHIELD WILL AWAIT YOU AT MARATHON.
MARATHON.

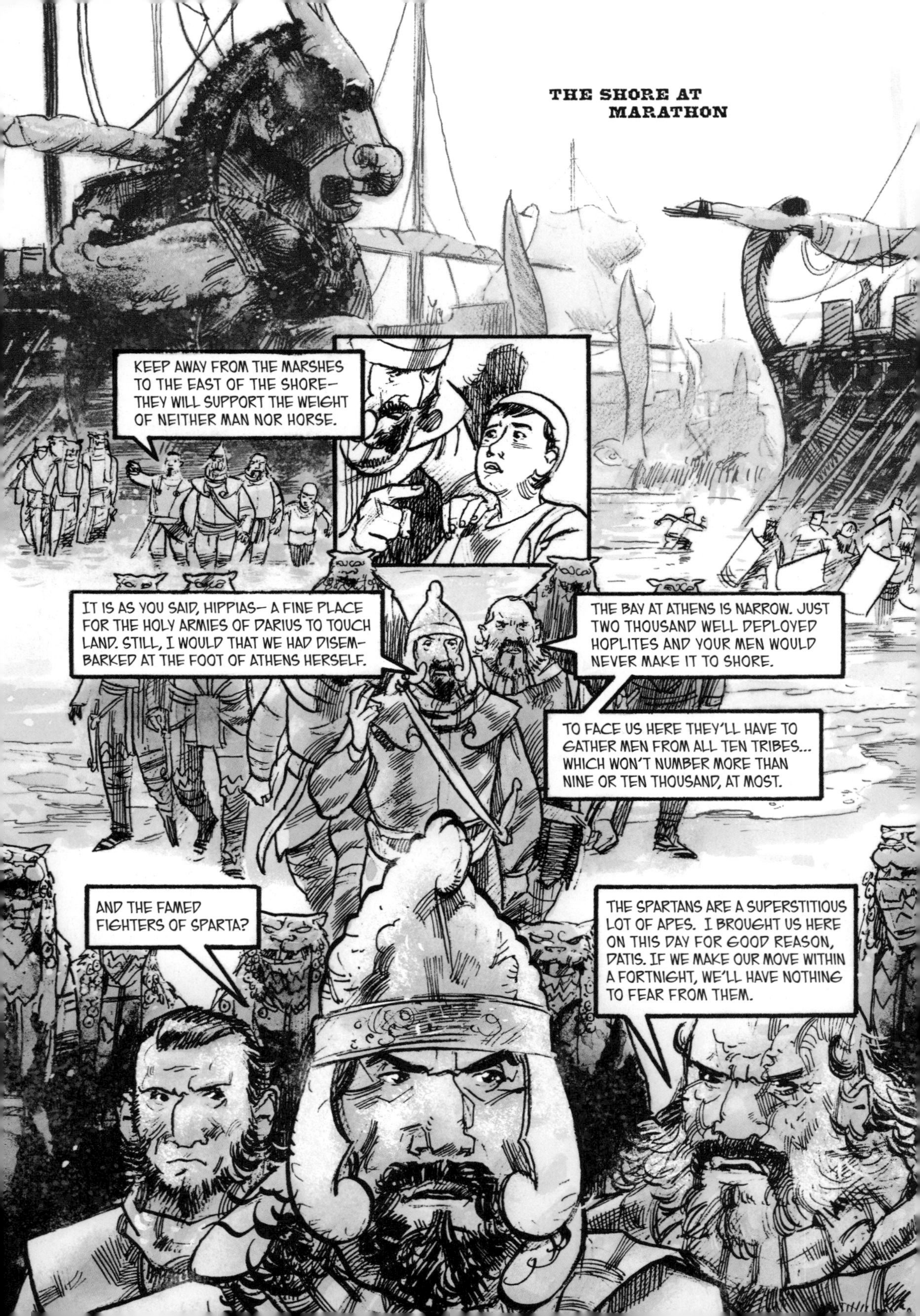
THE SHORE AT MARATHON
KEEP AWAY FROM THE MARSHES TO THE EAST OF THE SHORE— THEY WILL SUPPORT THE WEIGHT OF NEITHER MAN NOR HORSE.
IT IS AS YOU SAID, HIPPIAS— A FINE PLACE FOR THE HOLY ARMIES OF DARIUS TO TOUCH LAND. STILL, I WOULD THAT WE HAD DISEMBARKED AT THE FOOT OF ATHENS HERSELF.
THE BAY AT ATHENS IS NARROW. JUST TWO THOUSAND WELL DEPLOYED HOPLITES AND YOUR MEN WOULD NEVER MAKE IT TO SHORE.
TO FACE US HERE THEY'LL HAVE TO GATHER MEN FROM ALL TEN TRIBES... WHICH WON'T NUMBER MORE THAN NINE OR TEN THOUSAND, AT MOST.
AND THE FAMED FIGHTERS OF SPARTA?
THE SPARTANS ARE A SUPERSTITIOUS LOT OF APES. I BROUGHT US HERE ON THIS DAY FOR GOOD REASON, DATIS. IF WE MAKE OUR MOVE WITHIN A FORTNIGHT, WE'LL HAVE NOTHING TO FEAR FROM THEM.

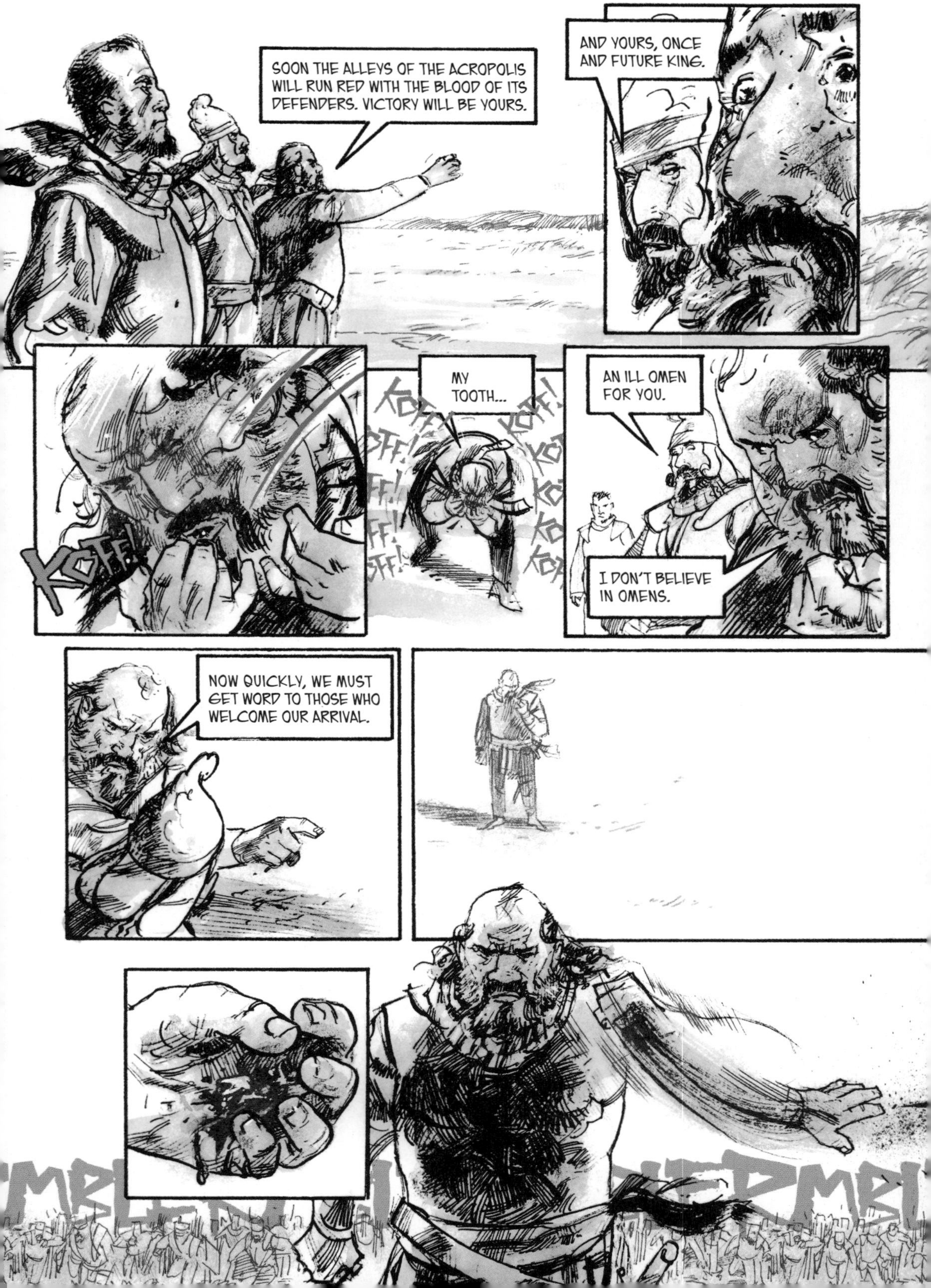
SOON THE ALLEYS OF THE ACROPOLIS WILL RUN RED WITH THE BLOOD OF ITS DEFENDERS. VICTORY WILL BE YOURS.
AND YOURS, ONCE AND FUTURE KING.
KOFF!
MY TOOTH...
AN ILL OMEN FOR YOU.
I DON'T BELIEVE IN OMENS.
NOW QUICKLY, WE MUST GET WORD TO THOSE WHO WELCOME OUR ARRIVAL.

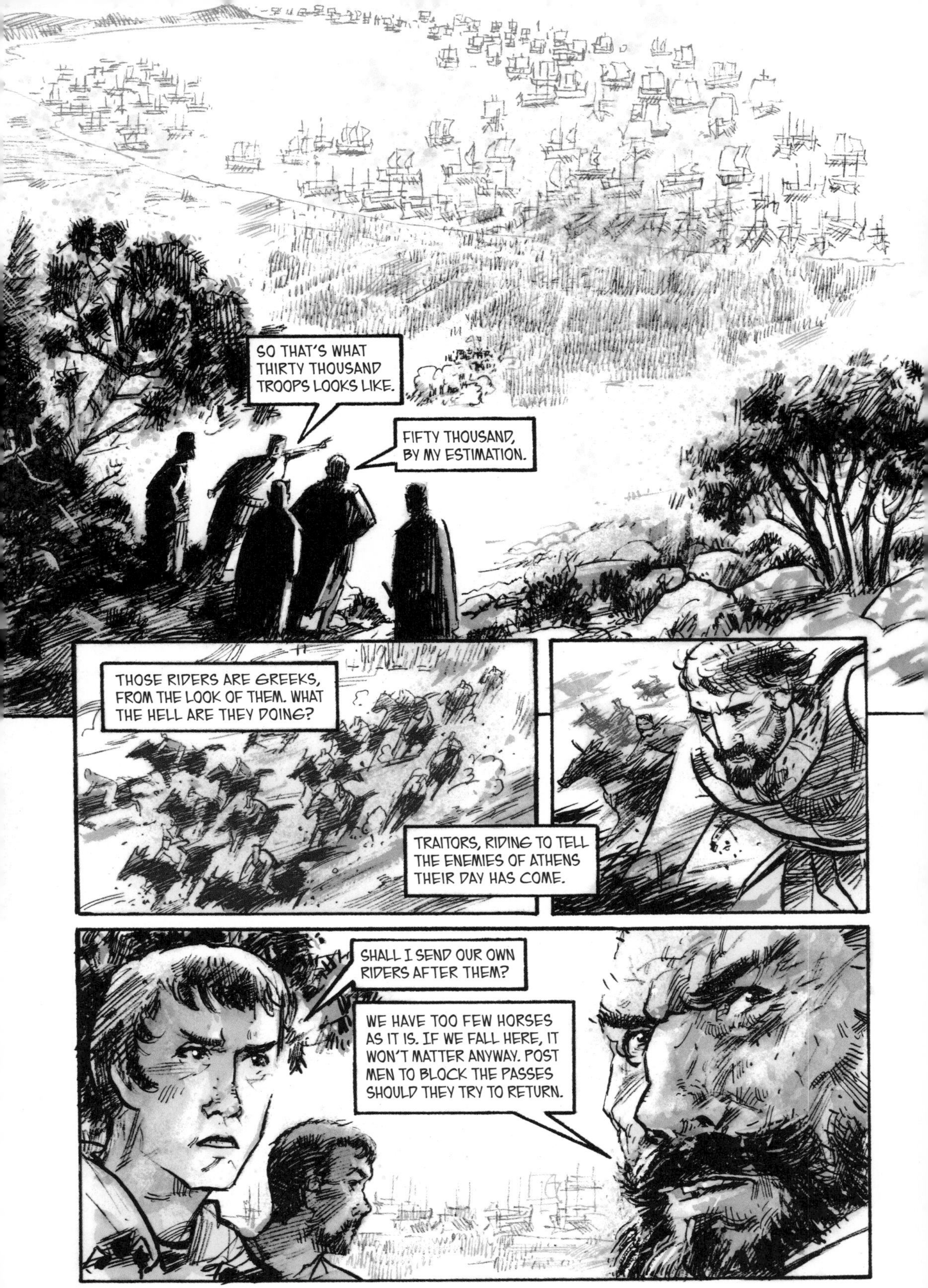
SO THAT'S WHAT THIRTY THOUSAND TROOPS LOOKS LIKE.
FIFTY THOUSAND, BY MY ESTIMATION.
THOSE RIDERS ARE GREEKS, FROM THE LOOK OF THEM. WHAT THE HELL ARE THEY DOING?
TRAITORS, RIDING TO TELL THE ENEMIES OF ATHENS THEIR DAY HAS COME.
SHALL I SEND OUR OWN RIDERS AFTER THEM?
WE HAVE TOO FEW HORSES AS IT IS. IF WE FALL HERE, IT WON'T MATTER ANYWAY. POST MEN TO BLOCK THE PASSES SHOULD THEY TRY TO RETURN.

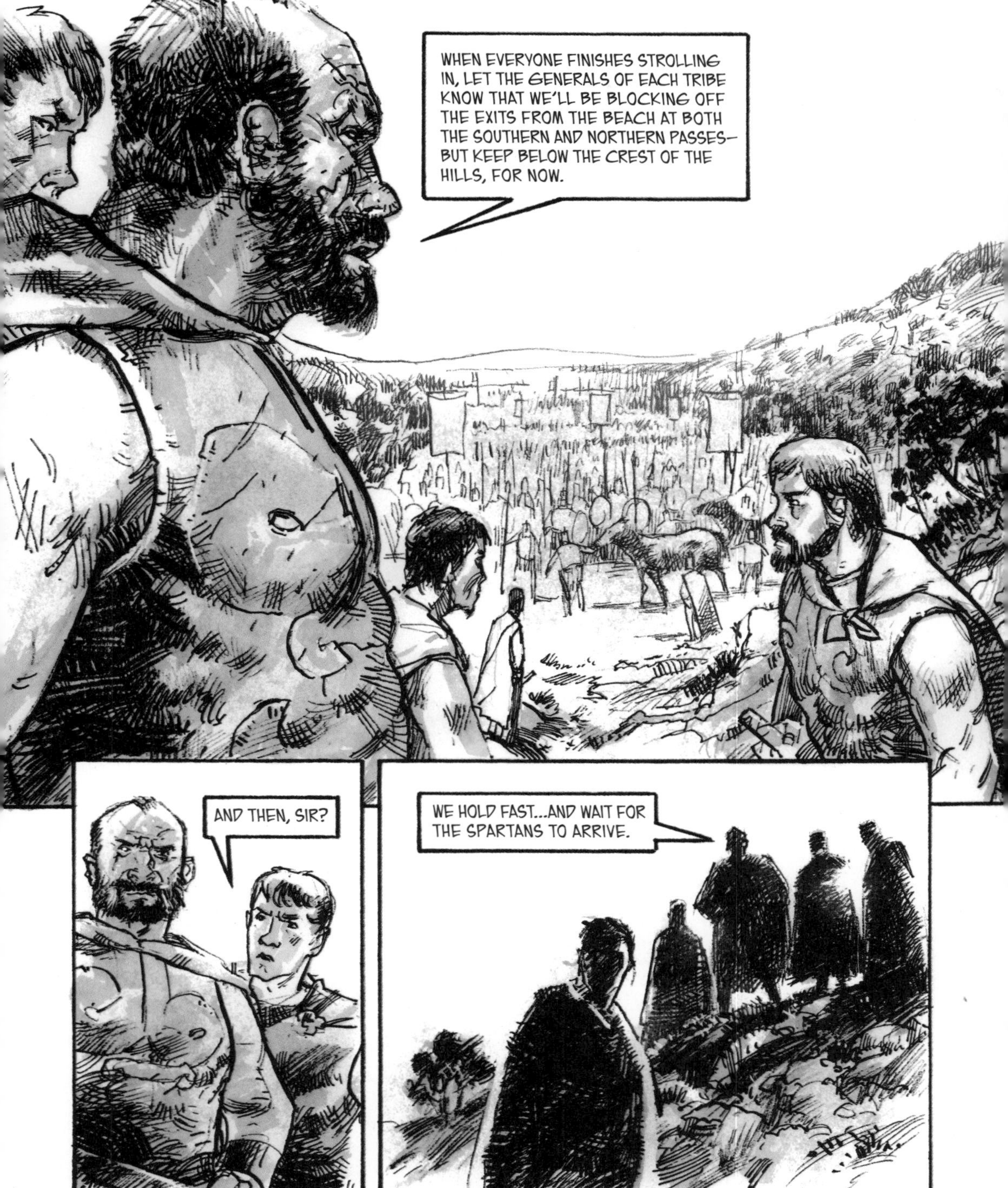
WHEN EVERYONE FINISHES STROLLING IN, LET THE GENERALS OF EACH TRIBE KNOW THAT WE'LL BE BLOCKING OFF THE EXITS FROM THE BEACH AT BOTH THE SOUTHERN AND NORTHERN PASSES—BUT KEEP BELOW THE CREST OF THE HILLS, FOR NOW.
AND THEN, SIR?
WE HOLD FAST...AND WAIT FOR THE SPARTANS TO ARRIVE.

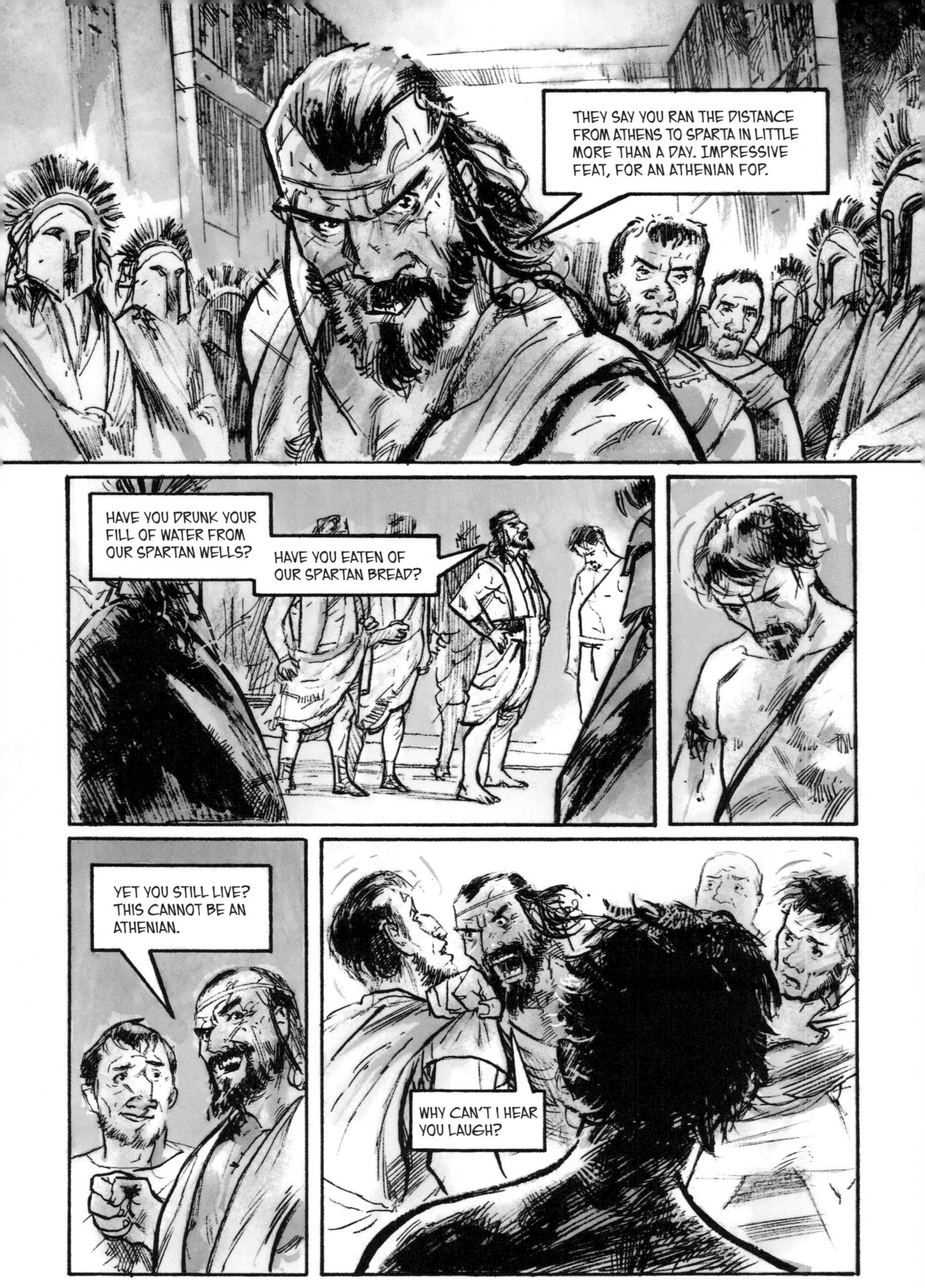
THEY SAY YOU RAN THE DISTANCE FROM ATHENS TO SPARTA IN LITTLE MORE THAN A DAY. IMPRESSIVE FEAT, FOR AN ATHENIAN FOP.
HAVE YOU DRUNK YOUR FILL OF WATER FROM OUR SPARTAN WELLS?
HAVE YOU EATEN OF OUR SPARTAN BREAD?
YET YOU STILL LIVE? THIS CANNOT BE AN ATHENIAN.
WHY CAN'T I HEAR YOU LAUGH?

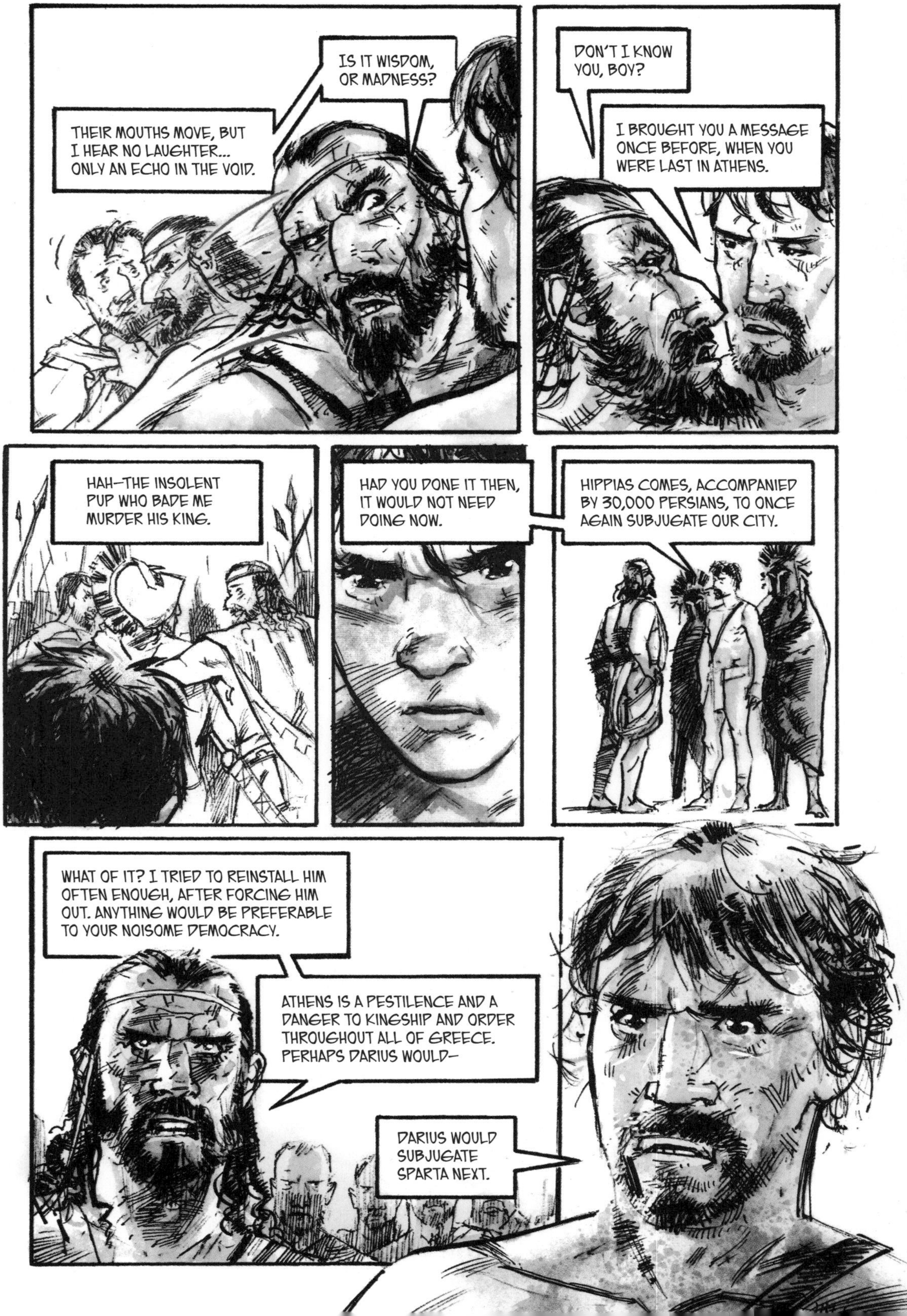
THEIR MOUTHS MOVE, BUT I HEAR NO LAUGHTER... ONLY AN ECHO IN THE VOID.
IS IT WISDOM, OR MADNESS?
DON'T I KNOW YOU, BOY?
I BROUGHT YOU A MESSAGE ONCE BEFORE, WHEN YOU WERE LAST IN ATHENS.
HAH—THE INSOLENT PUP WHO BADE ME MURDER HIS KING.
HAD YOU DONE IT THEN, IT WOULD NOT NEED DOING NOW.
HIPPIAS COMES, ACCOMPANIED BY 30,000 PERSIANS, TO ONCE AGAIN SUBJUGATE OUR CITY.
WHAT OF IT? I TRIED TO REINSTALL HIM OFTEN ENOUGH, AFTER FORCING HIM OUT. ANYTHING WOULD BE PREFERABLE TO YOUR NOISOME DEMOCRACY.
ATHENS IS A PESTILENCE AND A DANGER TO KINGSHIP AND ORDER THROUGHOUT ALL OF GREECE. PERHAPS DARIUS WOULD—
DARIUS WOULD SUBJUGATE SPARTA NEXT.

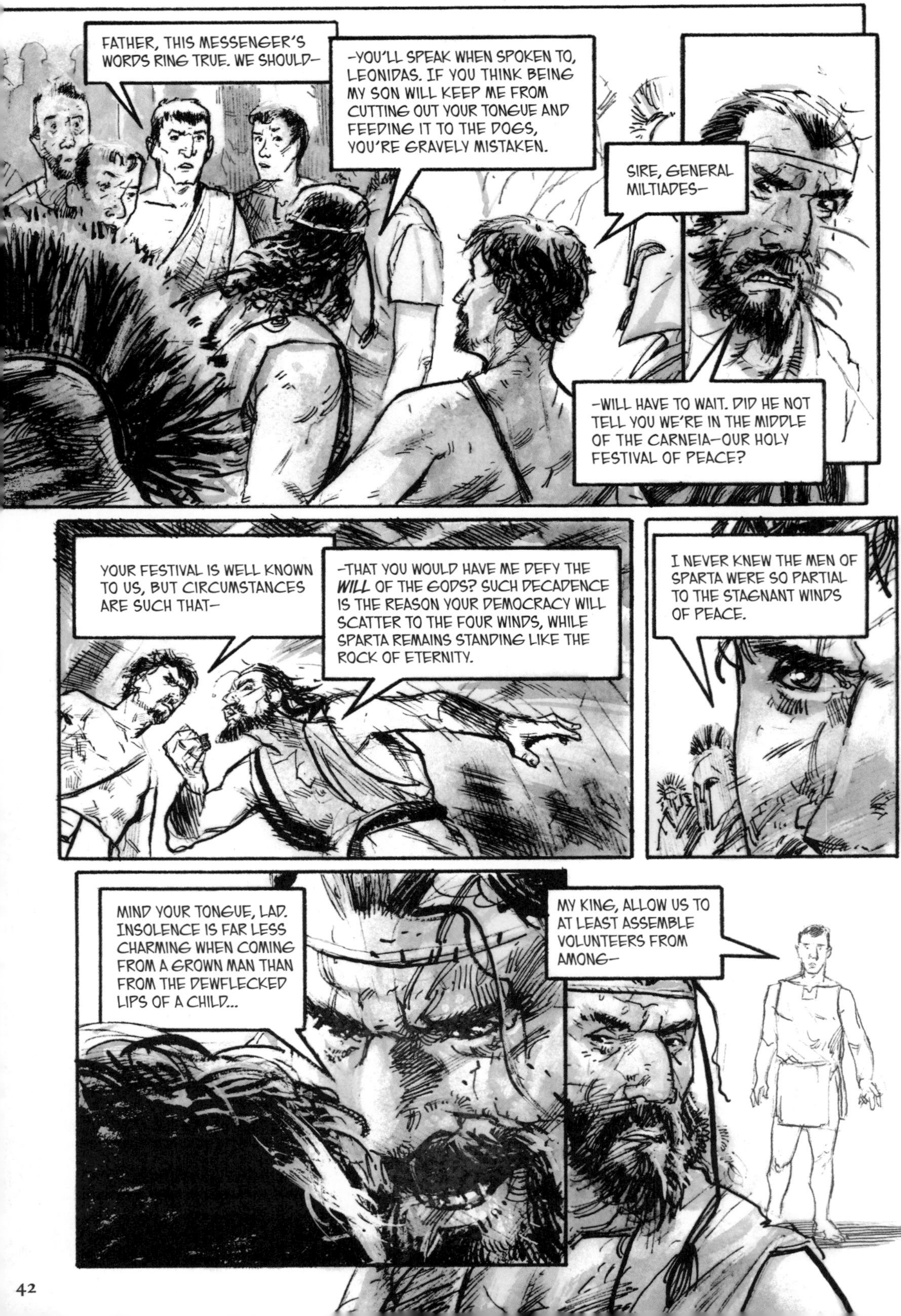
FATHER, THIS MESSENGER'S WORDS RING TRUE. WE SHOULD–
–YOU'LL SPEAK WHEN SPOKEN TO, LEONIDAS. IF YOU THINK BEING MY SON WILL KEEP ME FROM CUTTING OUT YOUR TONGUE AND FEEDING IT TO THE DOGS, YOU'RE GRAVELY MISTAKEN.
SIRE, GENERAL MILTIADES–
–WILL HAVE TO WAIT. DID HE NOT TELL YOU WE'RE IN THE MIDDLE OF THE CARNEIA–OUR HOLY FESTIVAL OF PEACE?
YOUR FESTIVAL IS WELL KNOWN TO US, BUT CIRCUMSTANCES ARE SUCH THAT–
–THAT YOU WOULD HAVE ME DEFY THE *WILL* OF THE GODS? SUCH DECADENCE IS THE REASON YOUR DEMOCRACY WILL SCATTER TO THE FOUR WINDS, WHILE SPARTA REMAINS STANDING LIKE THE ROCK OF ETERNITY.
I NEVER KNEW THE MEN OF SPARTA WERE SO PARTIAL TO THE STAGNANT WINDS OF PEACE.
MIND YOUR TONGUE, LAD. INSOLENCE IS FAR LESS CHARMING WHEN COMING FROM A GROWN MAN THAN FROM THE DEWFLECKED LIPS OF A CHILD...
MY KING, ALLOW US TO AT LEAST ASSEMBLE VOLUNTEERS FROM AMONG–

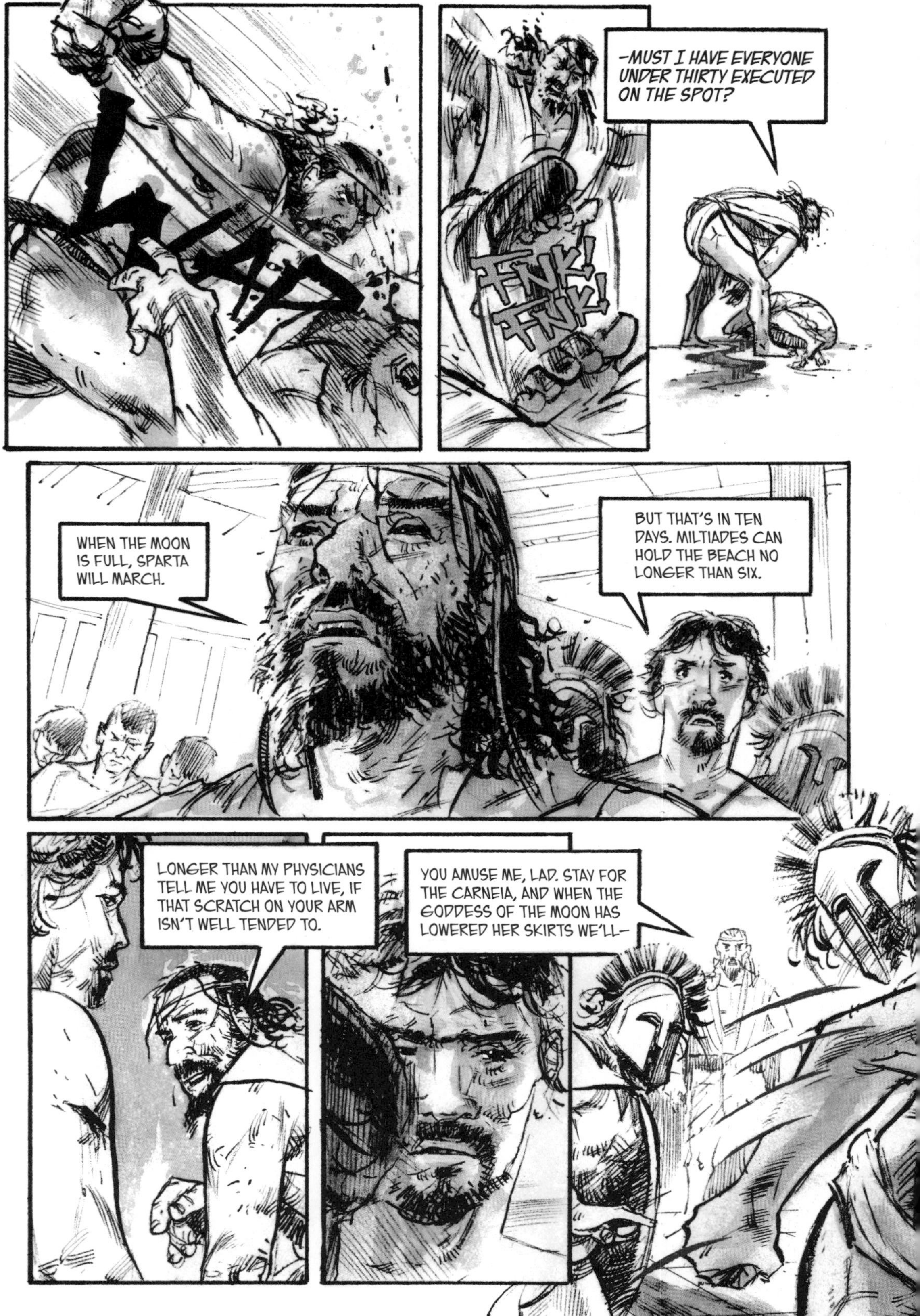
FNK! FNK!
–MUST I HAVE EVERYONE UNDER THIRTY EXECUTED ON THE SPOT?
WHEN THE MOON IS FULL, SPARTA WILL MARCH.
BUT THAT'S IN TEN DAYS. MILTIADES CAN HOLD THE BEACH NO LONGER THAN SIX.
LONGER THAN MY PHYSICIANS TELL ME YOU HAVE TO LIVE, IF THAT SCRATCH ON YOUR ARM ISN'T WELL TENDED TO.
YOU AMUSE ME, LAD. STAY FOR THE CARNEIA, AND WHEN THE GODDESS OF THE MOON HAS LOWERED HER SKIRTS WE'LL–

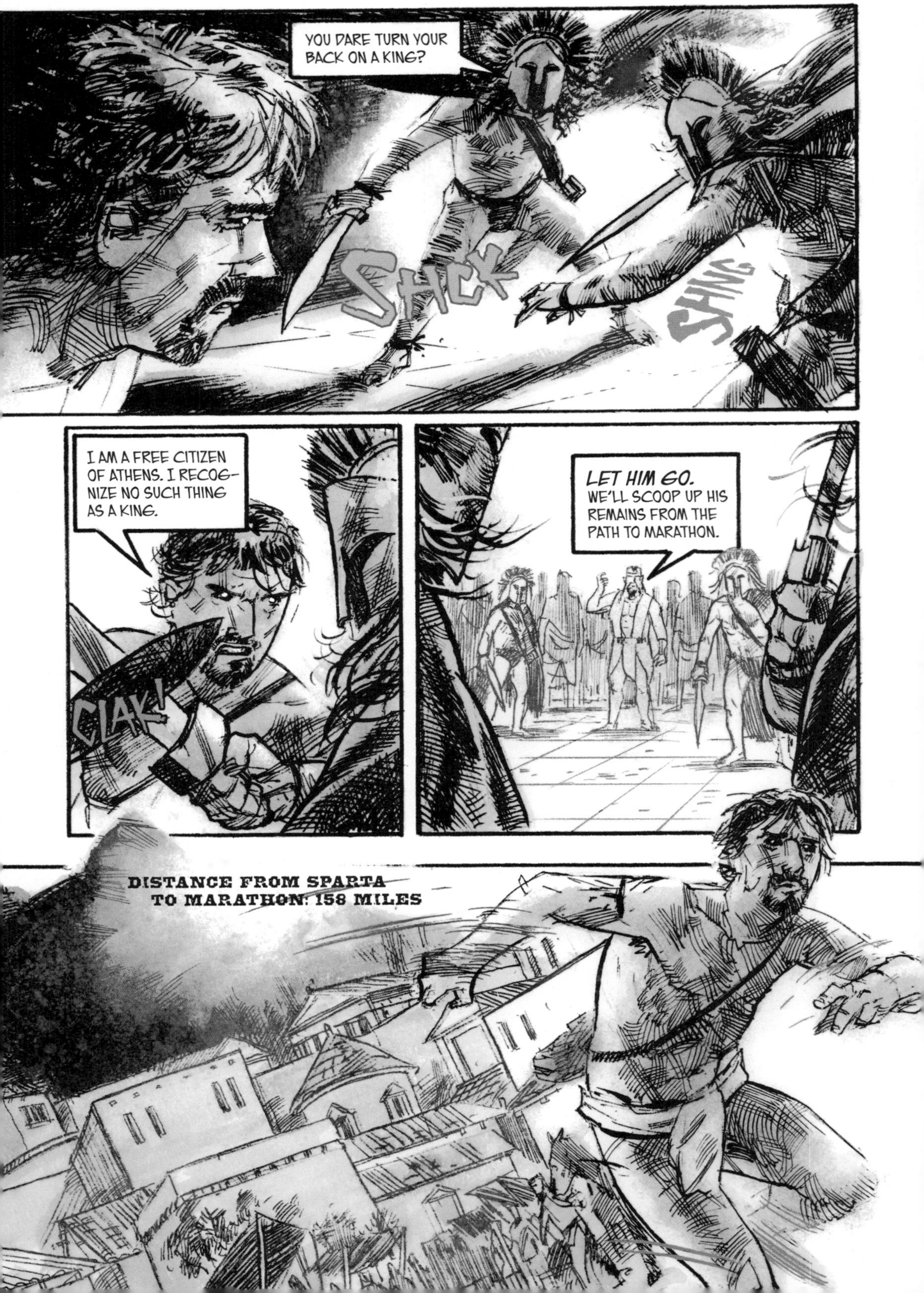
YOU DARE TURN YOUR BACK ON A KING?
SHCK
SHING
I AM A FREE CITIZEN OF ATHENS. I RECOG-NIZE NO SUCH THING AS A KING.
CLAK!
LET HIM GO. WE'LL SCOOP UP HIS REMAINS FROM THE PATH TO MARATHON.
DISTANCE FROM SPARTA TO MARATHON: 158 MILES

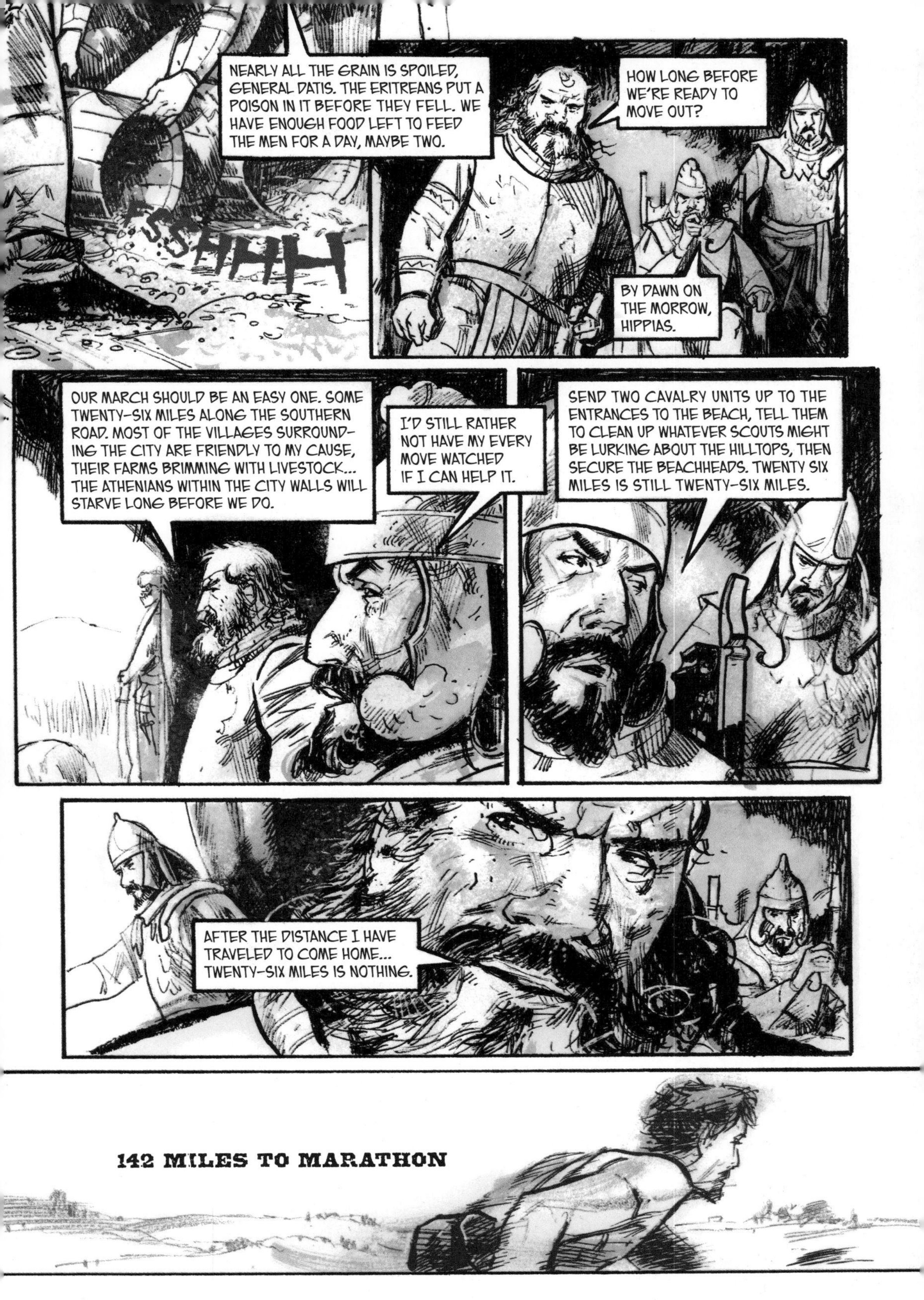
NEARLY ALL THE GRAIN IS SPOILED, GENERAL DATIS. THE ERITREANS PUT A POISON IN IT BEFORE THEY FELL. WE HAVE ENOUGH FOOD LEFT TO FEED THE MEN FOR A DAY, MAYBE TWO.
FSSHHH
HOW LONG BEFORE WE'RE READY TO MOVE OUT?
BY DAWN ON THE MORROW, HIPPIAS.
OUR MARCH SHOULD BE AN EASY ONE. SOME TWENTY-SIX MILES ALONG THE SOUTHERN ROAD. MOST OF THE VILLAGES SURROUNDING THE CITY ARE FRIENDLY TO MY CAUSE, THEIR FARMS BRIMMING WITH LIVESTOCK... THE ATHENIANS WITHIN THE CITY WALLS WILL STARVE LONG BEFORE WE DO.
I'D STILL RATHER NOT HAVE MY EVERY MOVE WATCHED IF I CAN HELP IT.
SEND TWO CAVALRY UNITS UP TO THE ENTRANCES TO THE BEACH, TELL THEM TO CLEAN UP WHATEVER SCOUTS MIGHT BE LURKING ABOUT THE HILLTOPS, THEN SECURE THE BEACHHEADS. TWENTY SIX MILES IS STILL TWENTY-SIX MILES.
AFTER THE DISTANCE I HAVE TRAVELED TO COME HOME... TWENTY-SIX MILES IS NOTHING.
142 MILES TO MARATHON

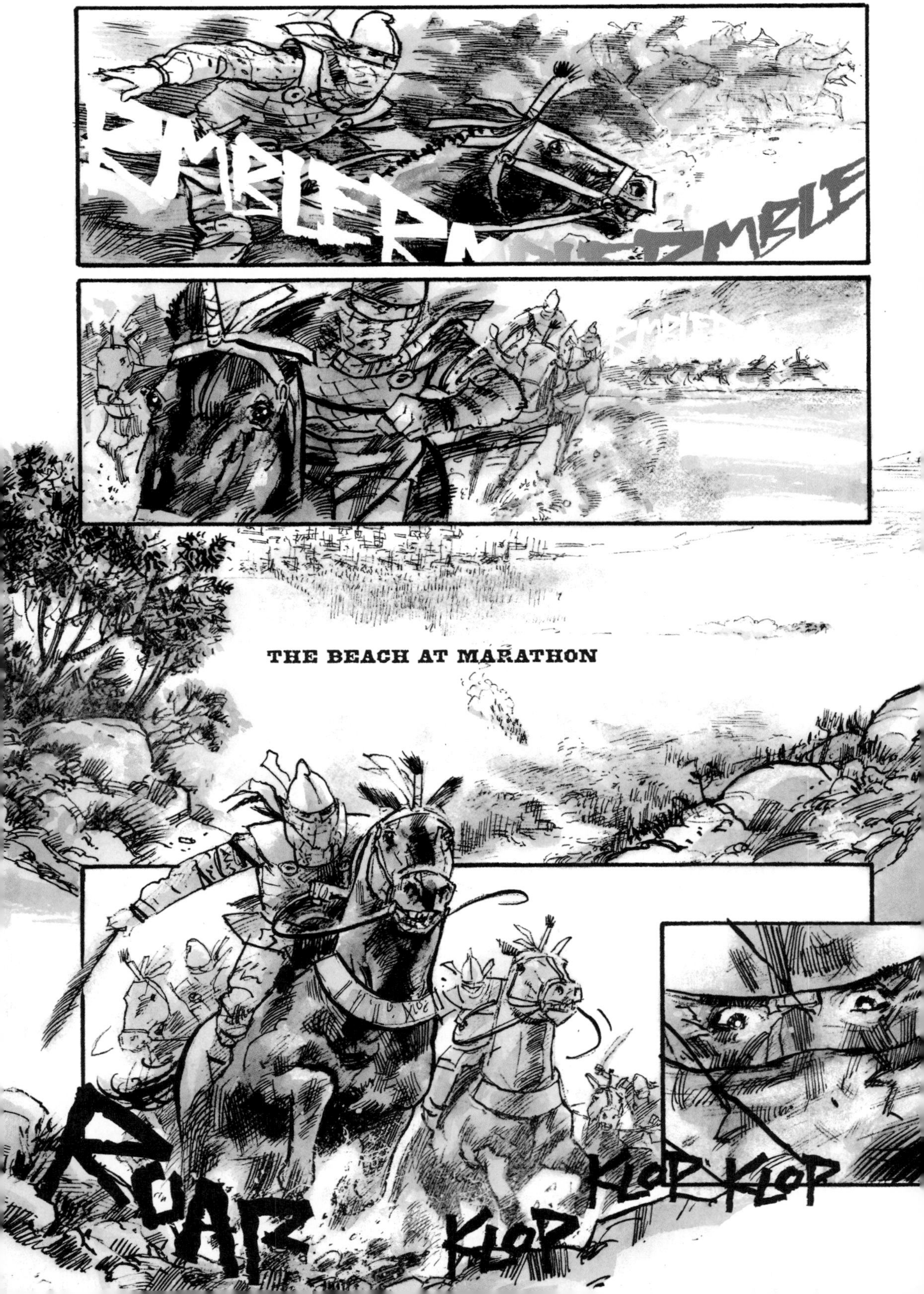
RUMBLE RUMBLE RUMBLE
THE BEACH AT MARATHON
ROAR
KLOP KLOP
KLOP

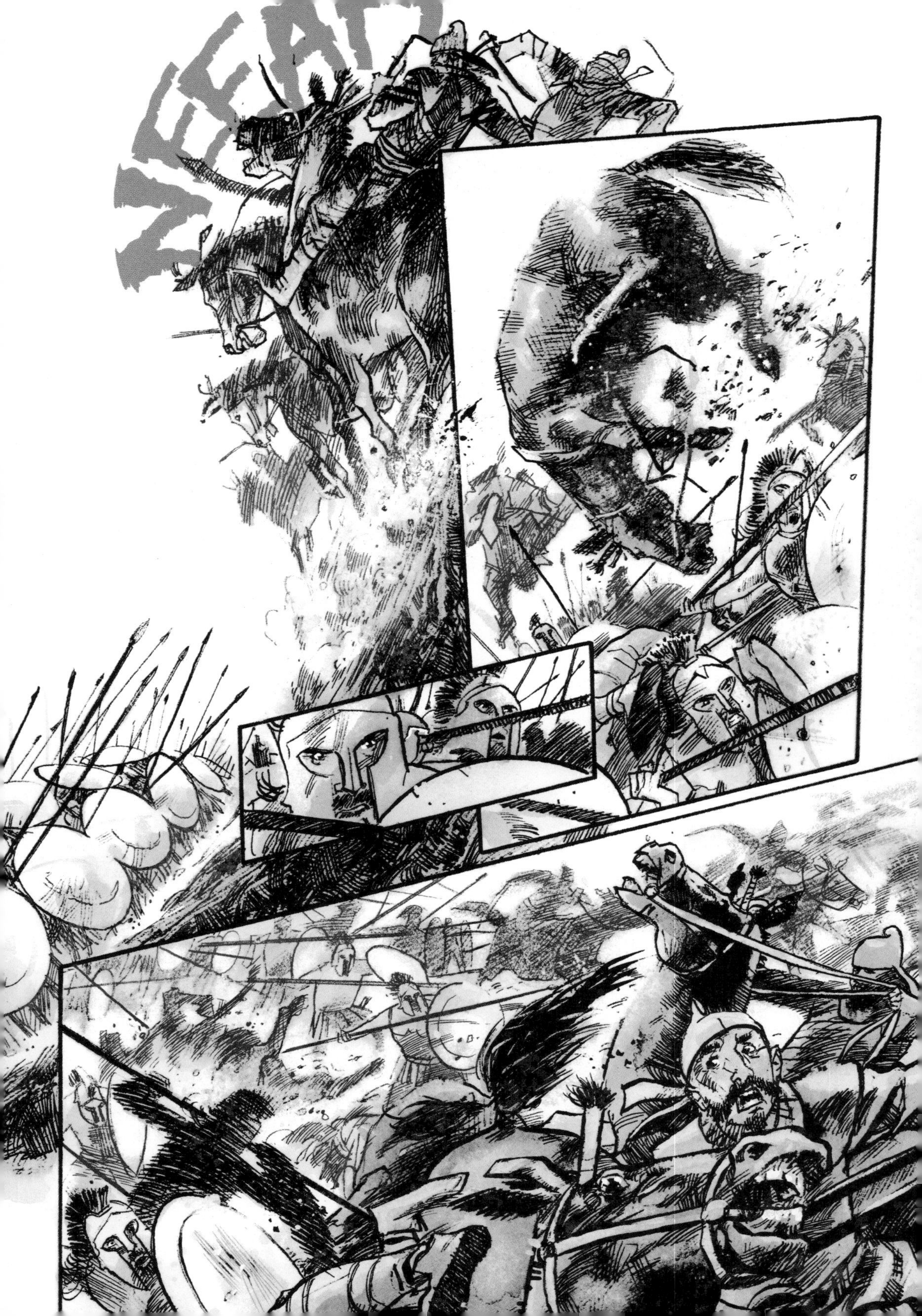
NEEA

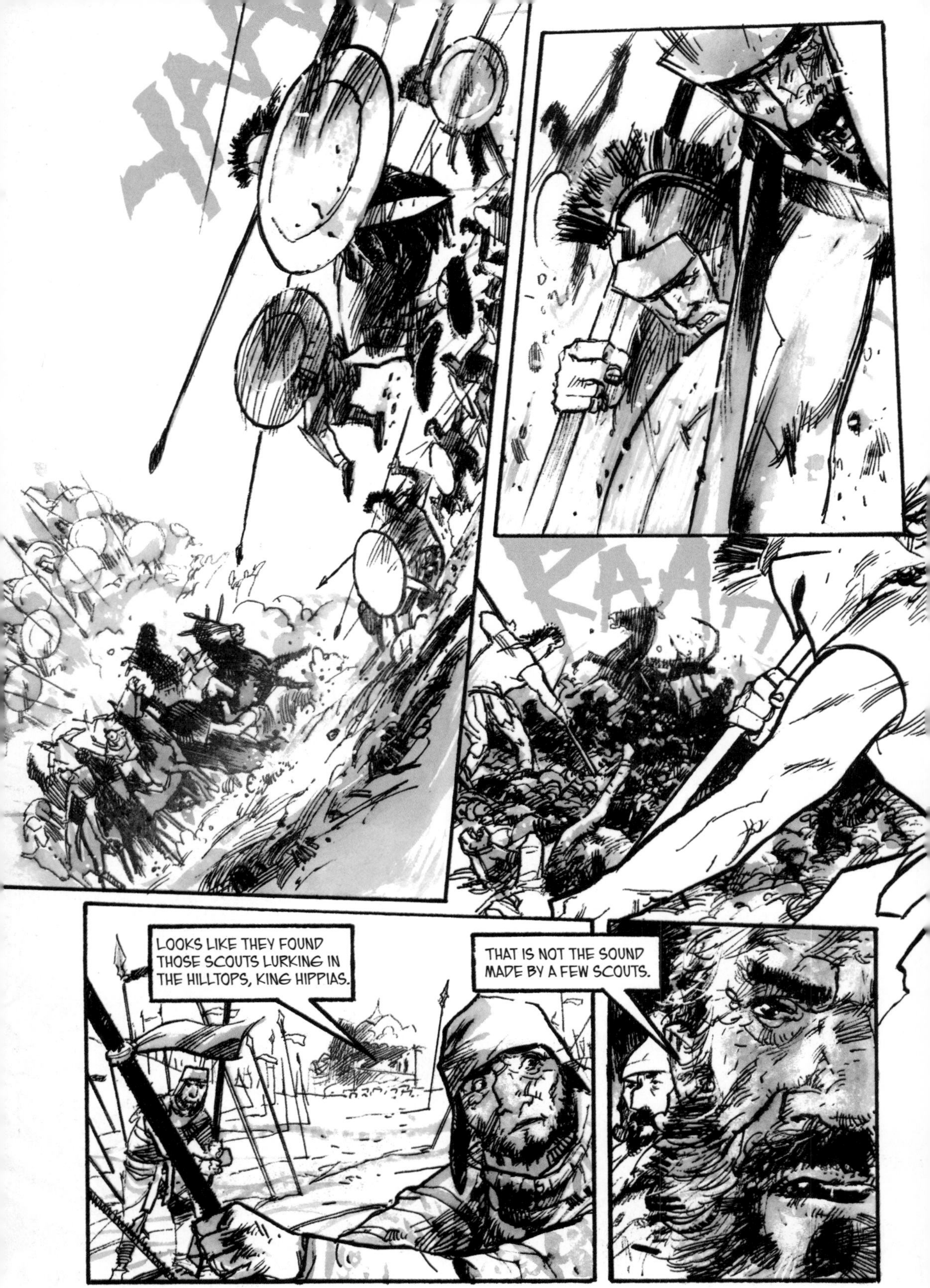
YAAA
RAAH
LOOKS LIKE THEY FOUND THOSE SCOUTS LURKING IN THE HILLTOPS, KING HIPPIAS.
THAT IS NOT THE SOUND MADE BY A FEW SCOUTS.

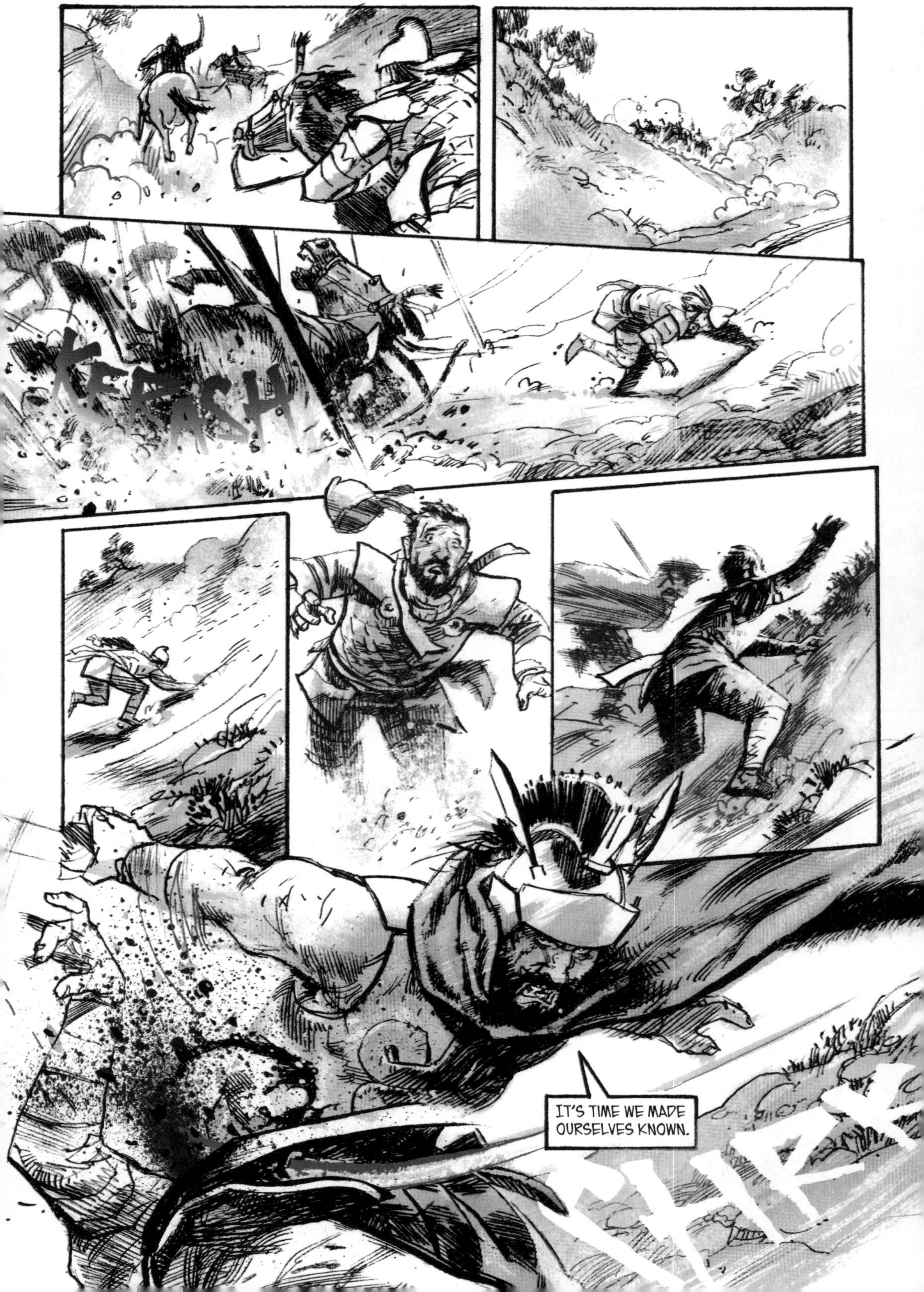
KERASH
IT'S TIME WE MADE OURSELVES KNOWN.

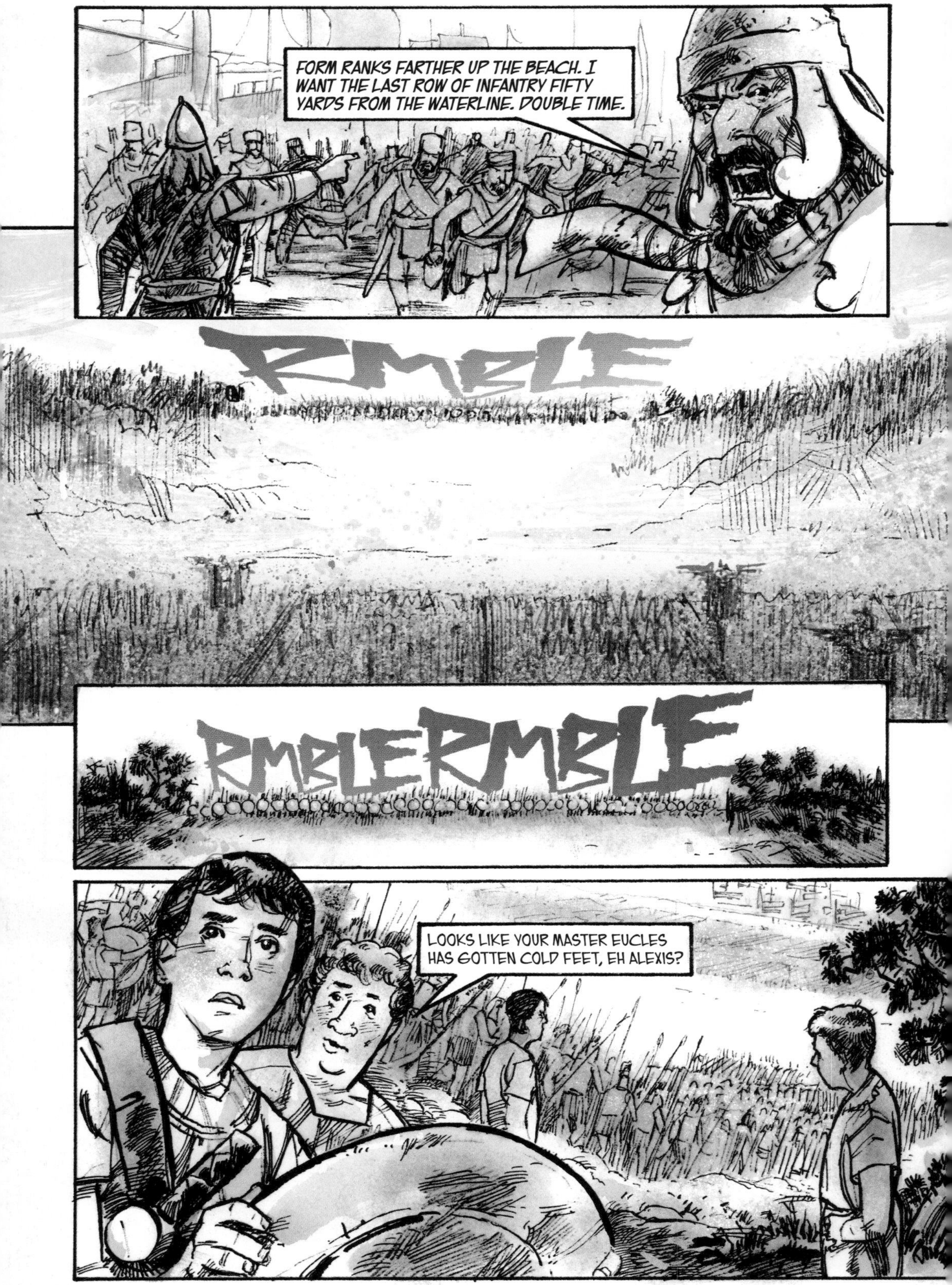
FORM RANKS FARTHER UP THE BEACH. I WANT THE LAST ROW OF INFANTRY FIFTY YARDS FROM THE WATERLINE. DOUBLE TIME.
RMBLE
RMBLERMBLE
LOOKS LIKE YOUR MASTER EUCLES HAS GOTTEN COLD FEET, EH ALEXIS?

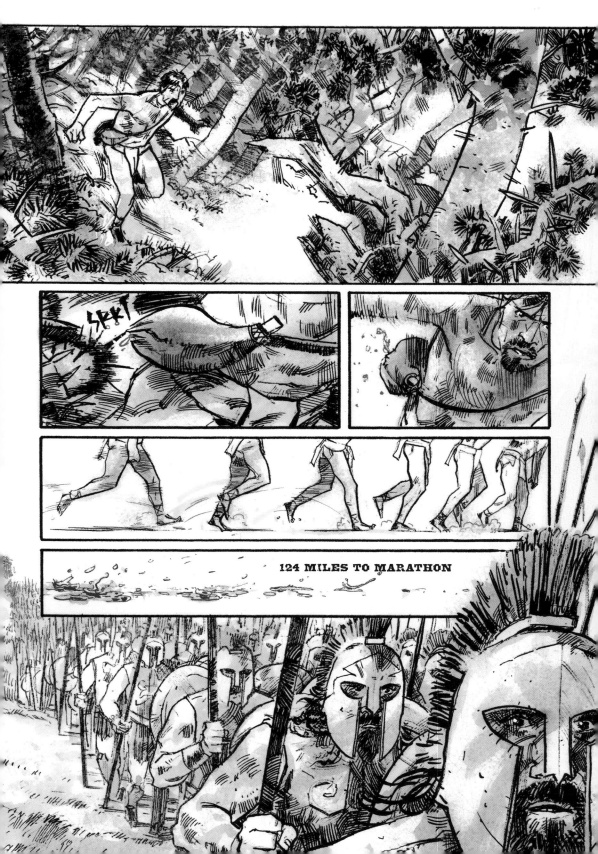

SKKT

124 MILES TO MARATHON

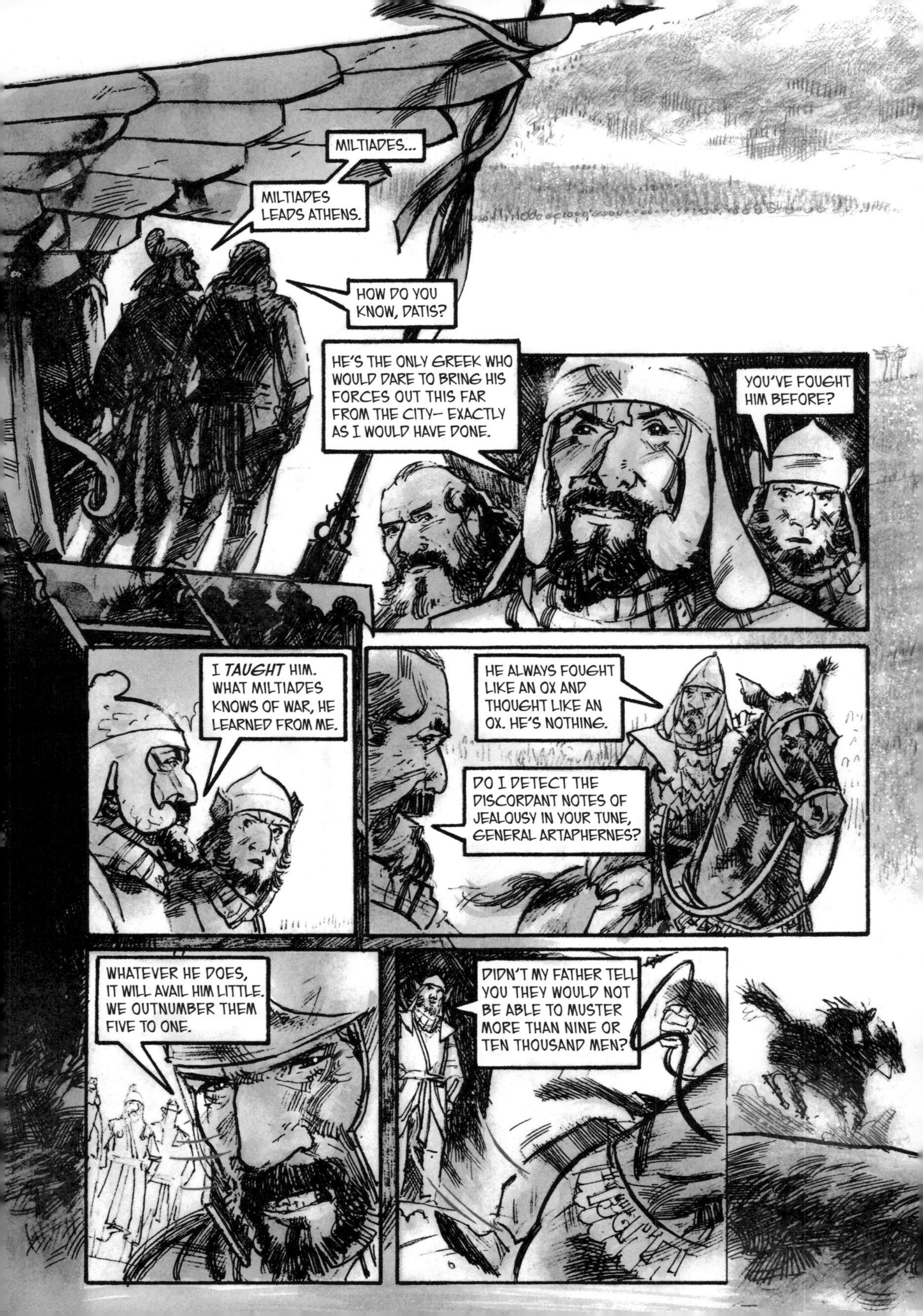
MILTIADES...
MILTIADES LEADS ATHENS.
HOW DO YOU KNOW, DATIS?
HE'S THE ONLY GREEK WHO WOULD DARE TO BRING HIS FORCES OUT THIS FAR FROM THE CITY— EXACTLY AS I WOULD HAVE DONE.
YOU'VE FOUGHT HIM BEFORE?
I *TAUGHT* HIM. WHAT MILTIADES KNOWS OF WAR, HE LEARNED FROM ME.
HE ALWAYS FOUGHT LIKE AN OX AND THOUGHT LIKE AN OX. HE'S NOTHING.
DO I DETECT THE DISCORDANT NOTES OF JEALOUSY IN YOUR TUNE, GENERAL ARTAPHERNES?
WHATEVER HE DOES, IT WILL AVAIL HIM LITTLE. WE OUTNUMBER THEM FIVE TO ONE.
DIDN'T MY FATHER TELL YOU THEY WOULD NOT BE ABLE TO MUSTER MORE THAN NINE OR TEN THOUSAND MEN?

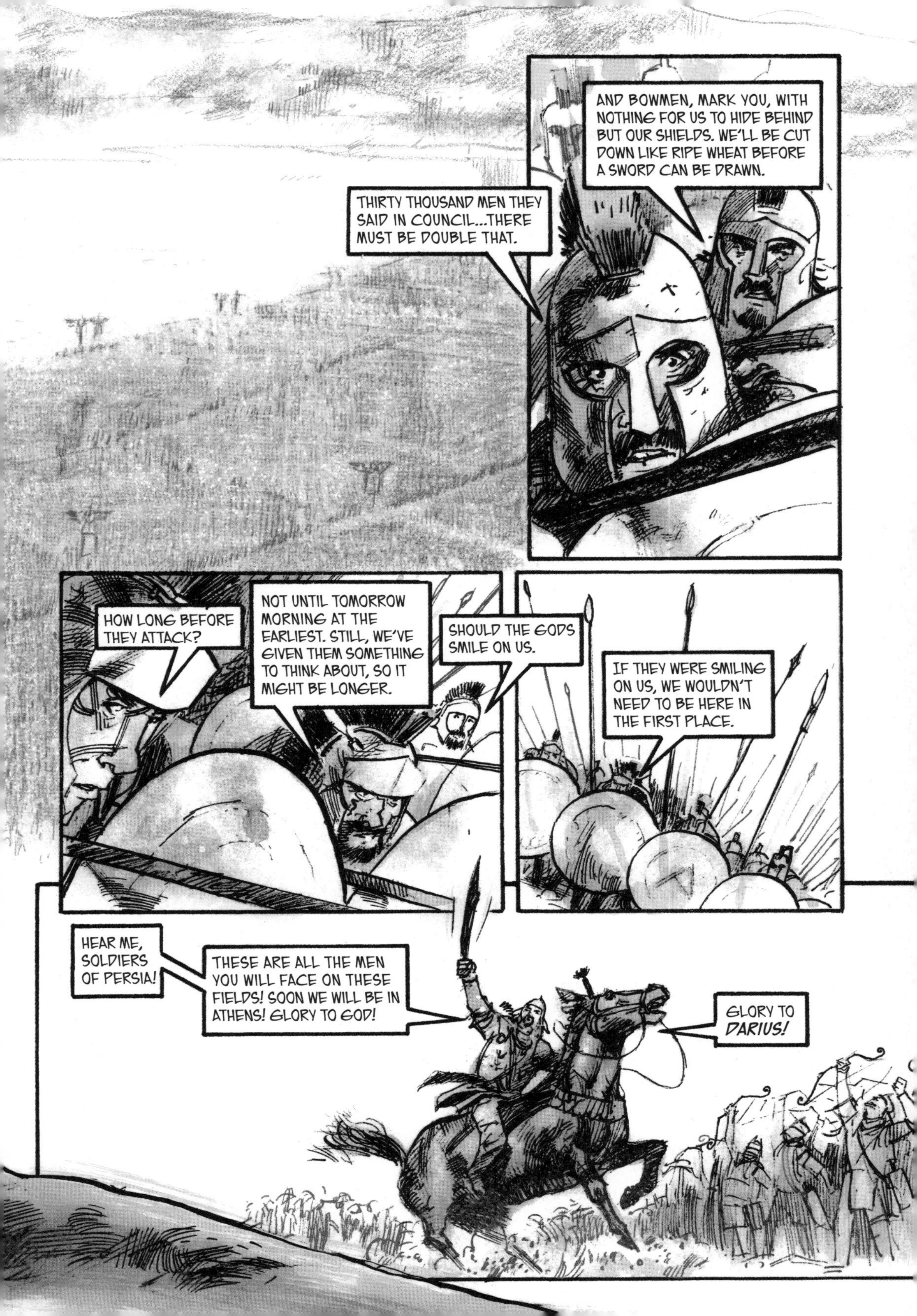
THIRTY THOUSAND MEN THEY SAID IN COUNCIL...THERE MUST BE DOUBLE THAT.
AND BOWMEN, MARK YOU, WITH NOTHING FOR US TO HIDE BEHIND BUT OUR SHIELDS. WE'LL BE CUT DOWN LIKE RIPE WHEAT BEFORE A SWORD CAN BE DRAWN.
HOW LONG BEFORE THEY ATTACK?
NOT UNTIL TOMORROW MORNING AT THE EARLIEST. STILL, WE'VE GIVEN THEM SOMETHING TO THINK ABOUT, SO IT MIGHT BE LONGER.
SHOULD THE GODS SMILE ON US.
IF THEY WERE SMILING ON US, WE WOULDN'T NEED TO BE HERE IN THE FIRST PLACE.
HEAR ME, SOLDIERS OF PERSIA!
THESE ARE ALL THE MEN YOU WILL FACE ON THESE FIELDS! SOON WE WILL BE IN ATHENS! GLORY TO GOD!
GLORY TO *DARIUS!*

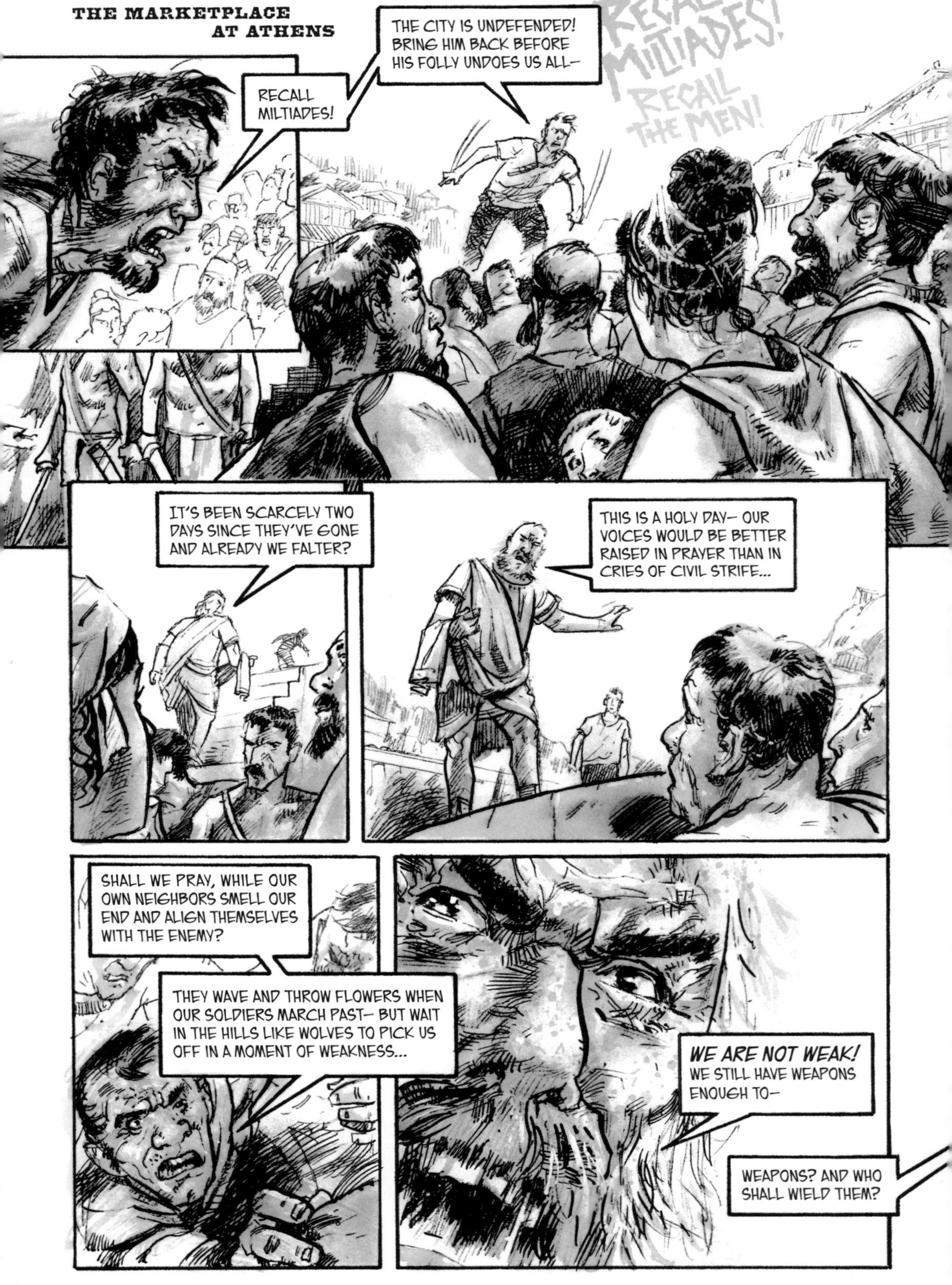
THE MARKETPLACE AT ATHENS
RECALL MILTIADES!
THE CITY IS UNDEFENDED! BRING HIM BACK BEFORE HIS FOLLY UNDOES US ALL—
RECALL MILTIADES! RECALL THE MEN!
IT'S BEEN SCARCELY TWO DAYS SINCE THEY'VE GONE AND ALREADY WE FALTER?
THIS IS A HOLY DAY— OUR VOICES WOULD BE BETTER RAISED IN PRAYER THAN IN CRIES OF CIVIL STRIFE...
SHALL WE PRAY, WHILE OUR OWN NEIGHBORS SMELL OUR END AND ALIGN THEMSELVES WITH THE ENEMY?
THEY WAVE AND THROW FLOWERS WHEN OUR SOLDIERS MARCH PAST— BUT WAIT IN THE HILLS LIKE WOLVES TO PICK US OFF IN A MOMENT OF WEAKNESS...
WE ARE NOT WEAK! WE STILL HAVE WEAPONS ENOUGH TO—
WEAPONS? AND WHO SHALL WIELD THEM?

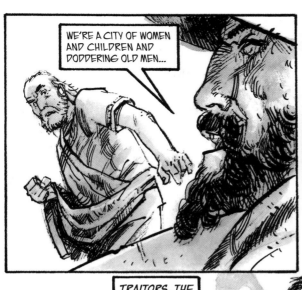

WE'RE A CITY OF WOMEN AND CHILDREN AND DODDERING OLD MEN...

MEN ENOUGH TO PUT AN END TO YOUR WHINING.

TRAITORS, THE LOT OF YOU—

ARTEMIS...

LOOK!

THE GODDESS ARTEMIS IS AMONG US!

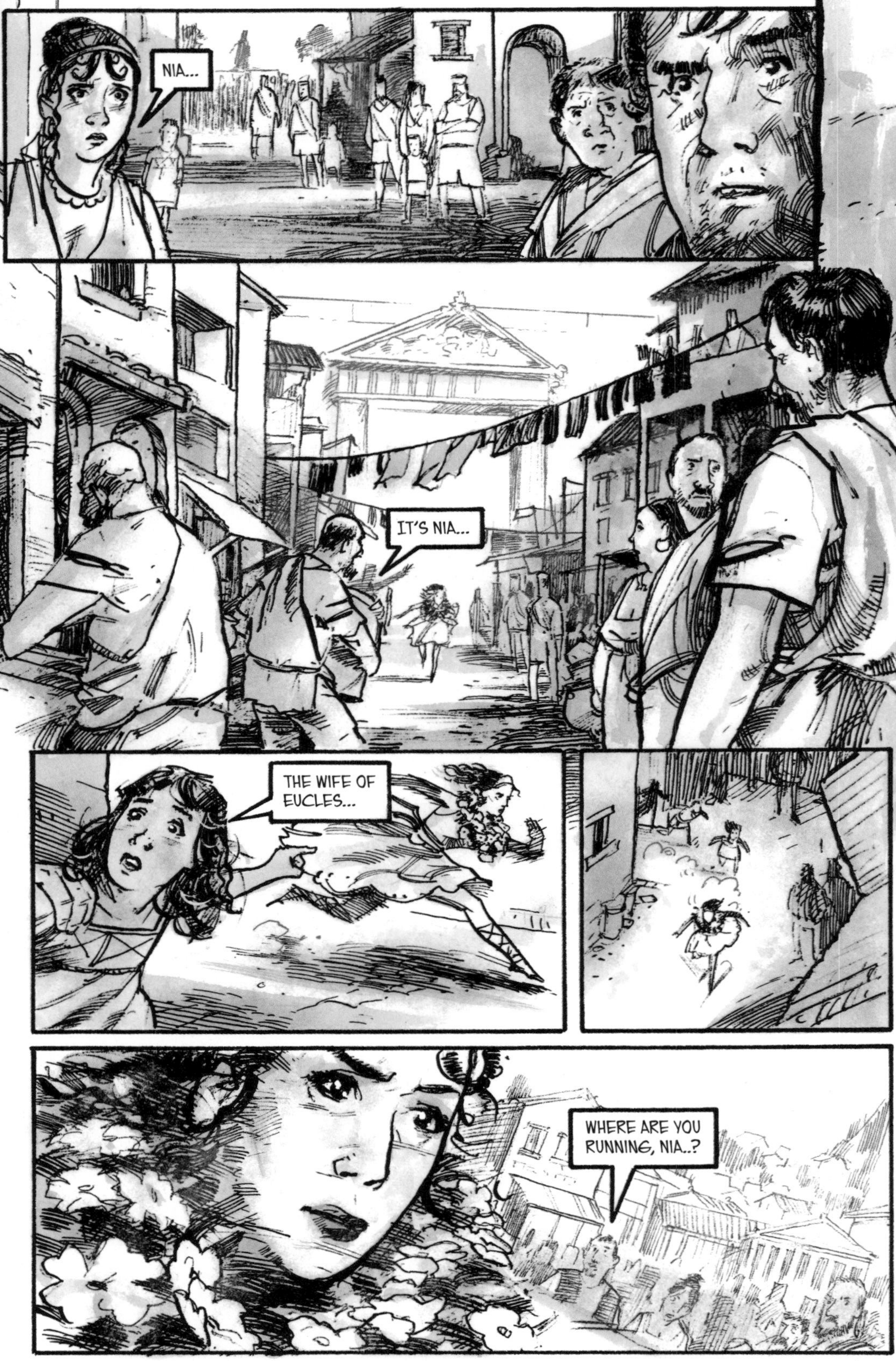
NIA...
IT'S NIA...
THE WIFE OF EUCLES...
WHERE ARE YOU RUNNING, NIA..?

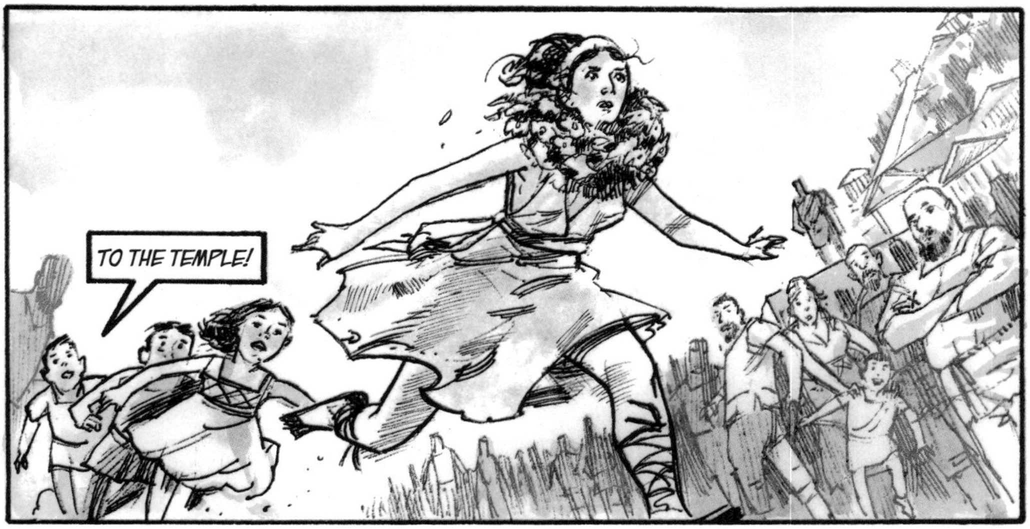
TO THE TEMPLE!

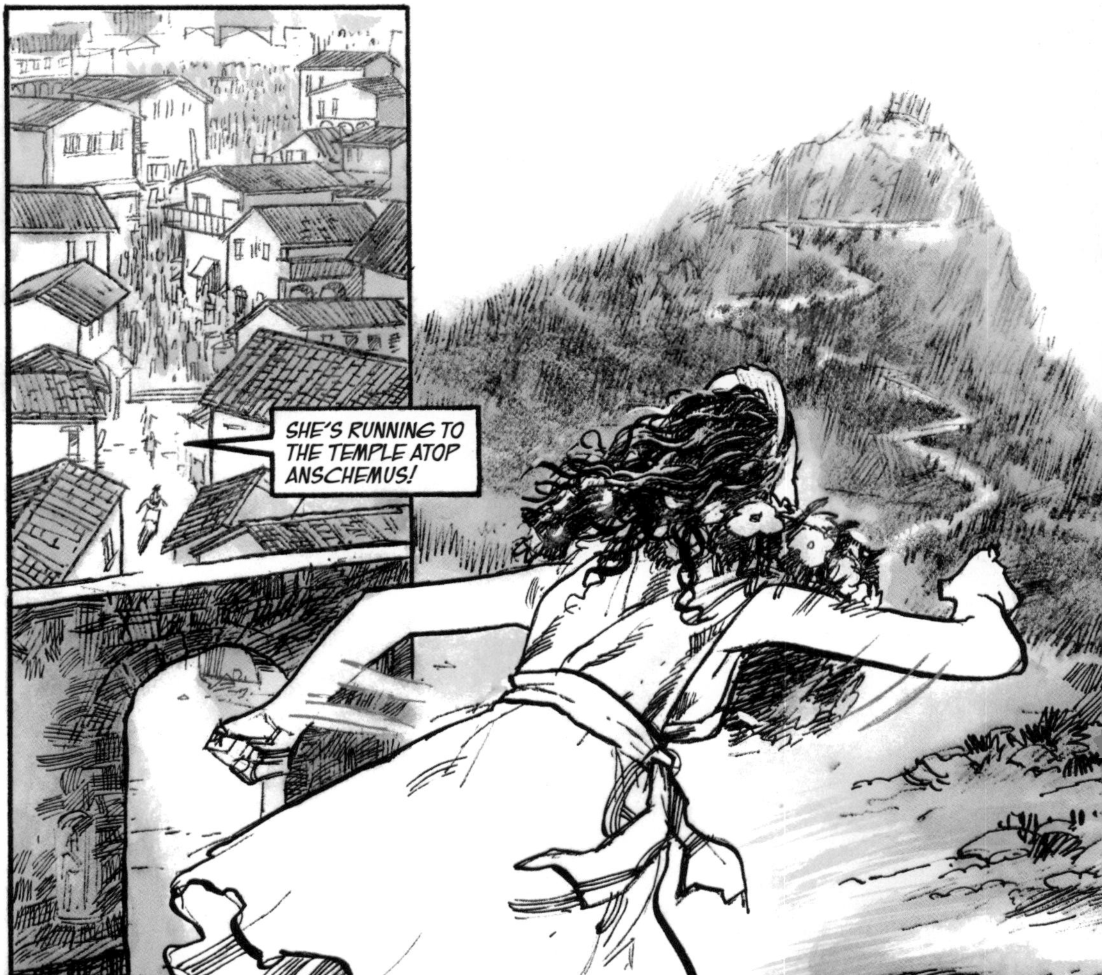
SHE'S RUNNING TO THE TEMPLE ATOP ANSCHEMUS!

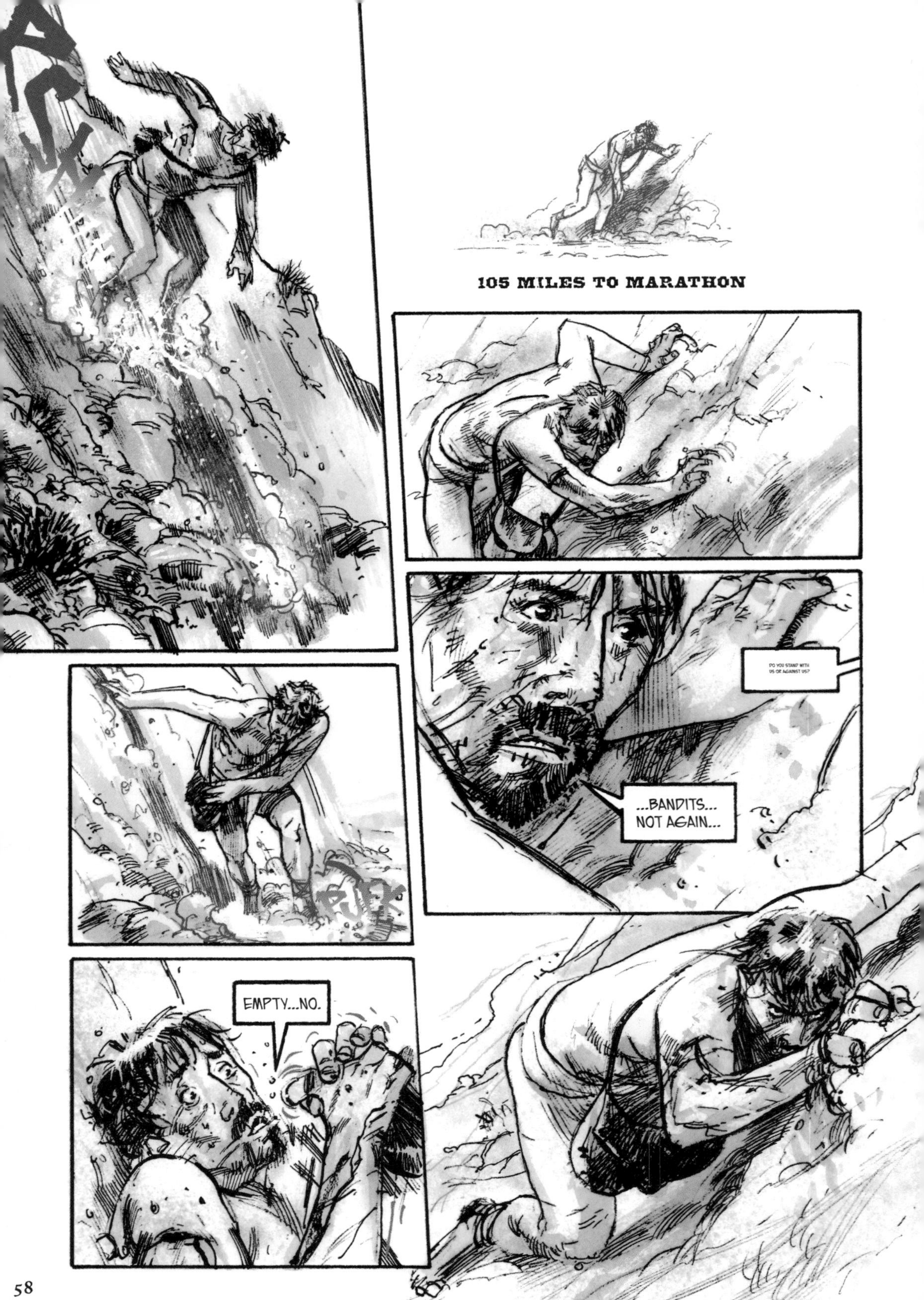
105 MILES TO MARATHON
DO YOU STAND WITH US OR AGAINST US?
...BANDITS... NOT AGAIN...
EMPTY...NO.

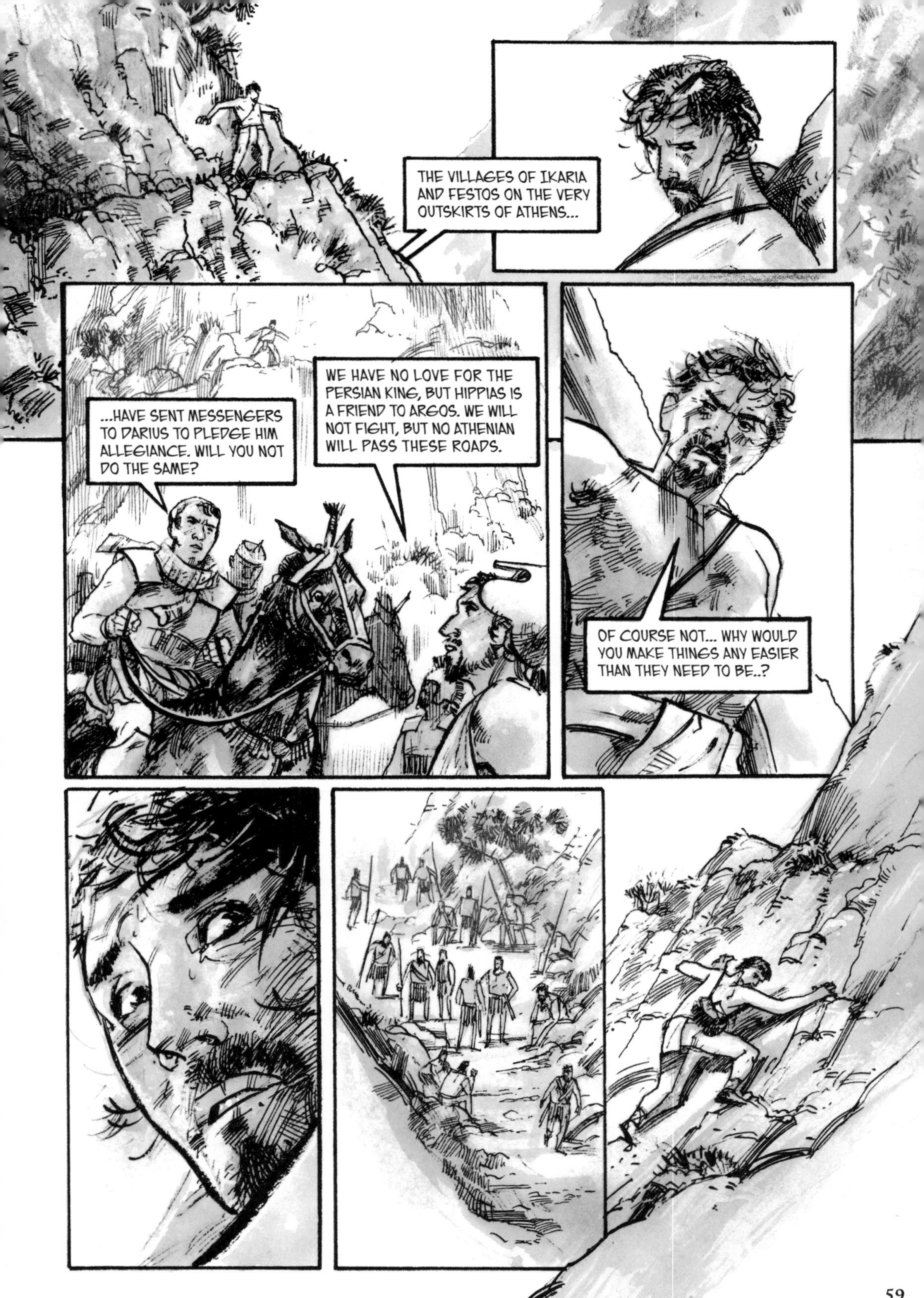
THE VILLAGES OF IKARIA AND FESTOS ON THE VERY OUTSKIRTS OF ATHENS...
...HAVE SENT MESSENGERS TO DARIUS TO PLEDGE HIM ALLEGIANCE. WILL YOU NOT DO THE SAME?
WE HAVE NO LOVE FOR THE PERSIAN KING, BUT HIPPIAS IS A FRIEND TO ARGOS. WE WILL NOT FIGHT, BUT NO ATHENIAN WILL PASS THESE ROADS.
OF COURSE NOT... WHY WOULD YOU MAKE THINGS ANY EASIER THAN THEY NEED TO BE..?

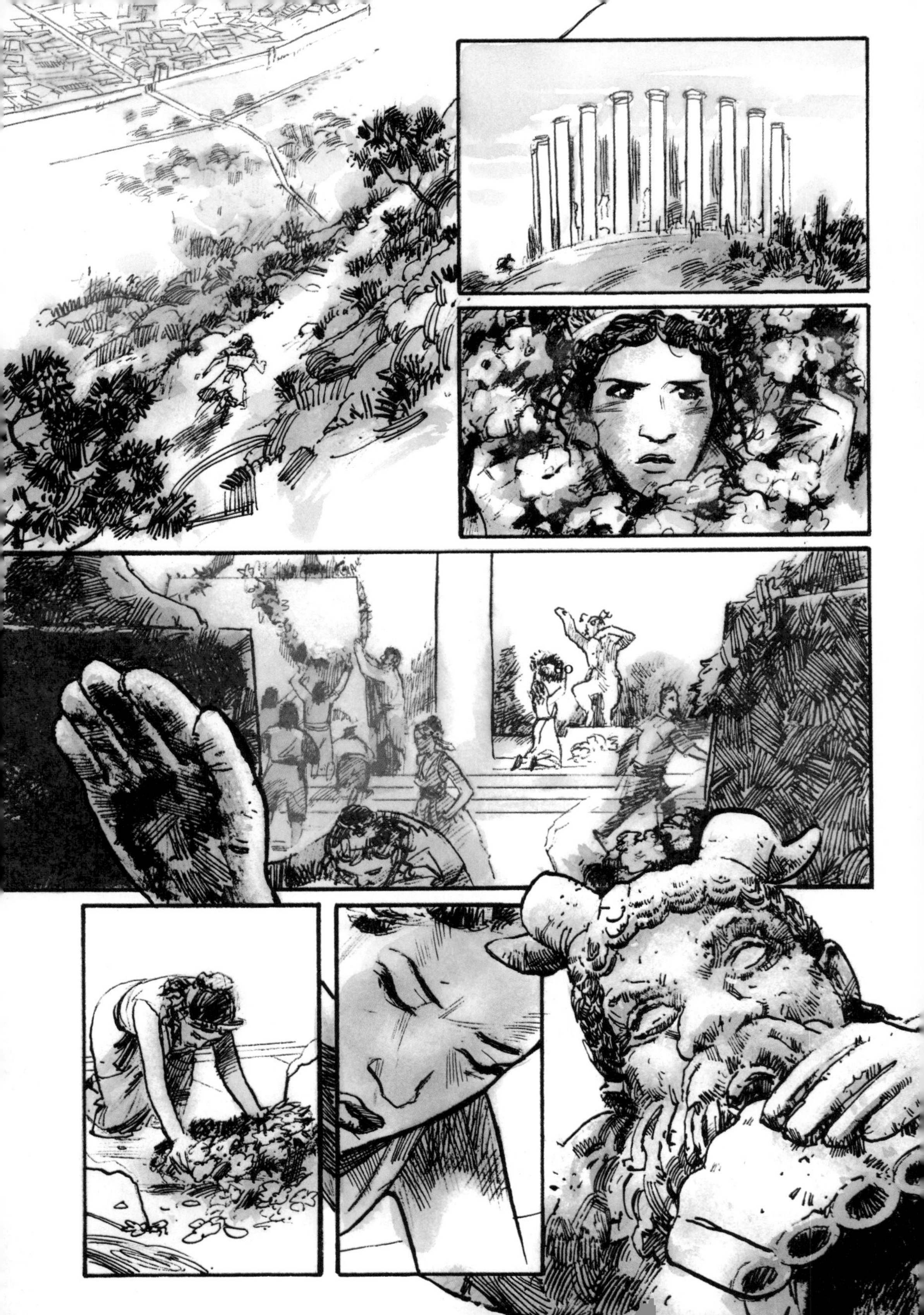

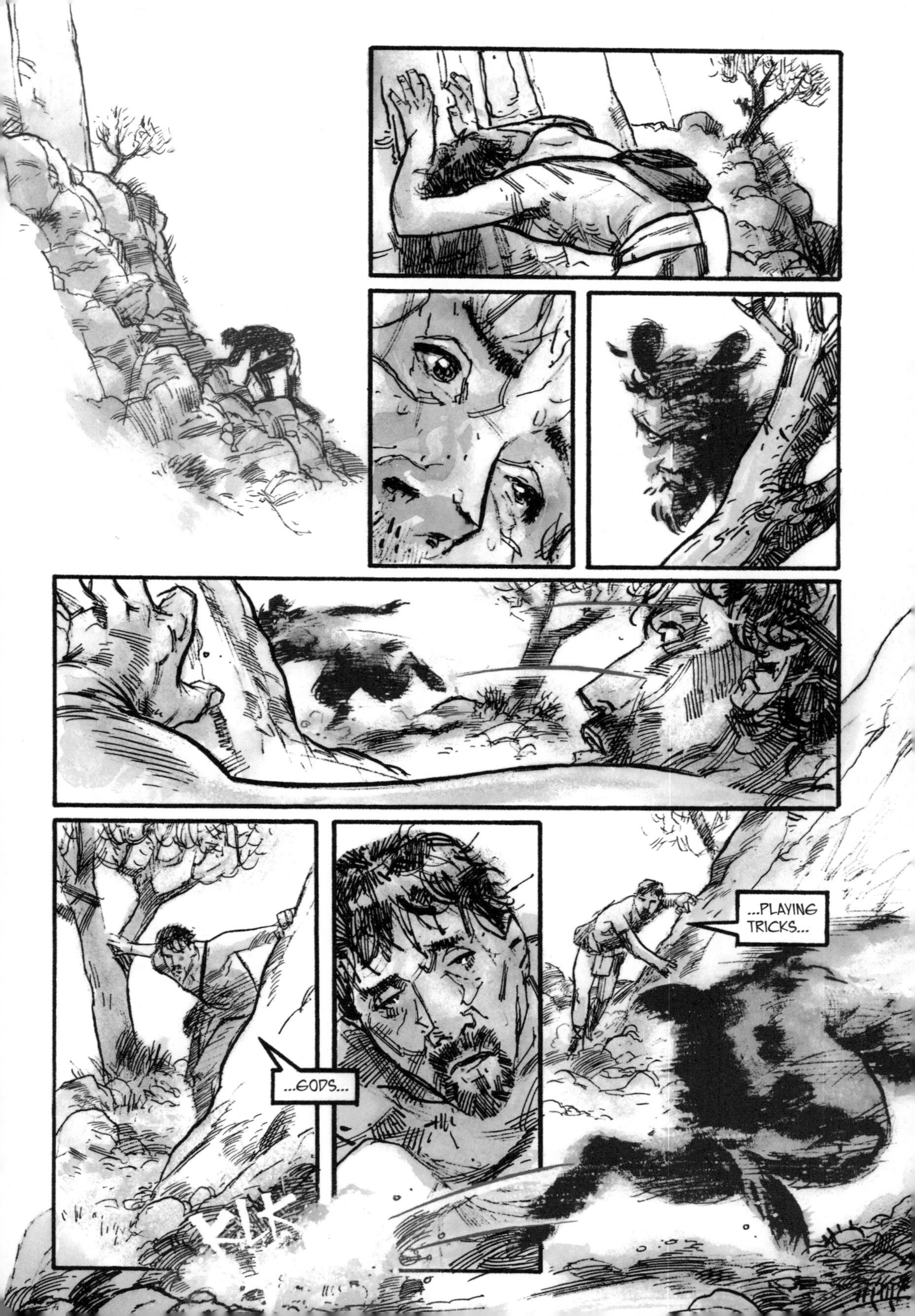
...GODS...
...PLAYING TRICKS...

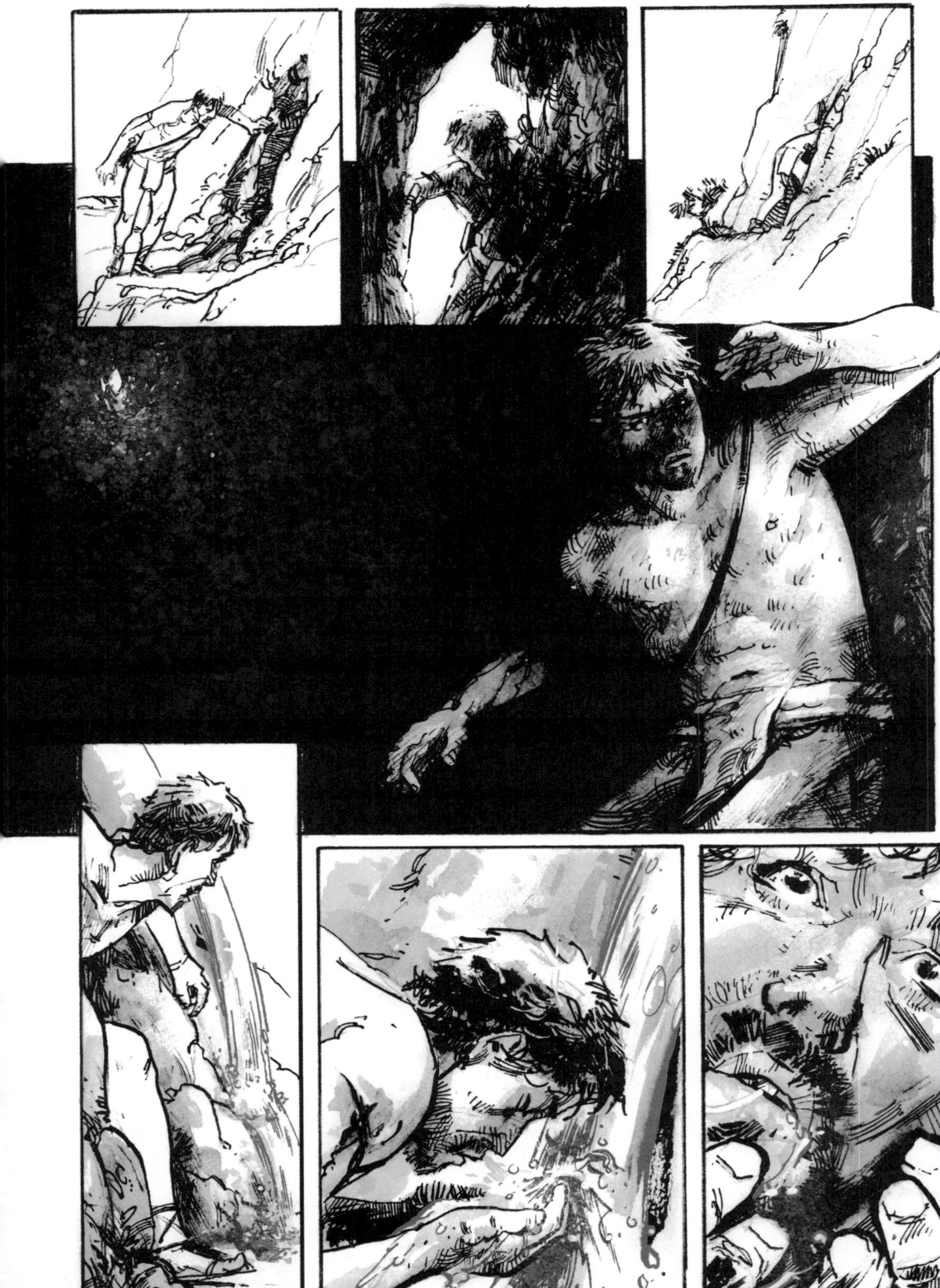

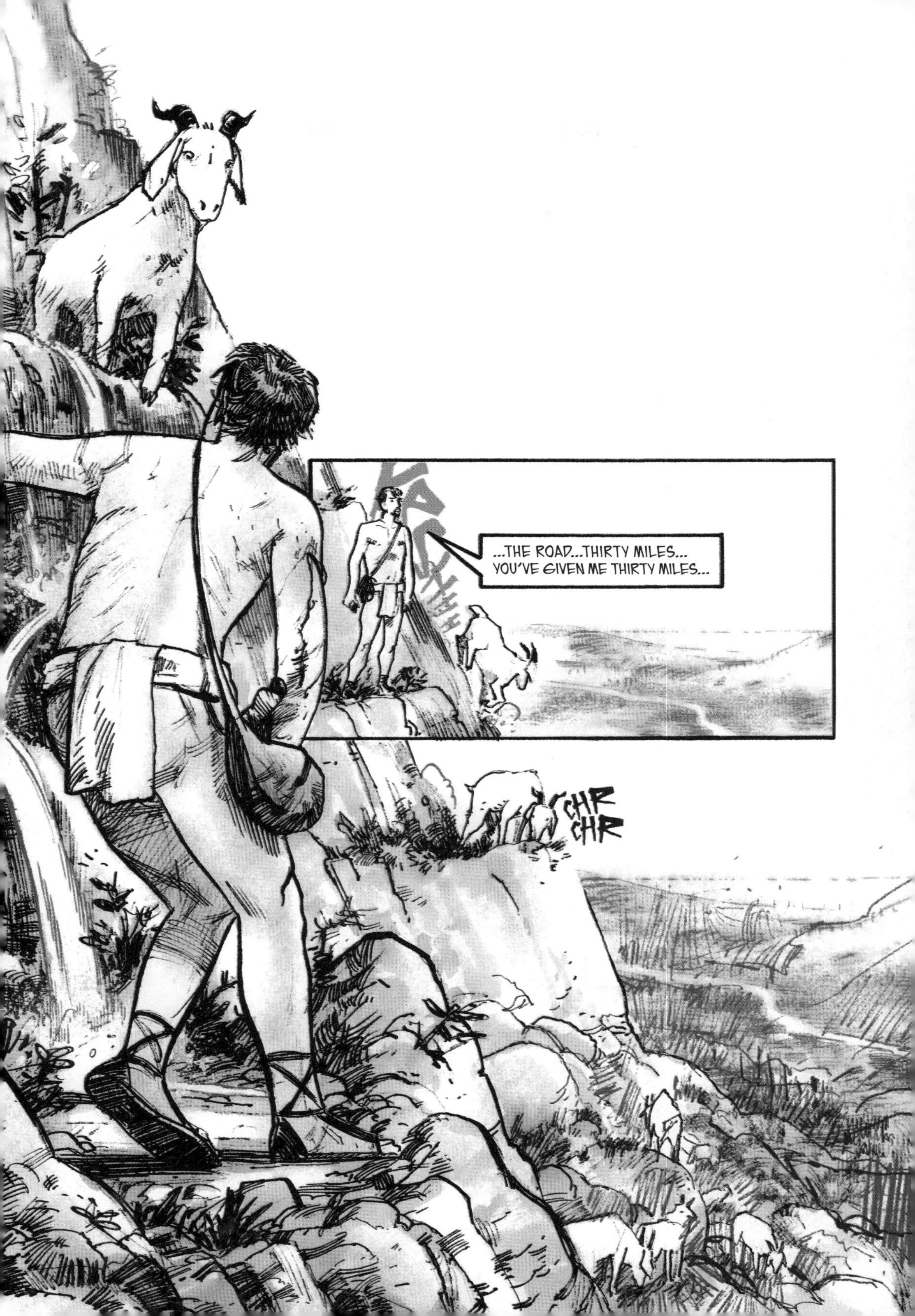
...THE ROAD...THIRTY MILES...
YOU'VE GIVEN ME THIRTY MILES...
CHR
CHR

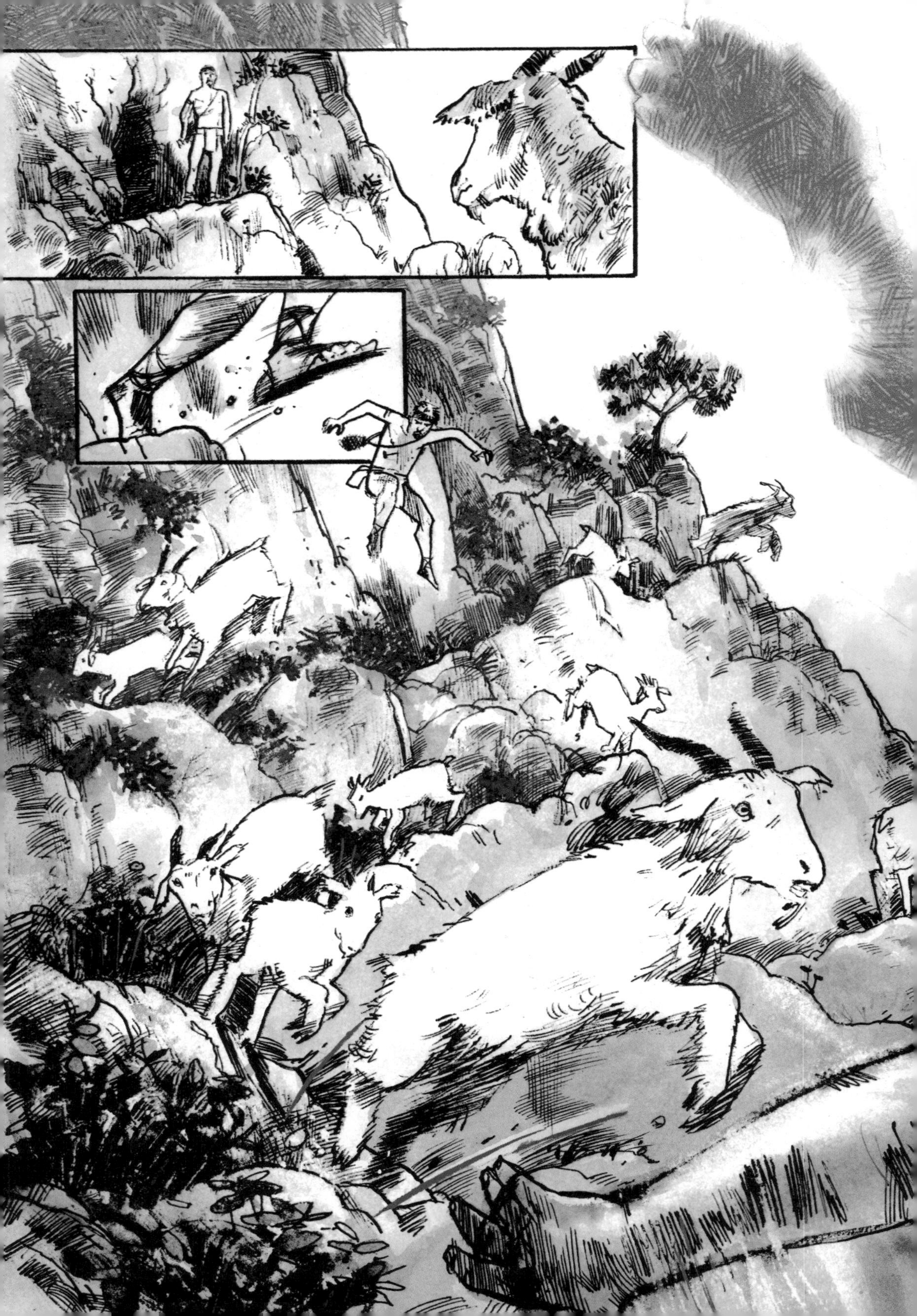

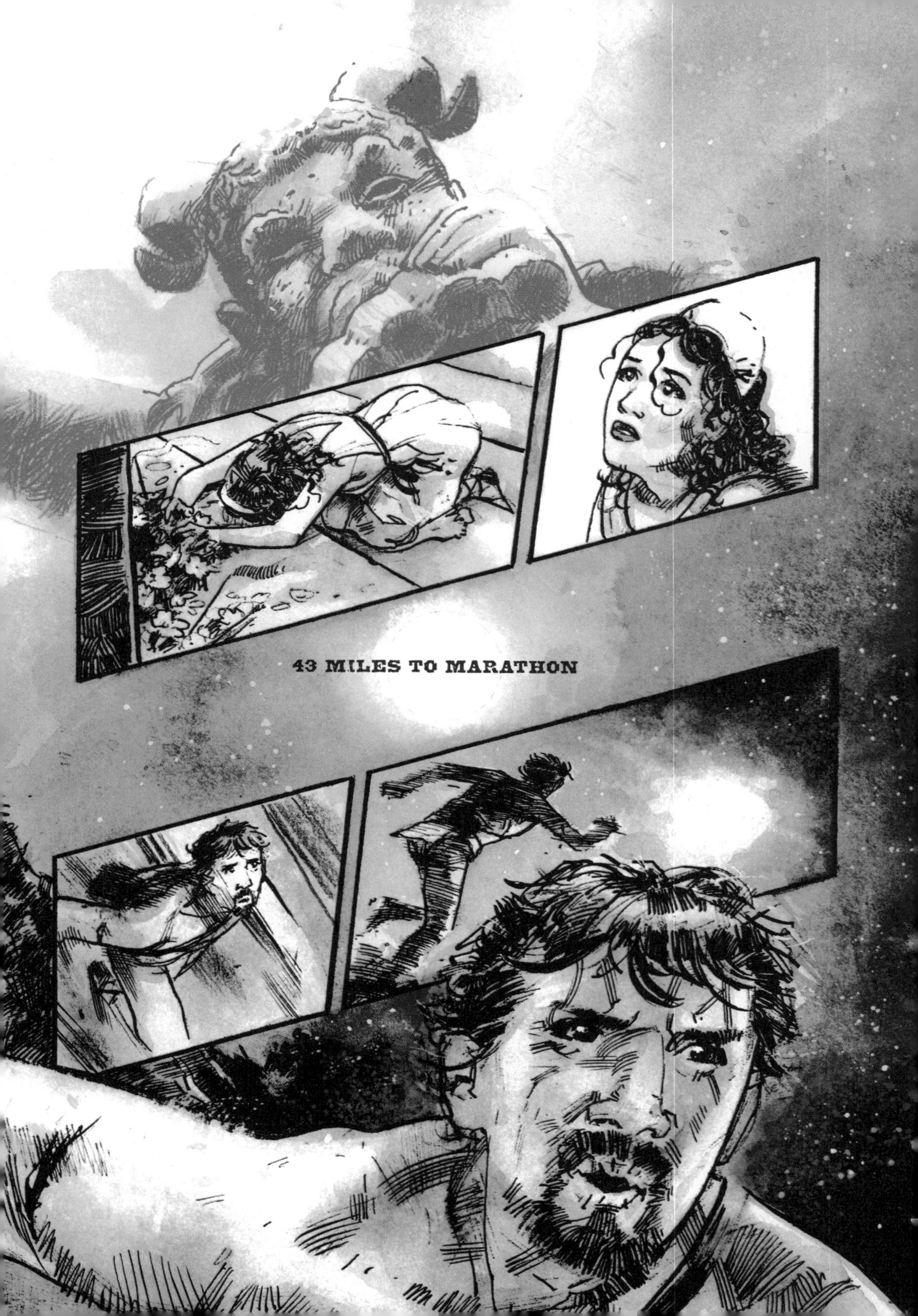
43 MILES TO MARATHON

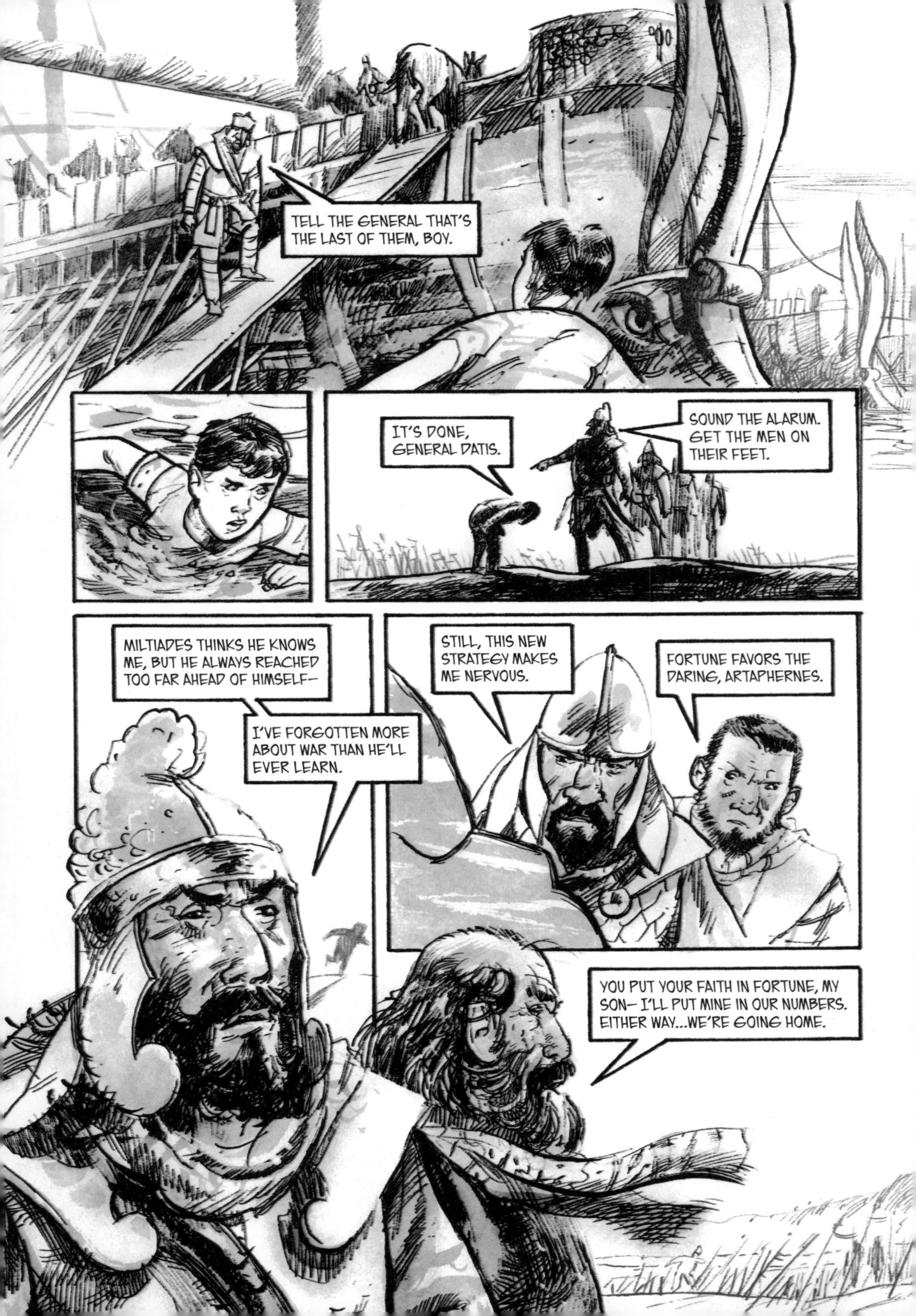
TELL THE GENERAL THAT'S THE LAST OF THEM, BOY.
IT'S DONE, GENERAL DATIS.
SOUND THE ALARUM. GET THE MEN ON THEIR FEET.
MILTIADES THINKS HE KNOWS ME, BUT HE ALWAYS REACHED TOO FAR AHEAD OF HIMSELF–
I'VE FORGOTTEN MORE ABOUT WAR THAN HE'LL EVER LEARN.
STILL, THIS NEW STRATEGY MAKES ME NERVOUS.
FORTUNE FAVORS THE DARING, ARTAPHERNES.
YOU PUT YOUR FAITH IN FORTUNE, MY SON– I'LL PUT MINE IN OUR NUMBERS. EITHER WAY...WE'RE GOING HOME.

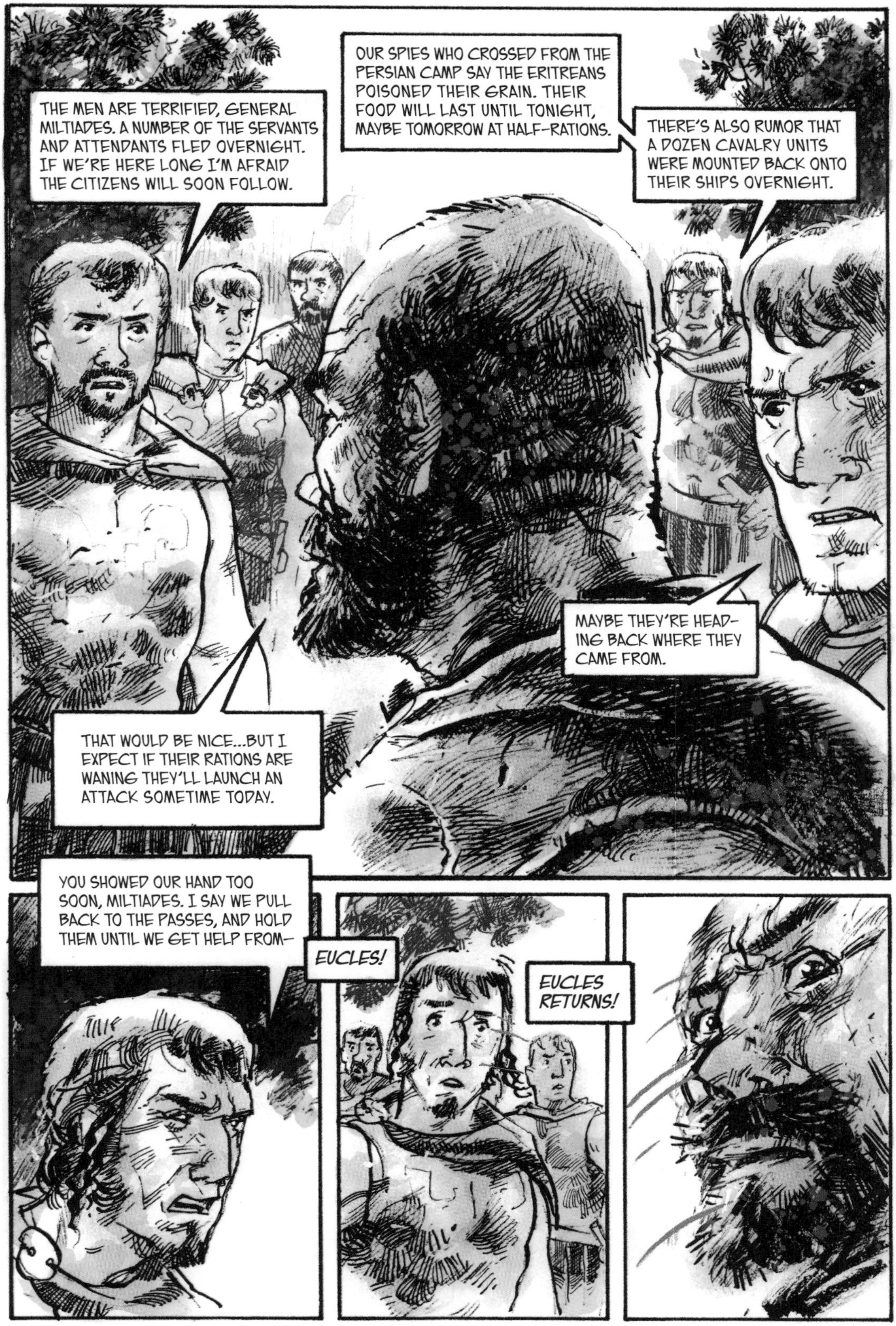
THE MEN ARE TERRIFIED, GENERAL MILTIADES. A NUMBER OF THE SERVANTS AND ATTENDANTS FLED OVERNIGHT. IF WE'RE HERE LONG I'M AFRAID THE CITIZENS WILL SOON FOLLOW.
OUR SPIES WHO CROSSED FROM THE PERSIAN CAMP SAY THE ERITREANS POISONED THEIR GRAIN. THEIR FOOD WILL LAST UNTIL TONIGHT, MAYBE TOMORROW AT HALF-RATIONS.
THERE'S ALSO RUMOR THAT A DOZEN CAVALRY UNITS WERE MOUNTED BACK ONTO THEIR SHIPS OVERNIGHT.
MAYBE THEY'RE HEADING BACK WHERE THEY CAME FROM.
THAT WOULD BE NICE...BUT I EXPECT IF THEIR RATIONS ARE WANING THEY'LL LAUNCH AN ATTACK SOMETIME TODAY.
YOU SHOWED OUR HAND TOO SOON, MILTIADES. I SAY WE PULL BACK TO THE PASSES, AND HOLD THEM UNTIL WE GET HELP FROM–
EUCLES!
EUCLES RETURNS!

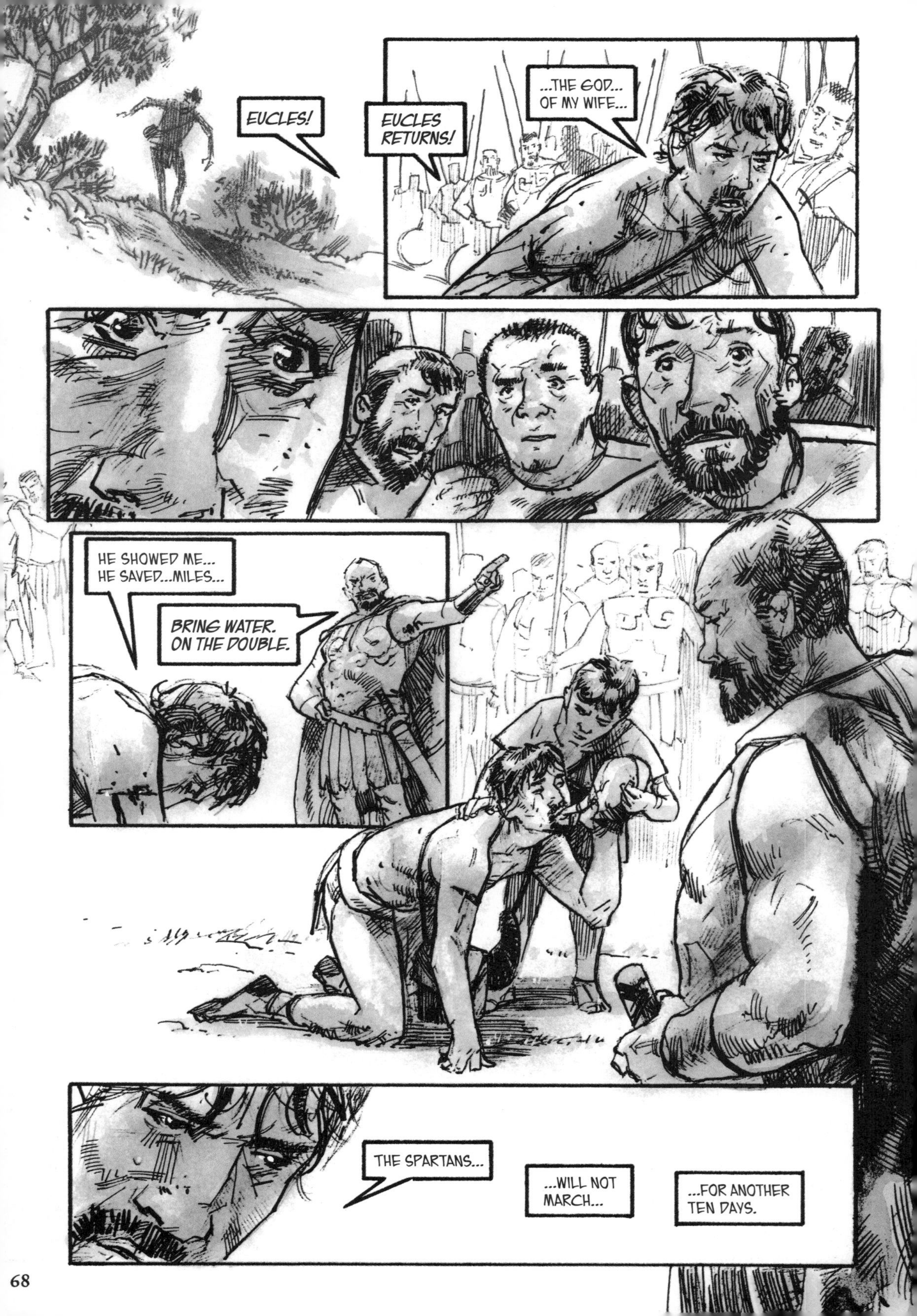
EUCLES!
EUCLES RETURNS!
...THE GOD... OF MY WIFE...
HE SHOWED ME... HE SAVED...MILES...
BRING WATER. ON THE DOUBLE.
THE SPARTANS...
...WILL NOT MARCH...
...FOR ANOTHER TEN DAYS.

THE HELL WITH THE SPARTANS.

THIS DAY WILL BE OUR GLORY, AND THEIR ETERNAL SHAME.

READY THE MEN. WE'LL ATTACK WHILE THE SUN IS STILL AT OUR BACKS.

ATTACK? FALL BACK AND HOLD THE BEACHHEADS!

—YOU HEARD WHAT OUR SPIES SAID...

—IF THERE'S EVEN THE CHANCE OF THEM LEAVING, I SAY LET THEM DO IT...

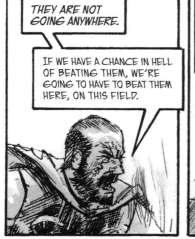

THEY ARE NOT GOING ANYWHERE.

IF WE HAVE A CHANCE IN HELL OF BEATING THEM, WE'RE GOING TO HAVE TO BEAT THEM HERE, ON THIS FIELD.

GENERAL MILTIADES...I AGREE WE MUST ATTACK. BUT IN FORMA-TION THEIR LINES STRETCH AT LEAST THREE TIMES THE LENGTH OF OUR OWN. OUR FLANKS WILL BE INDEFENSIBLE...

—IF WE EVEN GET THAT FAR. WHAT OF THEIR ARCHERS? WE HAVE NO COVER. WE'LL BE MASSACRED.

NOT IF YOU DO EXACTLY AS I SAY.

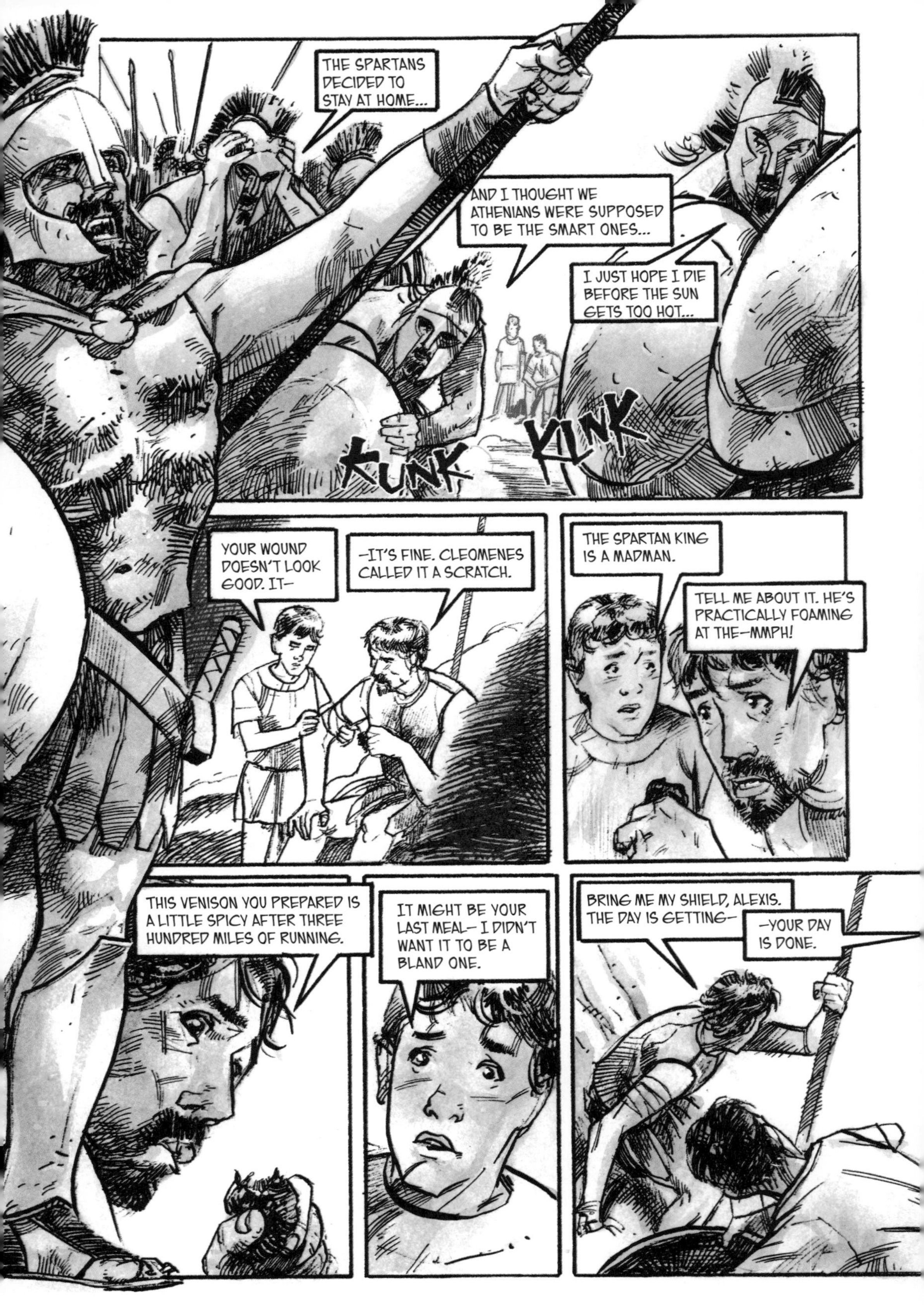
THE SPARTANS DECIDED TO STAY AT HOME...
AND I THOUGHT WE ATHENIANS WERE SUPPOSED TO BE THE SMART ONES...
I JUST HOPE I DIE BEFORE THE SUN GETS TOO HOT...
KUNK
KLINK
YOUR WOUND DOESN'T LOOK GOOD. IT—
—IT'S FINE. CLEOMENES CALLED IT A SCRATCH.
THE SPARTAN KING IS A MADMAN.
TELL ME ABOUT IT. HE'S PRACTICALLY FOAMING AT THE—MMPH!
THIS VENISON YOU PREPARED IS A LITTLE SPICY AFTER THREE HUNDRED MILES OF RUNNING.
IT MIGHT BE YOUR LAST MEAL— I DIDN'T WANT IT TO BE A BLAND ONE.
BRING ME MY SHIELD, ALEXIS. THE DAY IS GETTING—
—YOUR DAY IS DONE.

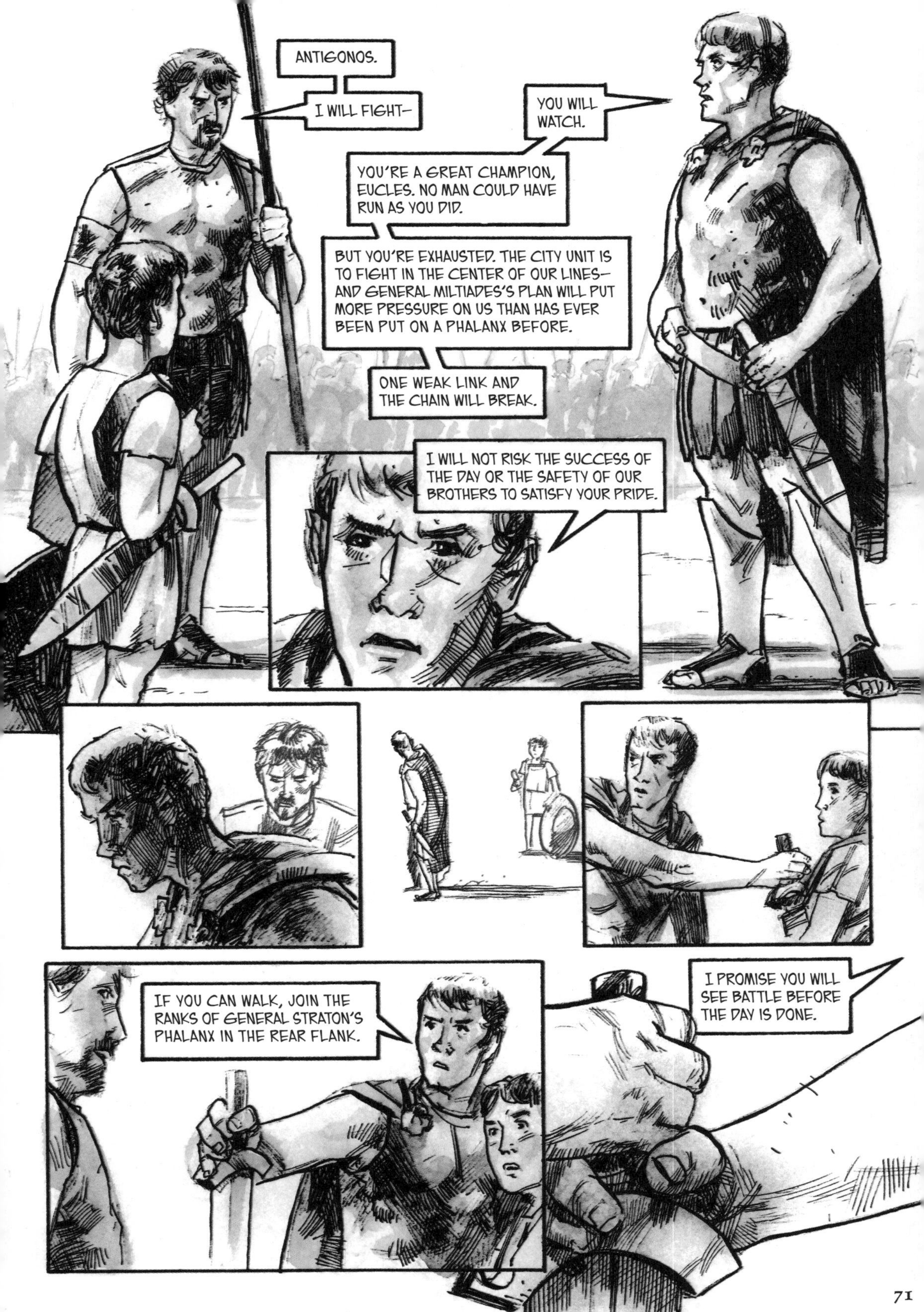
ANTIGONOS.
I WILL FIGHT—
YOU WILL WATCH.
YOU'RE A GREAT CHAMPION, EUCLES. NO MAN COULD HAVE RUN AS YOU DID.
BUT YOU'RE EXHAUSTED. THE CITY UNIT IS TO FIGHT IN THE CENTER OF OUR LINES— AND GENERAL MILTIADES'S PLAN WILL PUT MORE PRESSURE ON US THAN HAS EVER BEEN PUT ON A PHALANX BEFORE.
ONE WEAK LINK AND THE CHAIN WILL BREAK.
I WILL NOT RISK THE SUCCESS OF THE DAY OR THE SAFETY OF OUR BROTHERS TO SATISFY YOUR PRIDE.
IF YOU CAN WALK, JOIN THE RANKS OF GENERAL STRATON'S PHALANX IN THE REAR FLANK.
I PROMISE YOU WILL SEE BATTLE BEFORE THE DAY IS DONE.

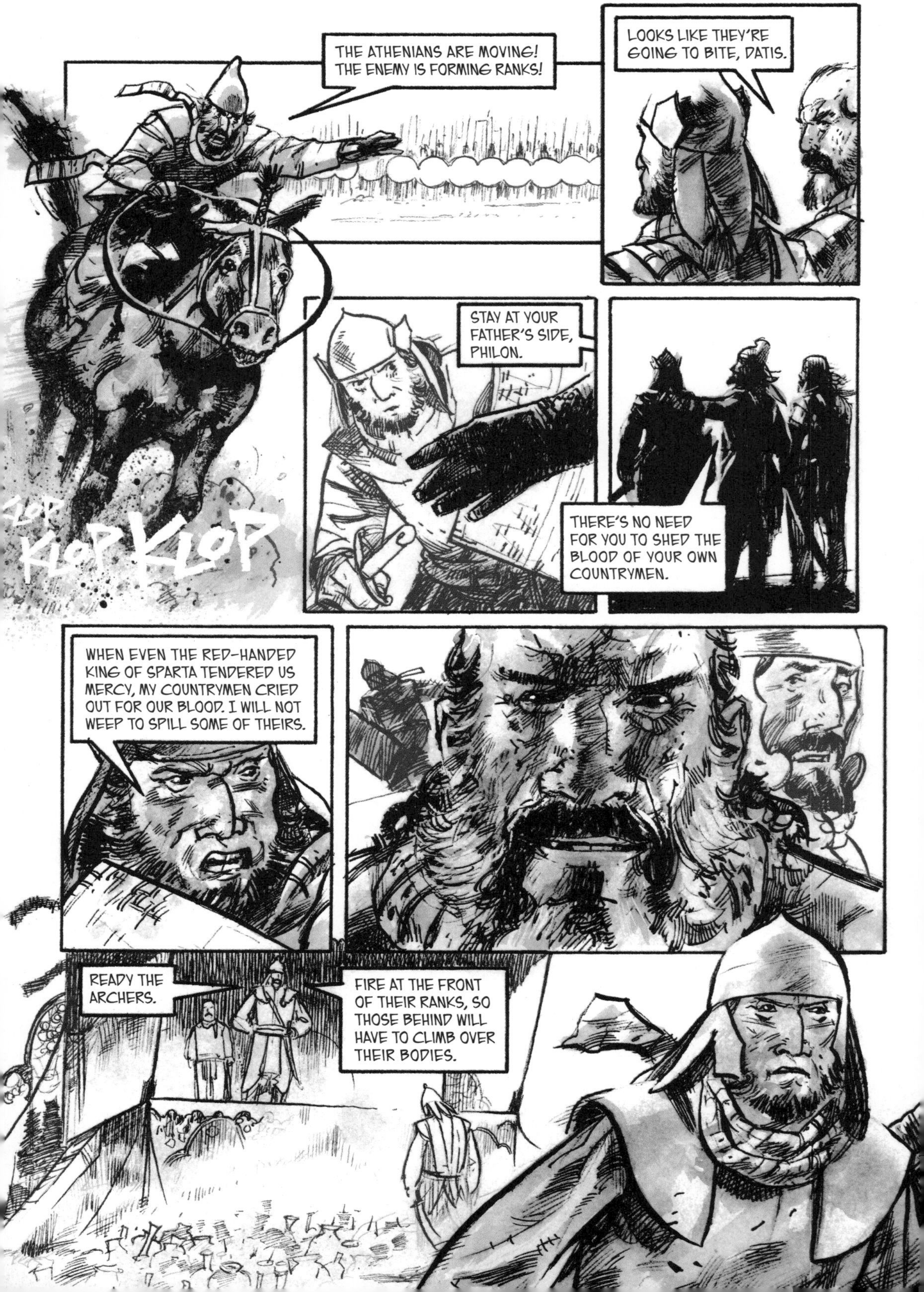
THE ATHENIANS ARE MOVING! THE ENEMY IS FORMING RANKS!
LOOKS LIKE THEY'RE GOING TO BITE, DATIS.
KLOP KLOP KLOP
STAY AT YOUR FATHER'S SIDE, PHILON.
THERE'S NO NEED FOR YOU TO SHED THE BLOOD OF YOUR OWN COUNTRYMEN.
WHEN EVEN THE RED-HANDED KING OF SPARTA TENDERED US MERCY, MY COUNTRYMEN CRIED OUT FOR OUR BLOOD. I WILL NOT WEEP TO SPILL SOME OF THEIRS.
READY THE ARCHERS.
FIRE AT THE FRONT OF THEIR RANKS, SO THOSE BEHIND WILL HAVE TO CLIMB OVER THEIR BODIES.

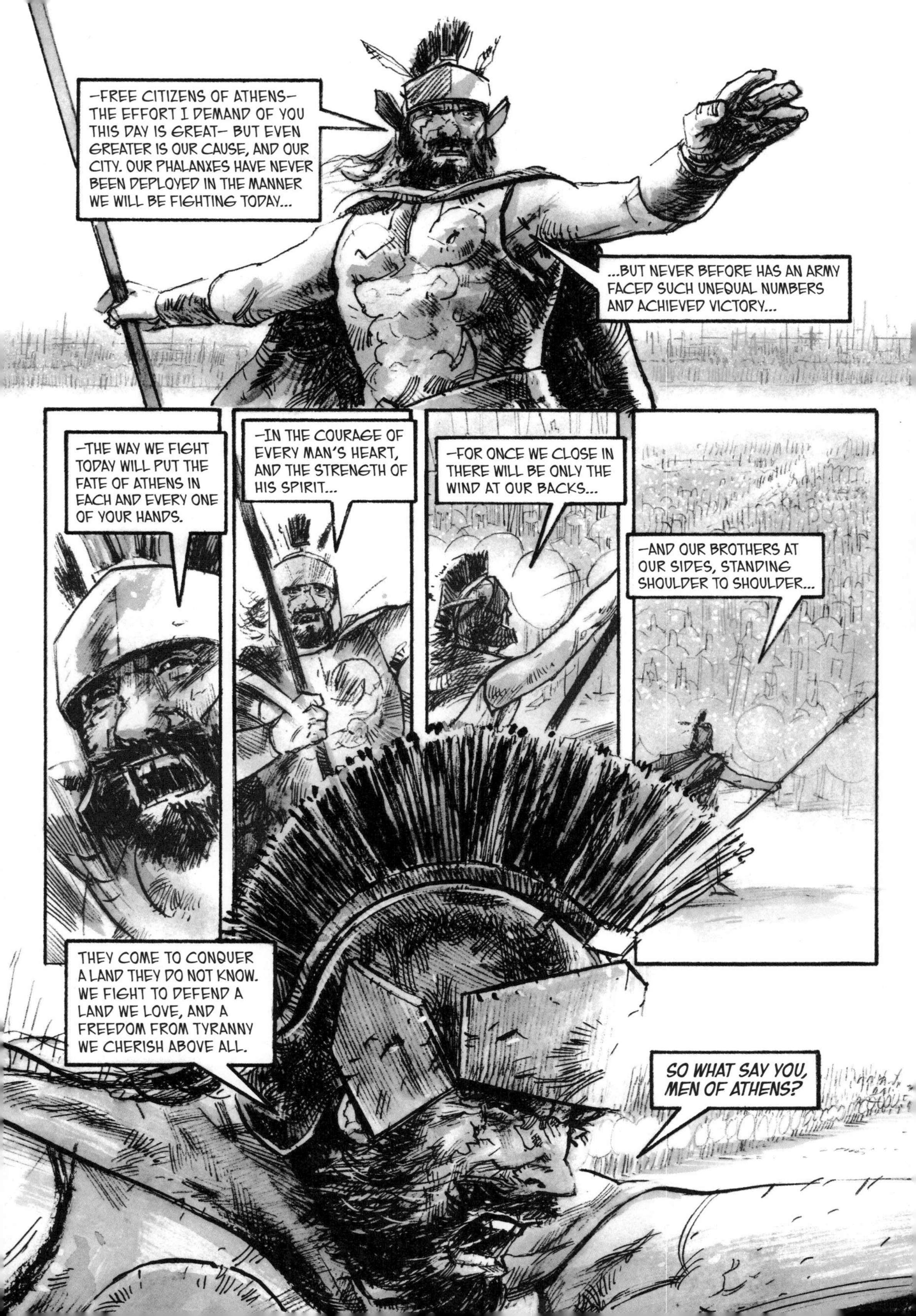
–FREE CITIZENS OF ATHENS– THE EFFORT I DEMAND OF YOU THIS DAY IS GREAT– BUT EVEN GREATER IS OUR CAUSE, AND OUR CITY. OUR PHALANXES HAVE NEVER BEEN DEPLOYED IN THE MANNER WE WILL BE FIGHTING TODAY...
...BUT NEVER BEFORE HAS AN ARMY FACED SUCH UNEQUAL NUMBERS AND ACHIEVED VICTORY...
–THE WAY WE FIGHT TODAY WILL PUT THE FATE OF ATHENS IN EACH AND EVERY ONE OF YOUR HANDS.
–IN THE COURAGE OF EVERY MAN'S HEART, AND THE STRENGTH OF HIS SPIRIT...
–FOR ONCE WE CLOSE IN THERE WILL BE ONLY THE WIND AT OUR BACKS...
–AND OUR BROTHERS AT OUR SIDES, STANDING SHOULDER TO SHOULDER...
THEY COME TO CONQUER A LAND THEY DO NOT KNOW. WE FIGHT TO DEFEND A LAND WE LOVE, AND A FREEDOM FROM TYRANNY WE CHERISH ABOVE ALL.
SO WHAT SAY YOU, MEN OF ATHENS?

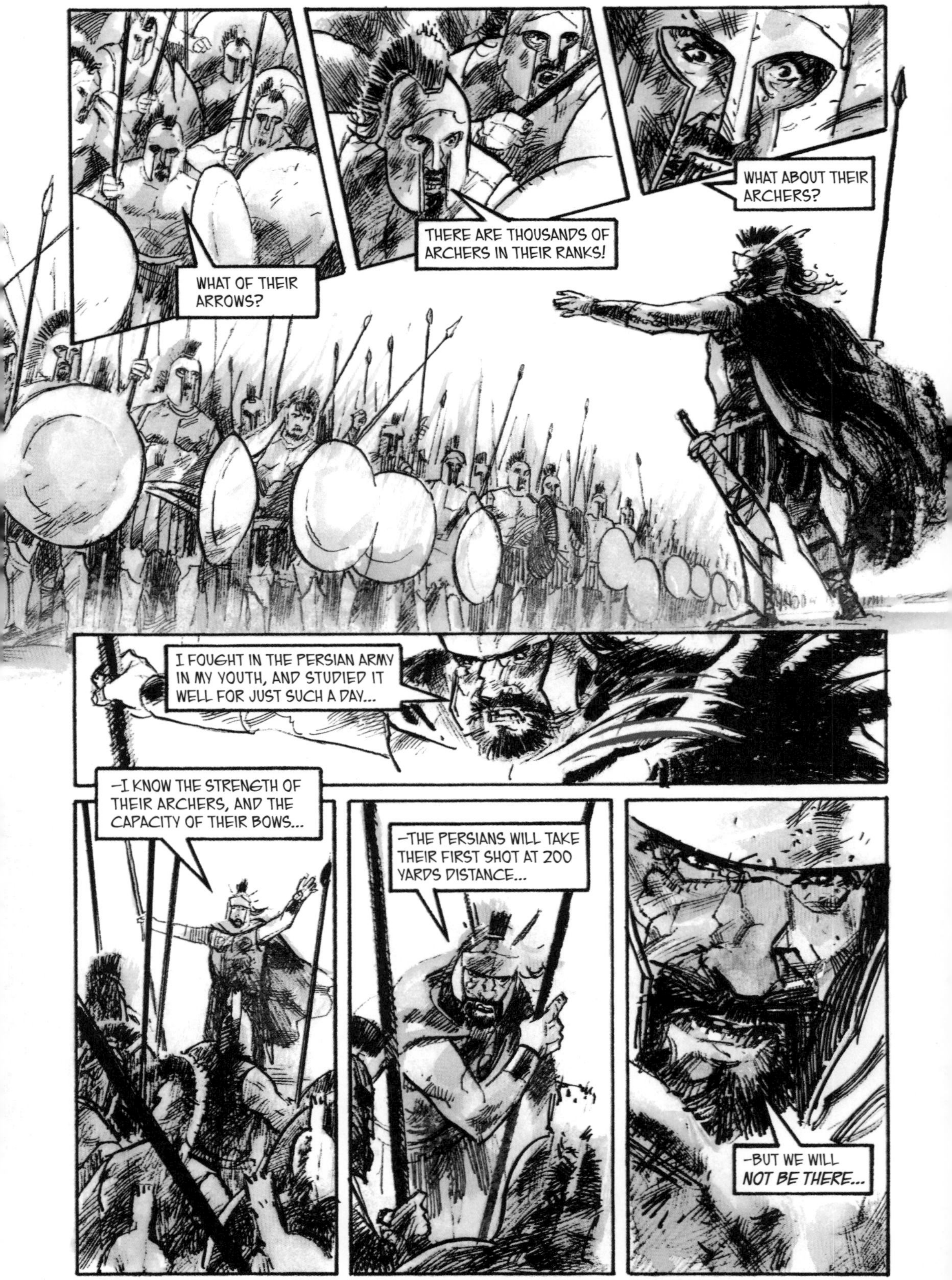
WHAT OF THEIR ARROWS?
THERE ARE THOUSANDS OF ARCHERS IN THEIR RANKS!
WHAT ABOUT THEIR ARCHERS?
I FOUGHT IN THE PERSIAN ARMY IN MY YOUTH, AND STUDIED IT WELL FOR JUST SUCH A DAY...
–I KNOW THE STRENGTH OF THEIR ARCHERS, AND THE CAPACITY OF THEIR BOWS...
–THE PERSIANS WILL TAKE THEIR FIRST SHOT AT 200 YARDS DISTANCE...
–BUT WE WILL *NOT BE THERE...*

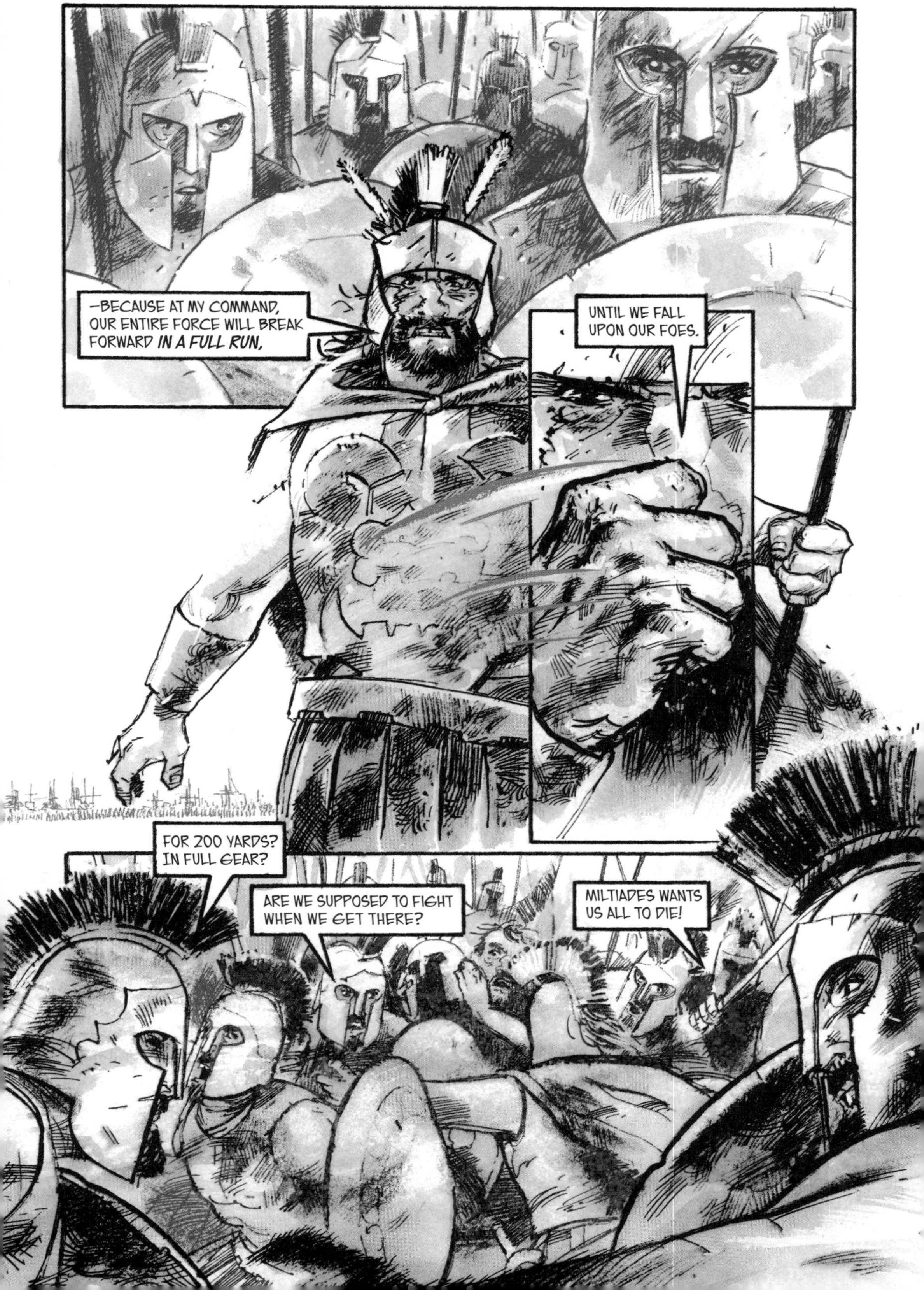
–BECAUSE AT MY COMMAND, OUR ENTIRE FORCE WILL BREAK FORWARD *IN A FULL RUN,*
UNTIL WE FALL UPON OUR FOES.
FOR 200 YARDS? IN FULL GEAR?
ARE WE SUPPOSED TO FIGHT WHEN WE GET THERE?
MILTIADES WANTS US ALL TO DIE!

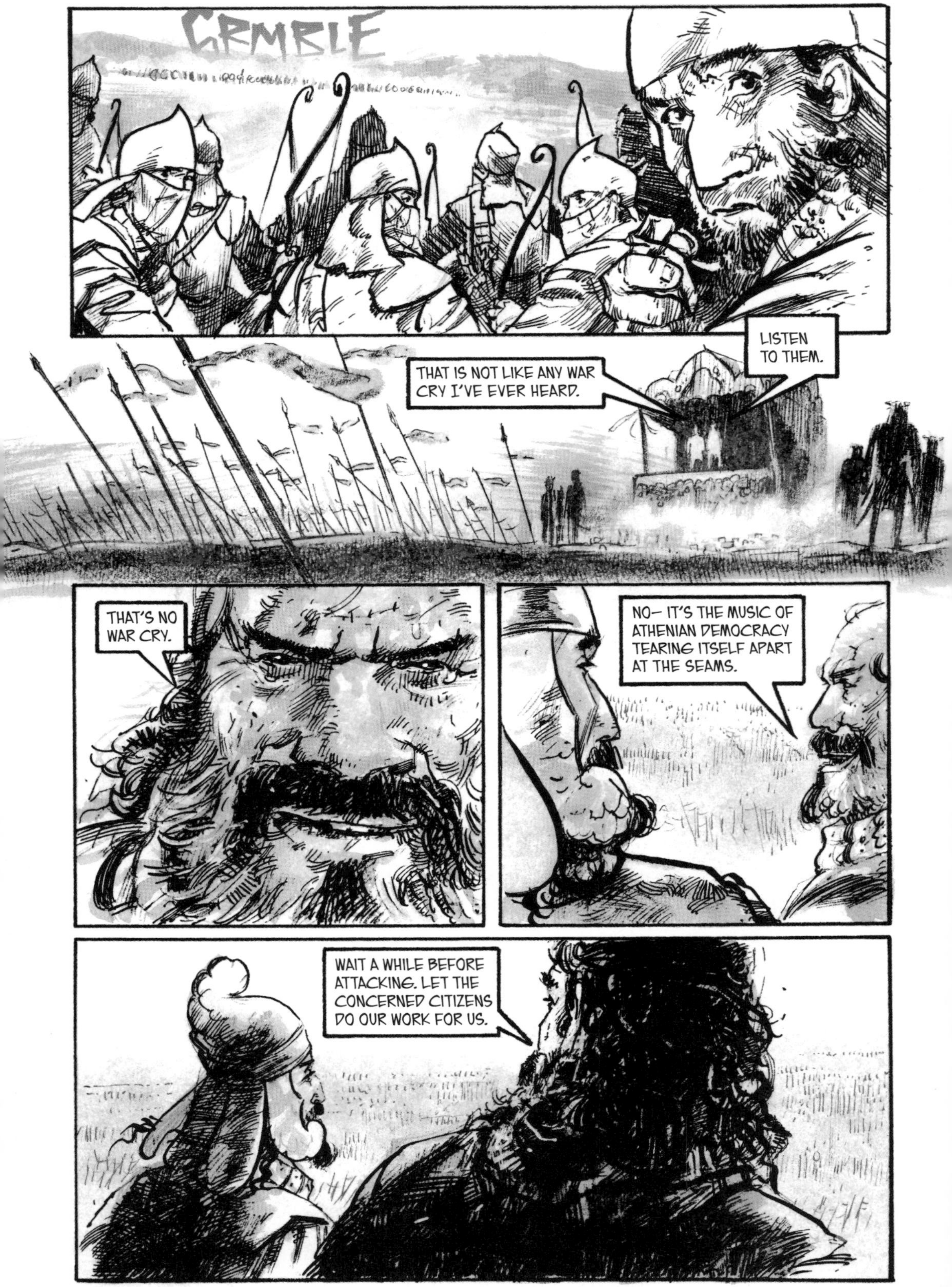
GRMBLE
THAT IS NOT LIKE ANY WAR CRY I'VE EVER HEARD.
LISTEN TO THEM.
THAT'S NO WAR CRY.
NO— IT'S THE MUSIC OF ATHENIAN DEMOCRACY TEARING ITSELF APART AT THE SEAMS.
WAIT A WHILE BEFORE ATTACKING. LET THE CONCERNED CITIZENS DO OUR WORK FOR US.

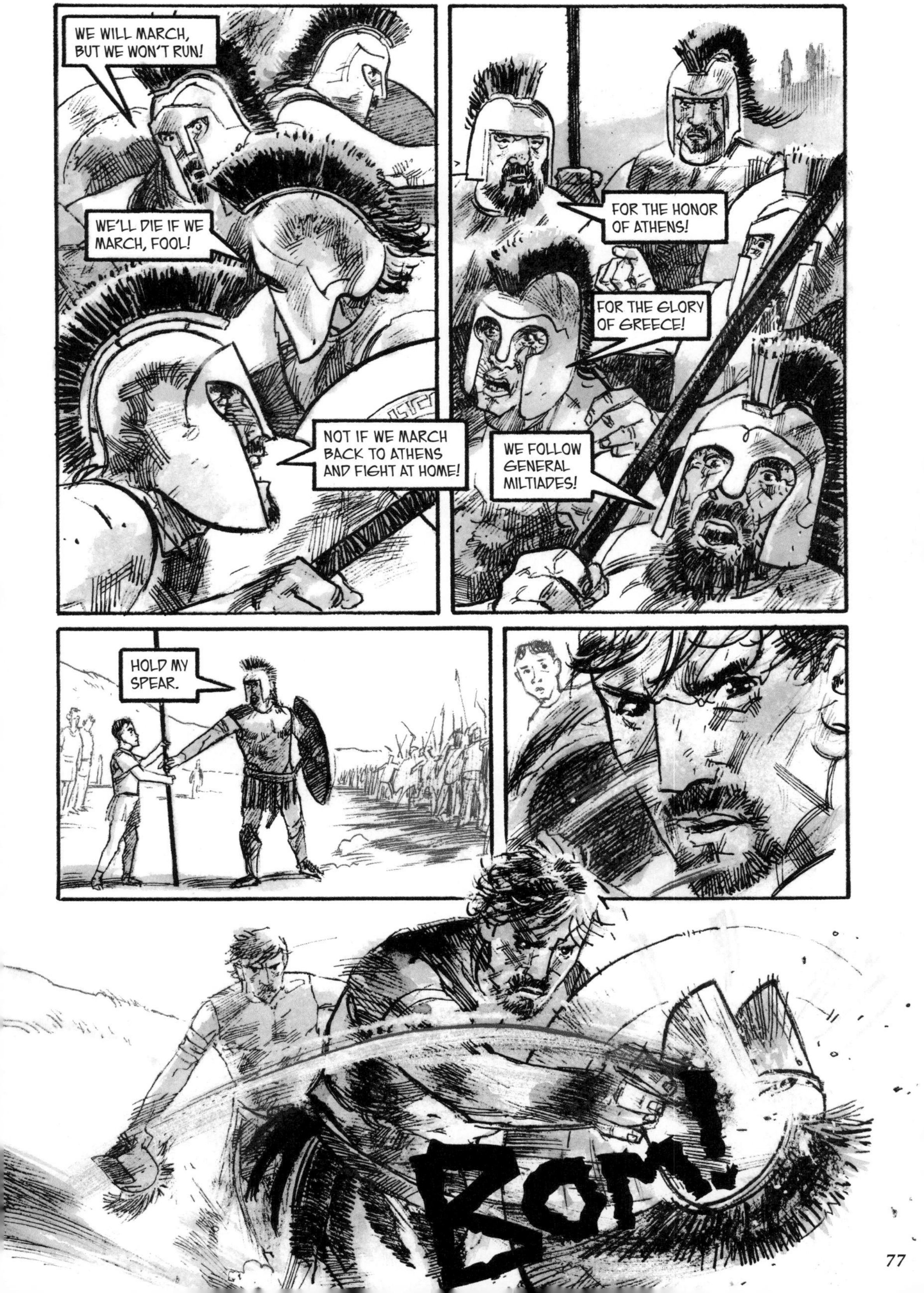
WE WILL MARCH, BUT WE WON'T RUN!
WE'LL DIE IF WE MARCH, FOOL!
NOT IF WE MARCH BACK TO ATHENS AND FIGHT AT HOME!
FOR THE HONOR OF ATHENS!
FOR THE GLORY OF GREECE!
WE FOLLOW GENERAL MILTIADES!
HOLD MY SPEAR.
BOM!

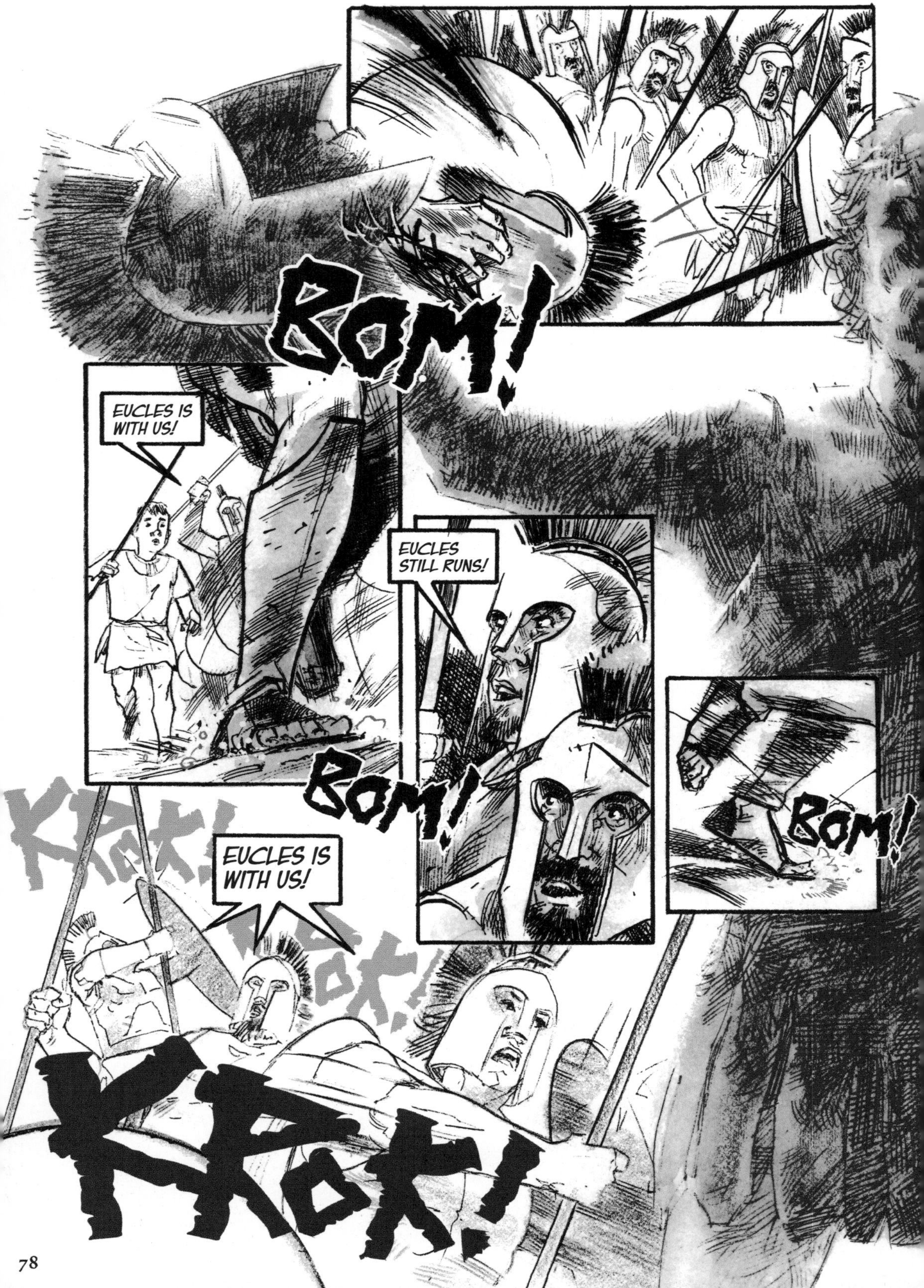
BOM!
EUCLES IS WITH US!
EUCLES STILL RUNS!
BOM!
BOM!
KRAK!
EUCLES IS WITH US!
KRAK!
KRAK!

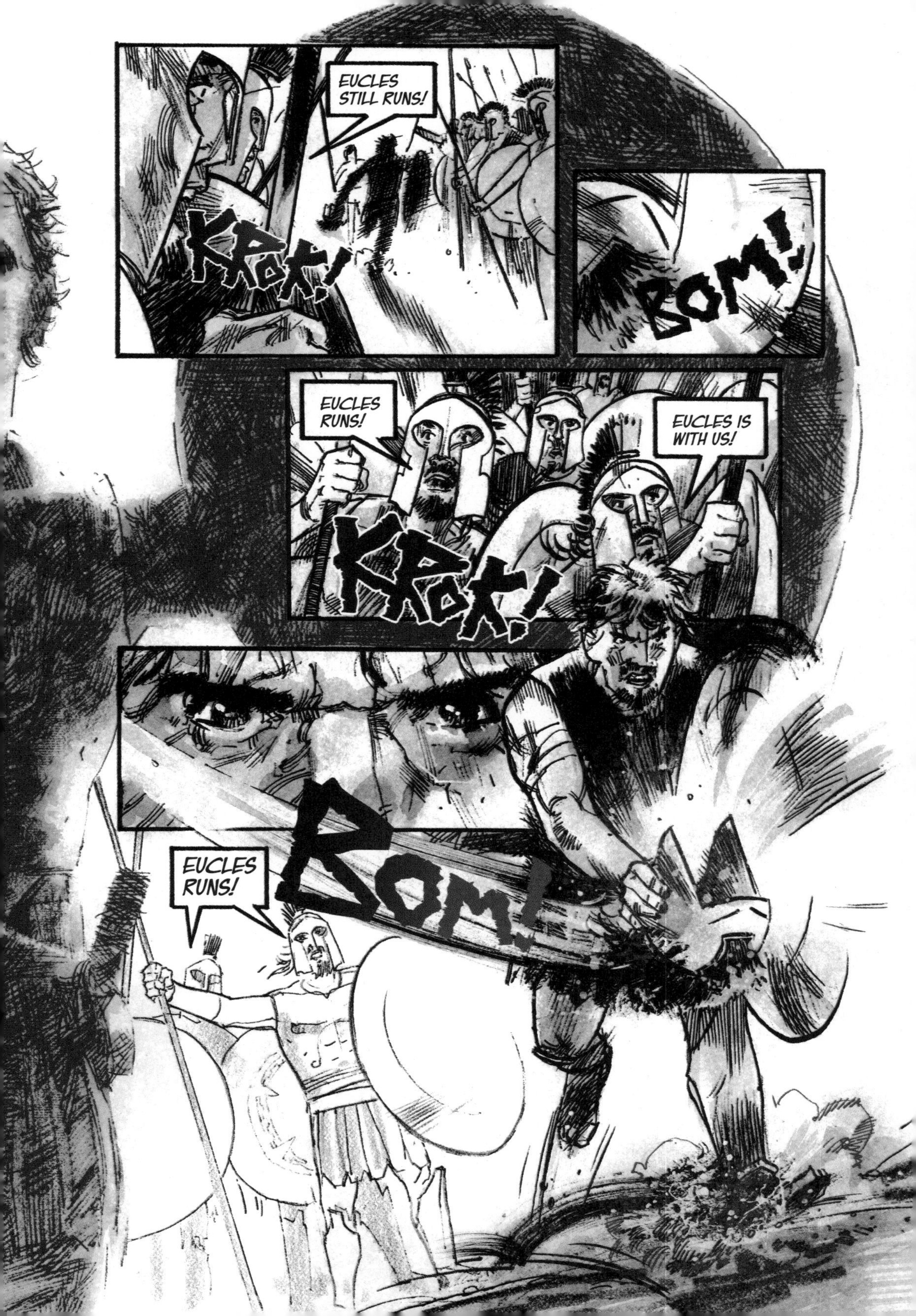
EUCLES STILL RUNS!
KRAK!
BOM!
EUCLES RUNS!
EUCLES IS WITH US!
KRAK!
BOM!
EUCLES RUNS!

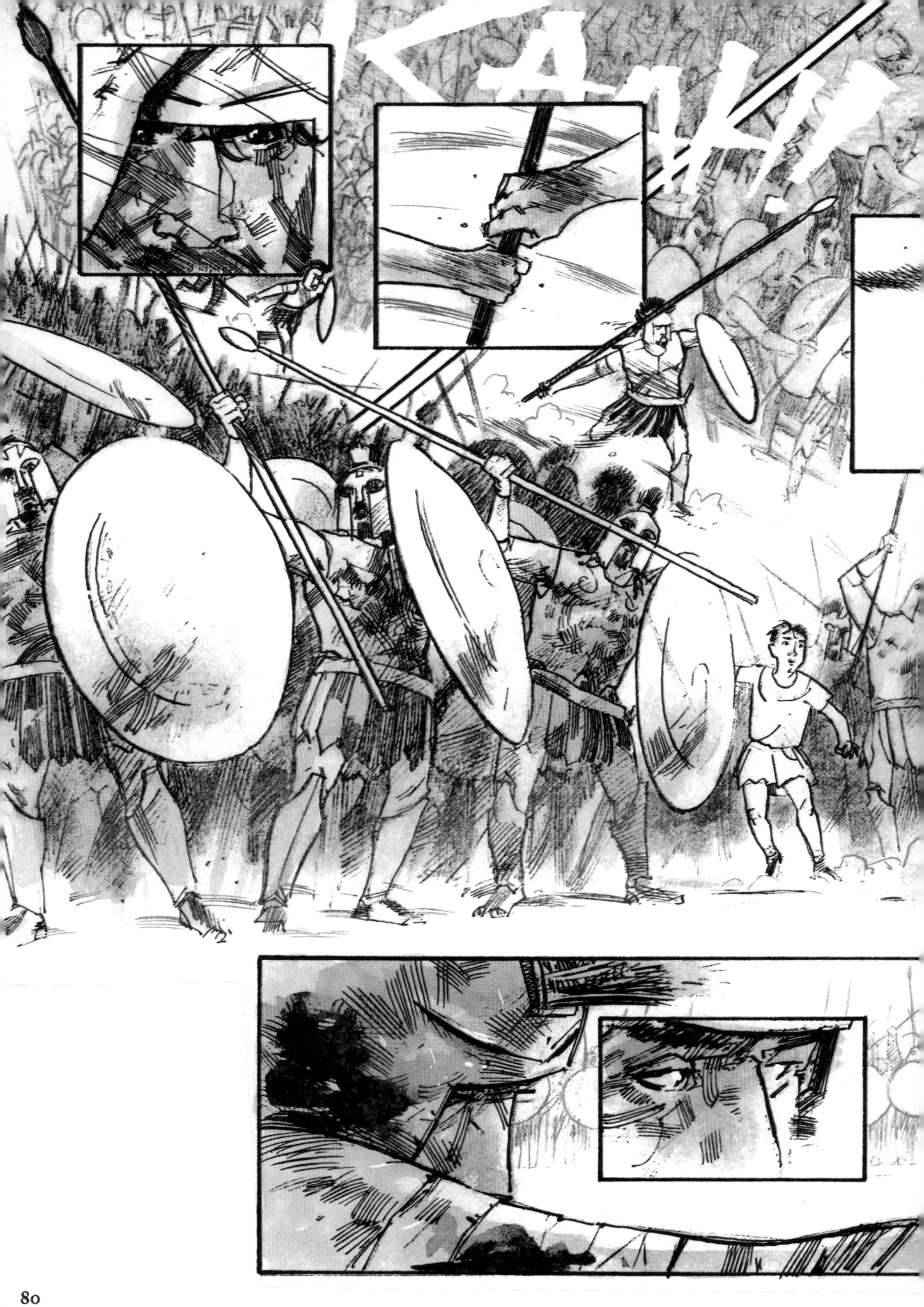

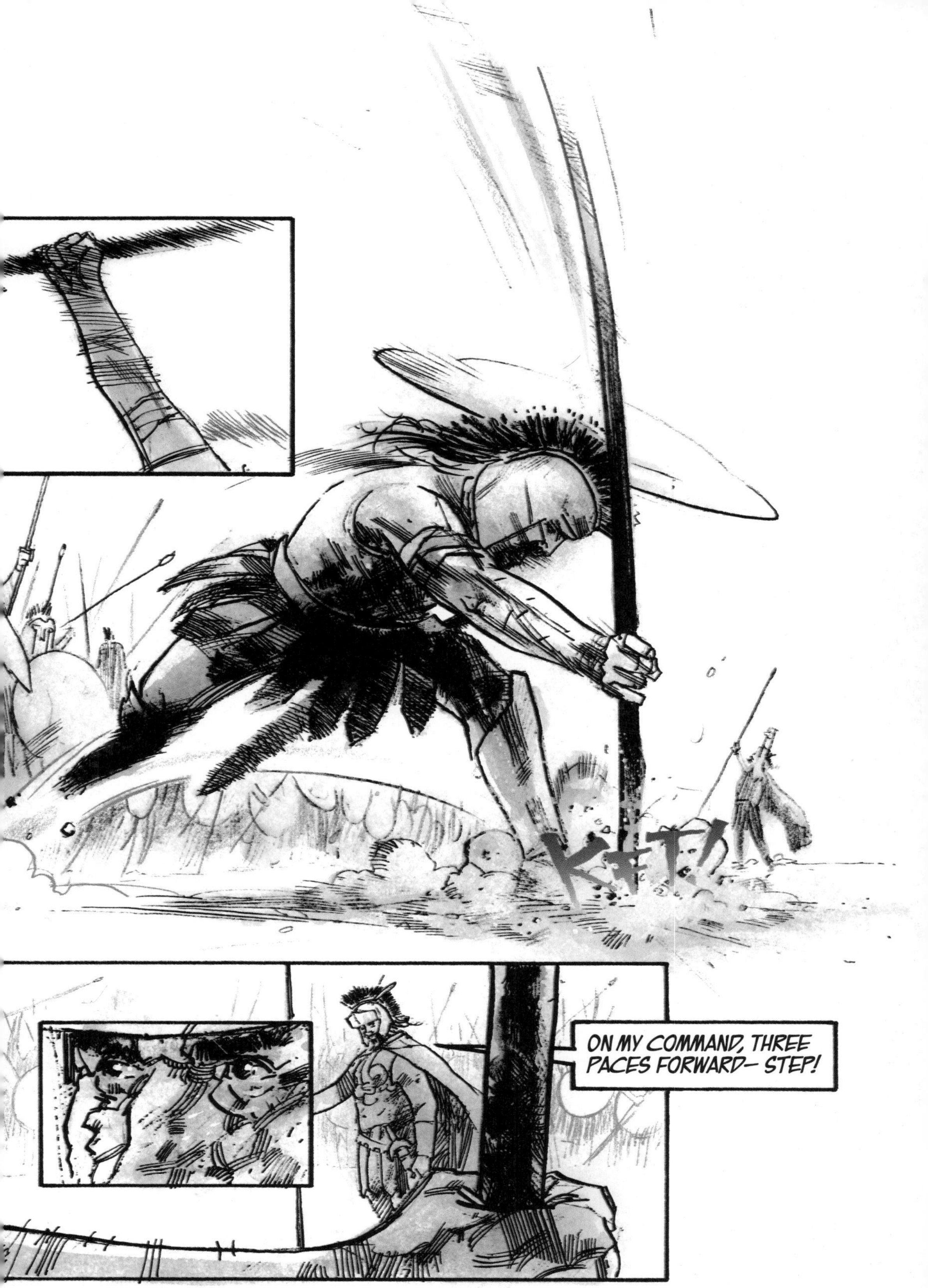
KFT!
ON MY COMMAND, THREE PACES FORWARD– STEP!

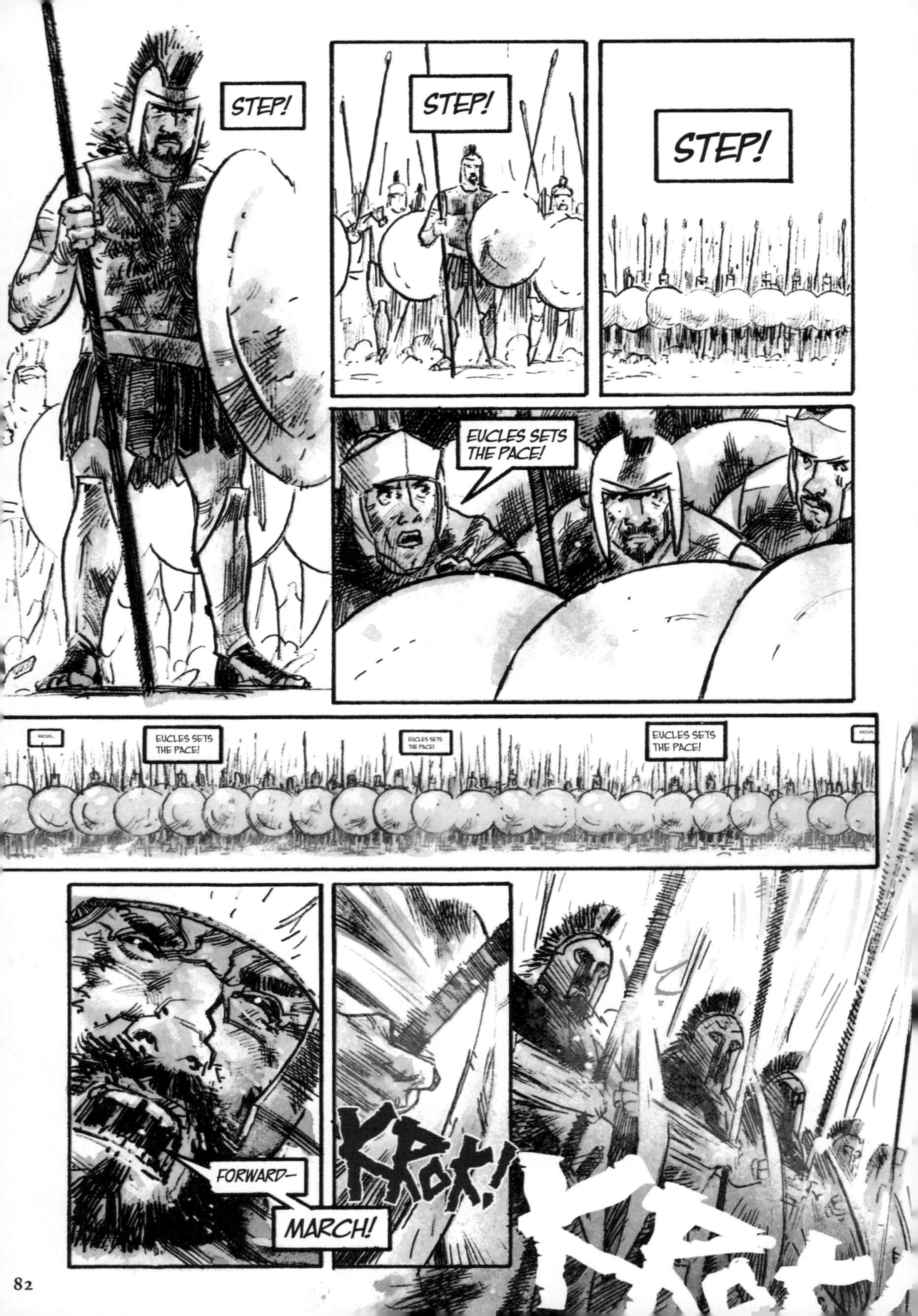
STEP!
STEP!
STEP!
EUCLES SETS THE PACE!
EUCLES SETS THE PACE!
EUCLES SETS THE PACE!
EUCLES SETS THE PACE!
FORWARD—
MARCH!
KRAK!

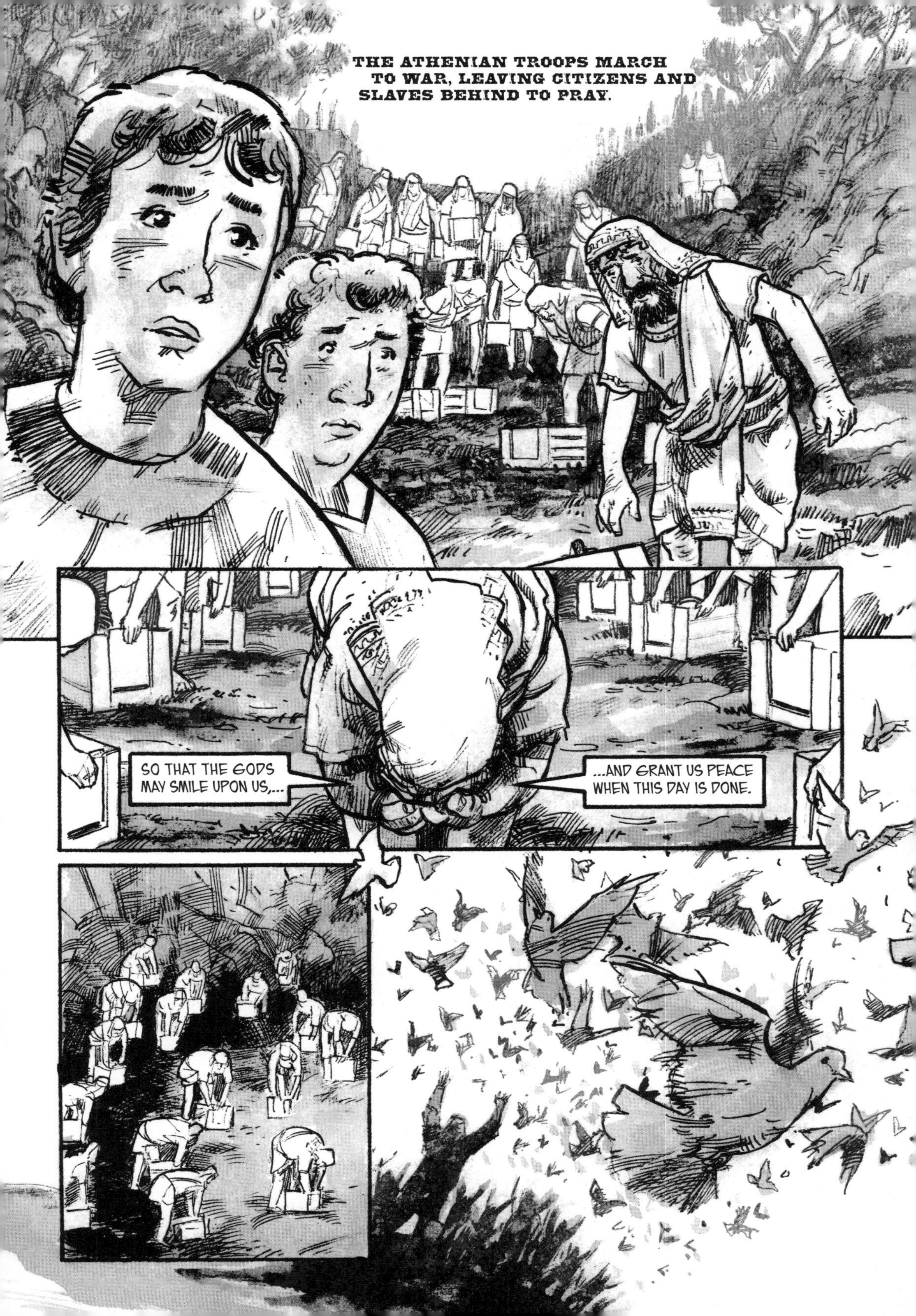
THE ATHENIAN TROOPS MARCH TO WAR, LEAVING CITIZENS AND SLAVES BEHIND TO PRAY.
SO THAT THE GODS MAY SMILE UPON US,...
...AND GRANT US PEACE WHEN THIS DAY IS DONE.

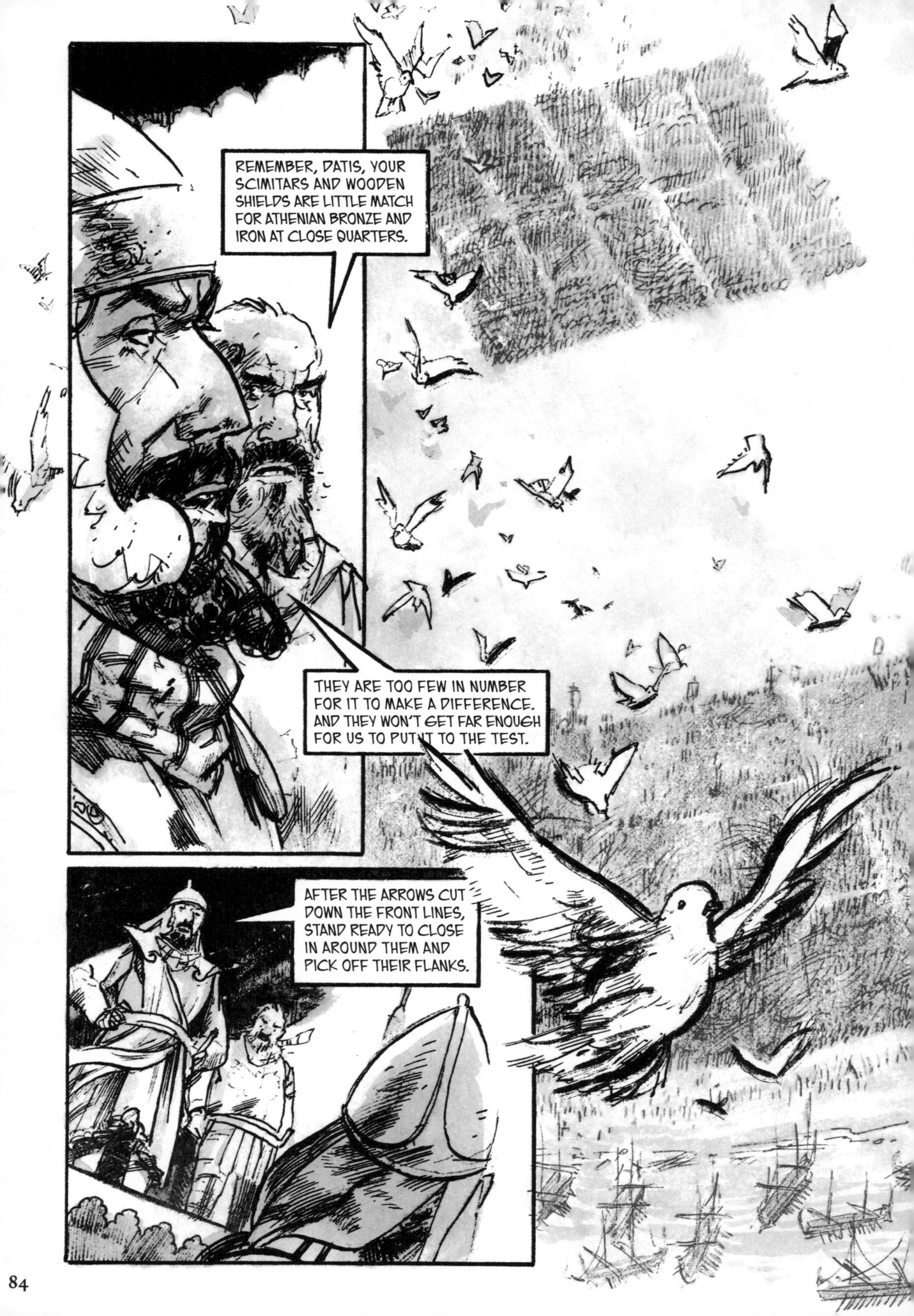
REMEMBER, DATIS, YOUR SCIMITARS AND WOODEN SHIELDS ARE LITTLE MATCH FOR ATHENIAN BRONZE AND IRON AT CLOSE QUARTERS.
THEY ARE TOO FEW IN NUMBER FOR IT TO MAKE A DIFFERENCE. AND THEY WON'T GET FAR ENOUGH FOR US TO PUT IT TO THE TEST.
AFTER THE ARROWS CUT DOWN THE FRONT LINES, STAND READY TO CLOSE IN AROUND THEM AND PICK OFF THEIR FLANKS.

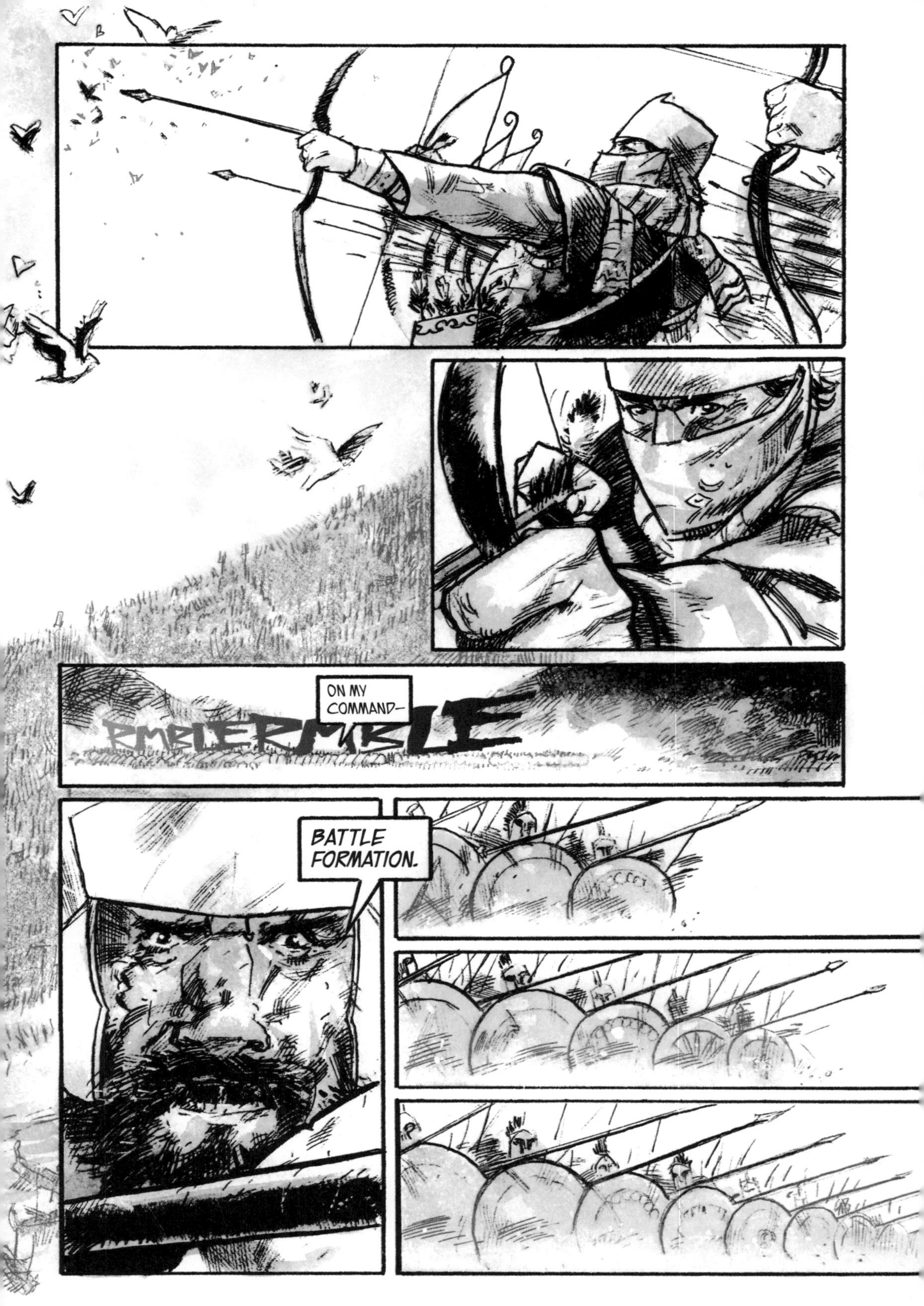
ON MY COMMAND–
RMBLERMBLE
BATTLE FORMATION.

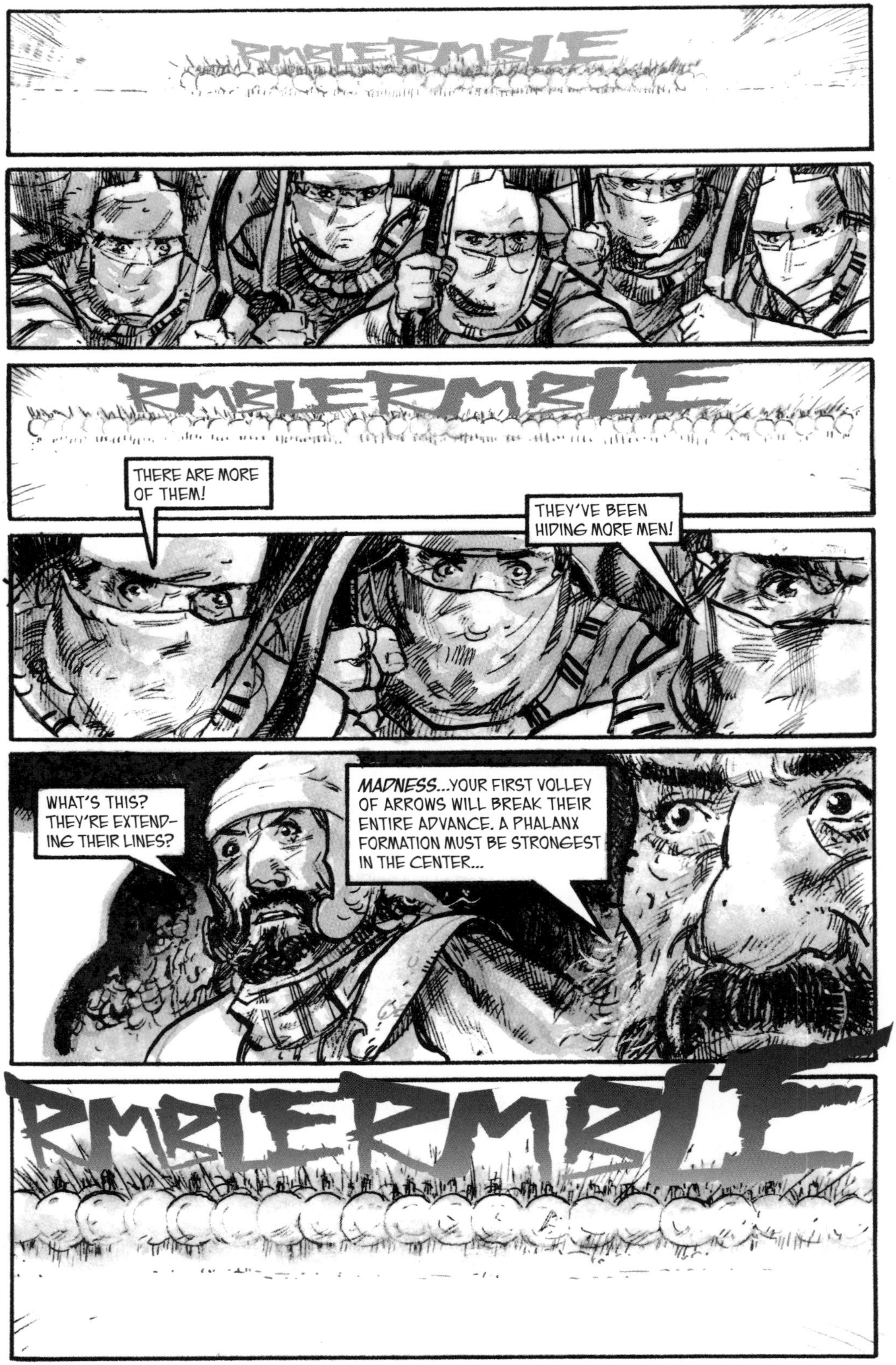
RMBLERMBLE
RMBLERMBLE
THERE ARE MORE OF THEM!
THEY'VE BEEN HIDING MORE MEN!
WHAT'S THIS? THEY'RE EXTENDING THEIR LINES?
MADNESS... YOUR FIRST VOLLEY OF ARROWS WILL BREAK THEIR ENTIRE ADVANCE. A PHALANX FORMATION MUST BE STRONGEST IN THE CENTER...
RMBLERMBLE

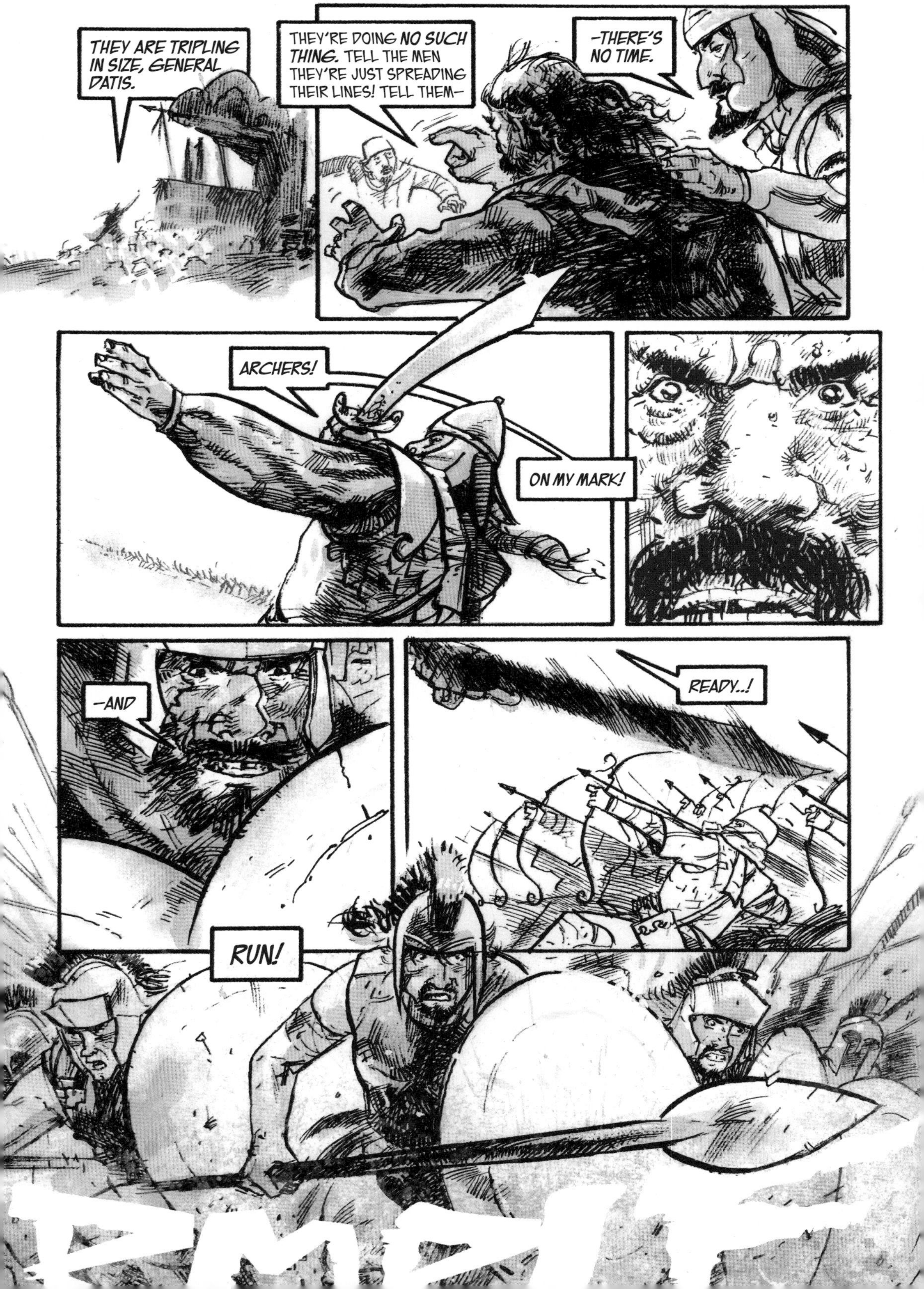

THEY ARE TRIPLING IN SIZE, GENERAL DATIS.
THEY'RE DOING NO SUCH THING. TELL THE MEN THEY'RE JUST SPREADING THEIR LINES! TELL THEM—
—THERE'S NO TIME.
ARCHERS!
ON MY MARK!
—AND
READY...!
RUN!

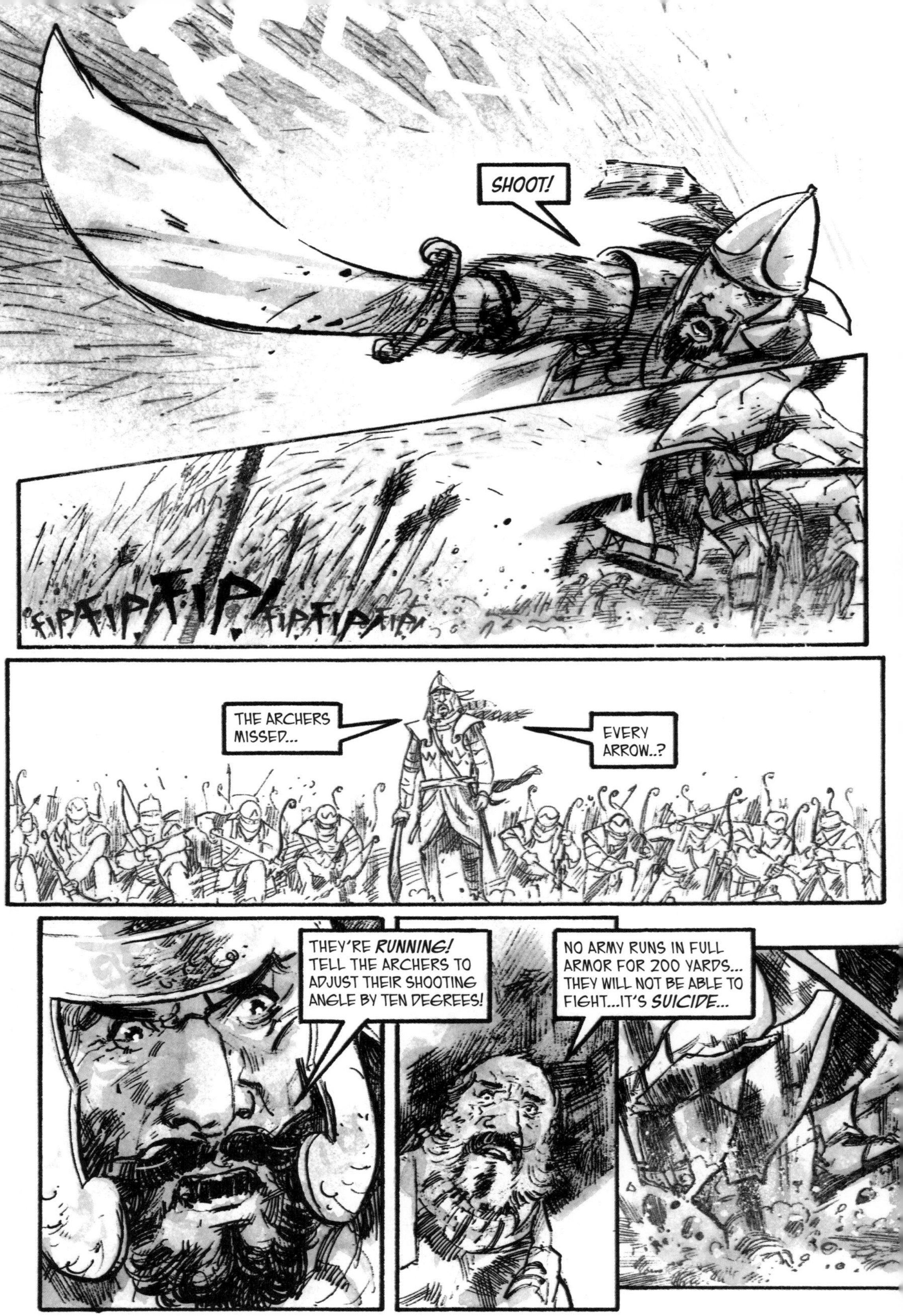

SHOOT!
FIP FIP FIP FIP FIP FIP FIP
THE ARCHERS MISSED...
EVERY ARROW..?
THEY'RE *RUNNING!* TELL THE ARCHERS TO ADJUST THEIR SHOOTING ANGLE BY TEN DEGREES!
NO ARMY RUNS IN FULL ARMOR FOR 200 YARDS... THEY WILL NOT BE ABLE TO FIGHT...IT'S *SUICIDE*...

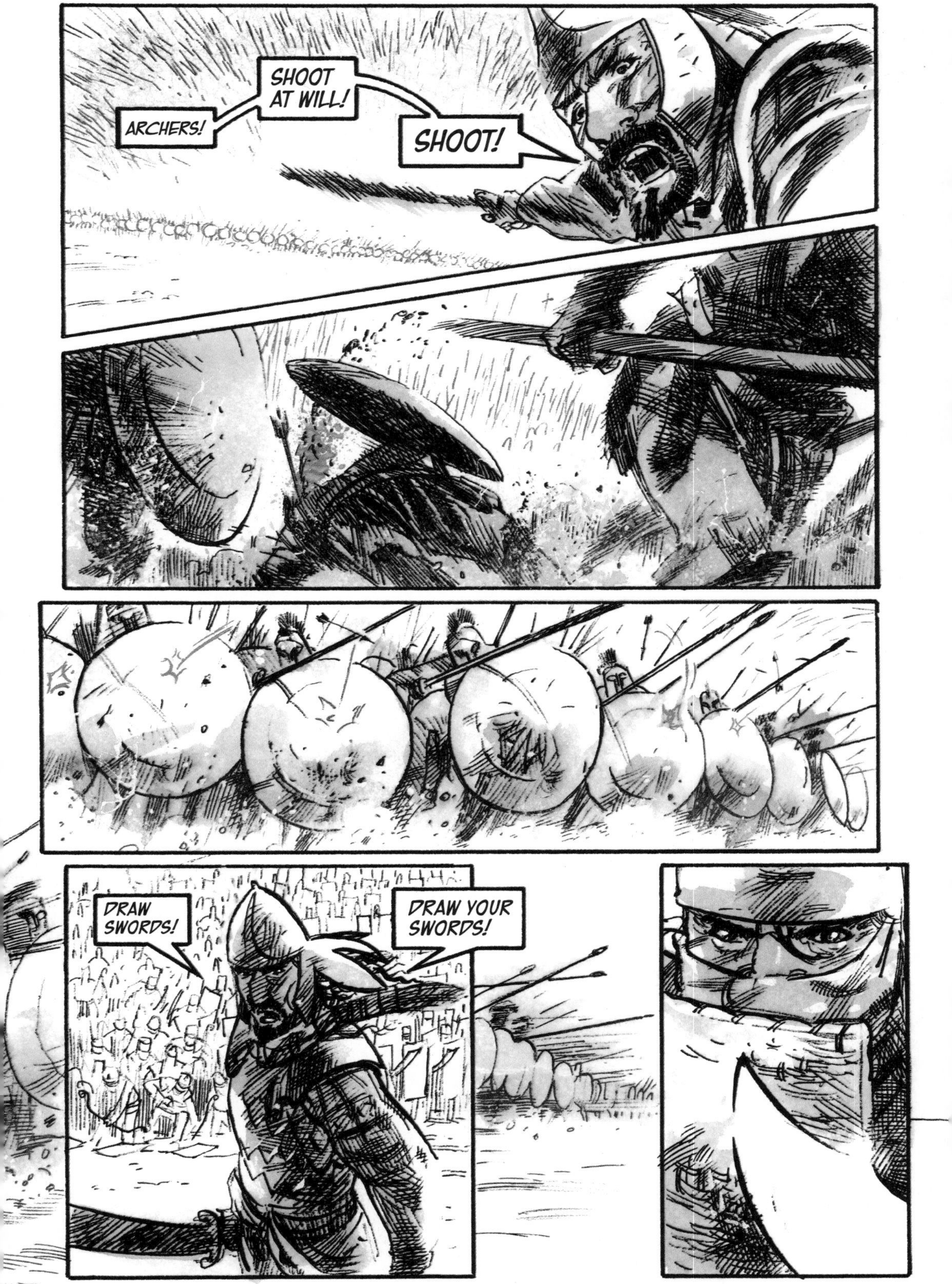
ARCHERS!
SHOOT AT WILL!
SHOOT!
DRAW SWORDS!
DRAW YOUR SWORDS!

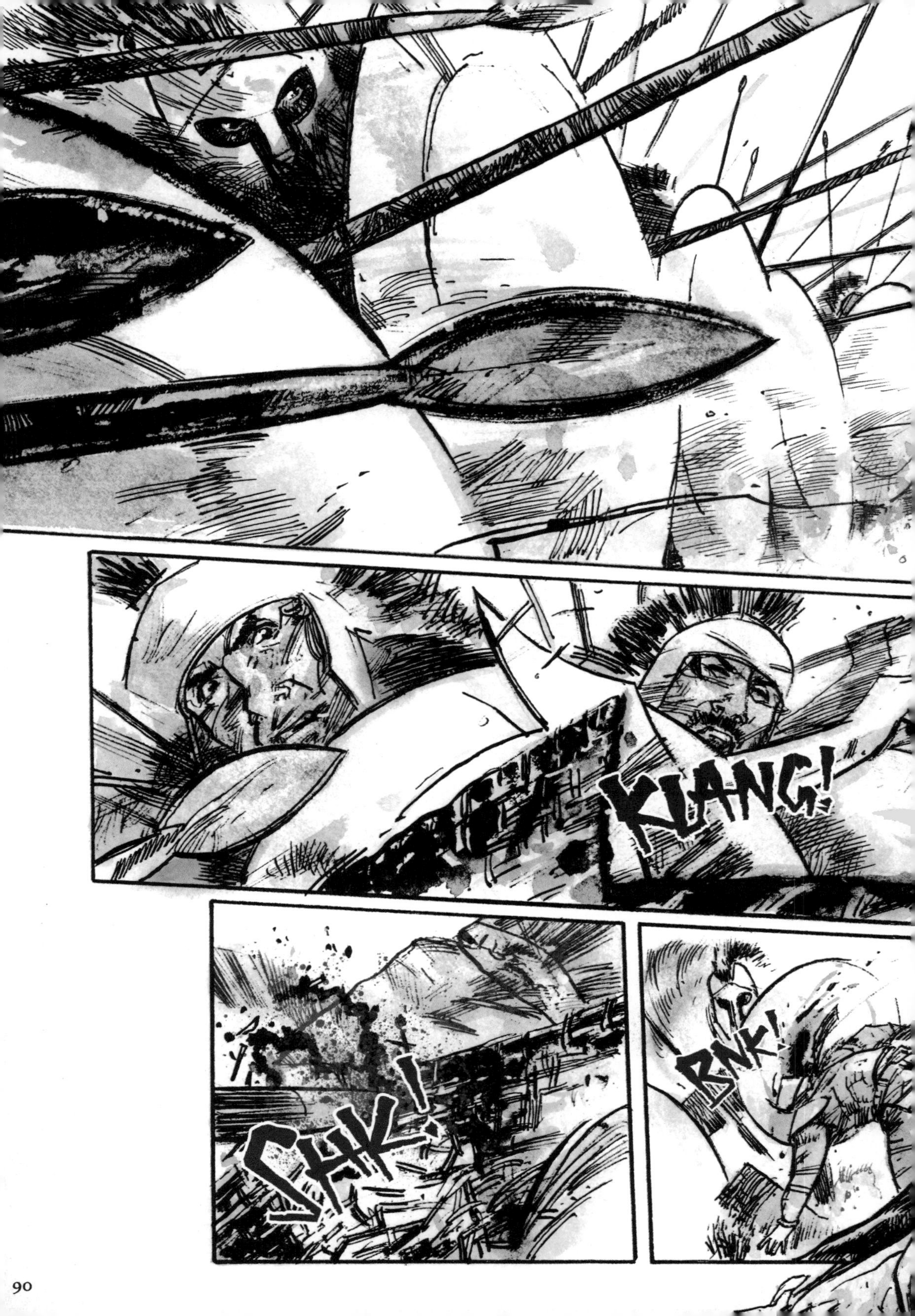
KLANG!
SHK!
BNK!

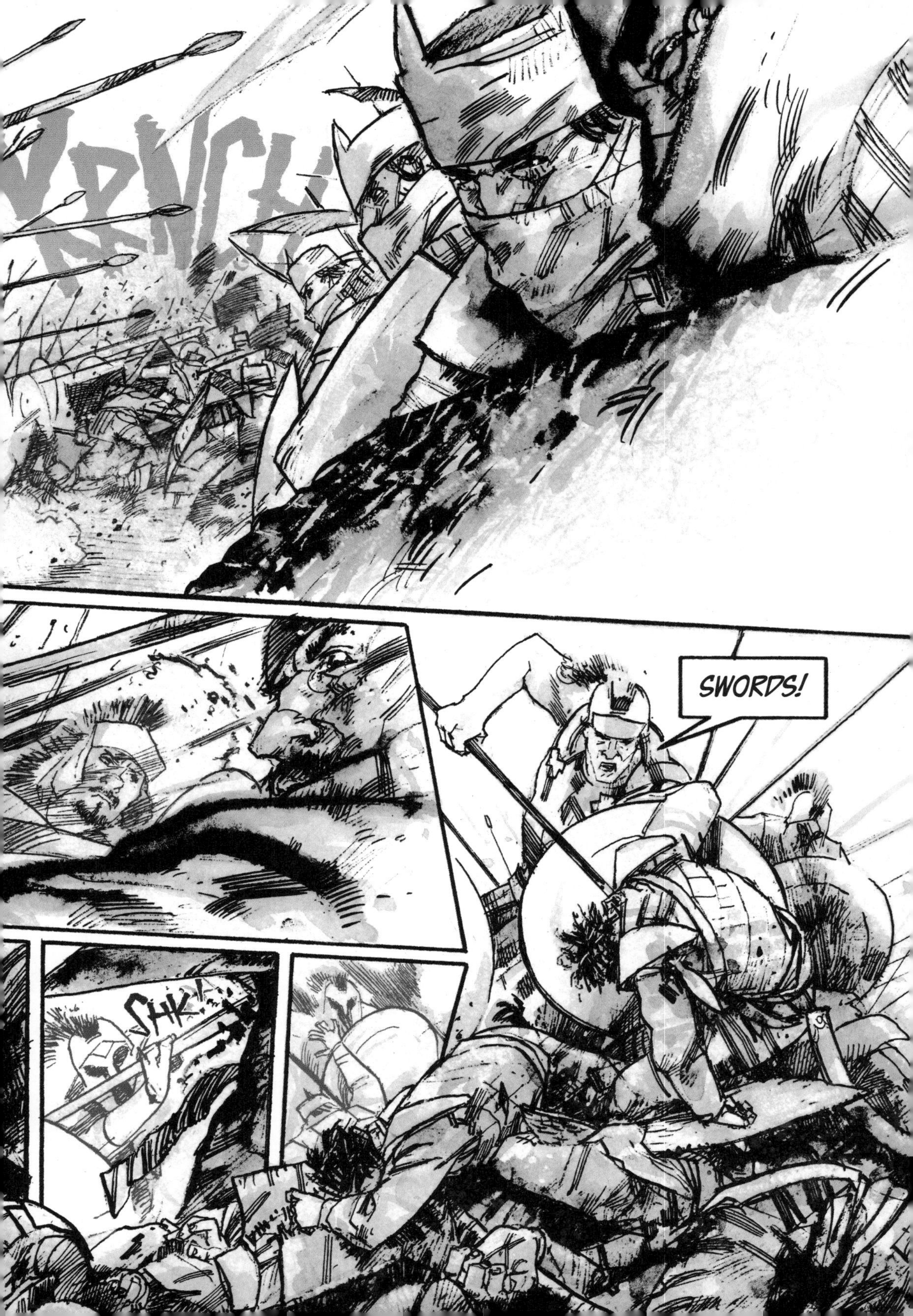

KRNCH!
SWORDS!
SHK!

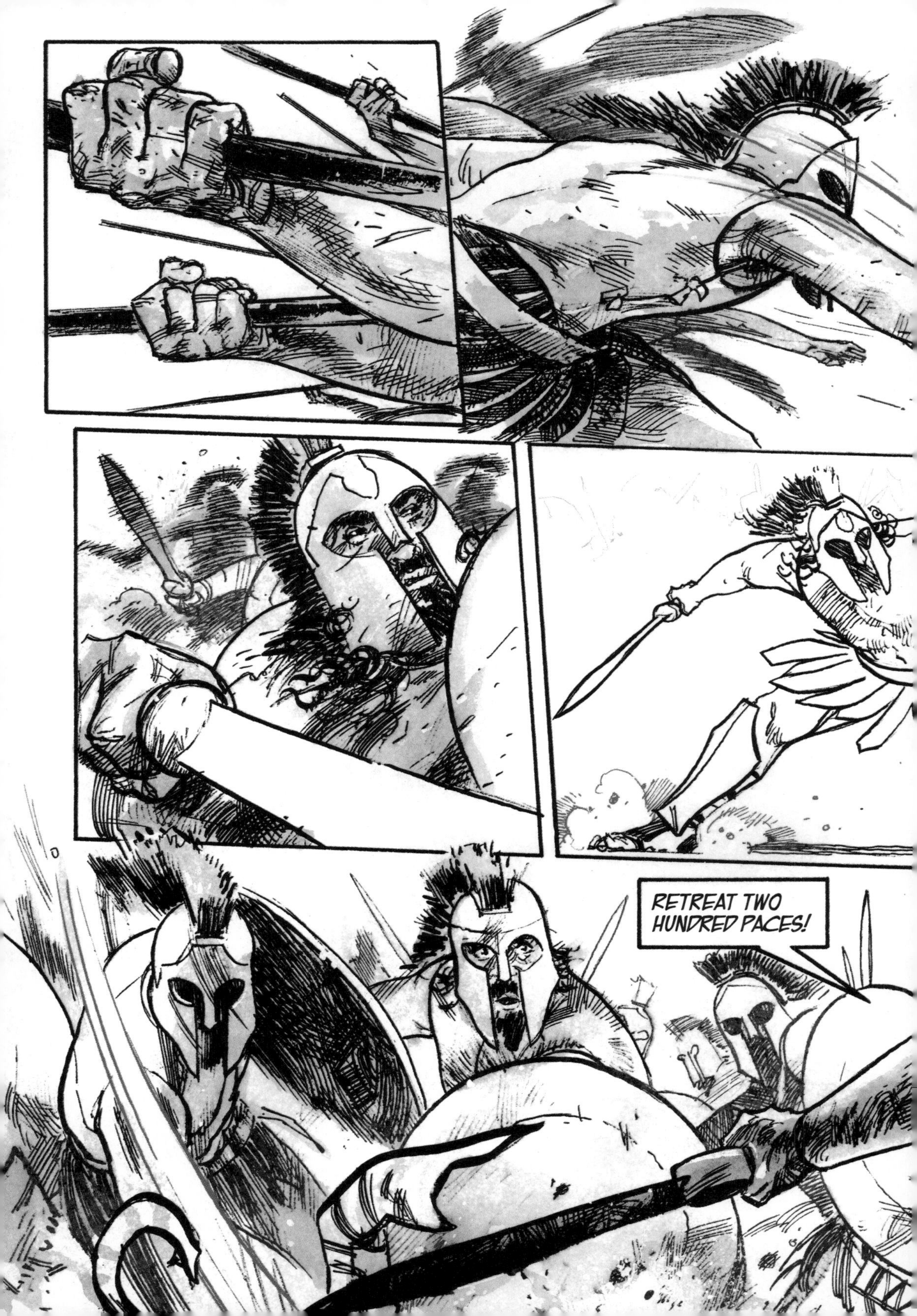
RETREAT TWO HUNDRED PACES!

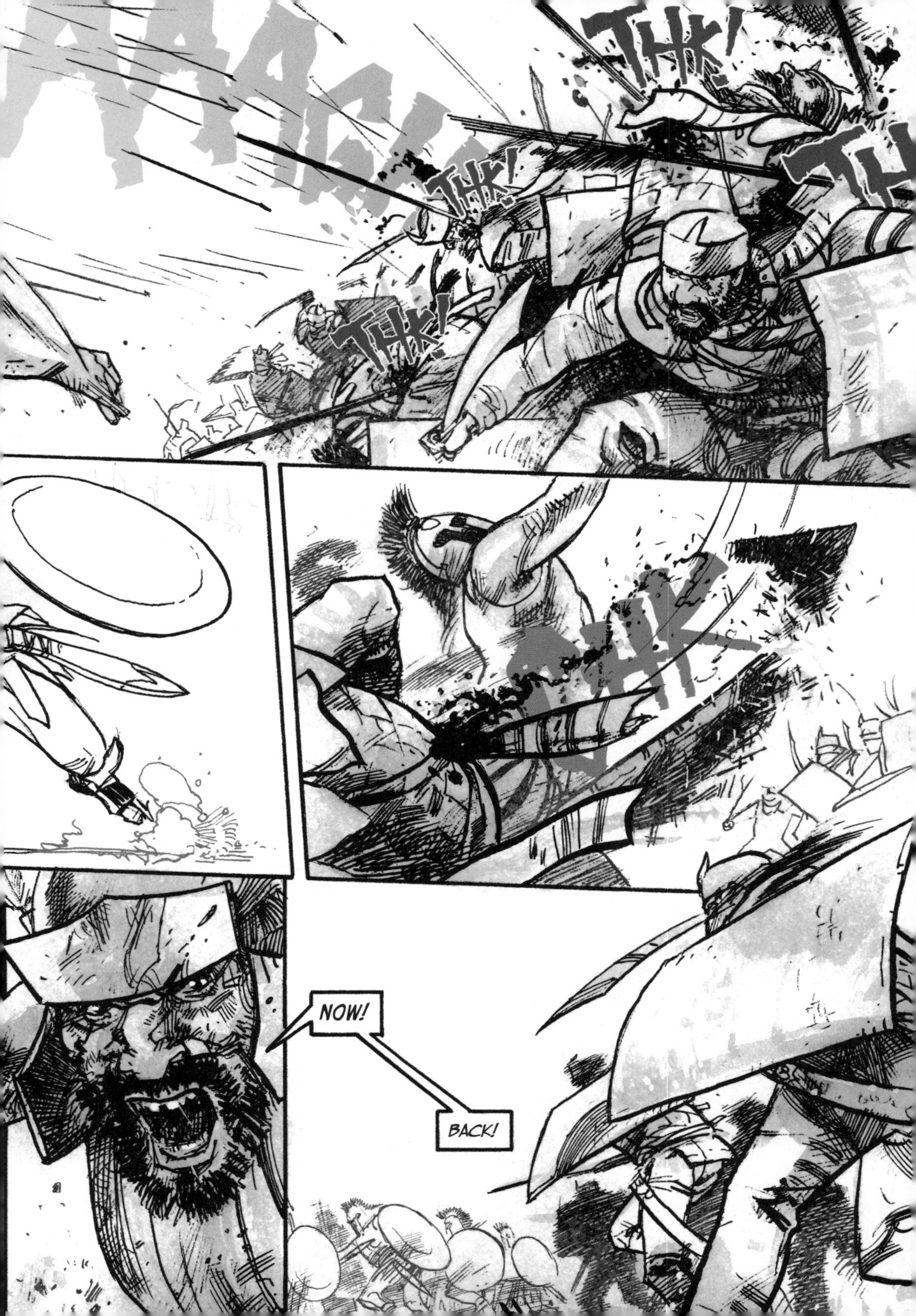
AAAGH
THK!
THK!
THK!
TH
THK
NOW!
BACK!

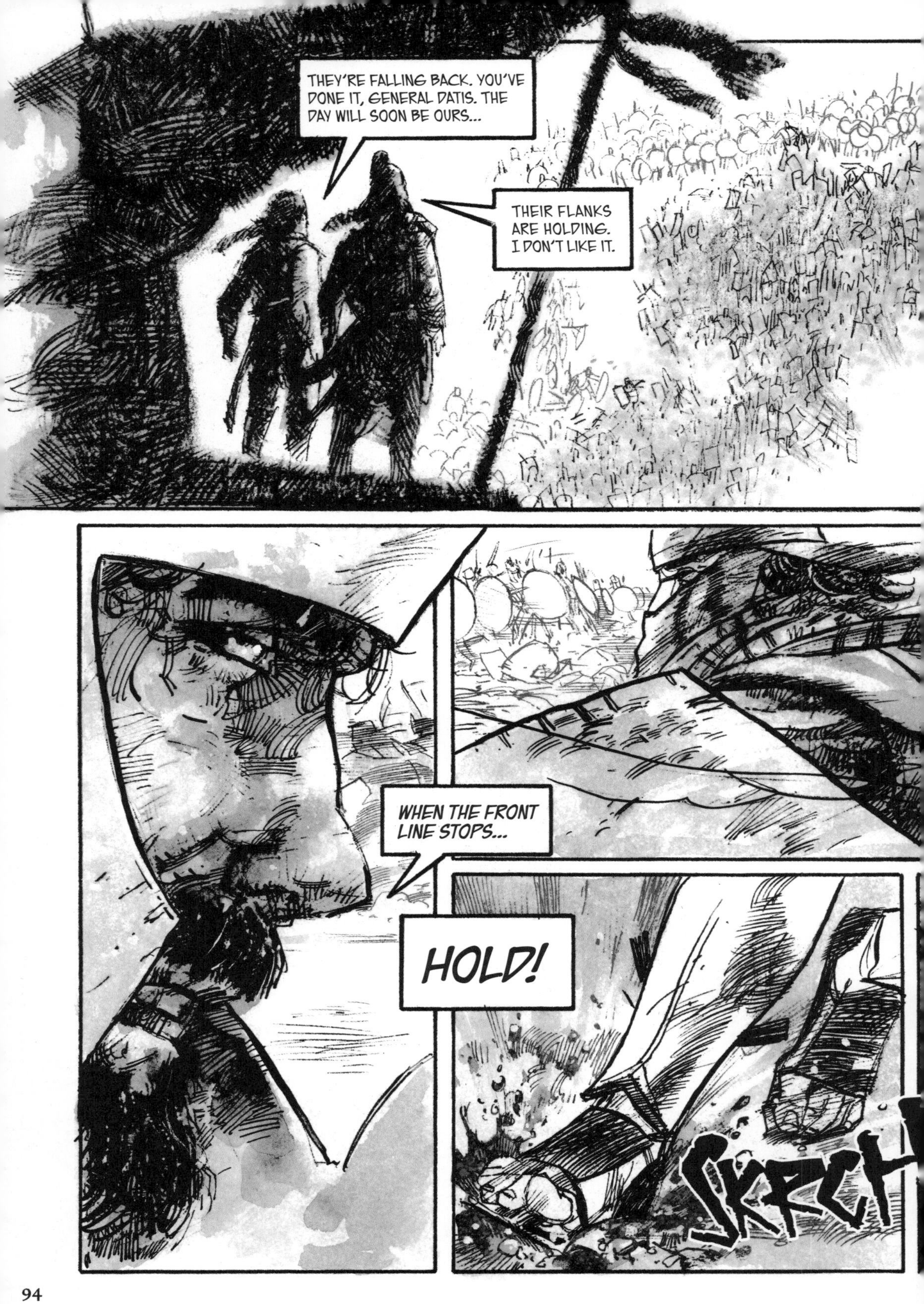
THEY'RE FALLING BACK. YOU'VE DONE IT, GENERAL DATIS. THE DAY WILL SOON BE OURS...
THEIR FLANKS ARE HOLDING. I DON'T LIKE IT.
WHEN THE FRONT LINE STOPS...
HOLD!
SKRCH

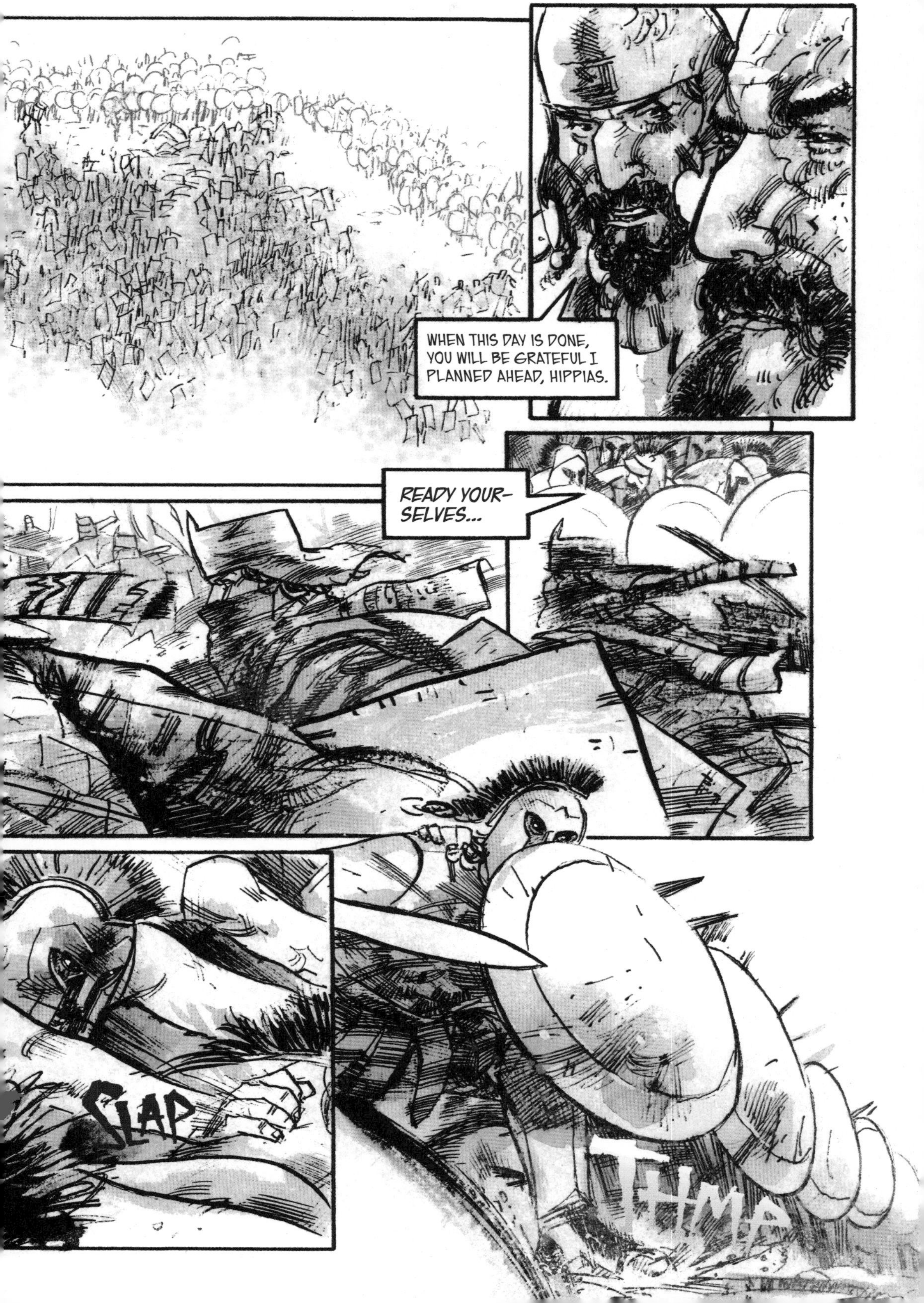
WHEN THIS DAY IS DONE, YOU WILL BE GRATEFUL I PLANNED AHEAD, HIPPIAS.
READY YOURSELVES...
SLAP
THMP

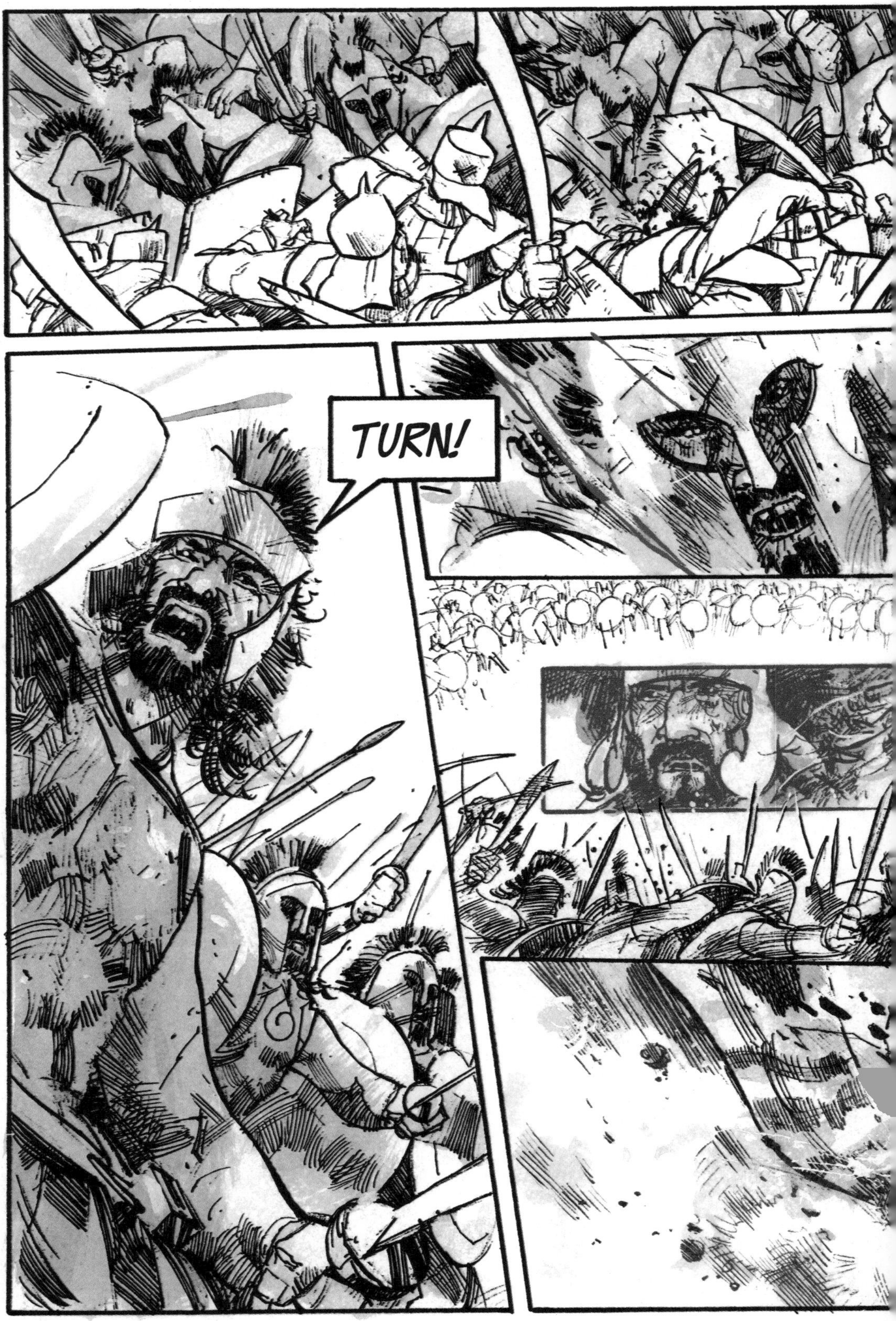
TURN!

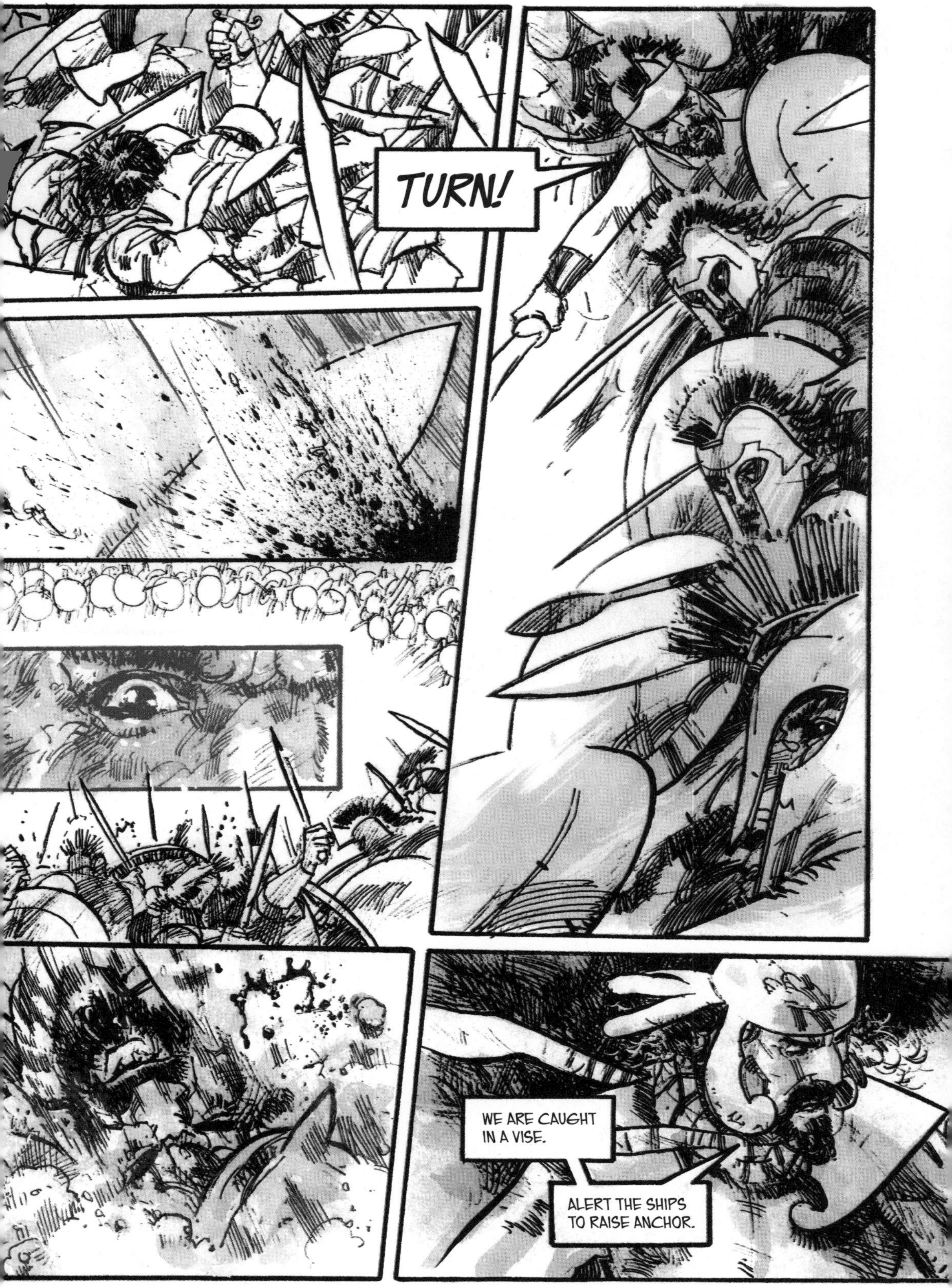
TURN!
WE ARE CAUGHT IN A VISE.
ALERT THE SHIPS TO RAISE ANCHOR.

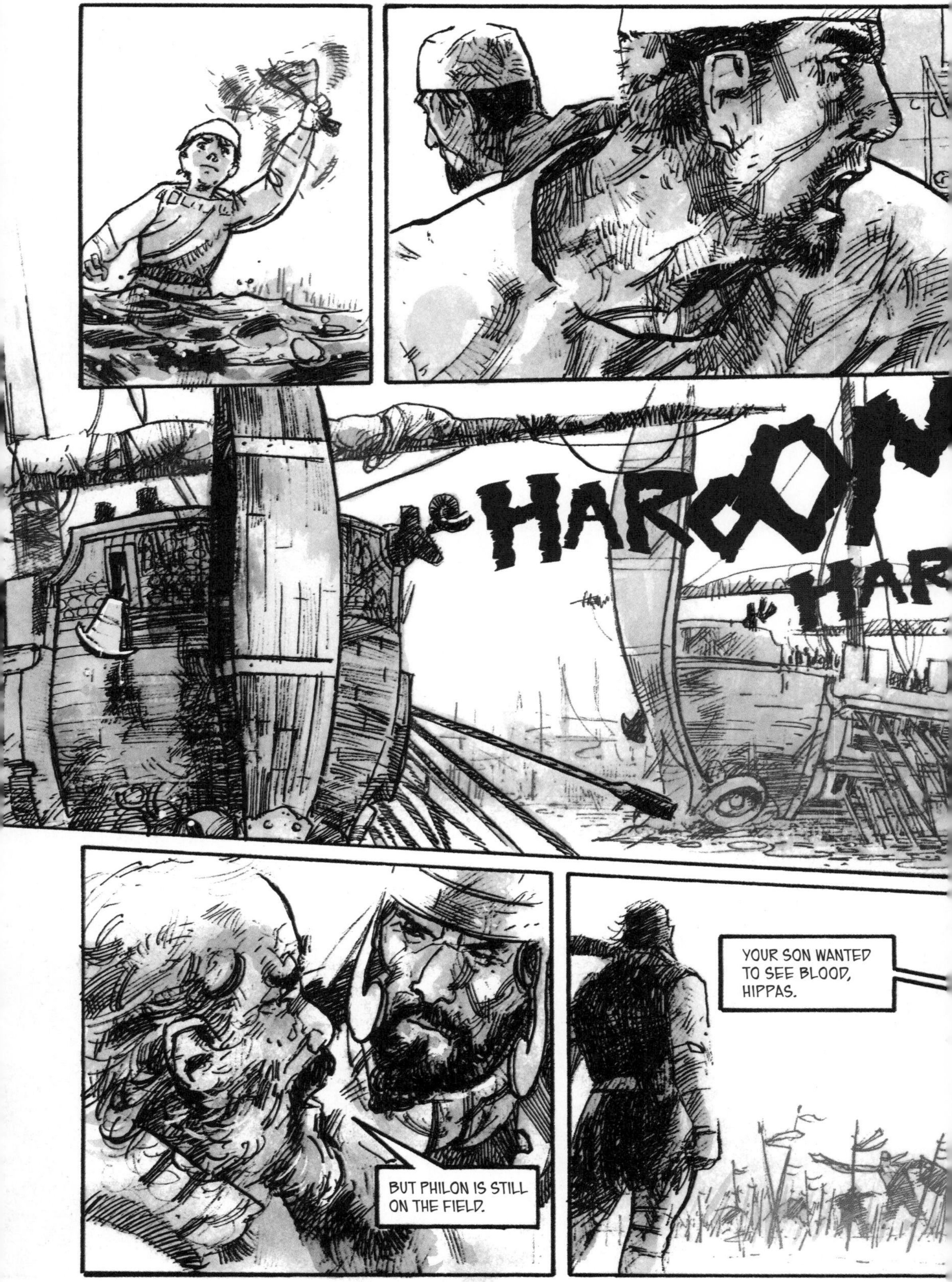
HAROOM
HAR
BUT PHILON IS STILL ON THE FIELD.
YOUR SON WANTED TO SEE BLOOD, HIPPAS.

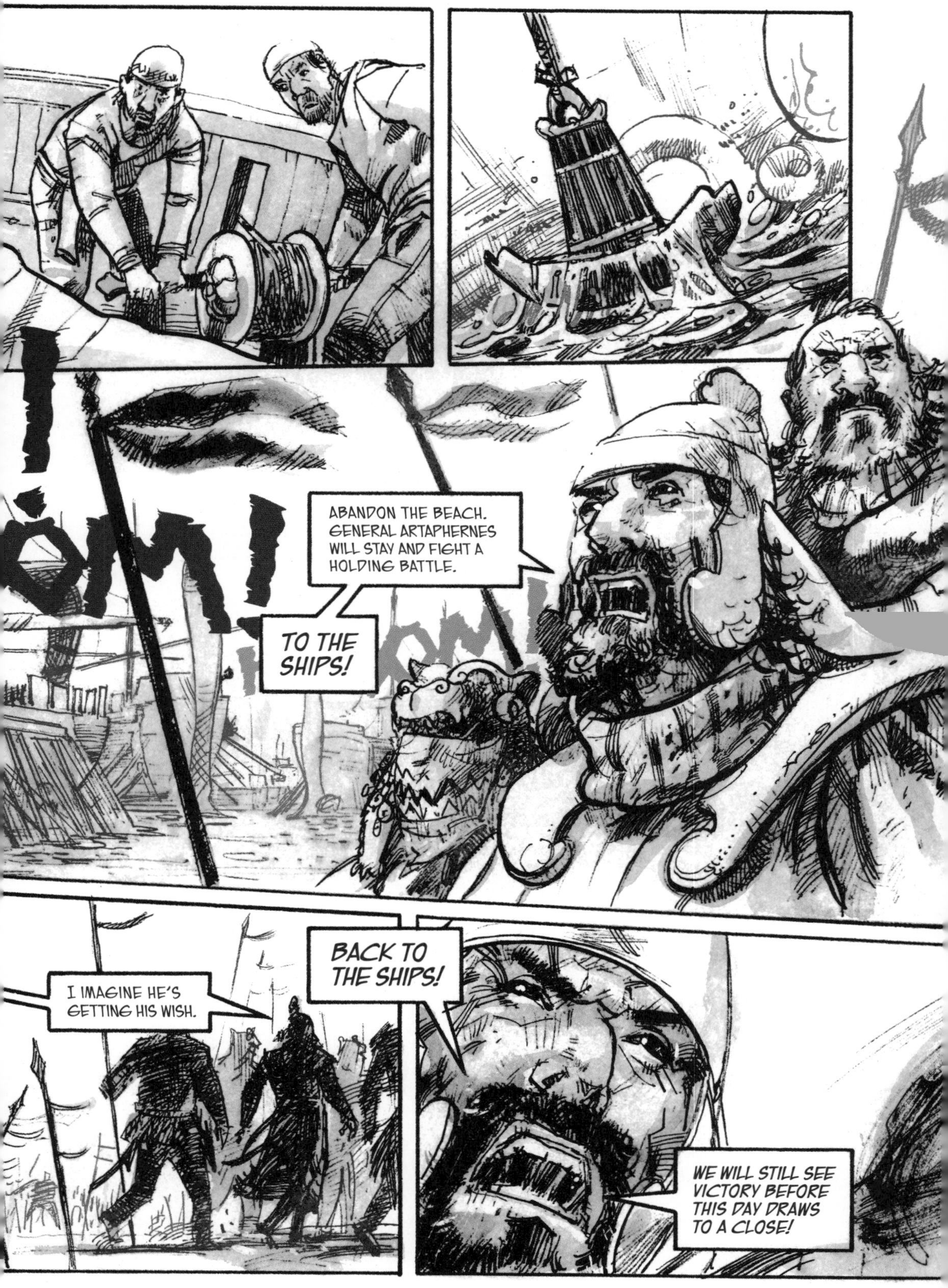

BOOM!
ABANDON THE BEACH. GENERAL ARTAPHERNES WILL STAY AND FIGHT A HOLDING BATTLE.
TO THE SHIPS!
I IMAGINE HE'S GETTING HIS WISH.
BACK TO THE SHIPS!
WE WILL STILL SEE VICTORY BEFORE THIS DAY DRAWS TO A CLOSE!

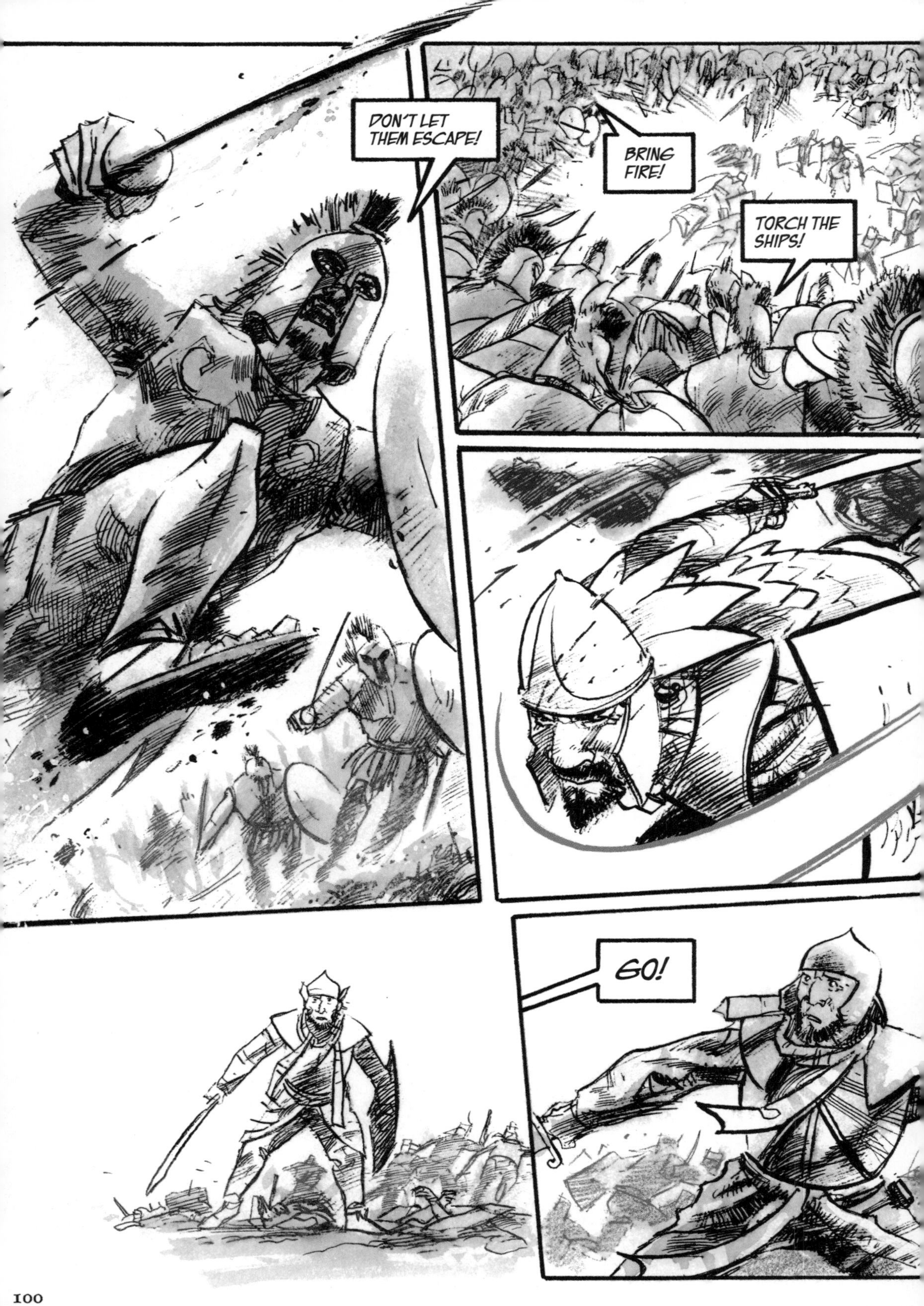
DON'T LET THEM ESCAPE!
BRING FIRE!
TORCH THE SHIPS!
GO!

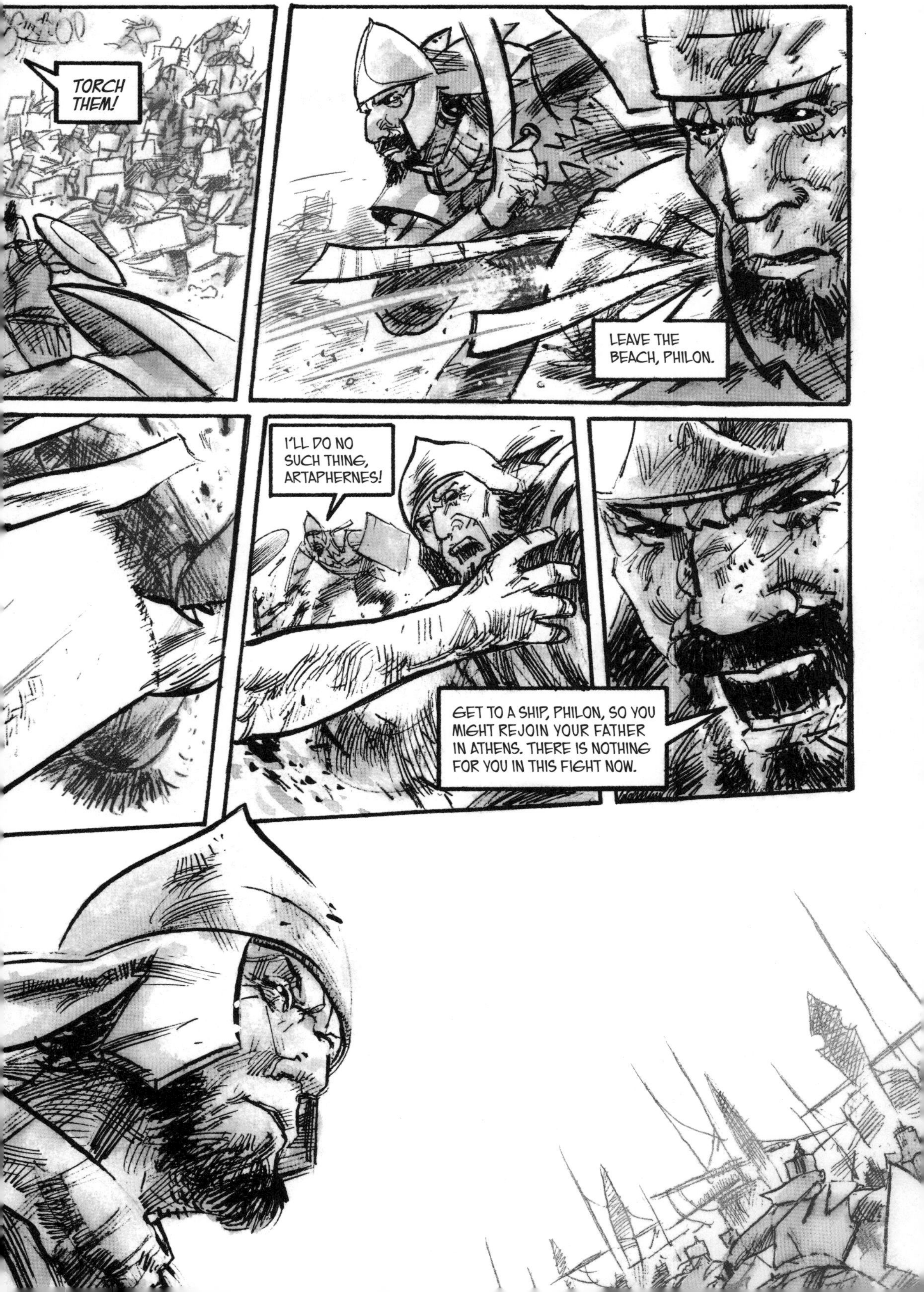
TORCH THEM!
LEAVE THE BEACH, PHILON.
I'LL DO NO SUCH THING, ARTAPHERNES!
GET TO A SHIP, PHILON, SO YOU MIGHT REJOIN YOUR FATHER IN ATHENS. THERE IS NOTHING FOR YOU IN THIS FIGHT NOW.

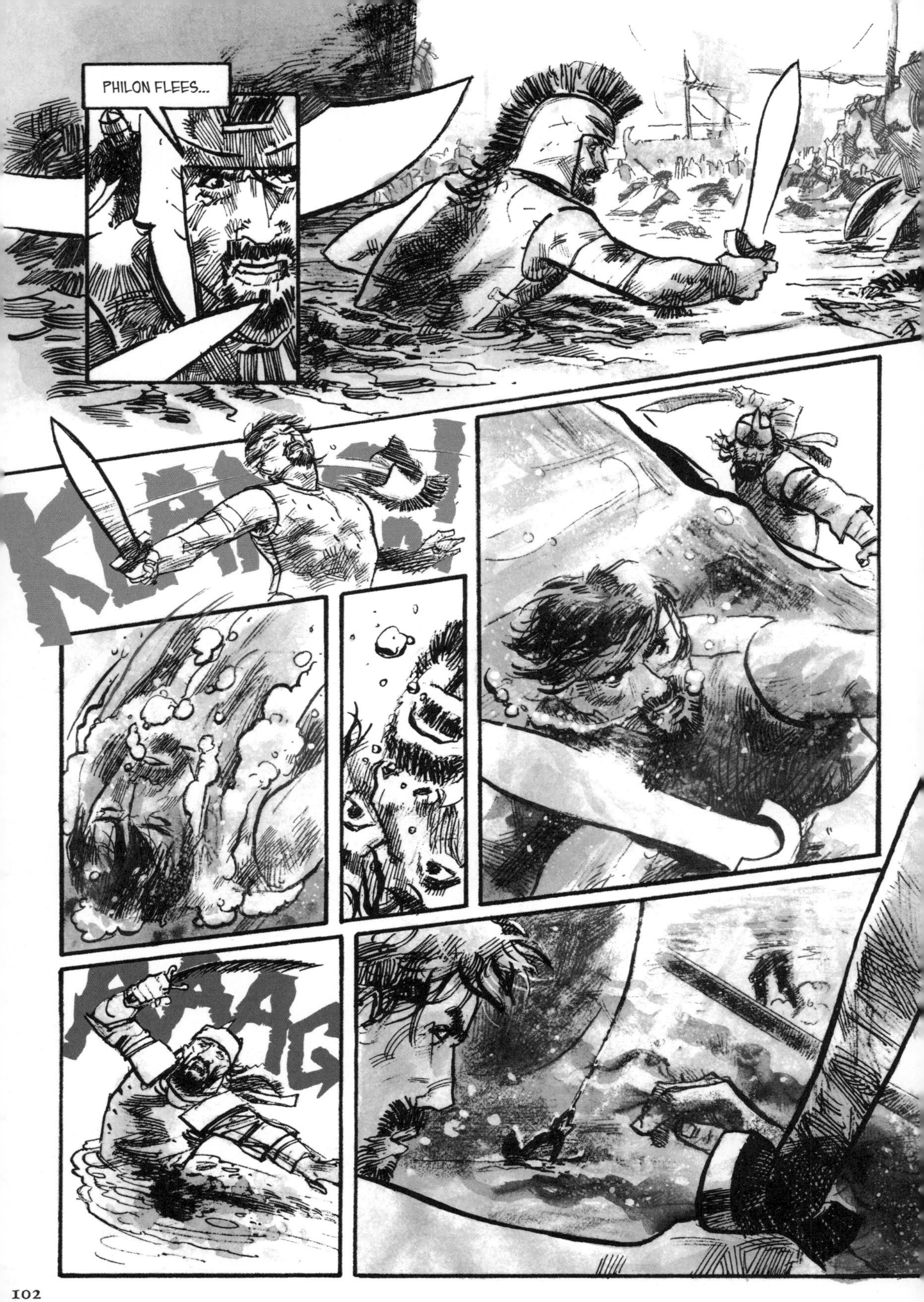
PHILON FLEES...

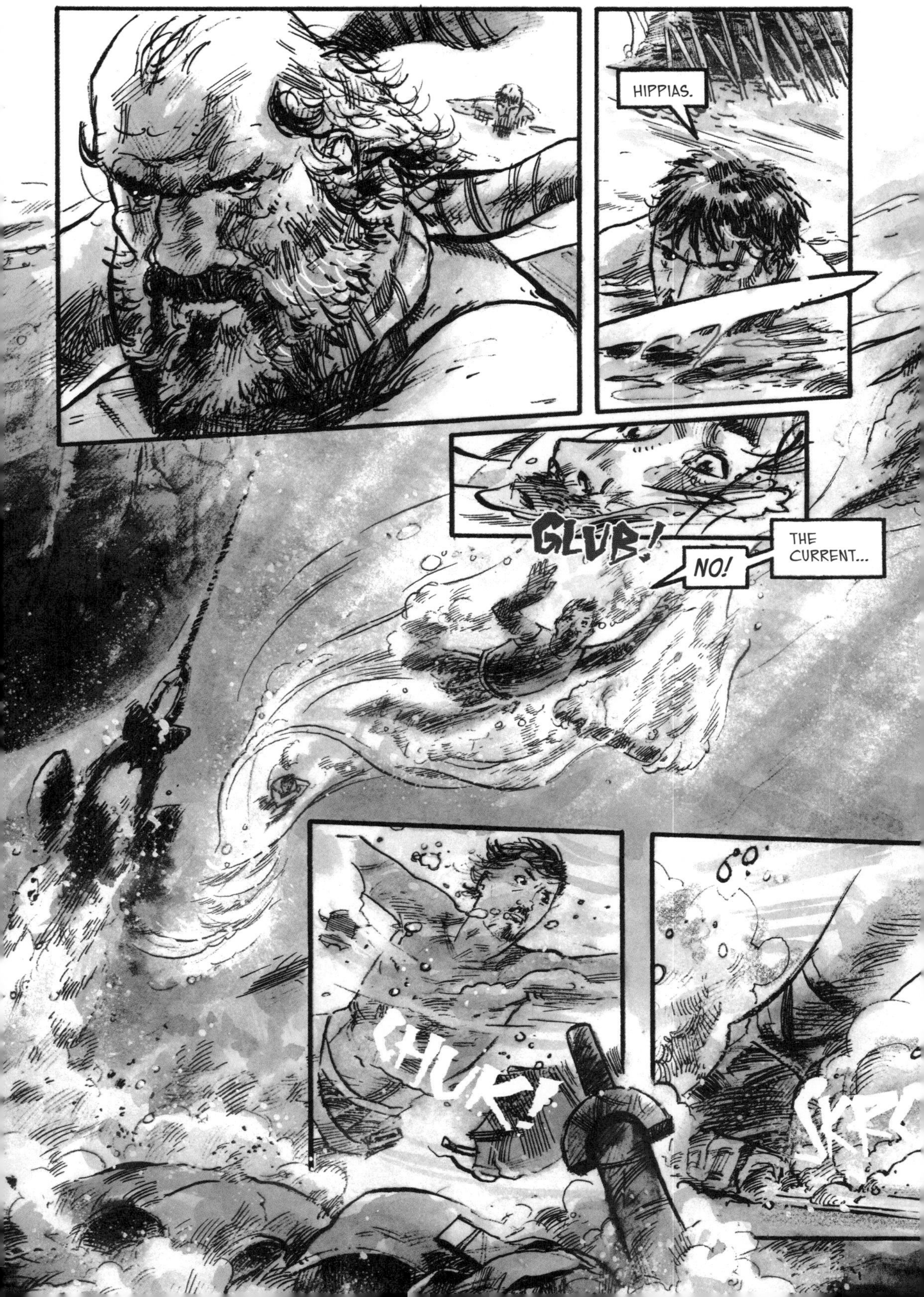

HIPPIAS.
GLUB!
NO!
THE CURRENT...
CHUK!

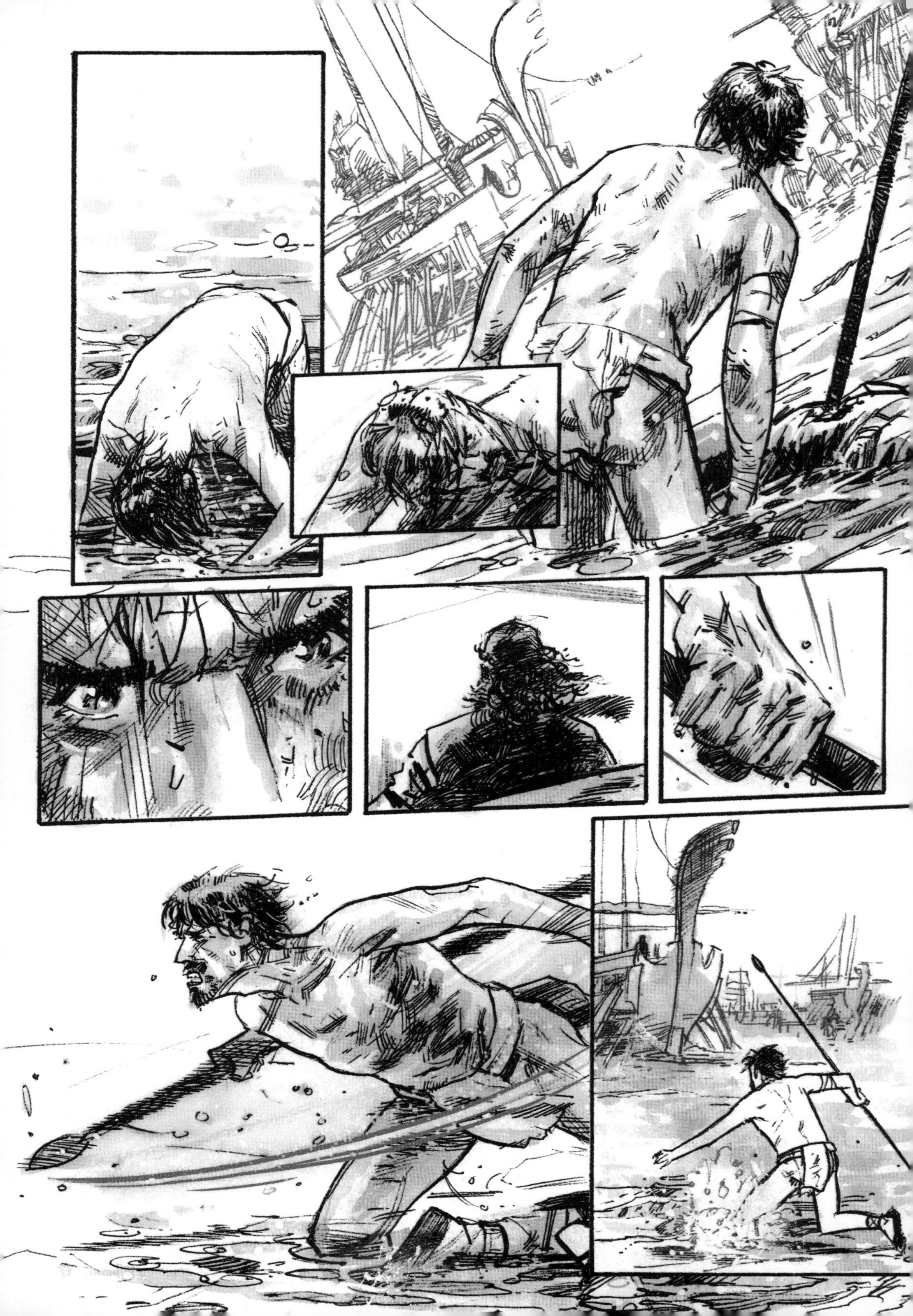

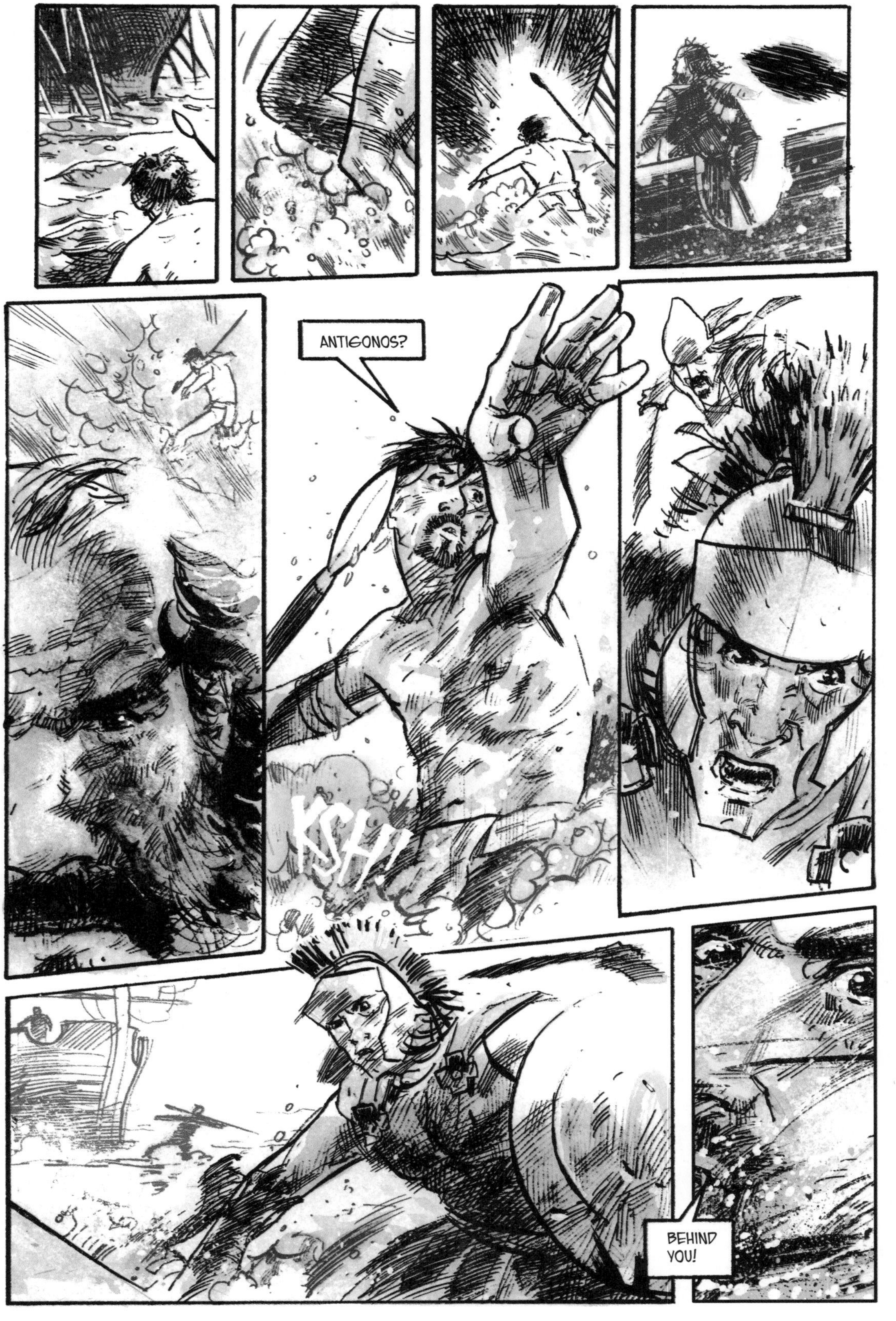
ANTIGONOS?
KSH!
BEHIND YOU!

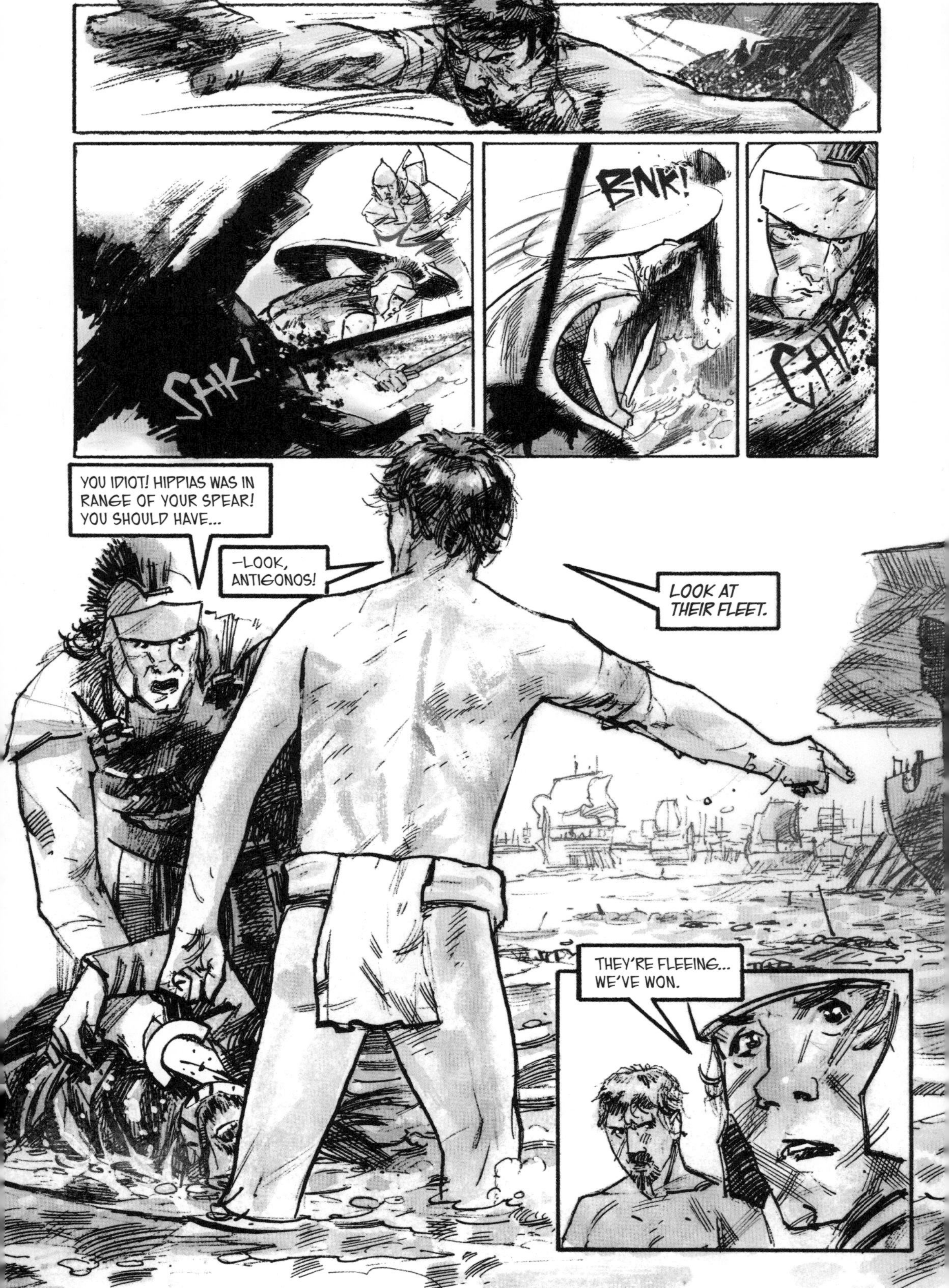
SHK!
BNK!
CHK!
YOU IDIOT! HIPPIAS WAS IN RANGE OF YOUR SPEAR! YOU SHOULD HAVE...
—LOOK, ANTIGONOS!
LOOK AT THEIR FLEET.
THEY'RE FLEEING... WE'VE WON.

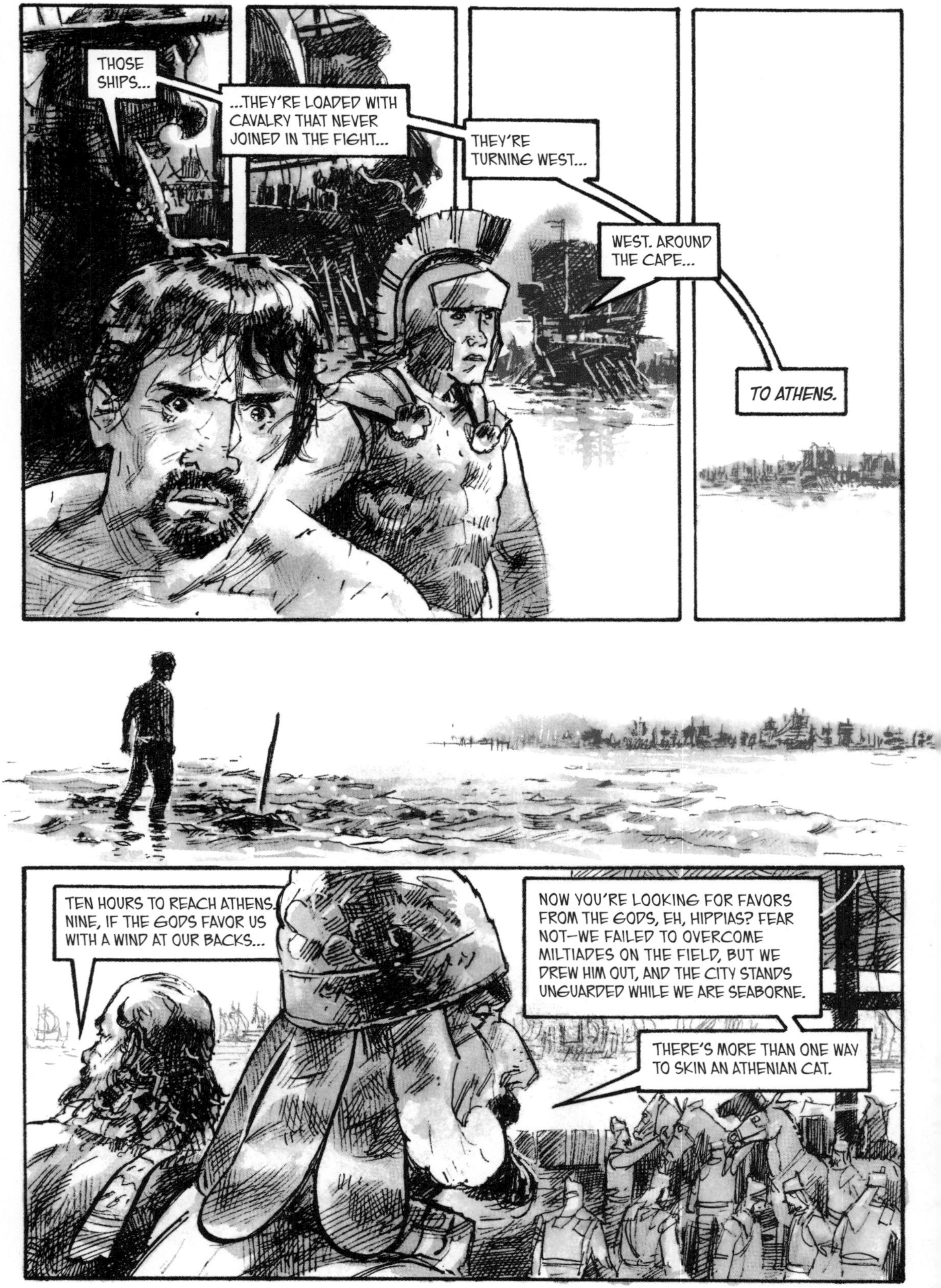
THOSE SHIPS...
...THEY'RE LOADED WITH CAVALRY THAT NEVER JOINED IN THE FIGHT...
THEY'RE TURNING WEST...
WEST. AROUND THE CAPE...
TO ATHENS.
TEN HOURS TO REACH ATHENS. NINE, IF THE GODS FAVOR US WITH A WIND AT OUR BACKS...
NOW YOU'RE LOOKING FOR FAVORS FROM THE GODS, EH, HIPPIAS? FEAR NOT—WE FAILED TO OVERCOME MILTIADES ON THE FIELD, BUT WE DREW HIM OUT, AND THE CITY STANDS UNGUARDED WHILE WE ARE SEABORNE.
THERE'S MORE THAN ONE WAY TO SKIN AN ATHENIAN CAT.

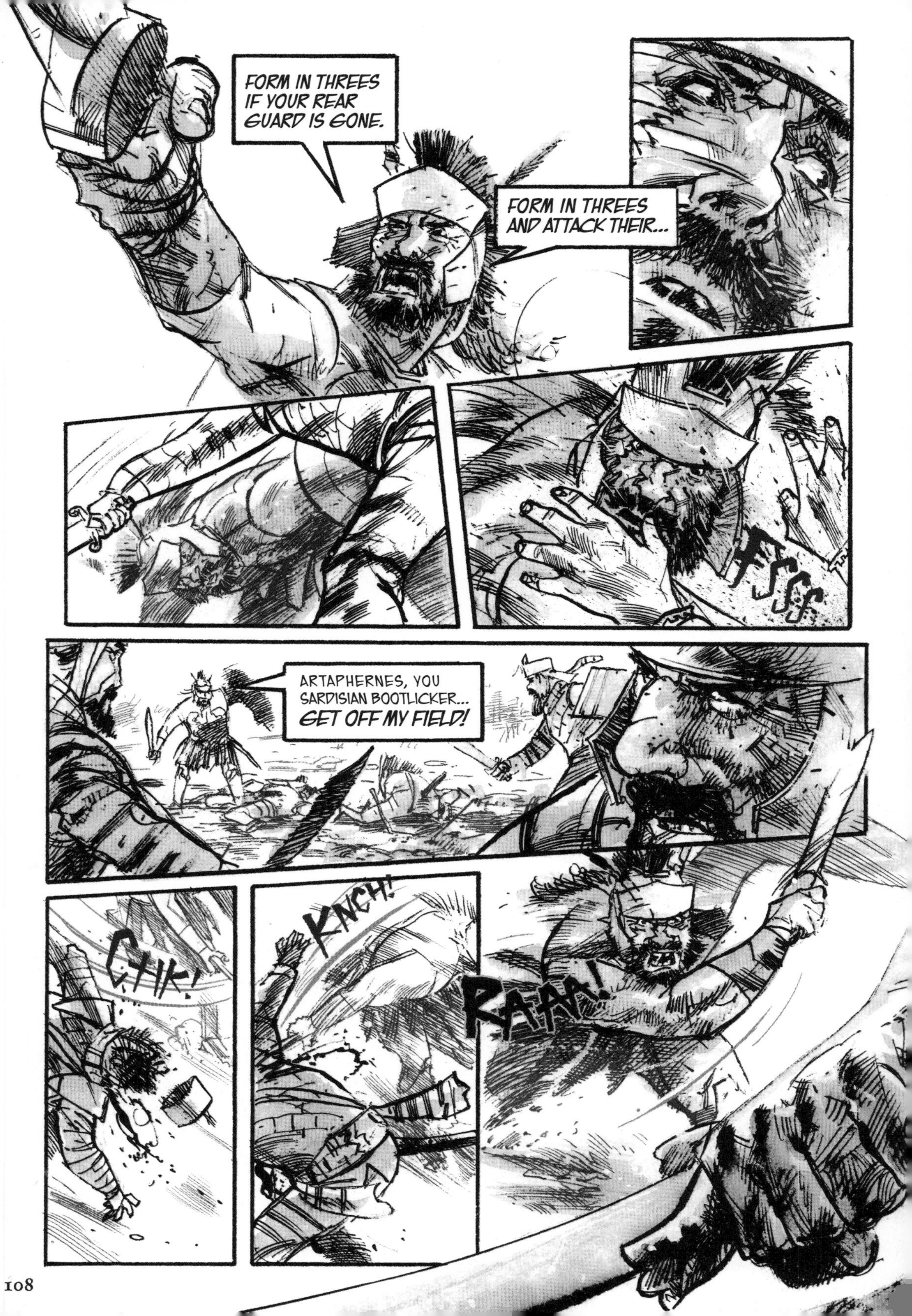
FORM IN THREES IF YOUR REAR GUARD IS GONE.
FORM IN THREES AND ATTACK THEIR...
FSSS
ARTAPHERNES, YOU SARDISIAN BOOTLICKER... GET OFF MY FIELD!
CHK!
KNCH!
RAAA!

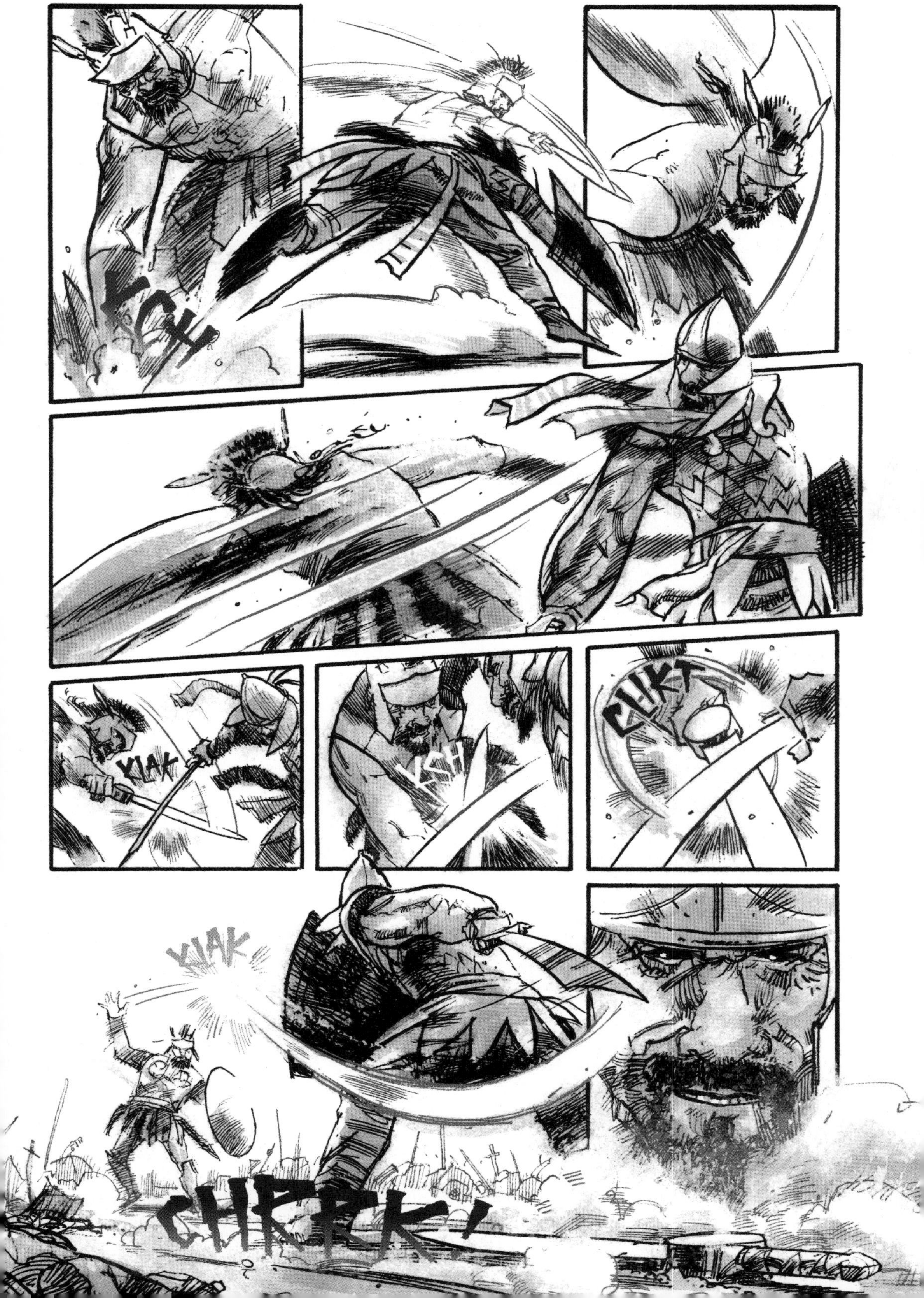
YCH
KLAK
YCH
CLIKT
KLAK
CHRRK!

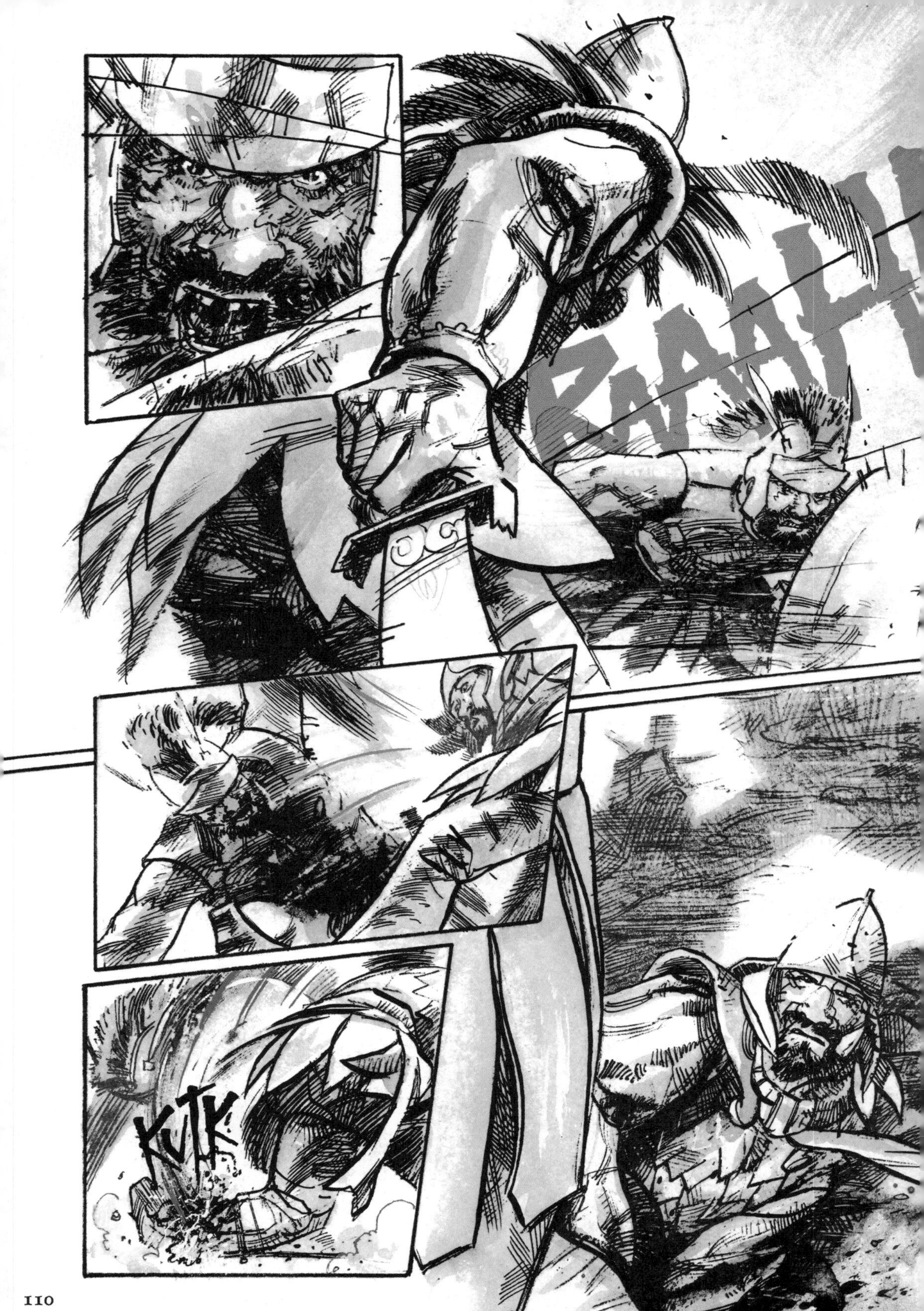
BAAAH
KUTK

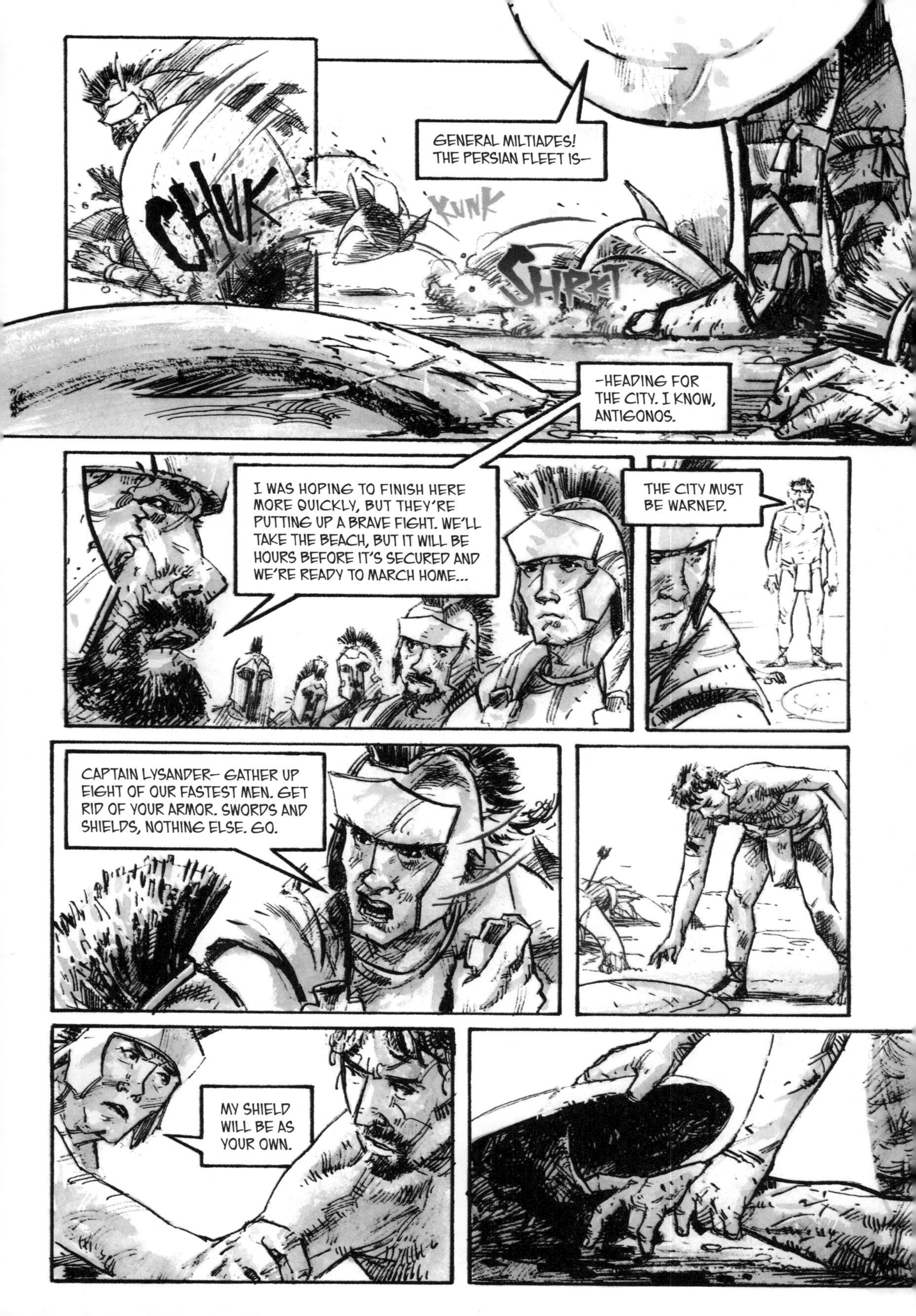
GENERAL MILTIADES! THE PERSIAN FLEET IS—
CHUK
KUNK
SHRKT
—HEADING FOR THE CITY. I KNOW, ANTIGONOS.
I WAS HOPING TO FINISH HERE MORE QUICKLY, BUT THEY'RE PUTTING UP A BRAVE FIGHT. WE'LL TAKE THE BEACH, BUT IT WILL BE HOURS BEFORE IT'S SECURED AND WE'RE READY TO MARCH HOME...
THE CITY MUST BE WARNED.
CAPTAIN LYSANDER— GATHER UP EIGHT OF OUR FASTEST MEN. GET RID OF YOUR ARMOR. SWORDS AND SHIELDS, NOTHING ELSE. GO.
MY SHIELD WILL BE AS YOUR OWN.

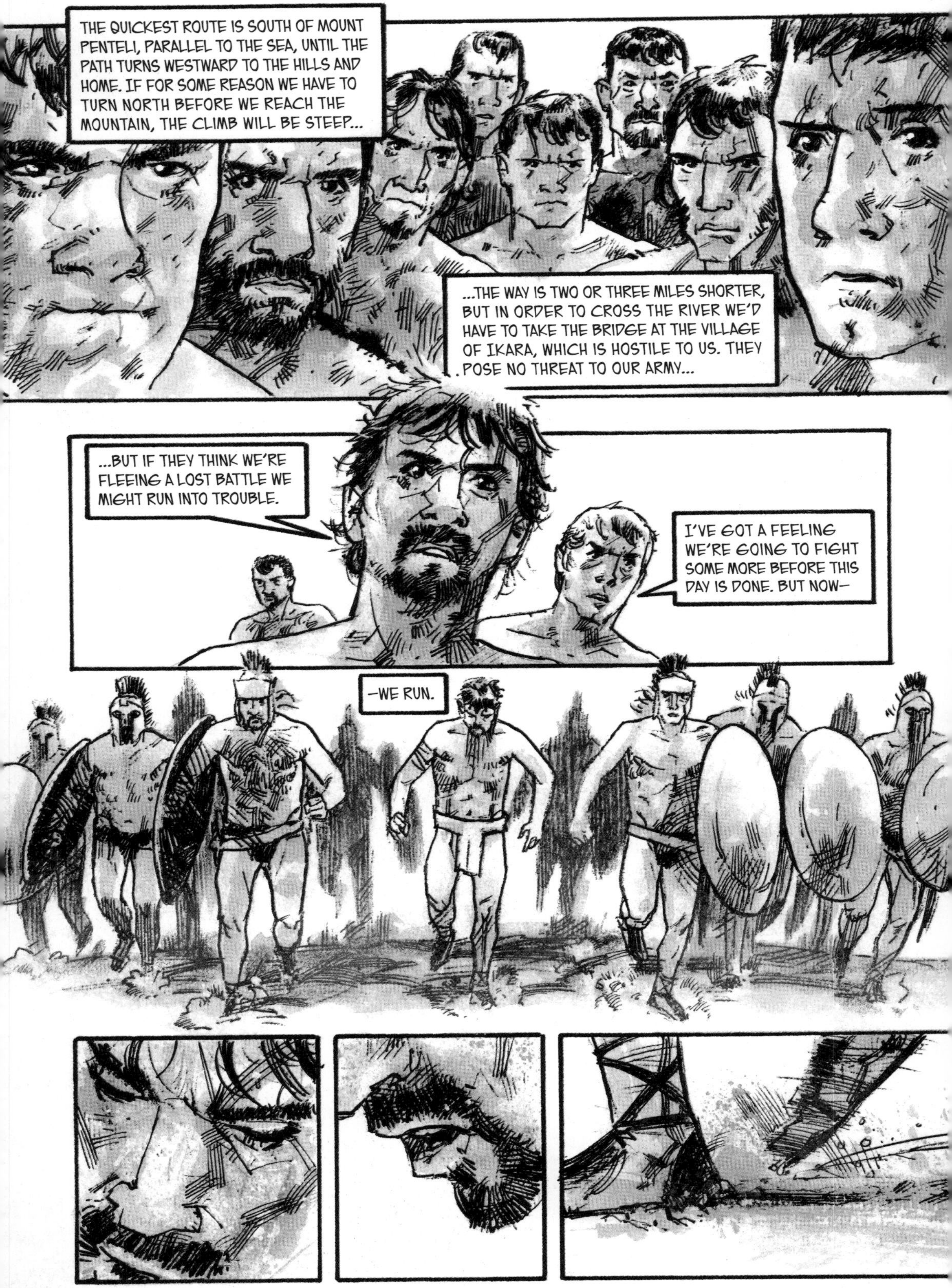

THE QUICKEST ROUTE IS SOUTH OF MOUNT PENTELI, PARALLEL TO THE SEA, UNTIL THE PATH TURNS WESTWARD TO THE HILLS AND HOME. IF FOR SOME REASON WE HAVE TO TURN NORTH BEFORE WE REACH THE MOUNTAIN, THE CLIMB WILL BE STEEP...
...THE WAY IS TWO OR THREE MILES SHORTER, BUT IN ORDER TO CROSS THE RIVER WE'D HAVE TO TAKE THE BRIDGE AT THE VILLAGE OF IKARA, WHICH IS HOSTILE TO US. THEY POSE NO THREAT TO OUR ARMY...
...BUT IF THEY THINK WE'RE FLEEING A LOST BATTLE WE MIGHT RUN INTO TROUBLE.
I'VE GOT A FEELING WE'RE GOING TO FIGHT SOME MORE BEFORE THIS DAY IS DONE. BUT NOW—
—WE RUN.

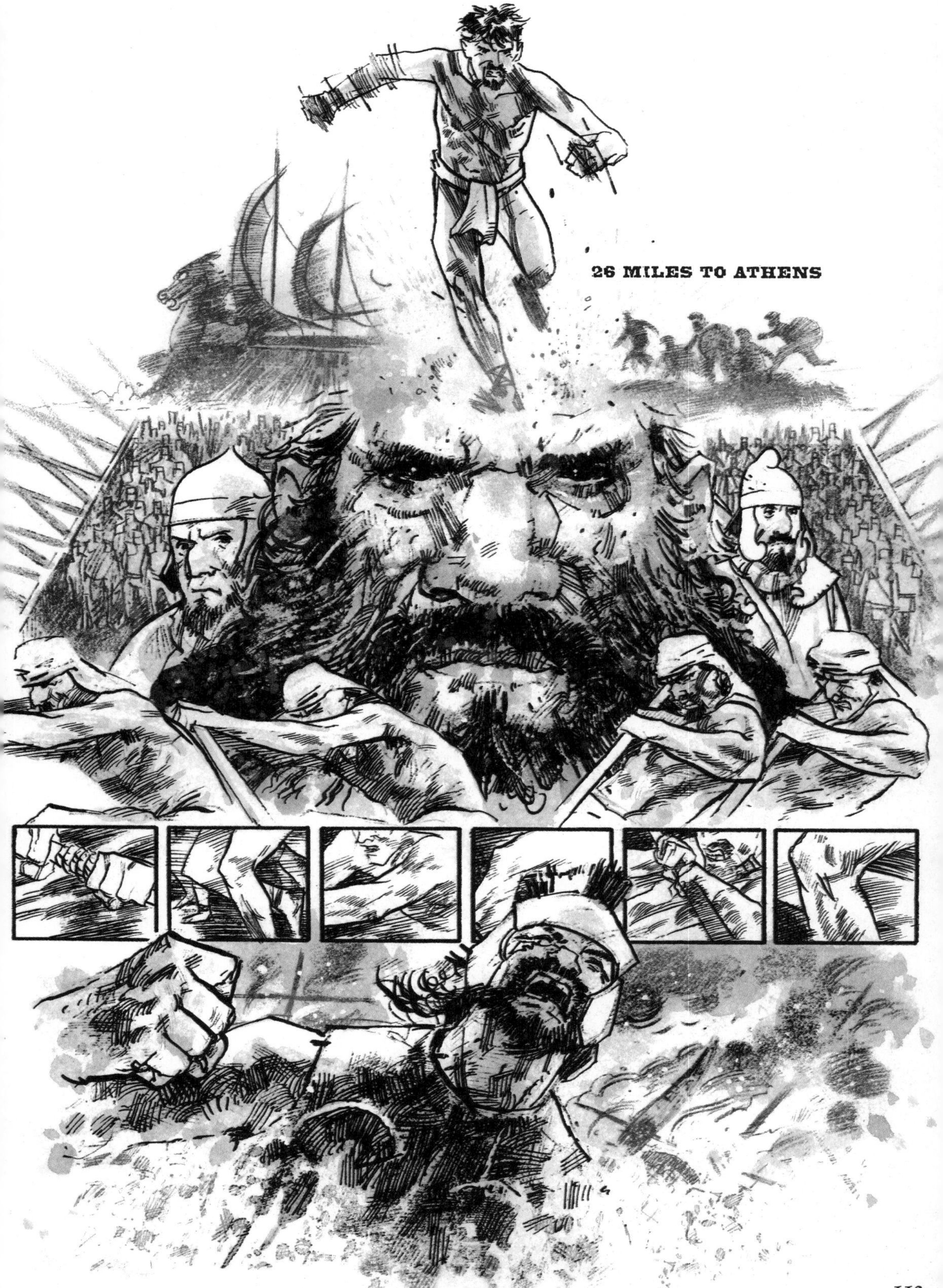
26 MILES TO ATHENS

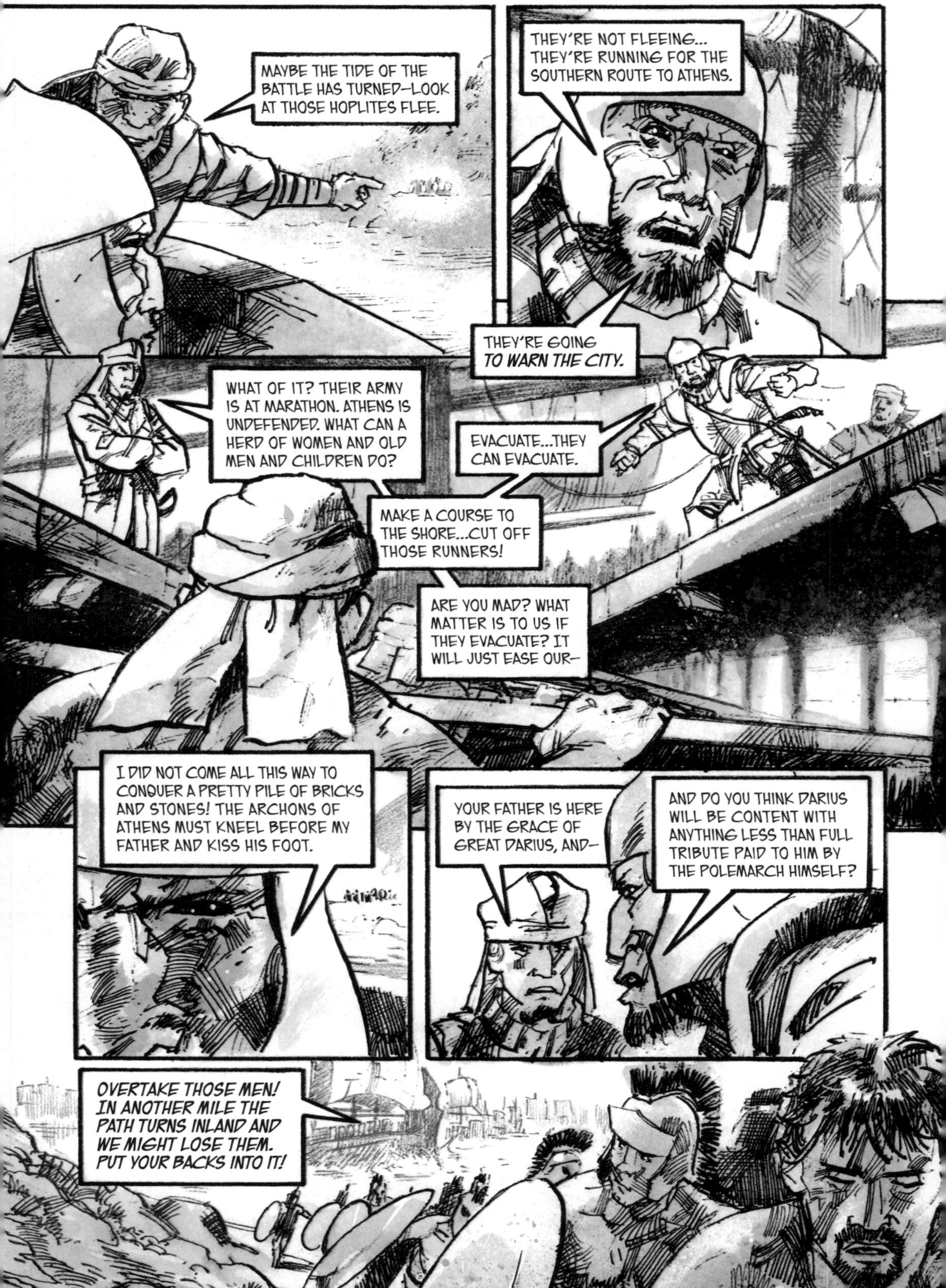
MAYBE THE TIDE OF THE BATTLE HAS TURNED—LOOK AT THOSE HOPLITES FLEE.
THEY'RE NOT FLEEING... THEY'RE RUNNING FOR THE SOUTHERN ROUTE TO ATHENS.
THEY'RE GOING *TO WARN THE CITY.*
WHAT OF IT? THEIR ARMY IS AT MARATHON. ATHENS IS UNDEFENDED. WHAT CAN A HERD OF WOMEN AND OLD MEN AND CHILDREN DO?
EVACUATE...THEY CAN EVACUATE.
MAKE A COURSE TO THE SHORE...CUT OFF THOSE RUNNERS!
ARE YOU MAD? WHAT MATTER IS TO US IF THEY EVACUATE? IT WILL JUST EASE OUR—
I DID NOT COME ALL THIS WAY TO CONQUER A PRETTY PILE OF BRICKS AND STONES! THE ARCHONS OF ATHENS MUST KNEEL BEFORE MY FATHER AND KISS HIS FOOT.
YOUR FATHER IS HERE BY THE GRACE OF GREAT DARIUS, AND—
AND DO YOU THINK DARIUS WILL BE CONTENT WITH ANYTHING LESS THAN FULL TRIBUTE PAID TO HIM BY THE POLEMARCH HIMSELF?
OVERTAKE THOSE MEN! IN ANOTHER MILE THE PATH TURNS INLAND AND WE MIGHT LOSE THEM. PUT YOUR BACKS INTO IT!

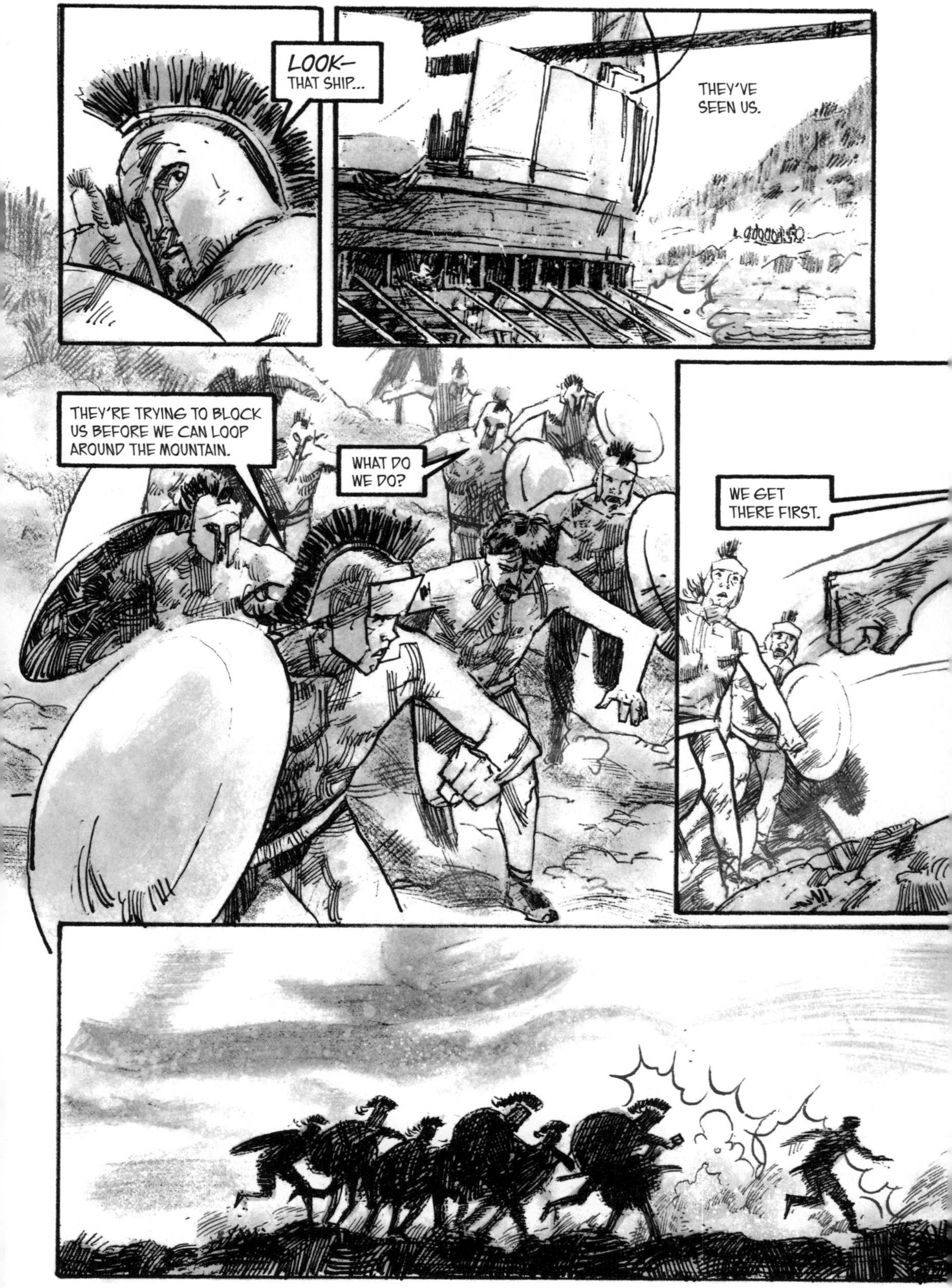
LOOK— THAT SHIP...
THEY'VE SEEN US.
THEY'RE TRYING TO BLOCK US BEFORE WE CAN LOOP AROUND THE MOUNTAIN.
WHAT DO WE DO?
WE GET THERE FIRST.

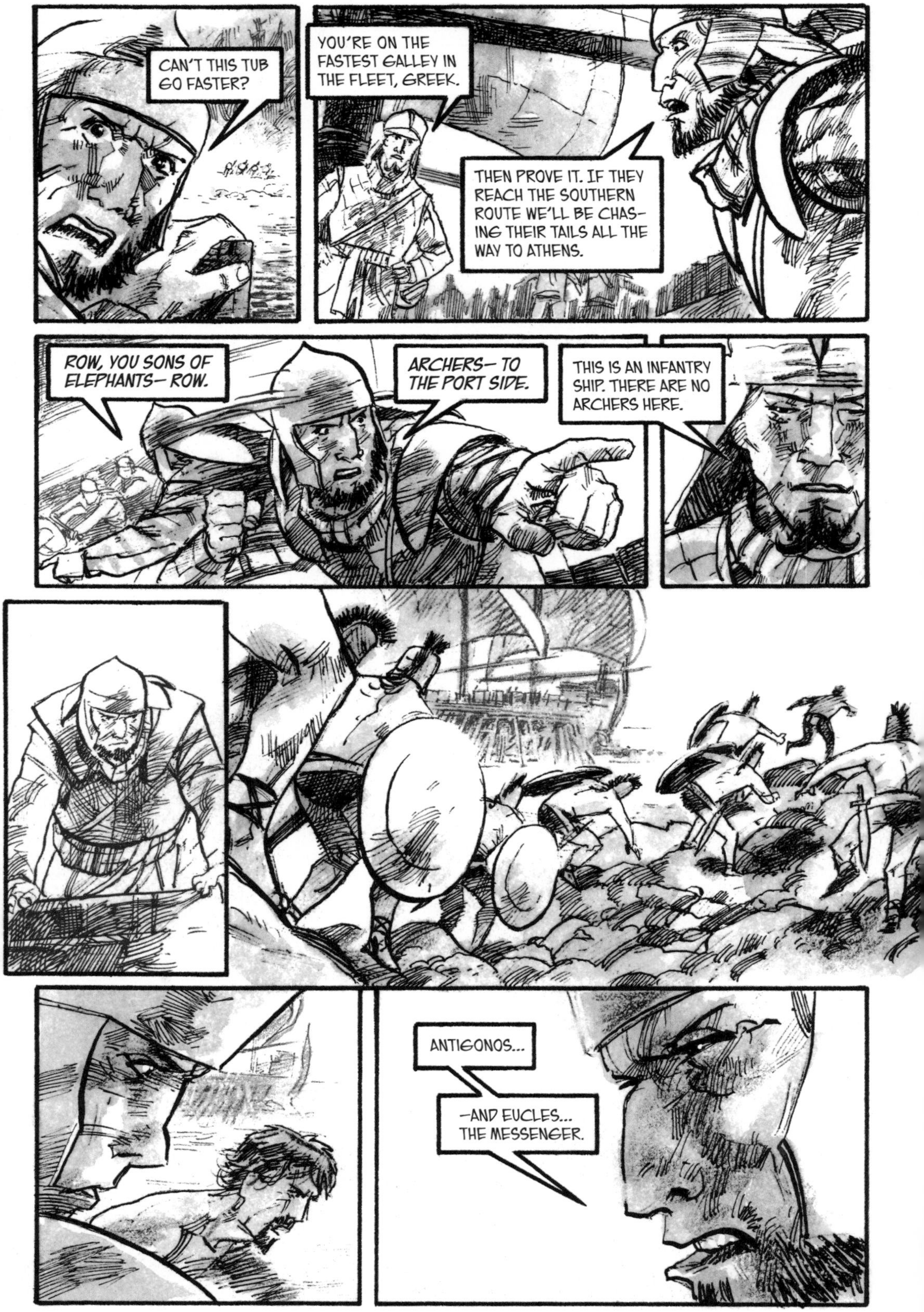
CAN'T THIS TUB GO FASTER?
YOU'RE ON THE FASTEST GALLEY IN THE FLEET, GREEK.
THEN PROVE IT. IF THEY REACH THE SOUTHERN ROUTE WE'LL BE CHASING THEIR TAILS ALL THE WAY TO ATHENS.
ROW, YOU SONS OF ELEPHANTS— ROW.
ARCHERS— TO THE PORT SIDE.
THIS IS AN INFANTRY SHIP. THERE ARE NO ARCHERS HERE.
ANTIGONOS...
—AND EUCLES... THE MESSENGER.

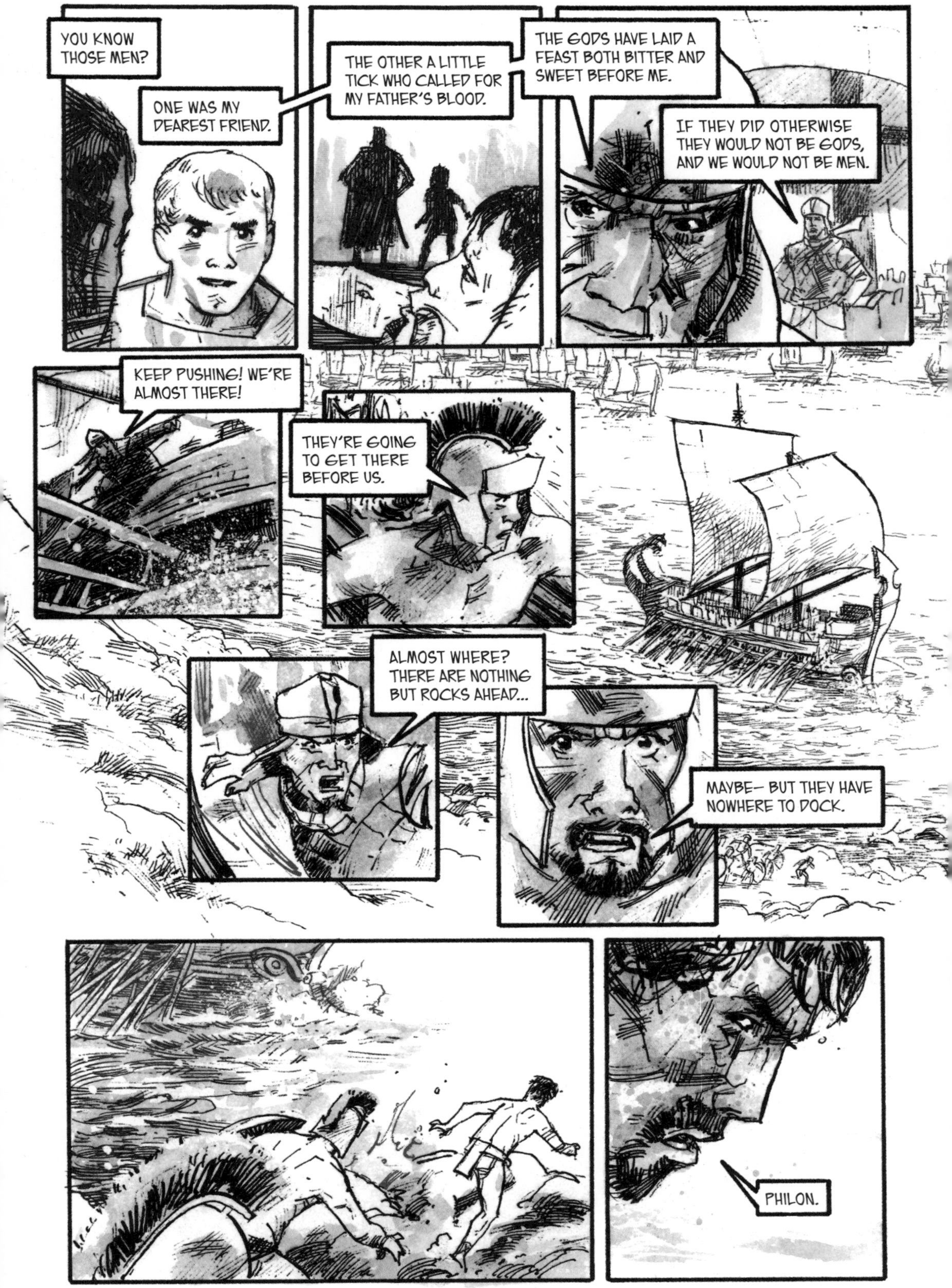
YOU KNOW THOSE MEN?
ONE WAS MY DEAREST FRIEND.
THE OTHER A LITTLE TICK WHO CALLED FOR MY FATHER'S BLOOD.
THE GODS HAVE LAID A FEAST BOTH BITTER AND SWEET BEFORE ME.
IF THEY DID OTHERWISE THEY WOULD NOT BE GODS, AND WE WOULD NOT BE MEN.
KEEP PUSHING! WE'RE ALMOST THERE!
THEY'RE GOING TO GET THERE BEFORE US.
ALMOST WHERE? THERE ARE NOTHING BUT ROCKS AHEAD...
MAYBE— BUT THEY HAVE NOWHERE TO DOCK.
PHILON.

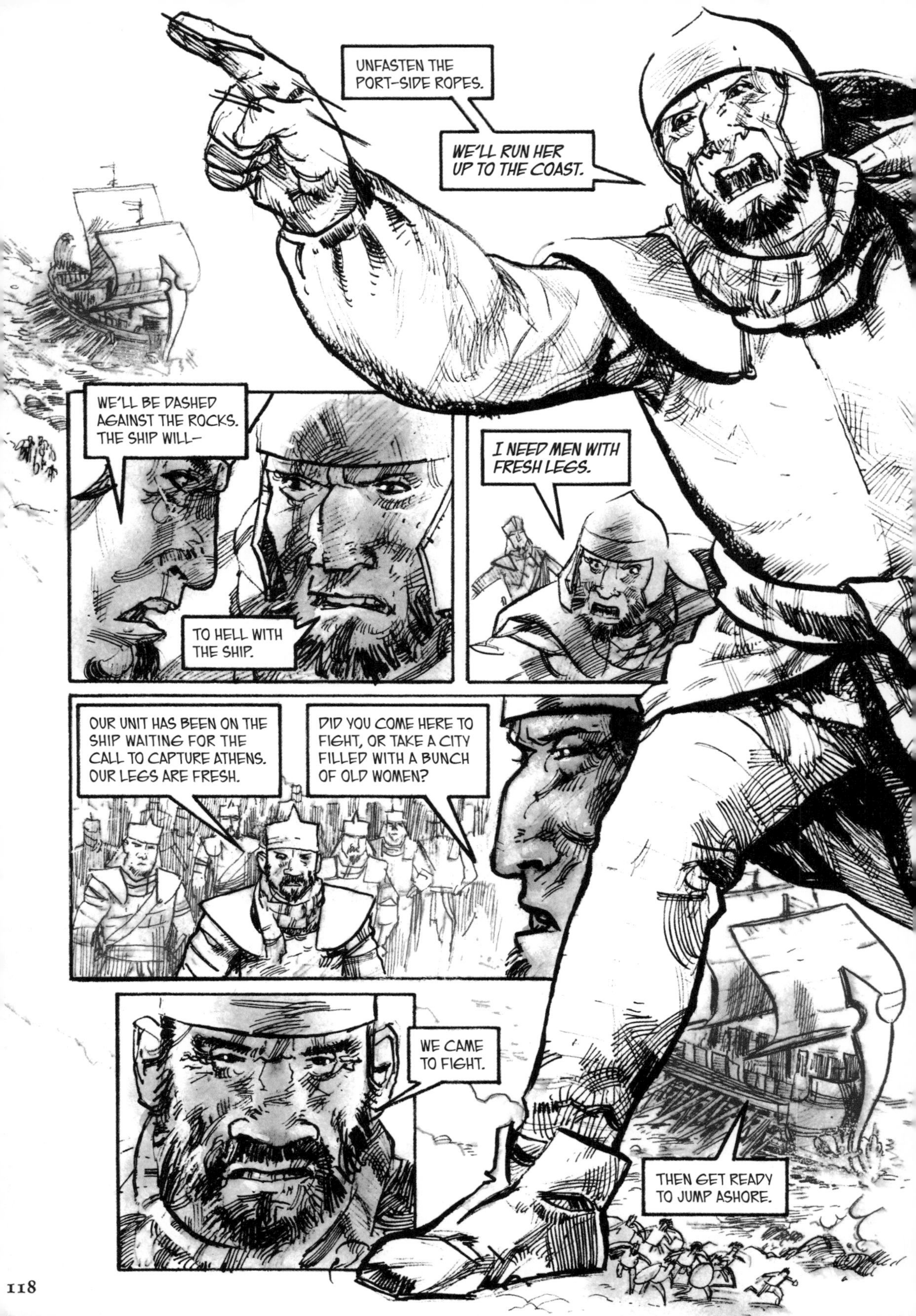
UNFASTEN THE PORT-SIDE ROPES.
WE'LL RUN HER UP TO THE COAST.
WE'LL BE DASHED AGAINST THE ROCKS. THE SHIP WILL-
TO HELL WITH THE SHIP.
I NEED MEN WITH FRESH LEGS.
OUR UNIT HAS BEEN ON THE SHIP WAITING FOR THE CALL TO CAPTURE ATHENS. OUR LEGS ARE FRESH.
DID YOU COME HERE TO FIGHT, OR TAKE A CITY FILLED WITH A BUNCH OF OLD WOMEN?
WE CAME TO FIGHT.
THEN GET READY TO JUMP ASHORE.

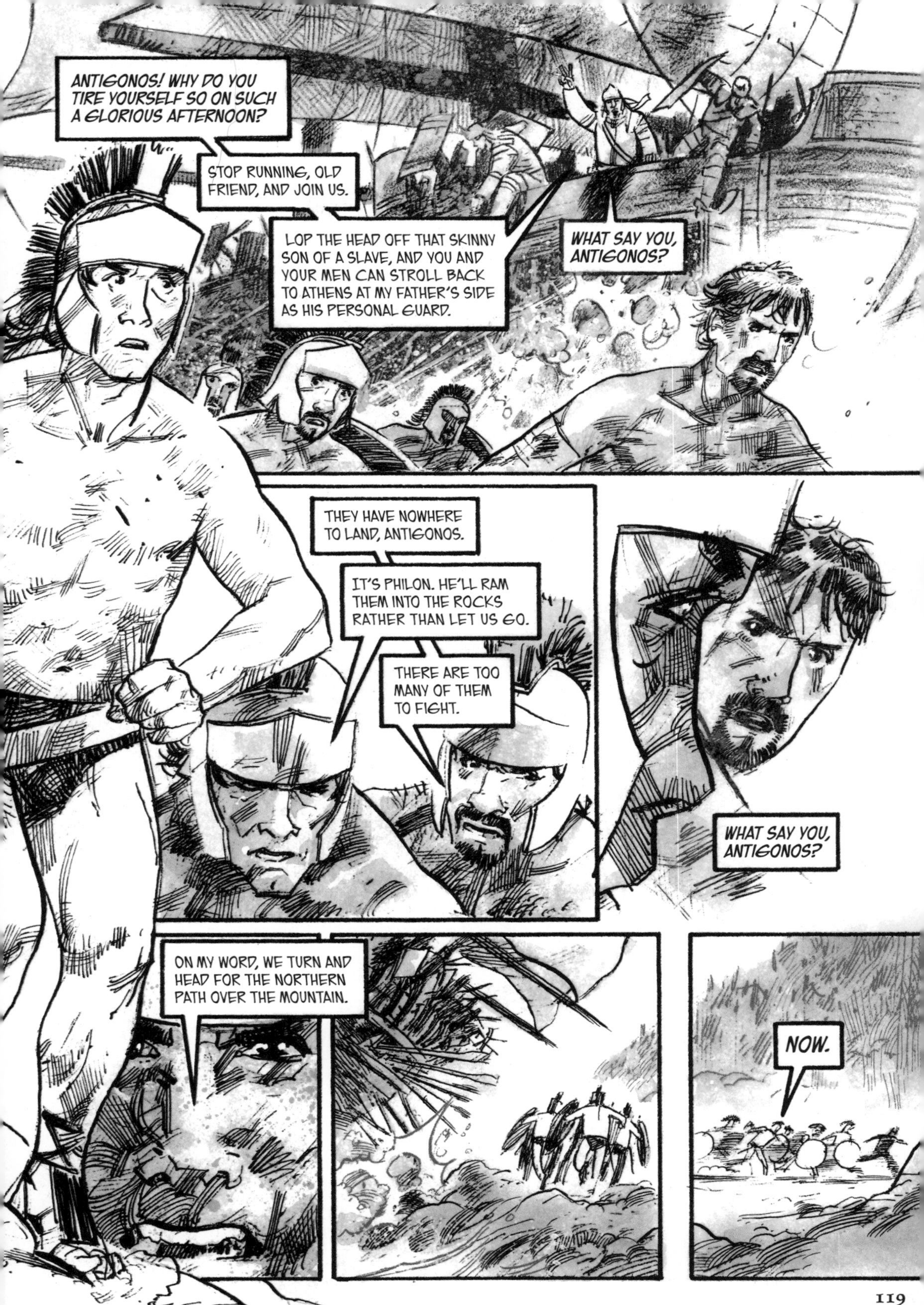
ANTIGONOS! WHY DO YOU TIRE YOURSELF SO ON SUCH A GLORIOUS AFTERNOON?
STOP RUNNING, OLD FRIEND, AND JOIN US.
LOP THE HEAD OFF THAT SKINNY SON OF A SLAVE, AND YOU AND YOUR MEN CAN STROLL BACK TO ATHENS AT MY FATHER'S SIDE AS HIS PERSONAL GUARD.
WHAT SAY YOU, ANTIGONOS?
THEY HAVE NOWHERE TO LAND, ANTIGONOS.
IT'S PHILON. HE'LL RAM THEM INTO THE ROCKS RATHER THAN LET US GO.
THERE ARE TOO MANY OF THEM TO FIGHT.
WHAT SAY YOU, ANTIGONOS?
ON MY WORD, WE TURN AND HEAD FOR THE NORTHERN PATH OVER THE MOUNTAIN.
NOW.

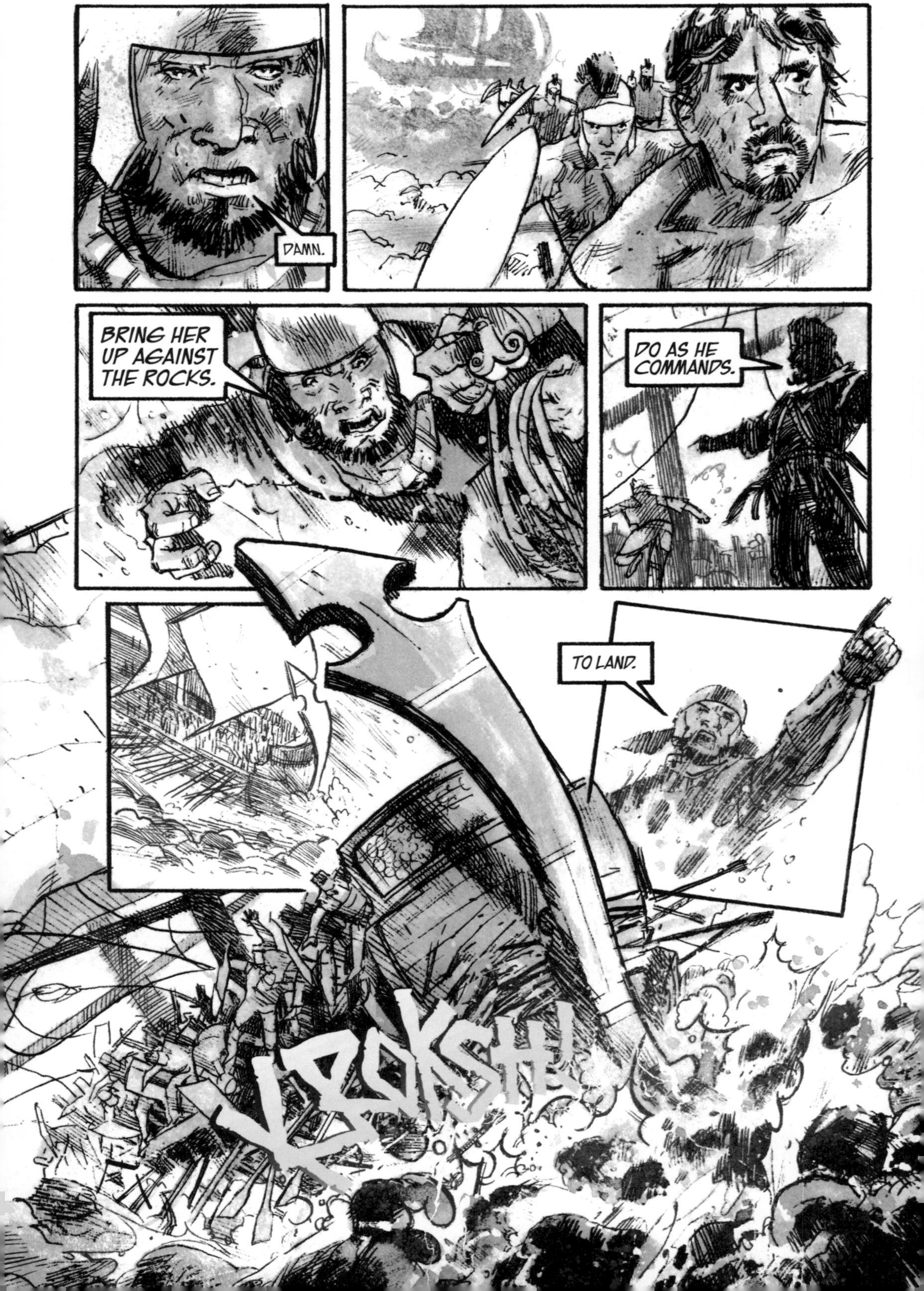
DAMN.
BRING HER UP AGAINST THE ROCKS.
DO AS HE COMMANDS.
TO LAND.
KROSH!

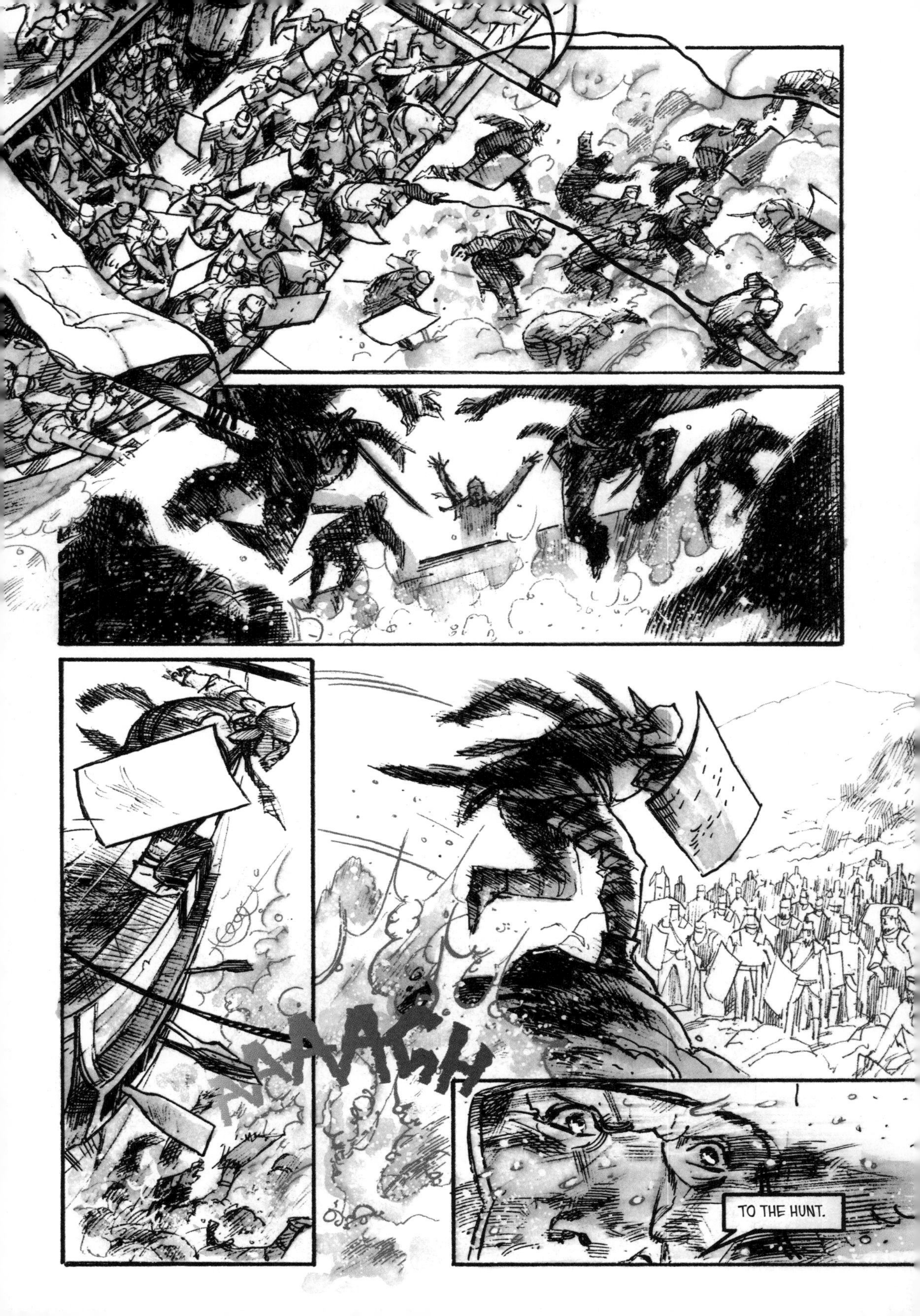
RAAAAGH
TO THE HUNT.

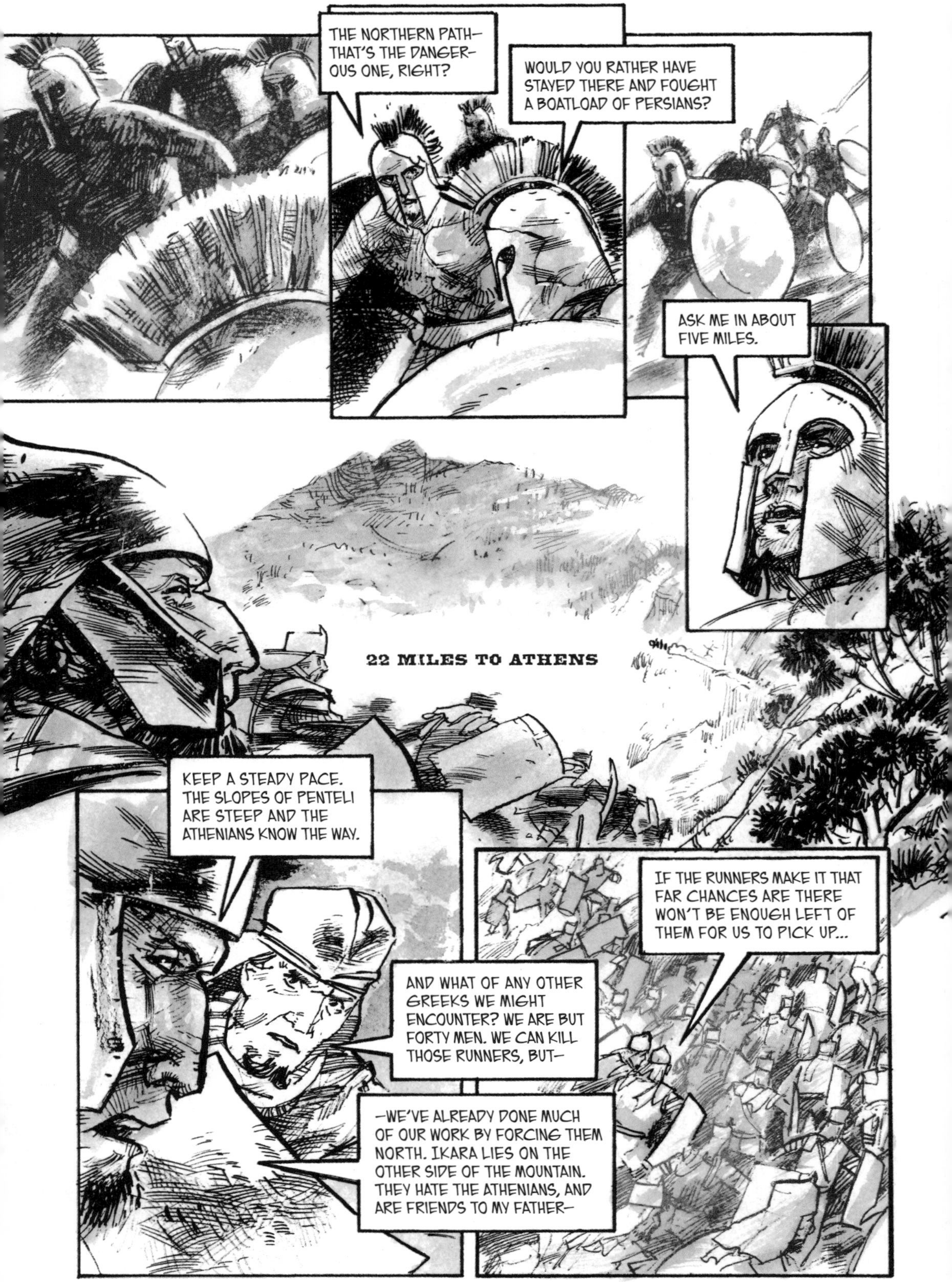
THE NORTHERN PATH— THAT'S THE DANGER-OUS ONE, RIGHT?
WOULD YOU RATHER HAVE STAYED THERE AND FOUGHT A BOATLOAD OF PERSIANS?
ASK ME IN ABOUT FIVE MILES.
22 MILES TO ATHENS
KEEP A STEADY PACE. THE SLOPES OF PENTELI ARE STEEP AND THE ATHENIANS KNOW THE WAY.
AND WHAT OF ANY OTHER GREEKS WE MIGHT ENCOUNTER? WE ARE BUT FORTY MEN. WE CAN KILL THOSE RUNNERS, BUT—
—WE'VE ALREADY DONE MUCH OF OUR WORK BY FORCING THEM NORTH. IKARA LIES ON THE OTHER SIDE OF THE MOUNTAIN. THEY HATE THE ATHENIANS, AND ARE FRIENDS TO MY FATHER—
IF THE RUNNERS MAKE IT THAT FAR CHANCES ARE THERE WON'T BE ENOUGH LEFT OF THEM FOR US TO PICK UP...

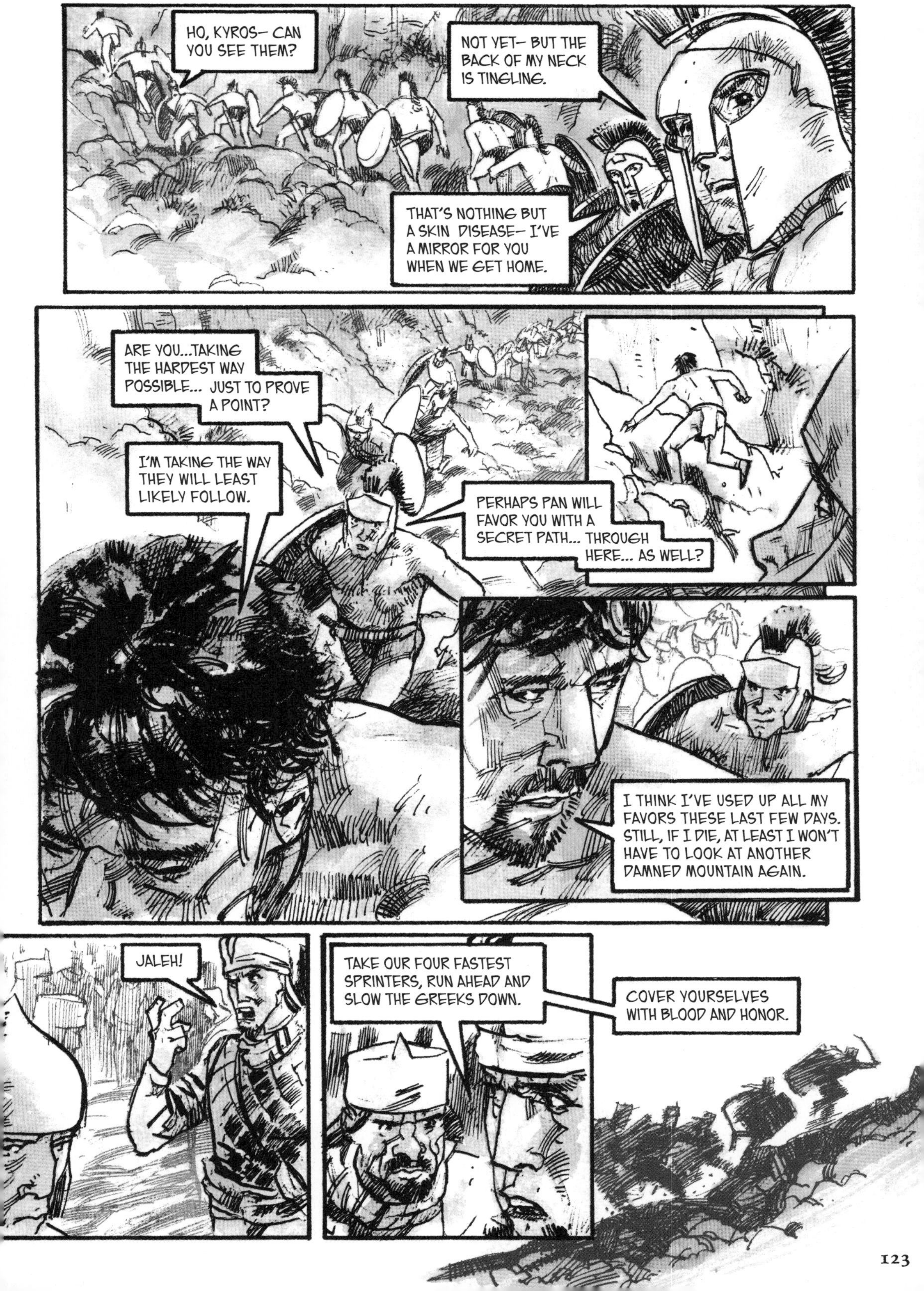
HO, KYROS— CAN YOU SEE THEM?
NOT YET— BUT THE BACK OF MY NECK IS TINGLING.
THAT'S NOTHING BUT A SKIN DISEASE— I'VE A MIRROR FOR YOU WHEN WE GET HOME.
ARE YOU...TAKING THE HARDEST WAY POSSIBLE... JUST TO PROVE A POINT?
I'M TAKING THE WAY THEY WILL LEAST LIKELY FOLLOW.
PERHAPS PAN WILL FAVOR YOU WITH A SECRET PATH... THROUGH HERE... AS WELL?
I THINK I'VE USED UP ALL MY FAVORS THESE LAST FEW DAYS. STILL, IF I DIE, AT LEAST I WON'T HAVE TO LOOK AT ANOTHER DAMNED MOUNTAIN AGAIN.
JALEH!
TAKE OUR FOUR FASTEST SPRINTERS, RUN AHEAD AND SLOW THE GREEKS DOWN.
COVER YOURSELVES WITH BLOOD AND HONOR.

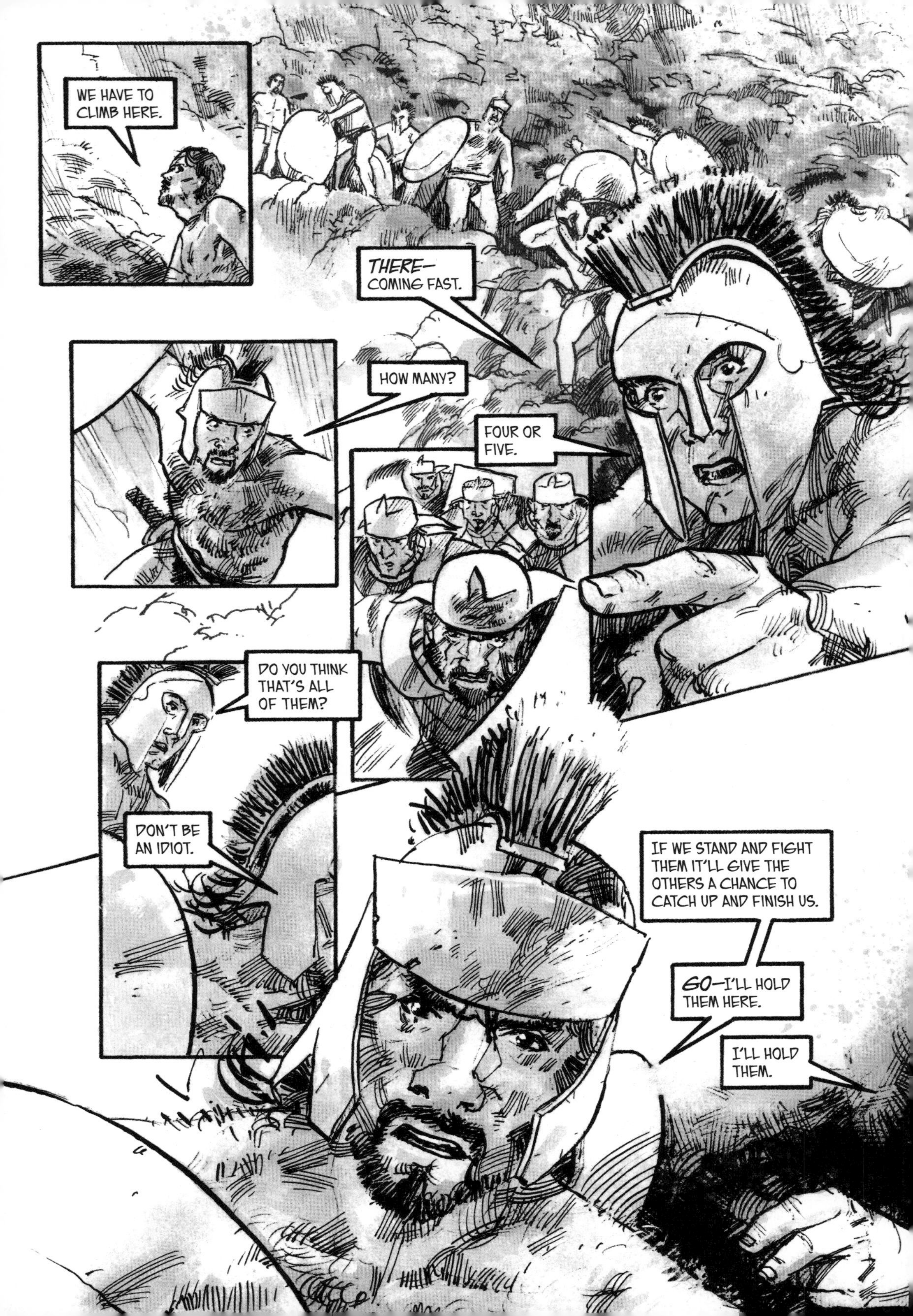
WE HAVE TO CLIMB HERE.
THERE—COMING FAST.
HOW MANY?
FOUR OR FIVE.
DO YOU THINK THAT'S ALL OF THEM?
DON'T BE AN IDIOT.
IF WE STAND AND FIGHT THEM IT'LL GIVE THE OTHERS A CHANCE TO CATCH UP AND FINISH US.
GO—I'LL HOLD THEM HERE.
I'LL HOLD THEM.

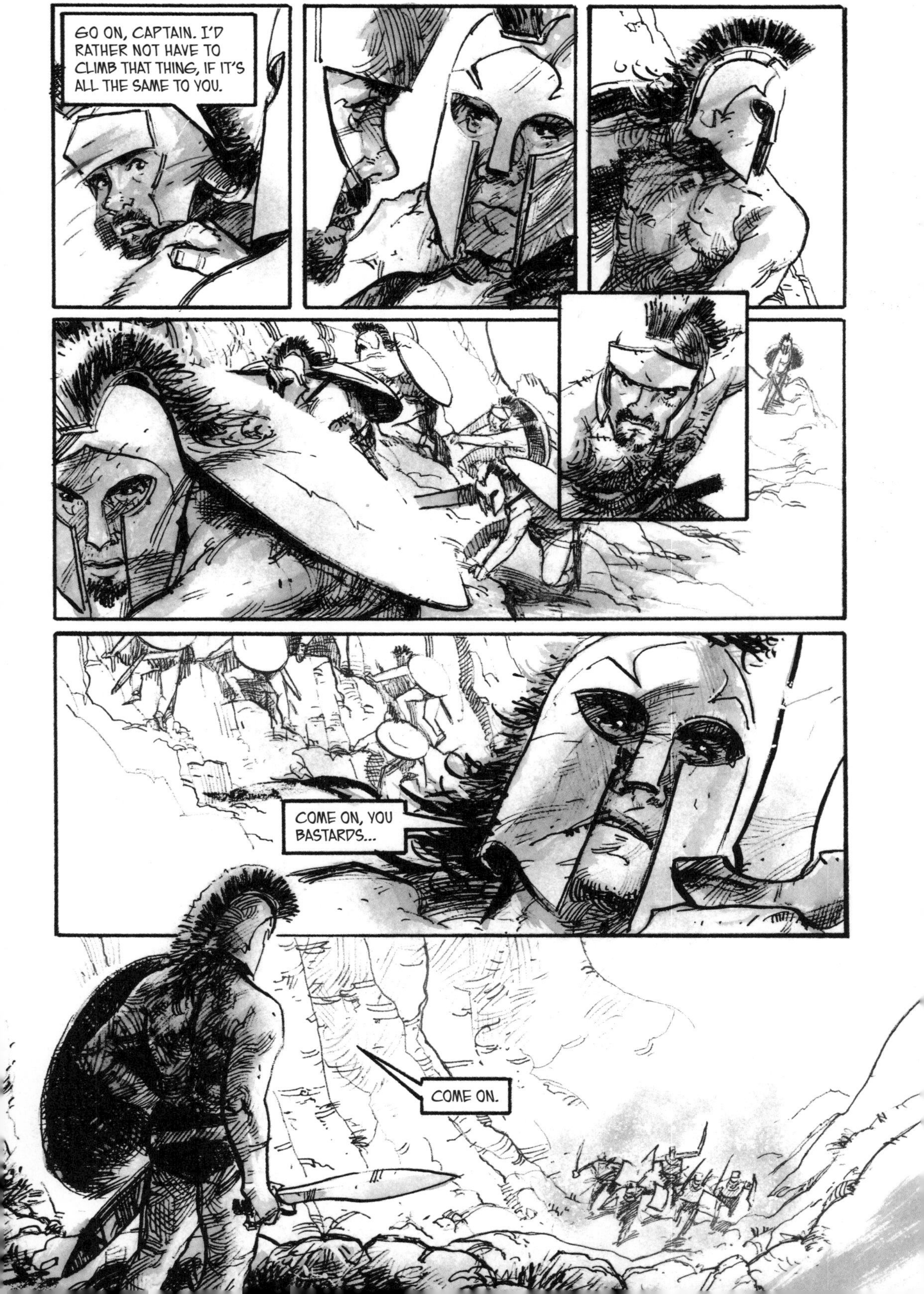
GO ON, CAPTAIN. I'D RATHER NOT HAVE TO CLIMB THAT THING, IF IT'S ALL THE SAME TO YOU.
COME ON, YOU BASTARDS...
COME ON.

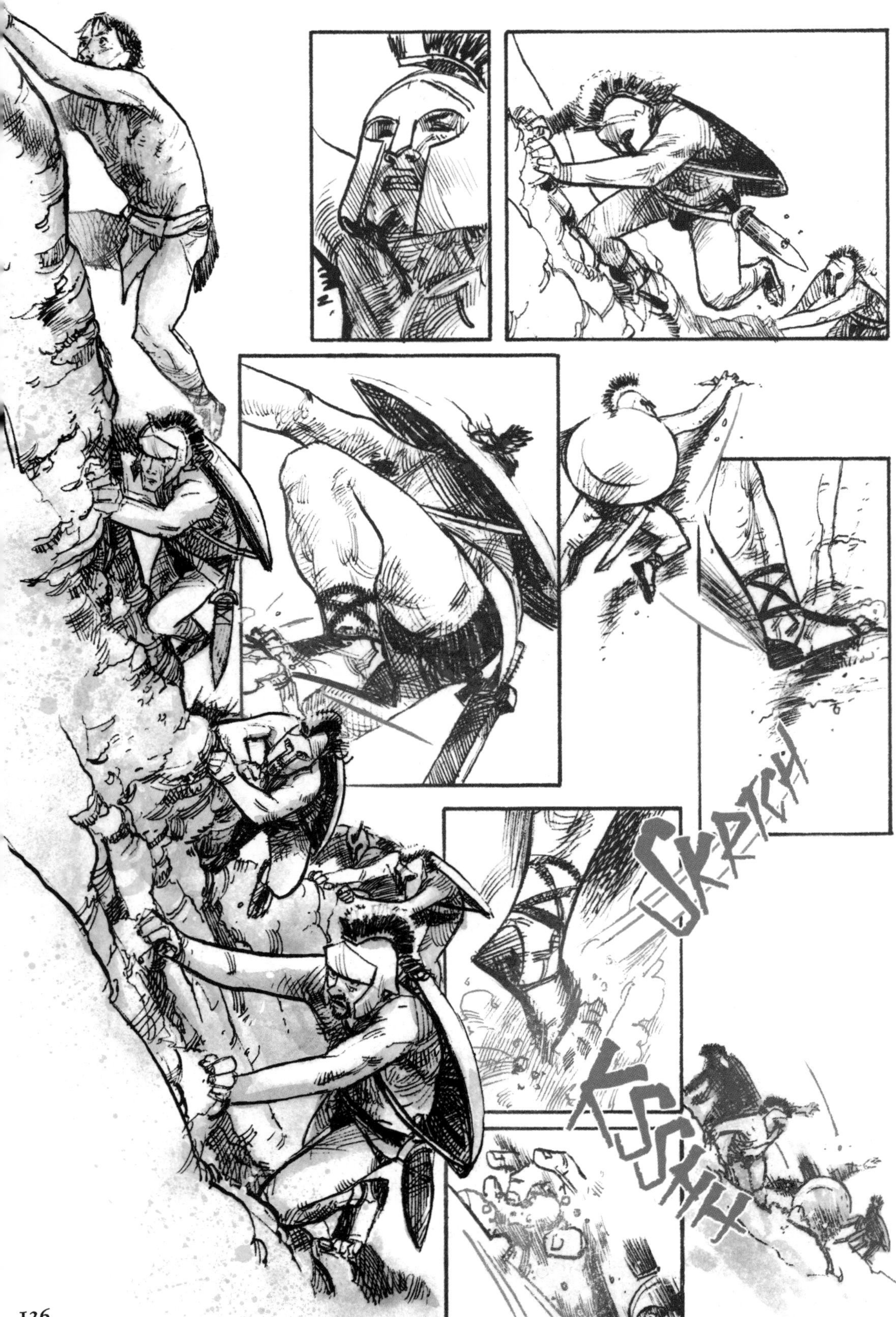
SKRTCH
KSSHH

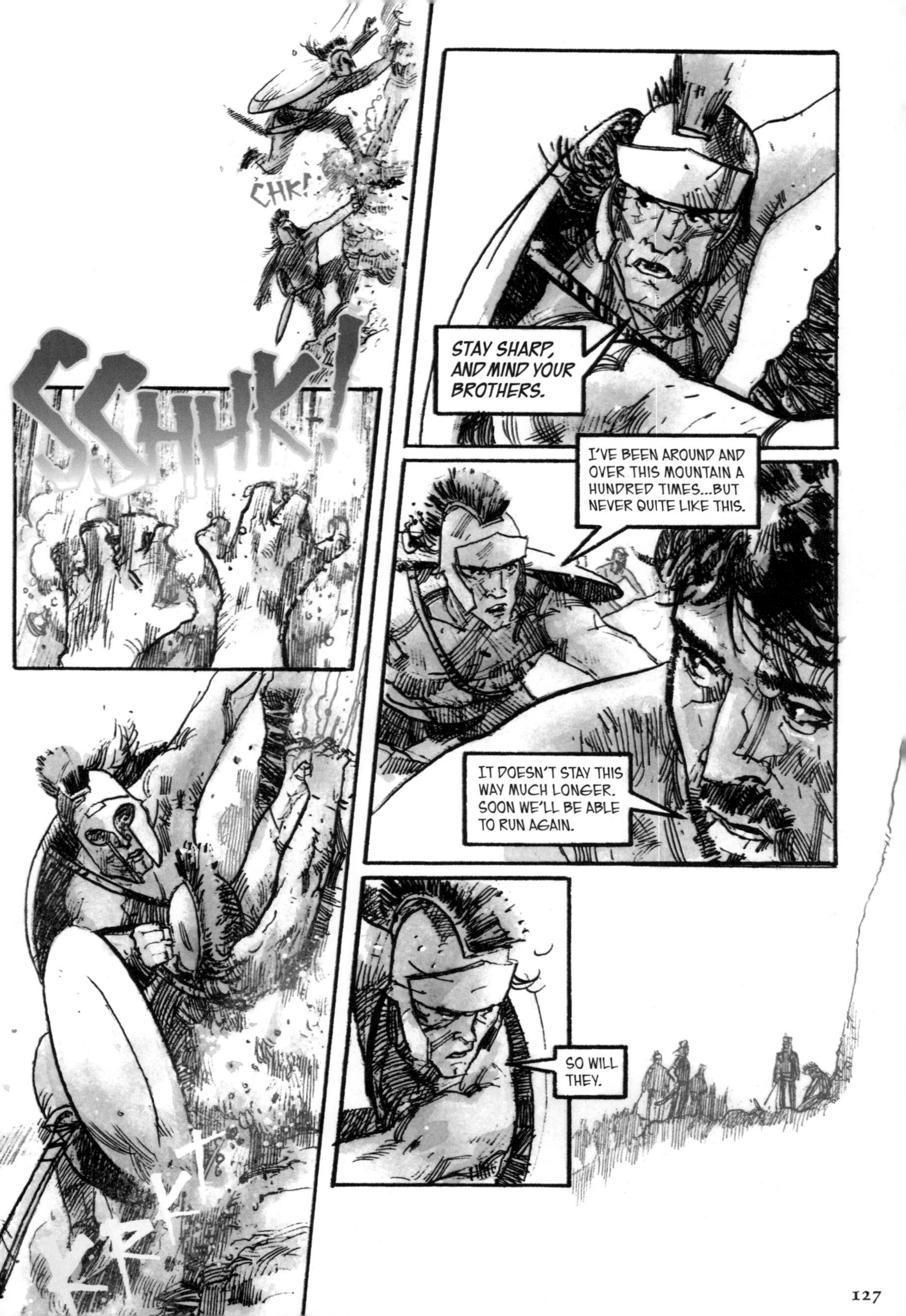
CHK!
SSHHK!
KRKT
STAY SHARP, AND MIND YOUR BROTHERS.
I'VE BEEN AROUND AND OVER THIS MOUNTAIN A HUNDRED TIMES...BUT NEVER QUITE LIKE THIS.
IT DOESN'T STAY THIS WAY MUCH LONGER. SOON WE'LL BE ABLE TO RUN AGAIN.
SO WILL THEY.

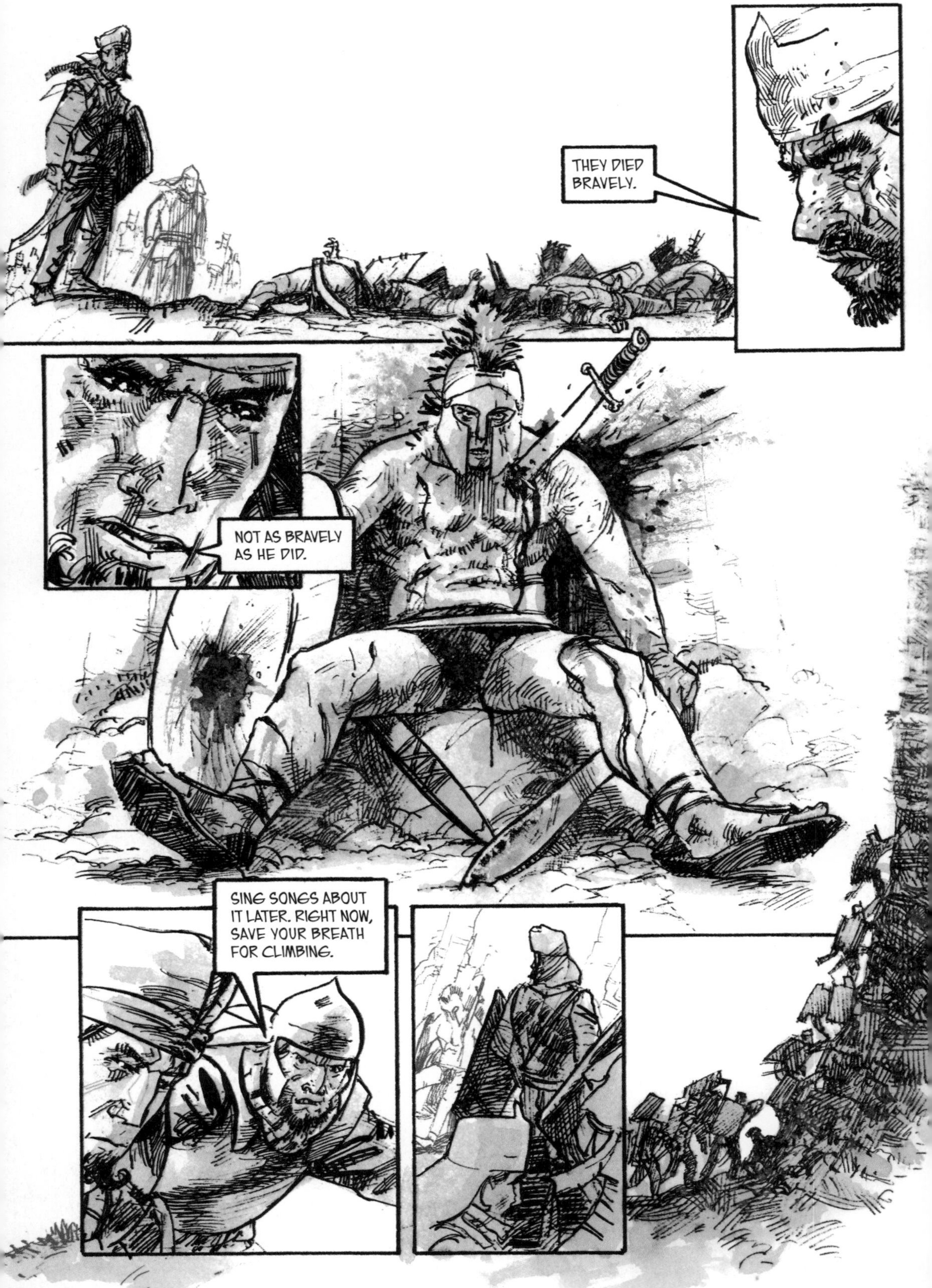
THEY DIED BRAVELY.
NOT AS BRAVELY AS HE DID.
SING SONGS ABOUT IT LATER. RIGHT NOW, SAVE YOUR BREATH FOR CLIMBING.

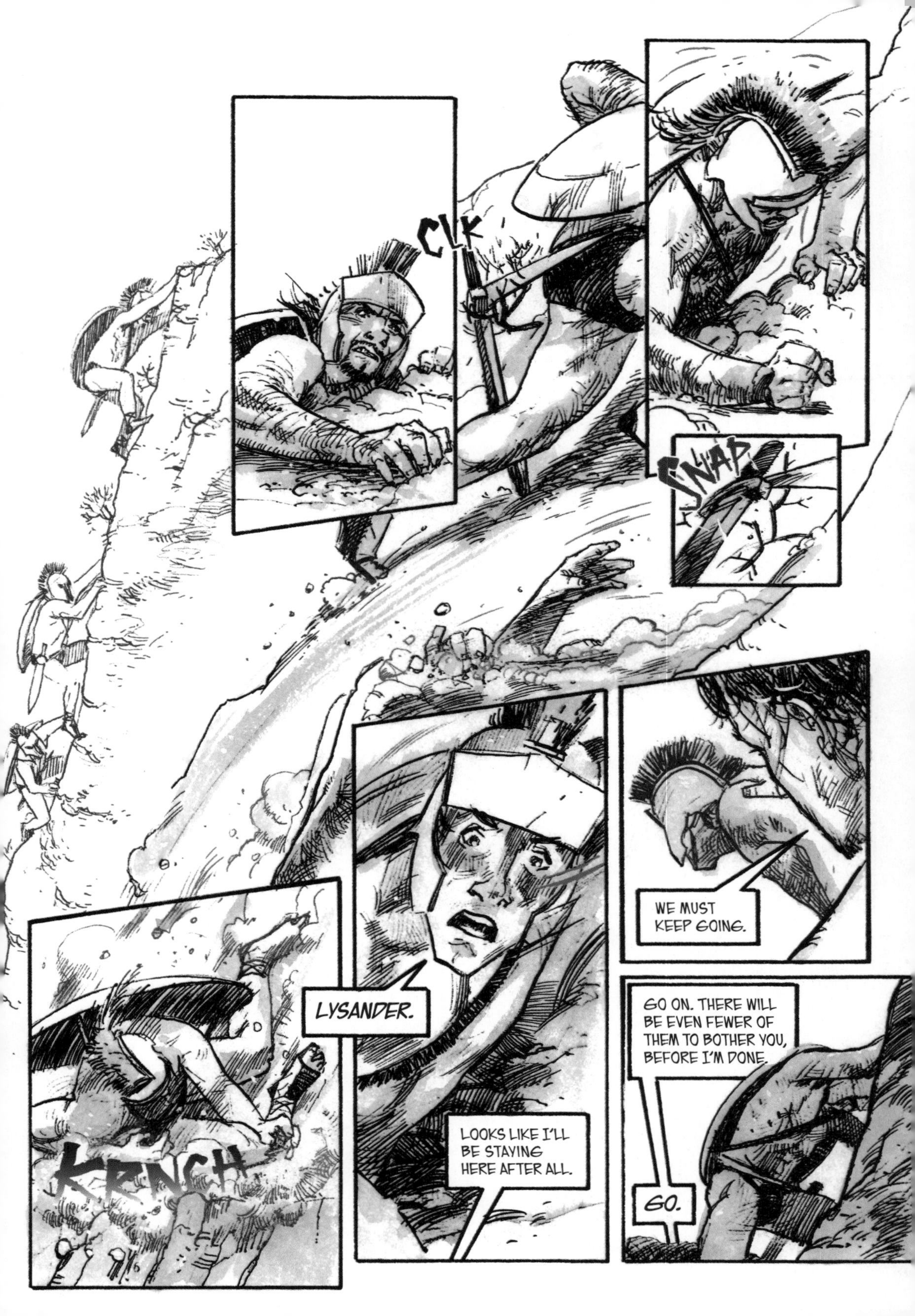
CLK
SNAP
KRNCH
LYSANDER.
LOOKS LIKE I'LL BE STAYING HERE AFTER ALL.
WE MUST KEEP GOING.
GO ON. THERE WILL BE EVEN FEWER OF THEM TO BOTHER YOU, BEFORE I'M DONE.
GO.

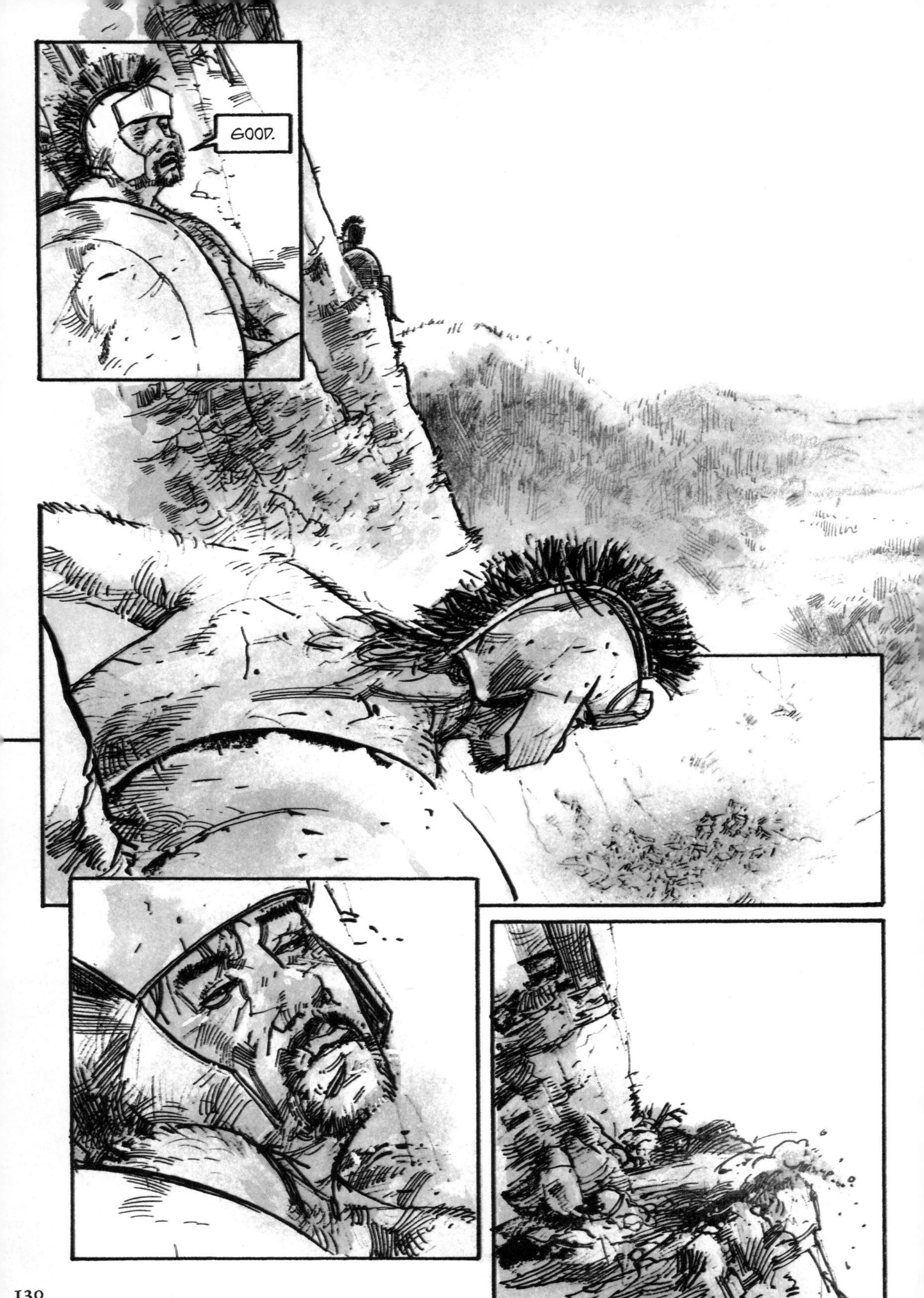
GOOD.

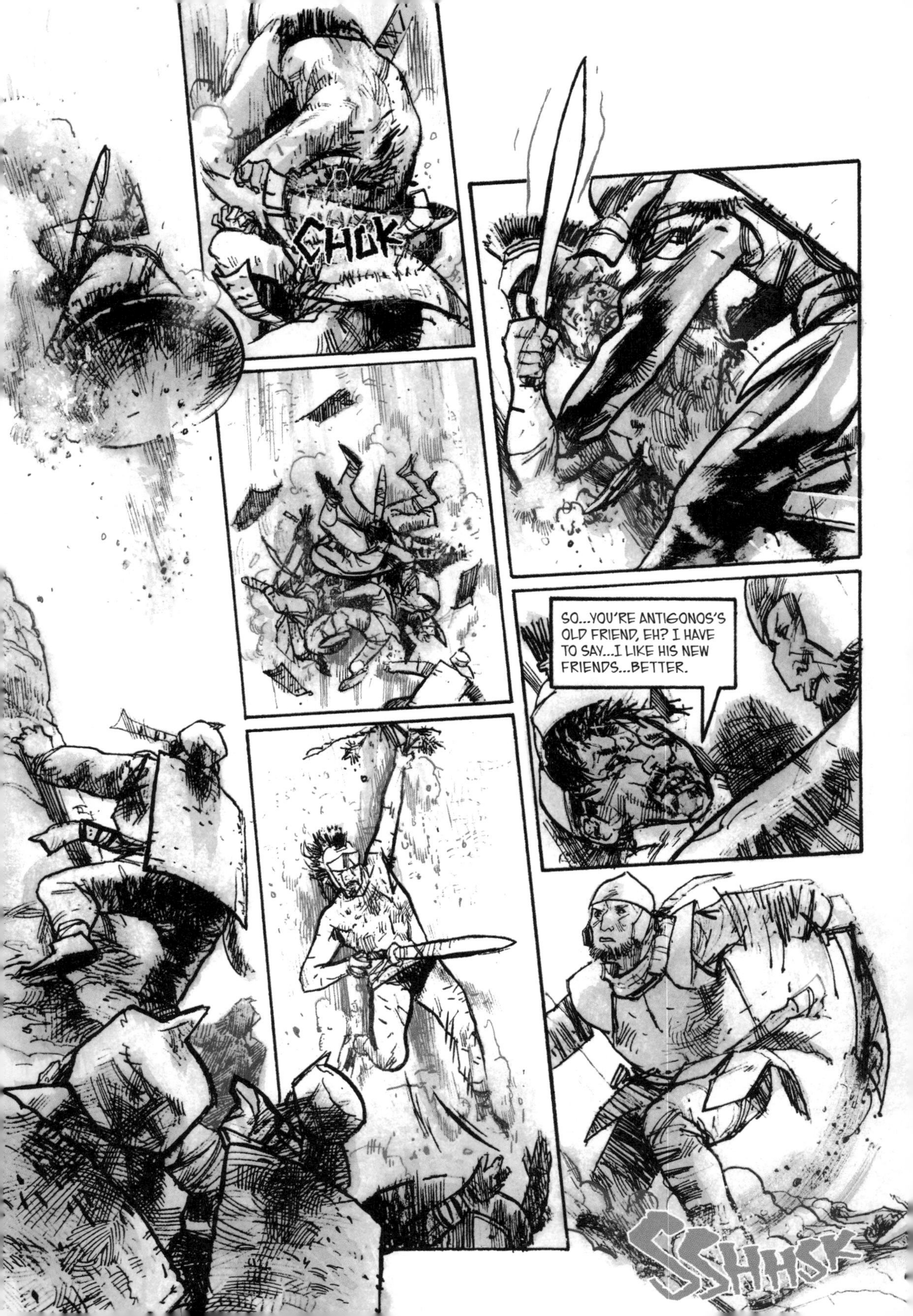
CHOK
SO...YOU'RE ANTIGONOS'S OLD FRIEND, EH? I HAVE TO SAY...I LIKE HIS NEW FRIENDS...BETTER.
SSHHSK

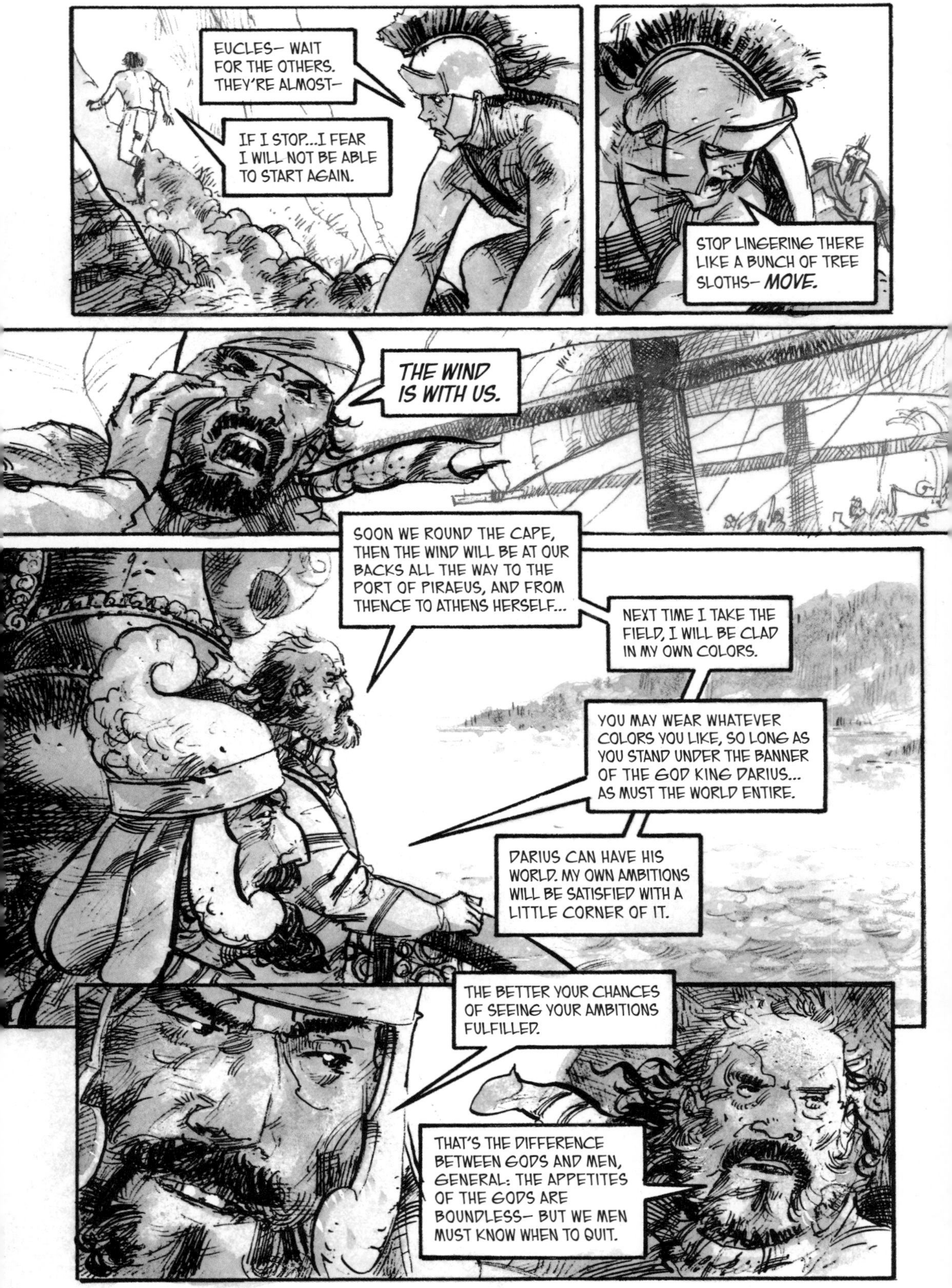

EUCLES— WAIT FOR THE OTHERS. THEY'RE ALMOST—
IF I STOP...I FEAR I WILL NOT BE ABLE TO START AGAIN.
STOP LINGERING THERE LIKE A BUNCH OF TREE SLOTHS— MOVE.
THE WIND IS WITH US.
SOON WE ROUND THE CAPE, THEN THE WIND WILL BE AT OUR BACKS ALL THE WAY TO THE PORT OF PIRAEUS, AND FROM THENCE TO ATHENS HERSELF...
NEXT TIME I TAKE THE FIELD, I WILL BE CLAD IN MY OWN COLORS.
YOU MAY WEAR WHATEVER COLORS YOU LIKE, SO LONG AS YOU STAND UNDER THE BANNER OF THE GOD KING DARIUS... AS MUST THE WORLD ENTIRE.
DARIUS CAN HAVE HIS WORLD. MY OWN AMBITIONS WILL BE SATISFIED WITH A LITTLE CORNER OF IT.
THE BETTER YOUR CHANCES OF SEEING YOUR AMBITIONS FULFILLED.
THAT'S THE DIFFERENCE BETWEEN GODS AND MEN, GENERAL: THE APPETITES OF THE GODS ARE BOUNDLESS— BUT WE MEN MUST KNOW WHEN TO QUIT.

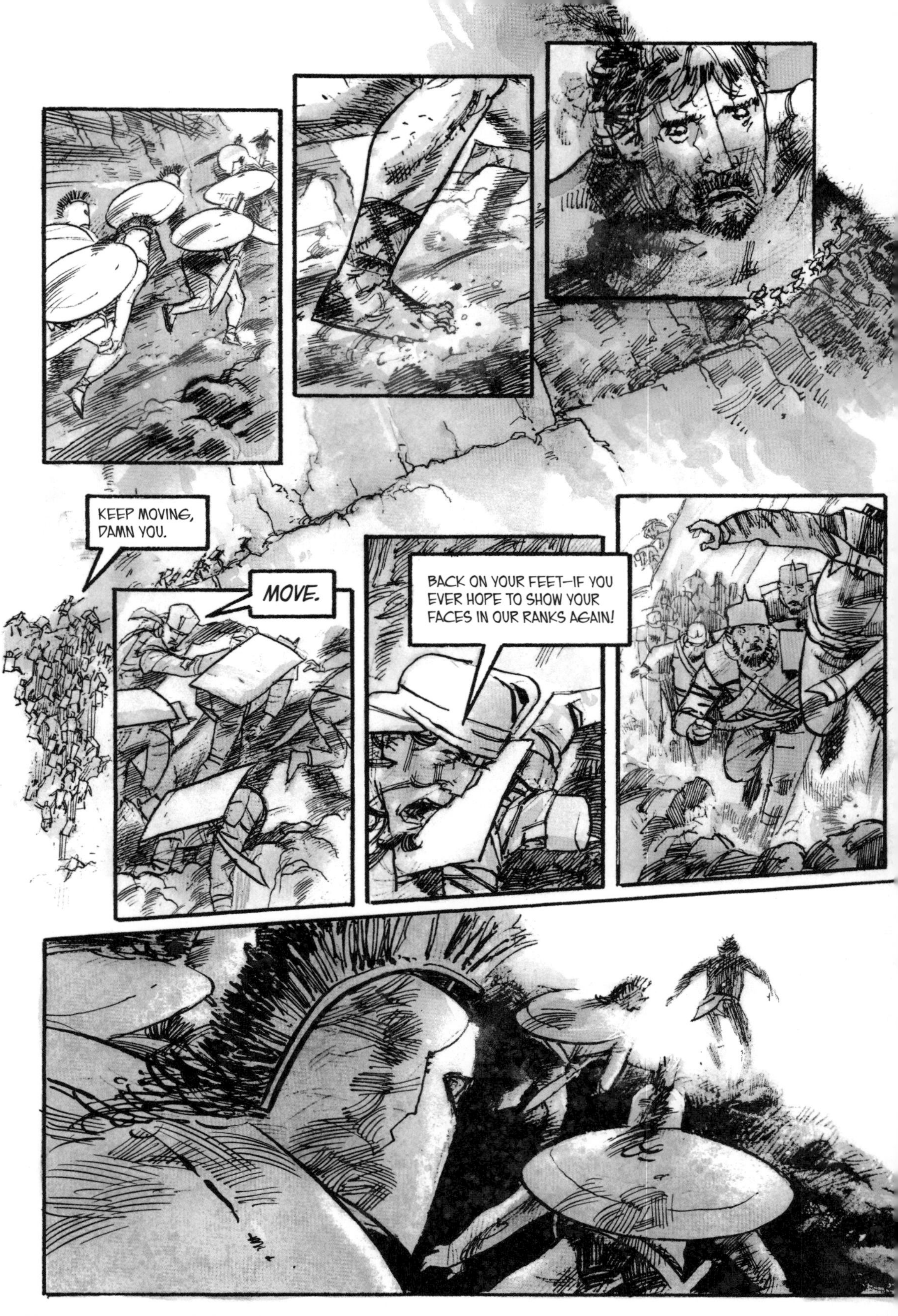
KEEP MOVING, DAMN YOU.
MOVE.
BACK ON YOUR FEET—IF YOU EVER HOPE TO SHOW YOUR FACES IN OUR RANKS AGAIN!

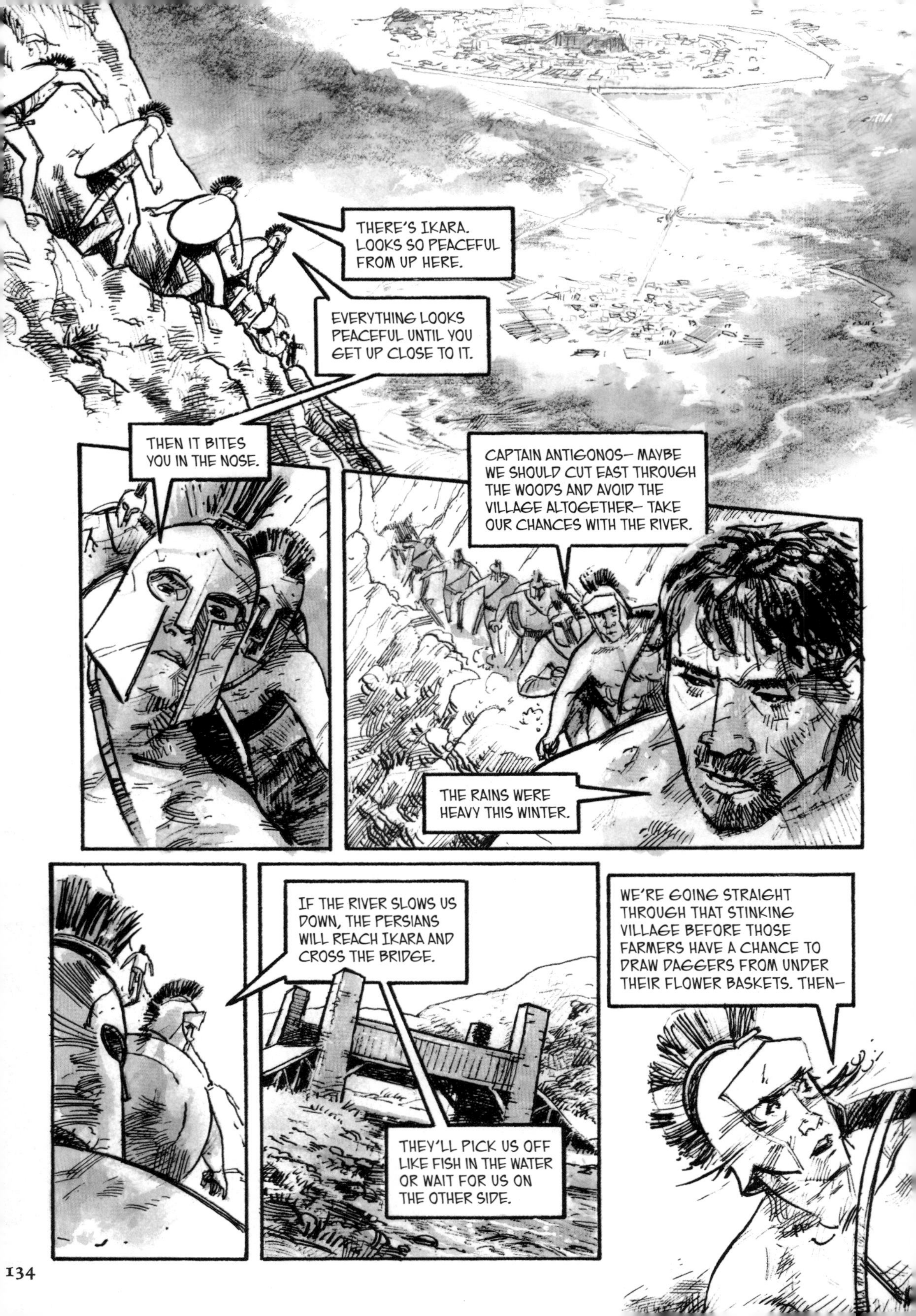
THERE'S IKARA. LOOKS SO PEACEFUL FROM UP HERE.
EVERYTHING LOOKS PEACEFUL UNTIL YOU GET UP CLOSE TO IT.
THEN IT BITES YOU IN THE NOSE.
CAPTAIN ANTIGONOS– MAYBE WE SHOULD CUT EAST THROUGH THE WOODS AND AVOID THE VILLAGE ALTOGETHER– TAKE OUR CHANCES WITH THE RIVER.
THE RAINS WERE HEAVY THIS WINTER.
IF THE RIVER SLOWS US DOWN, THE PERSIANS WILL REACH IKARA AND CROSS THE BRIDGE.
THEY'LL PICK US OFF LIKE FISH IN THE WATER OR WAIT FOR US ON THE OTHER SIDE.
WE'RE GOING STRAIGHT THROUGH THAT STINKING VILLAGE BEFORE THOSE FARMERS HAVE A CHANCE TO DRAW DAGGERS FROM UNDER THEIR FLOWER BASKETS. THEN–

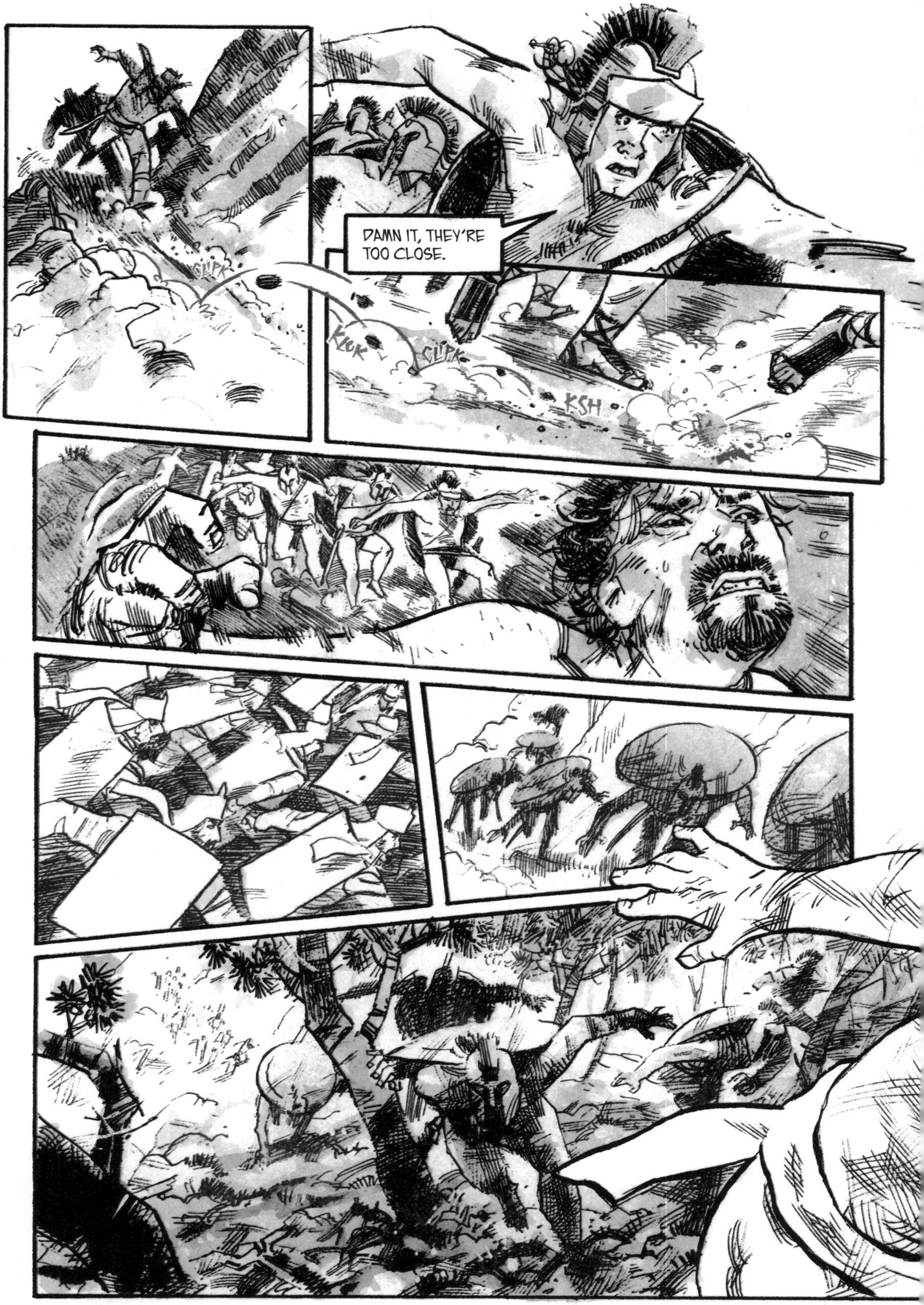
CLIPK
DAMN IT, THEY'RE TOO CLOSE.
KLUK
CLIPK
KSH

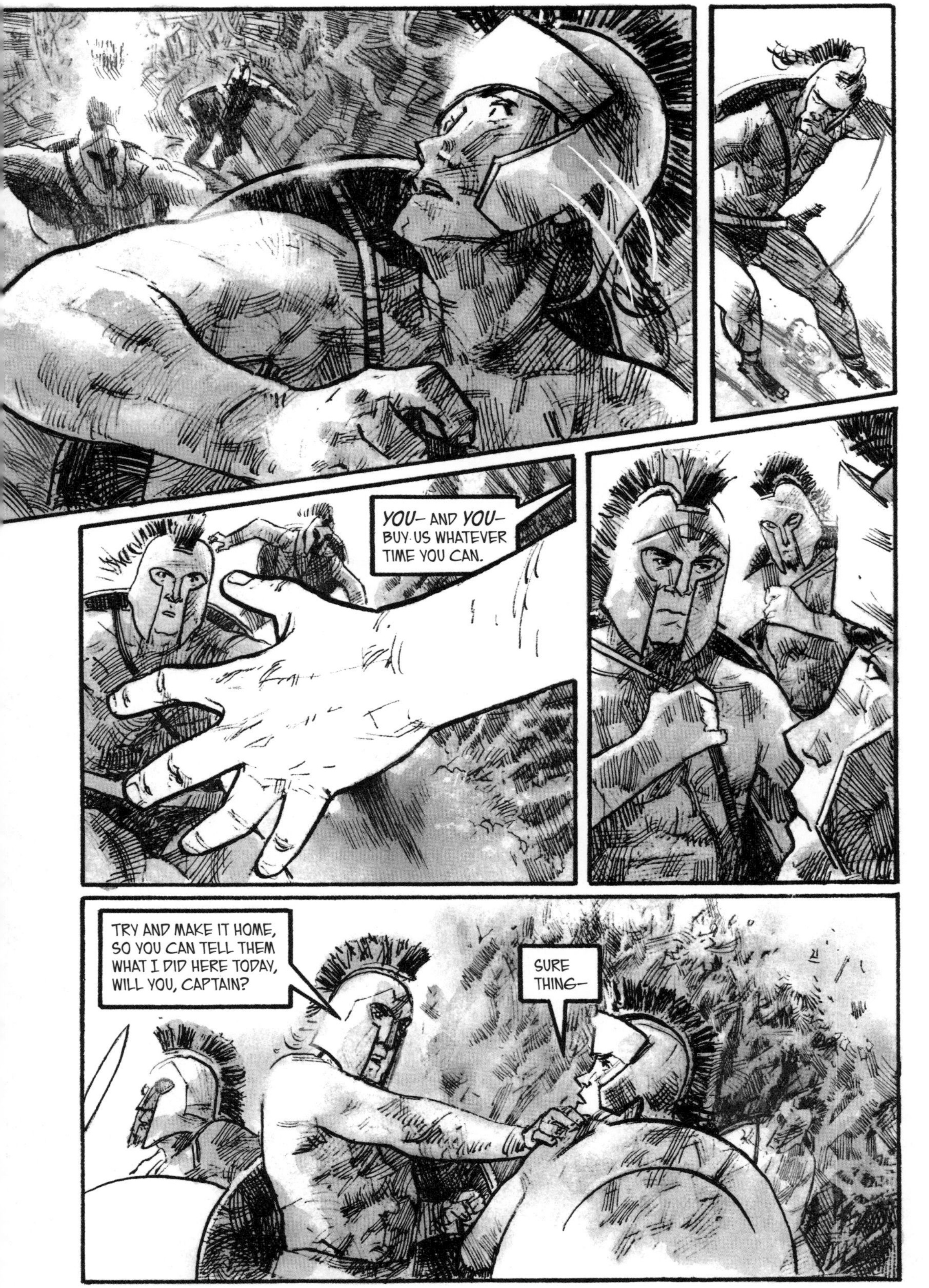
YOU– AND YOU– BUY US WHATEVER TIME YOU CAN.
TRY AND MAKE IT HOME, SO YOU CAN TELL THEM WHAT I DID HERE TODAY, WILL YOU, CAPTAIN?
SURE THING–

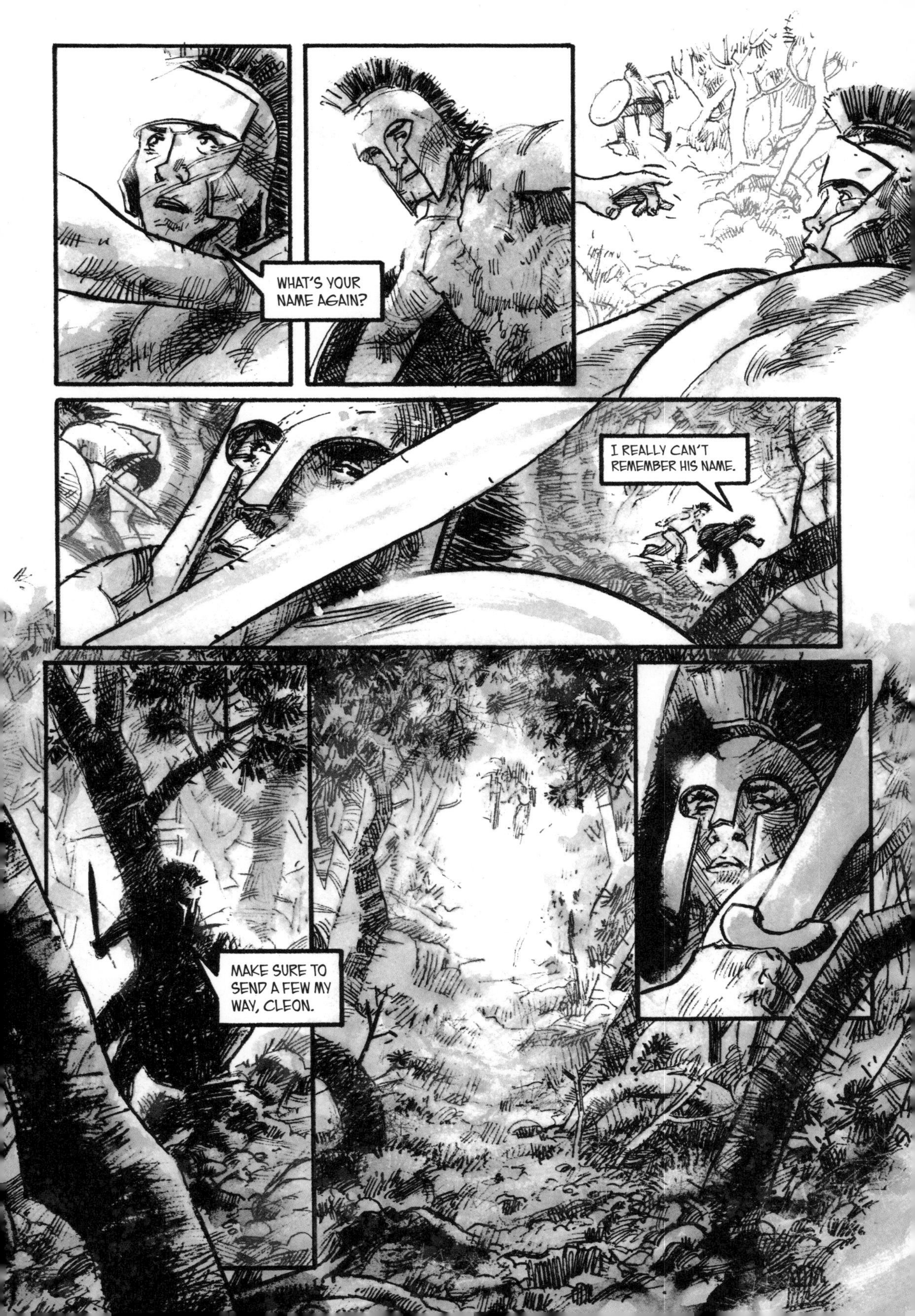
WHAT'S YOUR NAME AGAIN?
I REALLY CAN'T REMEMBER HIS NAME.
MAKE SURE TO SEND A FEW MY WAY, CLEON.

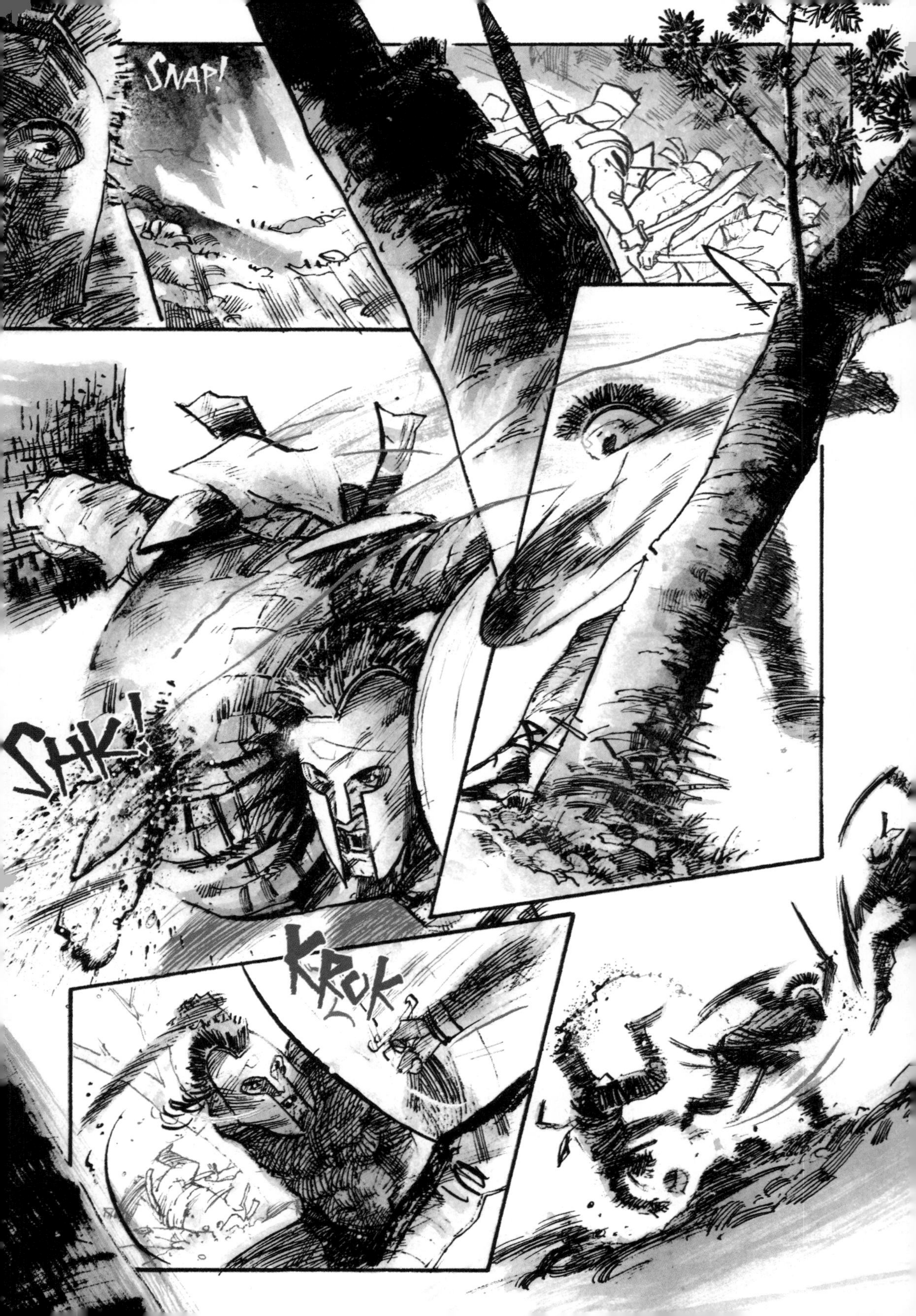
SNAP!
SHK!
KROK

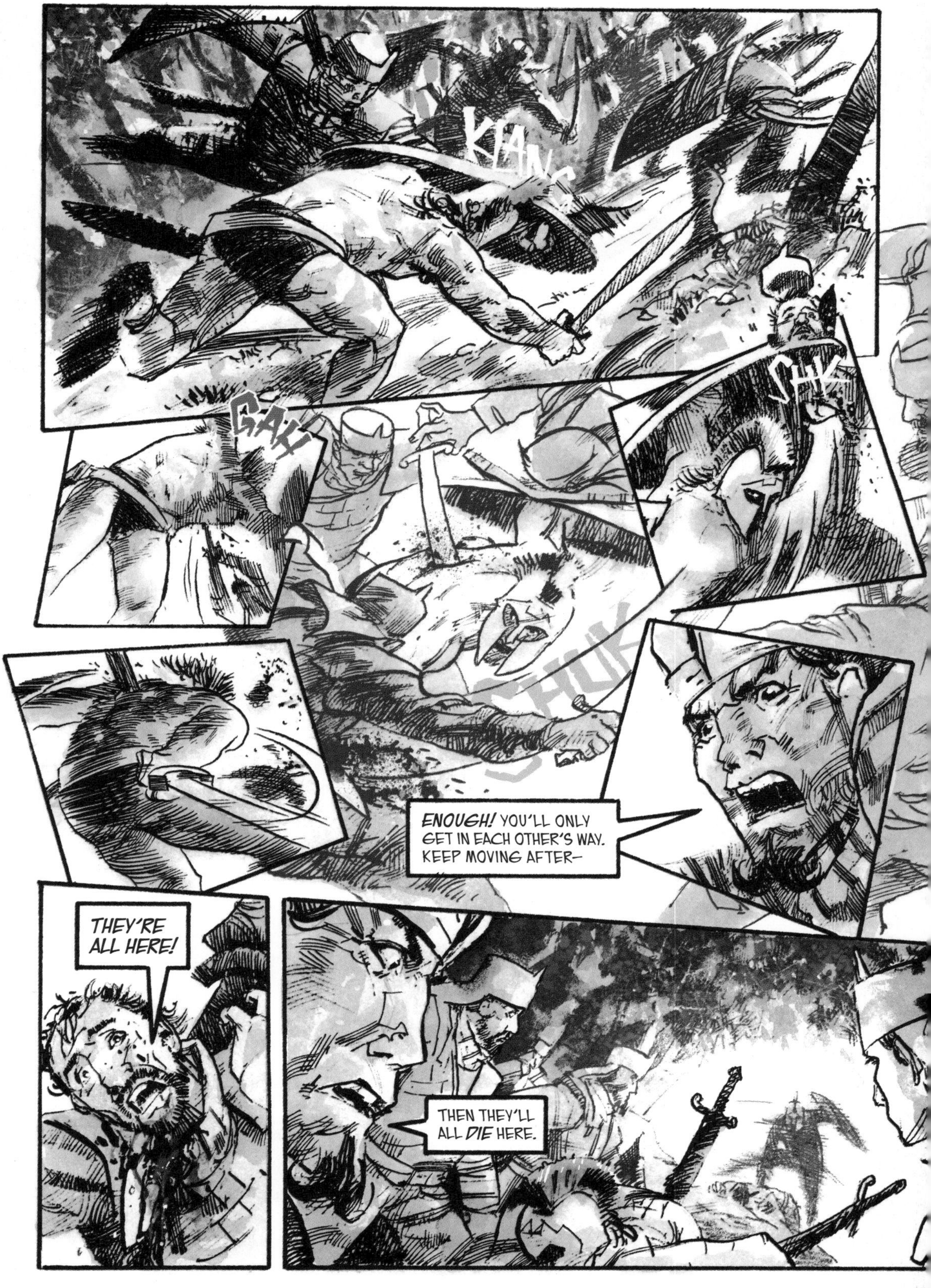
KLANG
GAH
SHK
SHUK
ENOUGH! YOU'LL ONLY GET IN EACH OTHER'S WAY. KEEP MOVING AFTER–
THEY'RE ALL HERE!
THEN THEY'LL ALL DIE HERE.

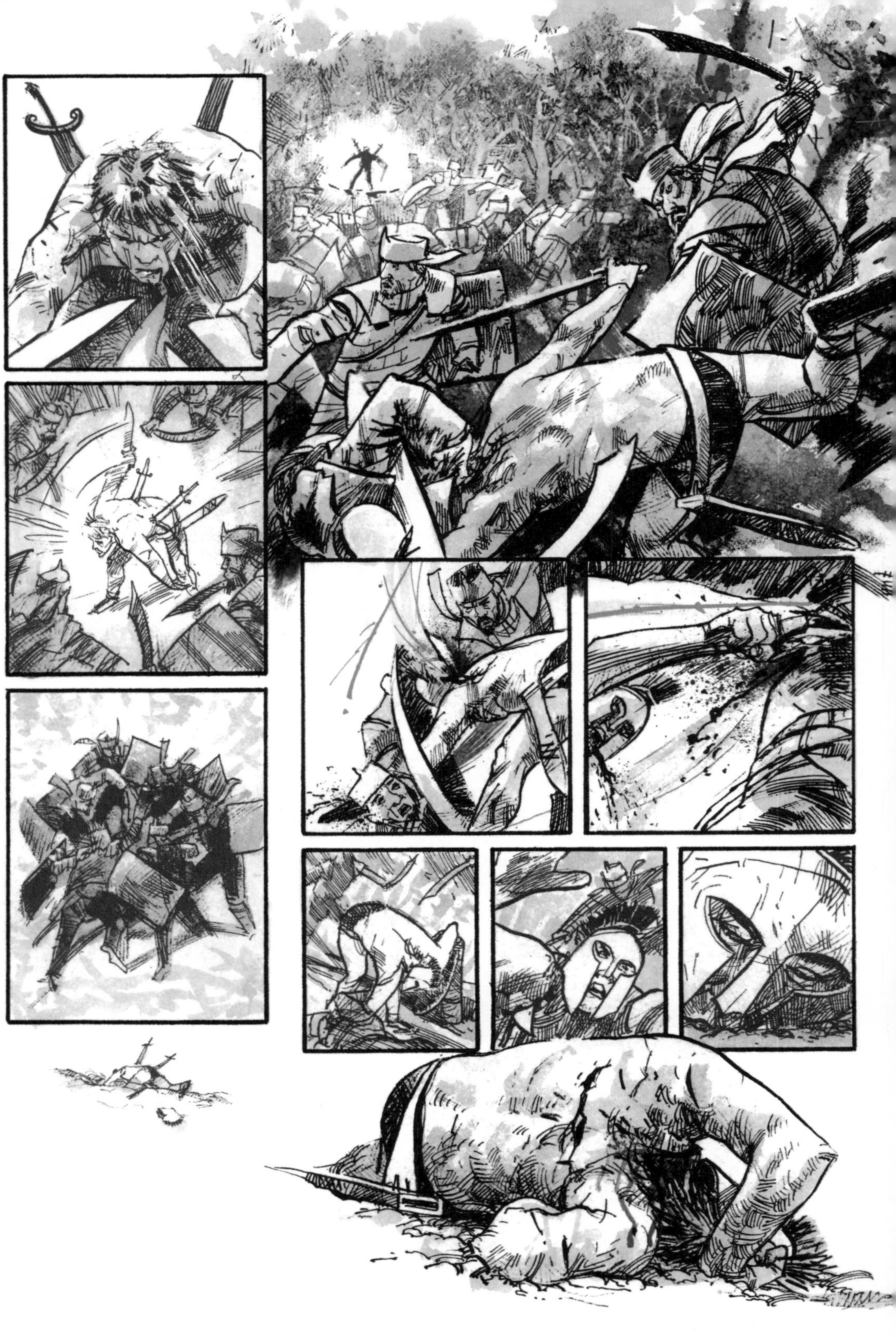

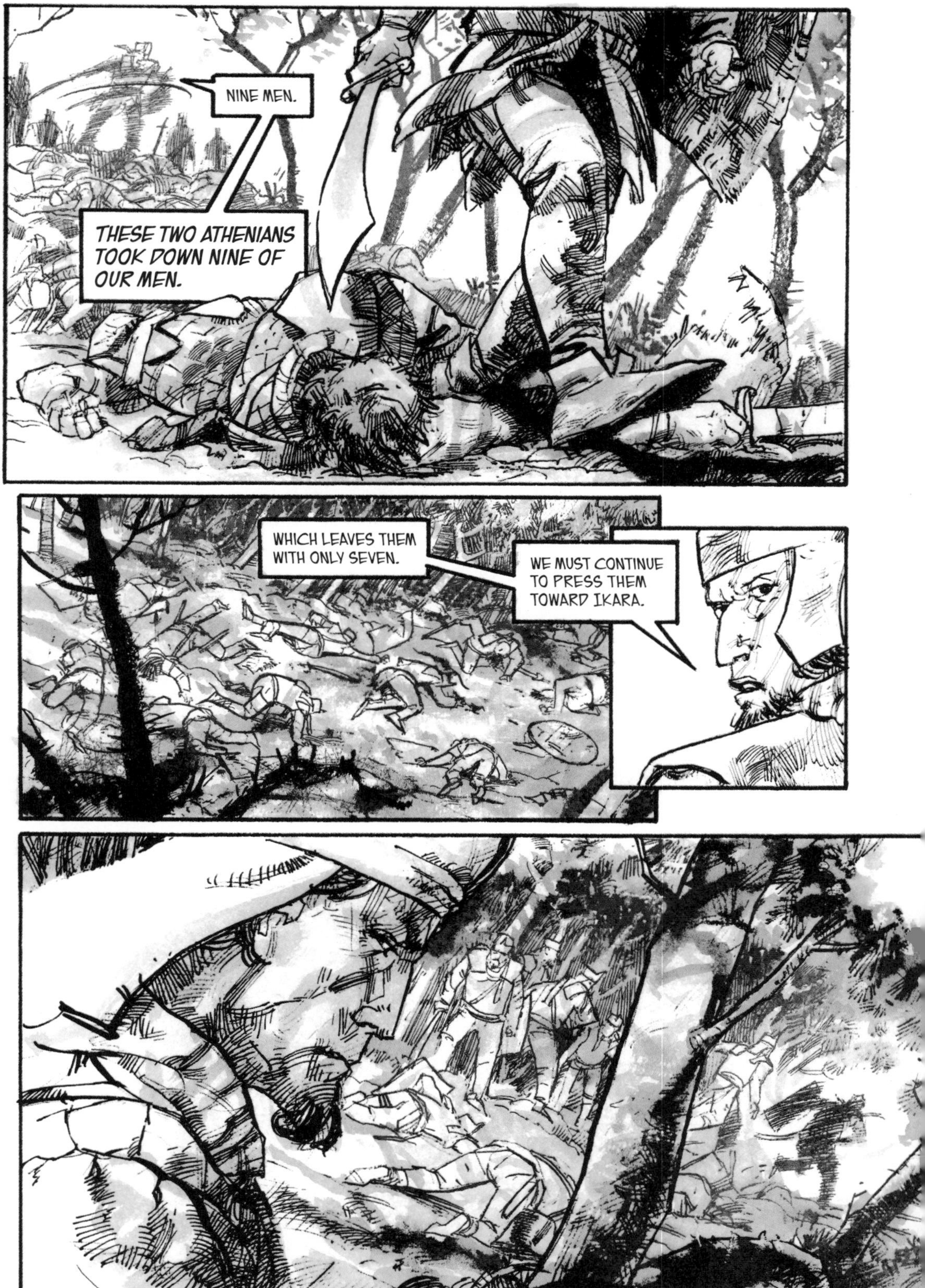
NINE MEN.
THESE TWO ATHENIANS TOOK DOWN NINE OF OUR MEN.
WHICH LEAVES THEM WITH ONLY SEVEN.
WE MUST CONTINUE TO PRESS THEM TOWARD IKARA.

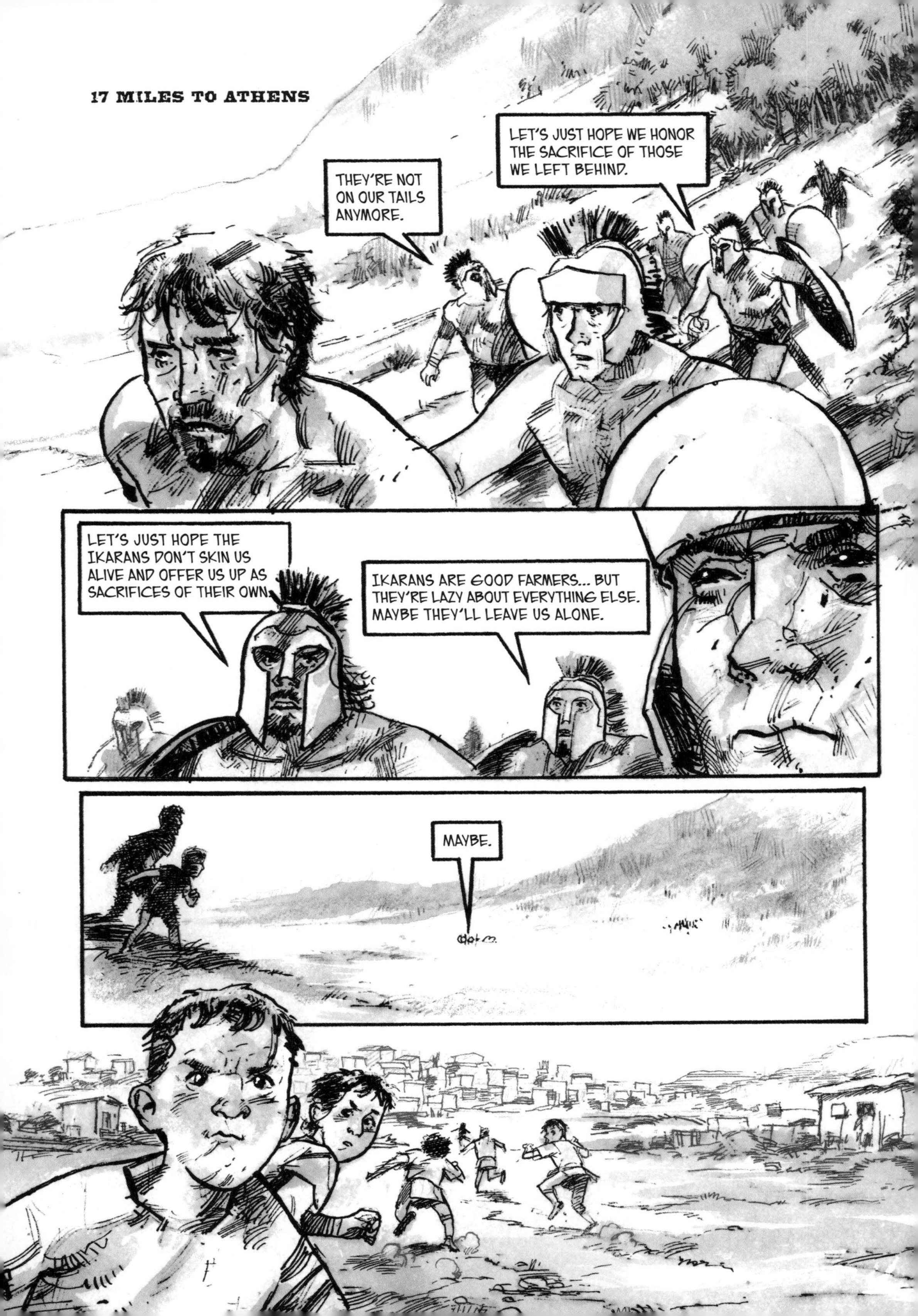
17 MILES TO ATHENS
THEY'RE NOT ON OUR TAILS ANYMORE.
LET'S JUST HOPE WE HONOR THE SACRIFICE OF THOSE WE LEFT BEHIND.
LET'S JUST HOPE THE IKARANS DON'T SKIN US ALIVE AND OFFER US UP AS SACRIFICES OF THEIR OWN.
IKARANS ARE GOOD FARMERS... BUT THEY'RE LAZY ABOUT EVERYTHING ELSE. MAYBE THEY'LL LEAVE US ALONE.
MAYBE.

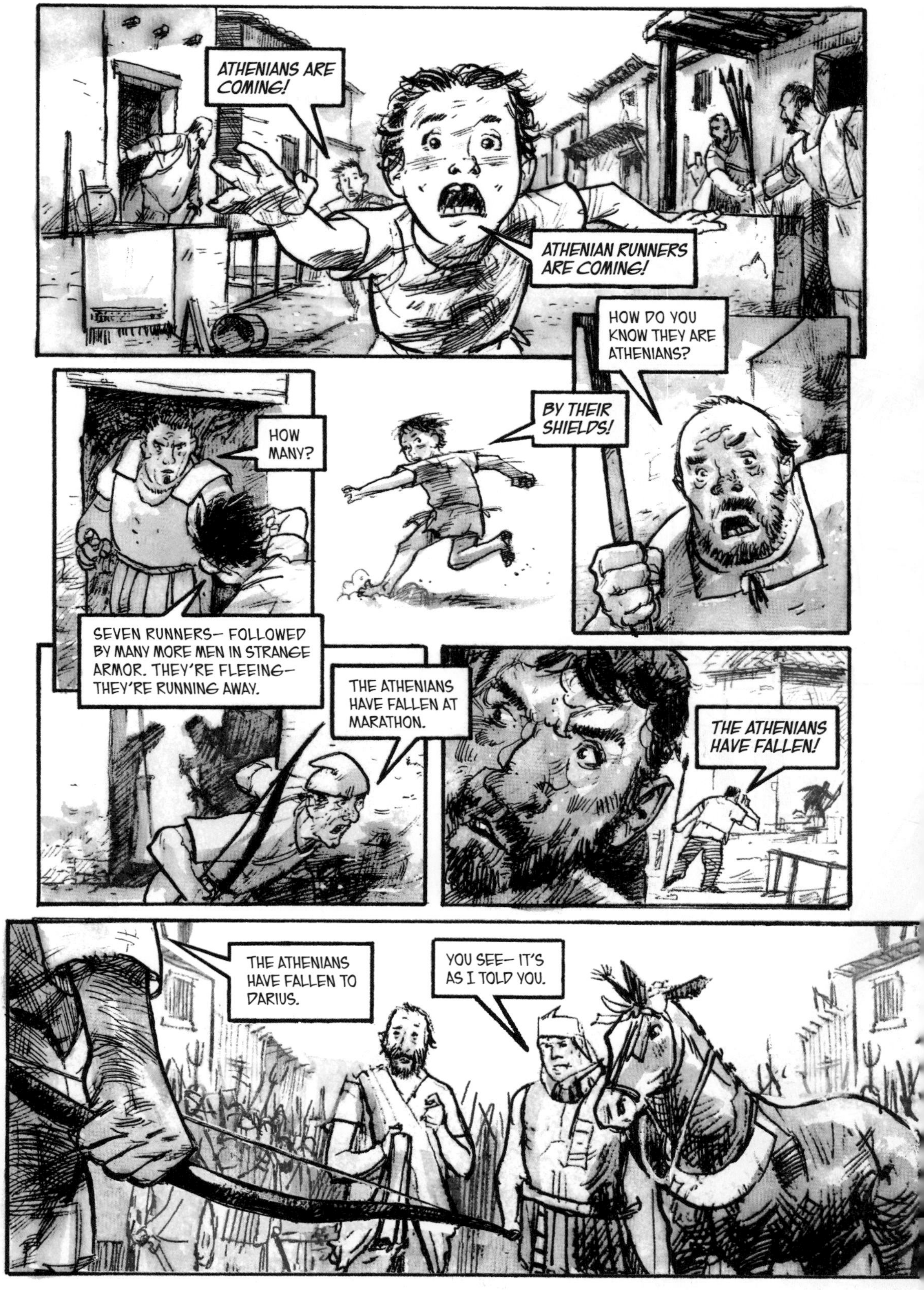
ATHENIANS ARE COMING!
ATHENIAN RUNNERS ARE COMING!
HOW MANY?
BY THEIR SHIELDS!
HOW DO YOU KNOW THEY ARE ATHENIANS?
SEVEN RUNNERS— FOLLOWED BY MANY MORE MEN IN STRANGE ARMOR. THEY'RE FLEEING— THEY'RE RUNNING AWAY.
THE ATHENIANS HAVE FALLEN AT MARATHON.
THE ATHENIANS HAVE FALLEN!
THE ATHENIANS HAVE FALLEN TO DARIUS.
YOU SEE— IT'S AS I TOLD YOU.

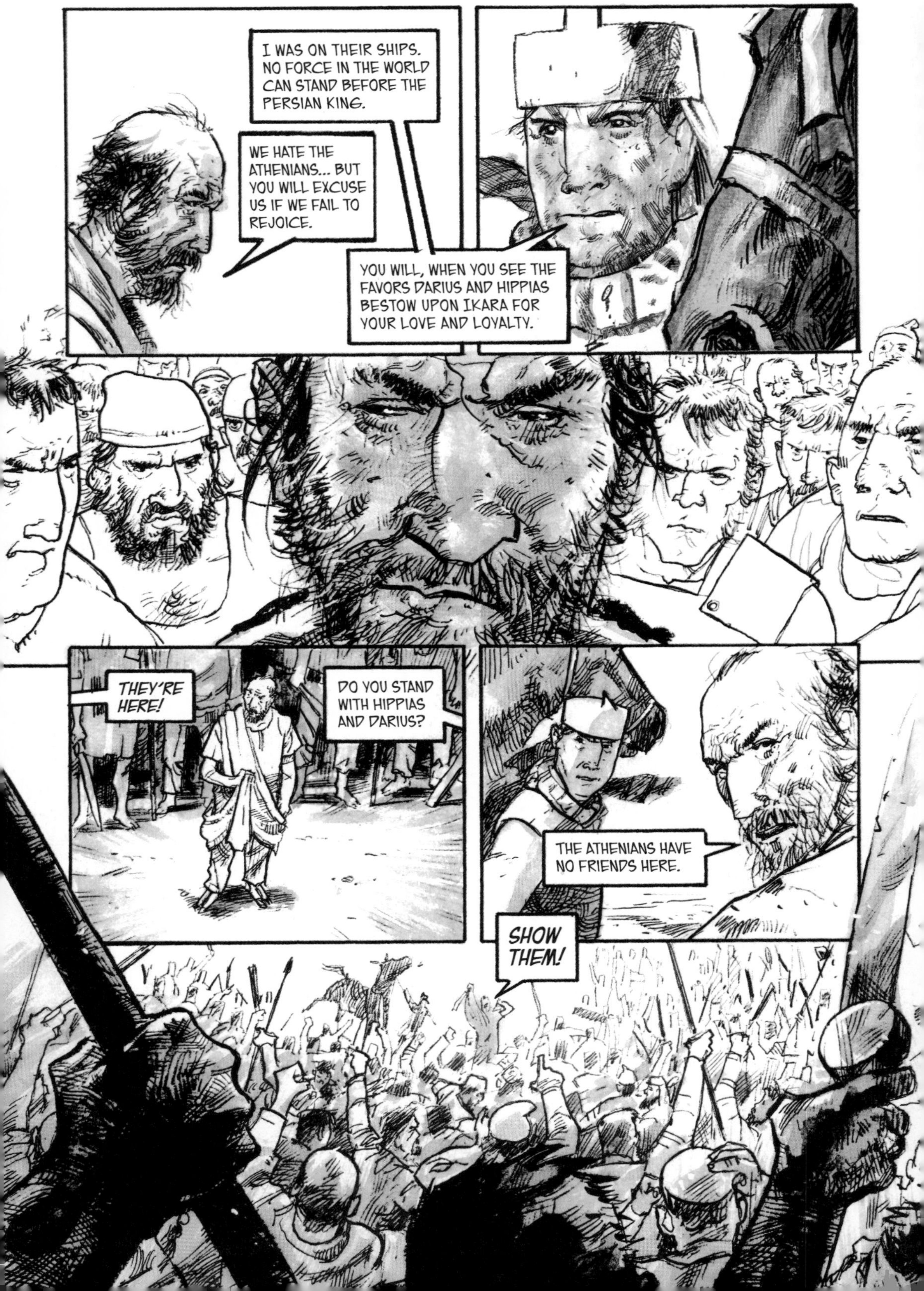
WE HATE THE ATHENIANS... BUT YOU WILL EXCUSE US IF WE FAIL TO REJOICE.
I WAS ON THEIR SHIPS. NO FORCE IN THE WORLD CAN STAND BEFORE THE PERSIAN KING.
YOU WILL, WHEN YOU SEE THE FAVORS DARIUS AND HIPPIAS BESTOW UPON IKARA FOR YOUR LOVE AND LOYALTY.
THEY'RE HERE!
DO YOU STAND WITH HIPPIAS AND DARIUS?
THE ATHENIANS HAVE NO FRIENDS HERE.
SHOW THEM!

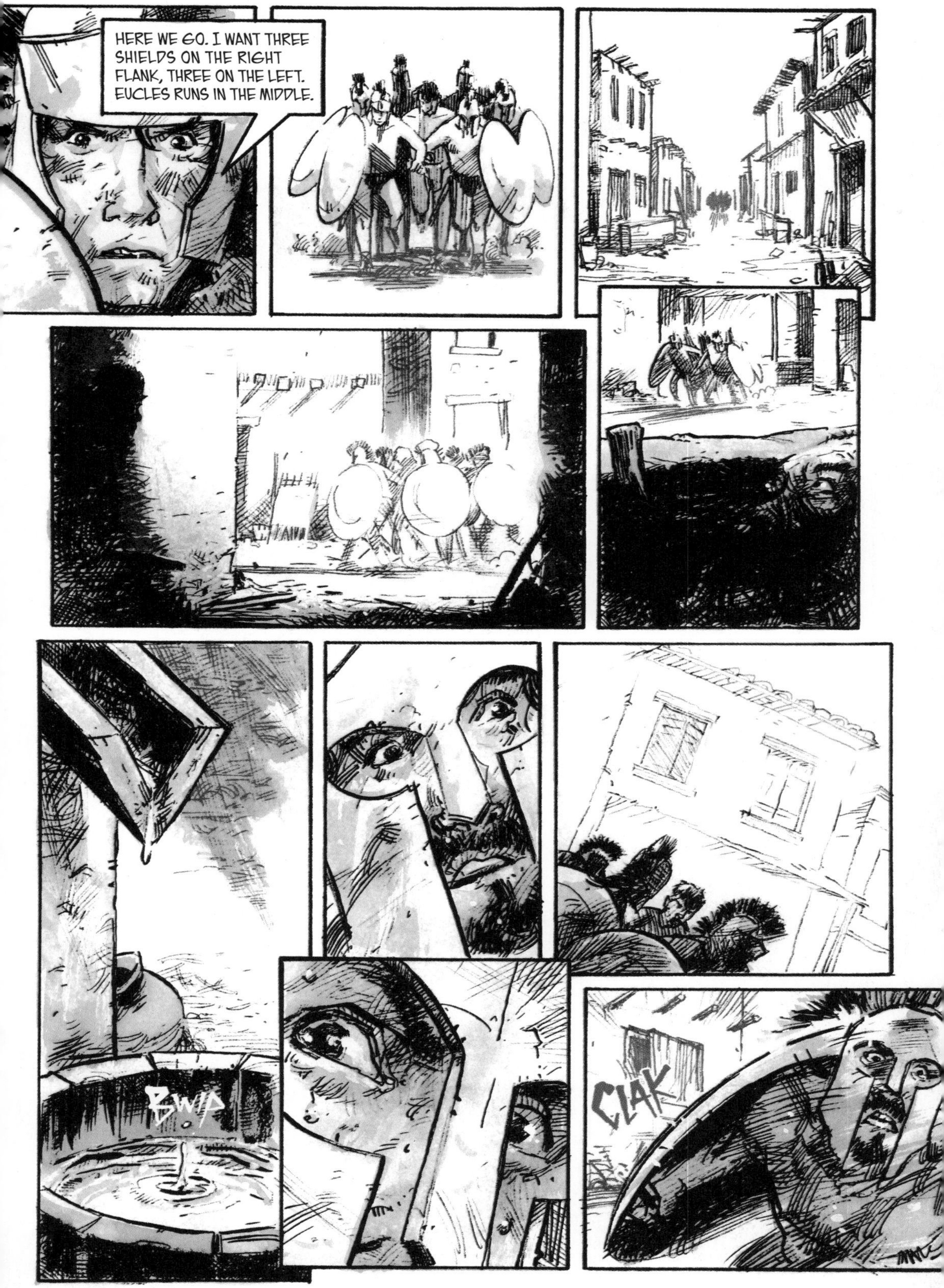
HERE WE GO. I WANT THREE SHIELDS ON THE RIGHT FLANK, THREE ON THE LEFT. EUCLES RUNS IN THE MIDDLE.
BWIP
CLAK

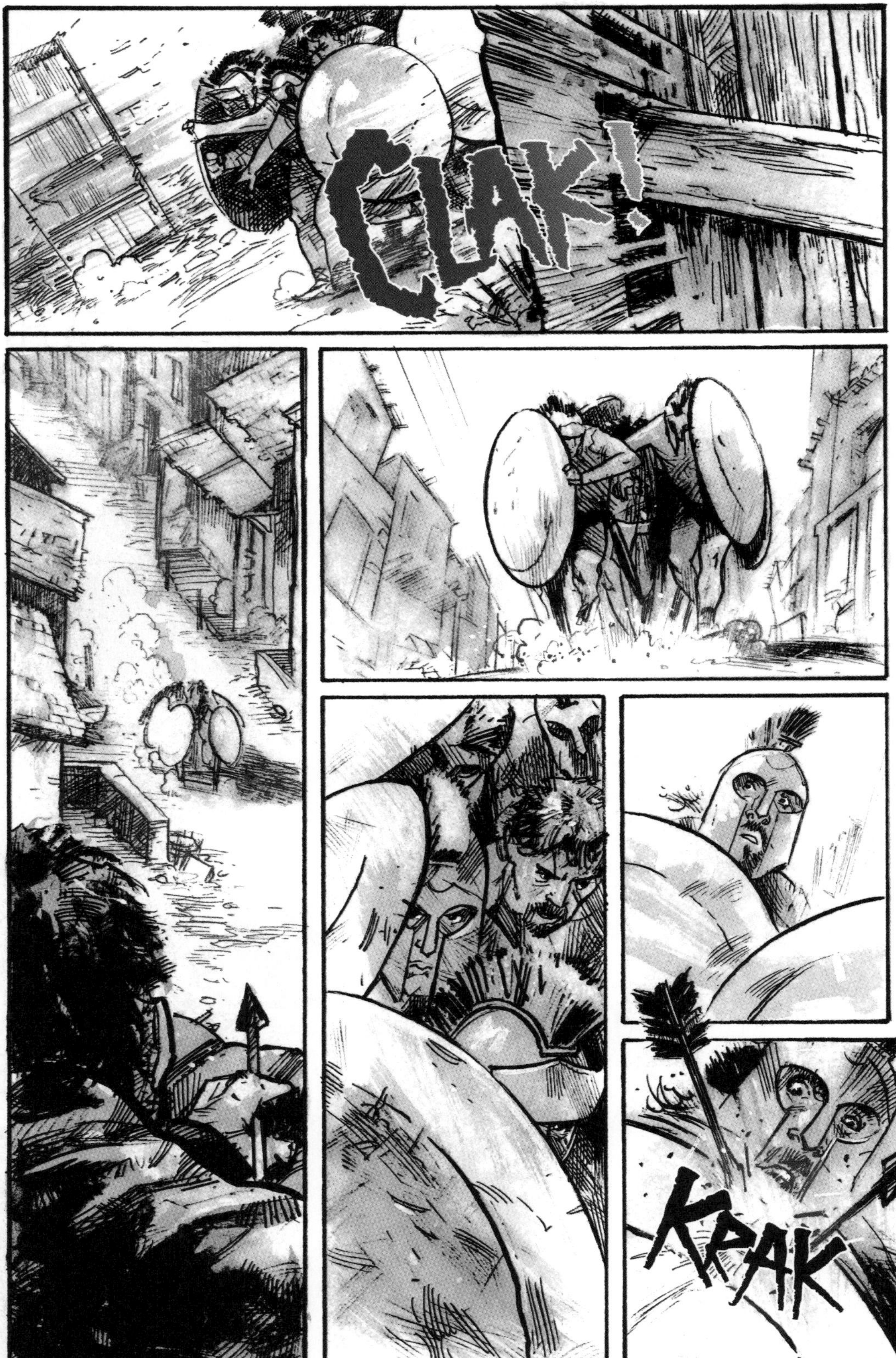
CLAK!
KRAK

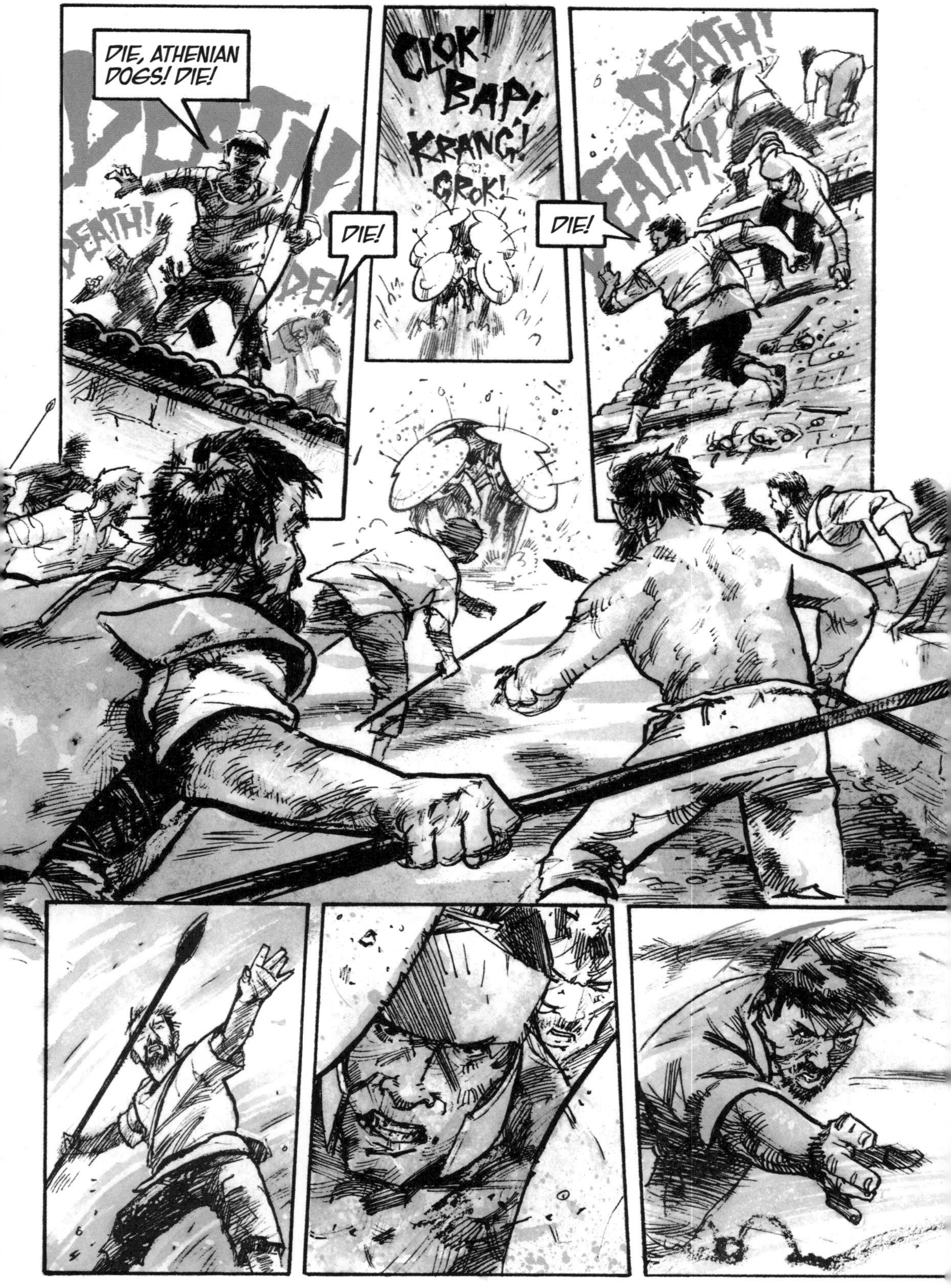
DIE, ATHENIAN DOGS! DIE!
DEATH!
DEATH!
DEATH!
DIE!
CLOK! BAP! KRANG! GROK!
DIE!
DEATH!
DEATH!

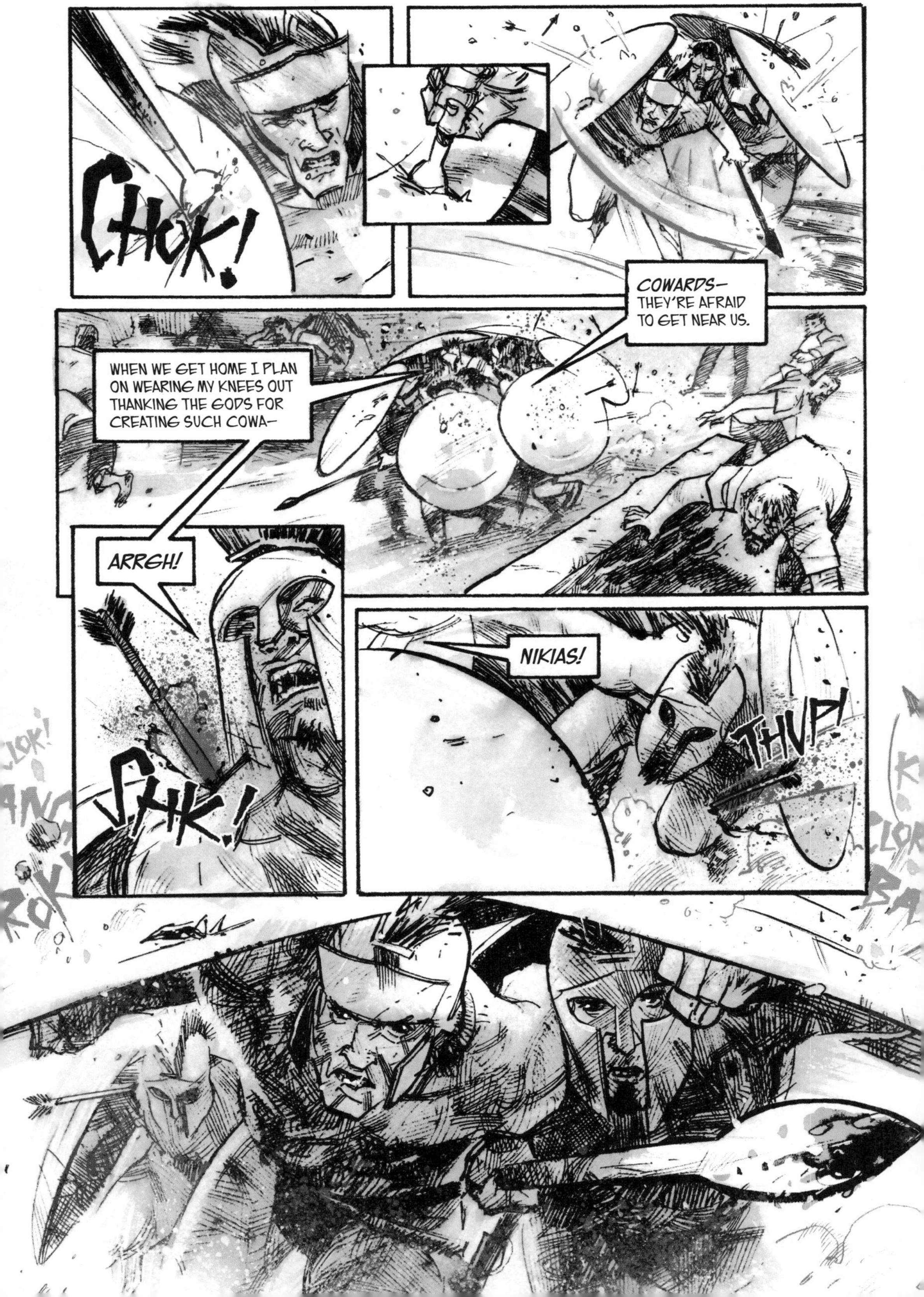
CHOK!
COWARDS— THEY'RE AFRAID TO GET NEAR US.
WHEN WE GET HOME I PLAN ON WEARING MY KNEES OUT THANKING THE GODS FOR CREATING SUCH COWA—
ARRGH!
SHK!
NIKIAS!
THUP!

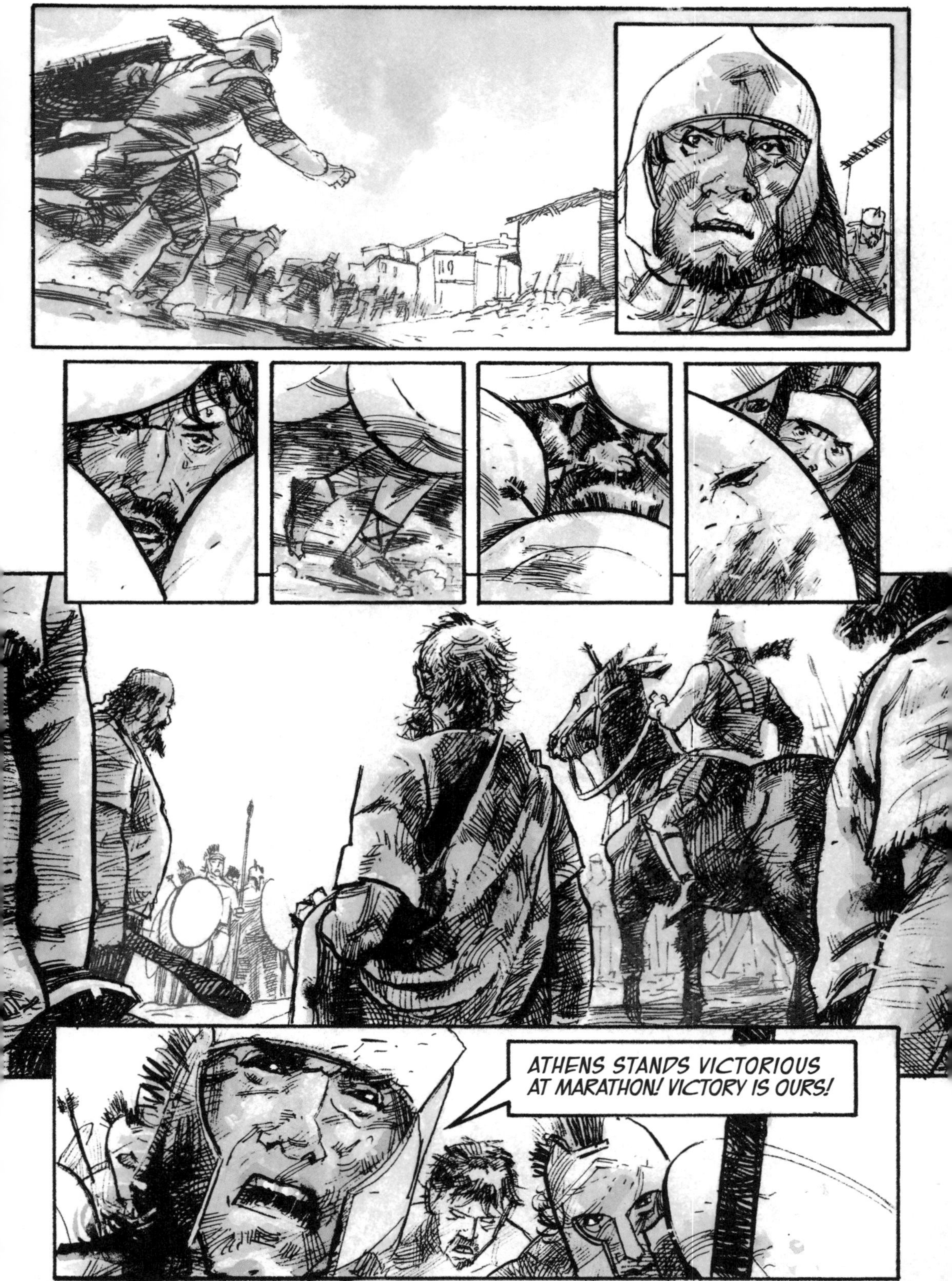
ATHENS STANDS VICTORIOUS AT MARATHON! VICTORY IS OURS!

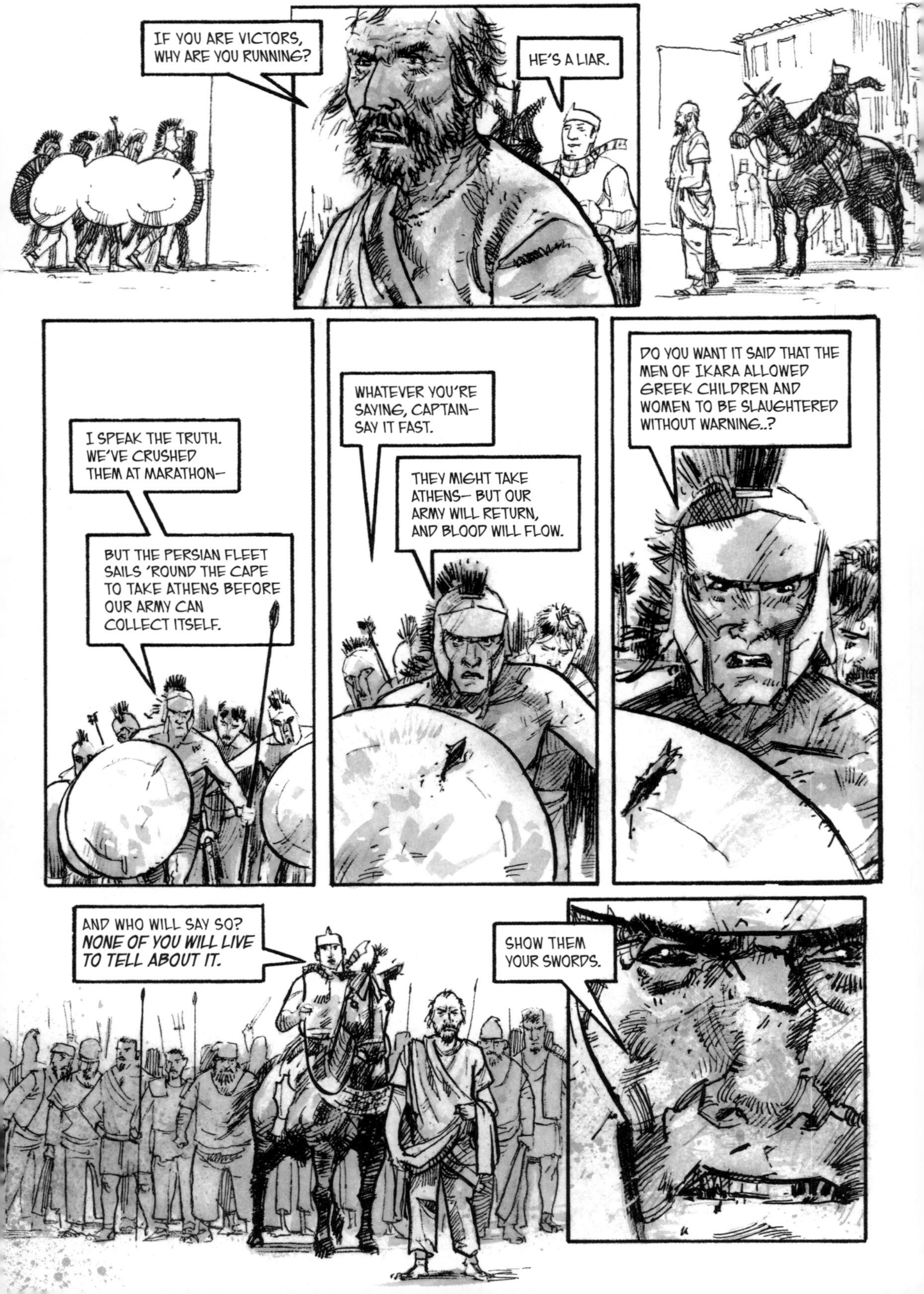
IF YOU ARE VICTORS, WHY ARE YOU RUNNING?
HE'S A LIAR.
I SPEAK THE TRUTH. WE'VE CRUSHED THEM AT MARATHON—
BUT THE PERSIAN FLEET SAILS 'ROUND THE CAPE TO TAKE ATHENS BEFORE OUR ARMY CAN COLLECT ITSELF.
WHATEVER YOU'RE SAYING, CAPTAIN— SAY IT FAST.
THEY MIGHT TAKE ATHENS— BUT OUR ARMY WILL RETURN, AND BLOOD WILL FLOW.
DO YOU WANT IT SAID THAT THE MEN OF IKARA ALLOWED GREEK CHILDREN AND WOMEN TO BE SLAUGHTERED WITHOUT WARNING..?
AND WHO WILL SAY SO? NONE OF YOU WILL LIVE TO TELL ABOUT IT.
SHOW THEM YOUR SWORDS.

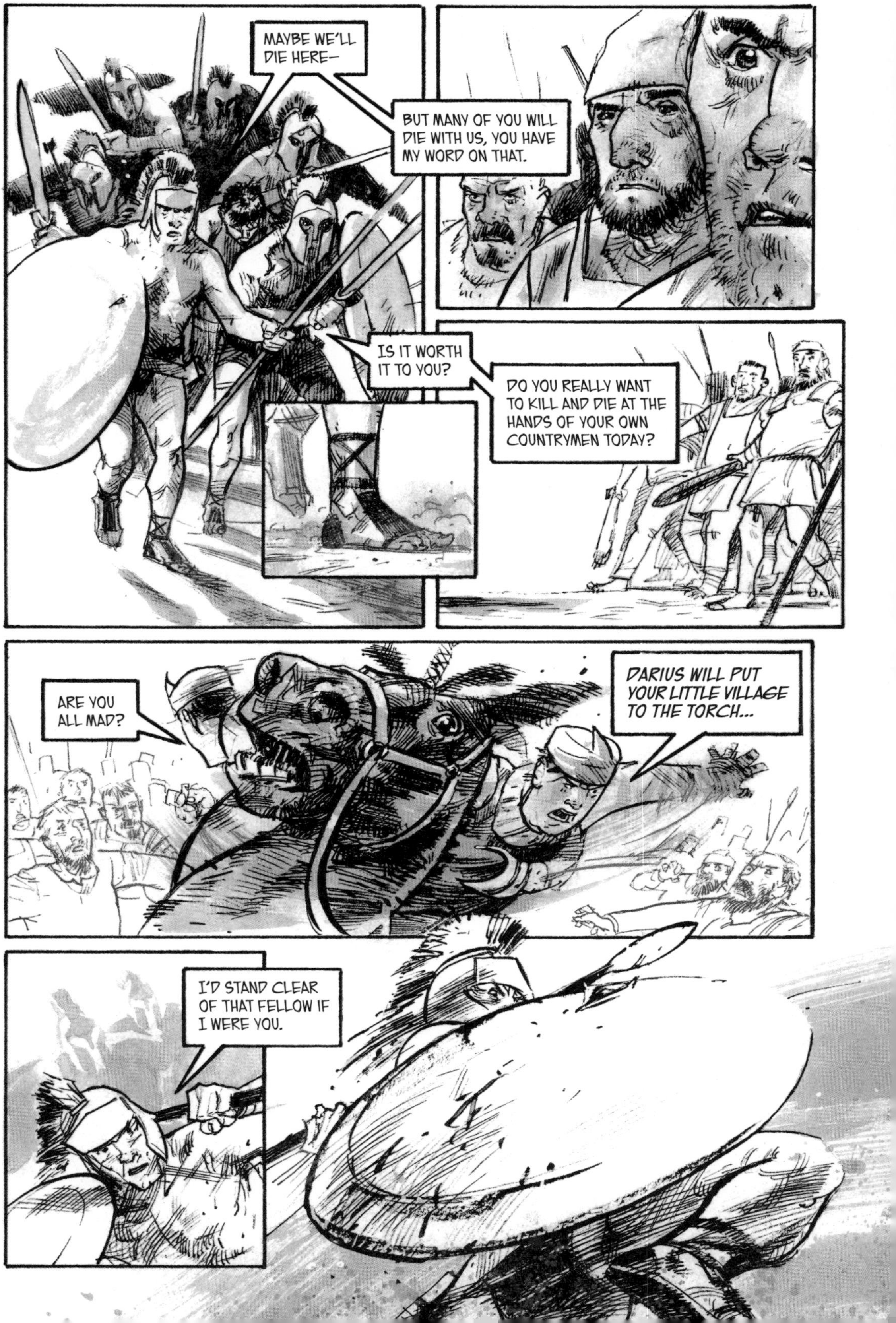
MAYBE WE'LL DIE HERE–
BUT MANY OF YOU WILL DIE WITH US, YOU HAVE MY WORD ON THAT.
IS IT WORTH IT TO YOU?
DO YOU REALLY WANT TO KILL AND DIE AT THE HANDS OF YOUR OWN COUNTRYMEN TODAY?
ARE YOU ALL MAD?
DARIUS WILL PUT YOUR LITTLE VILLAGE TO THE TORCH...
I'D STAND CLEAR OF THAT FELLOW IF I WERE YOU.

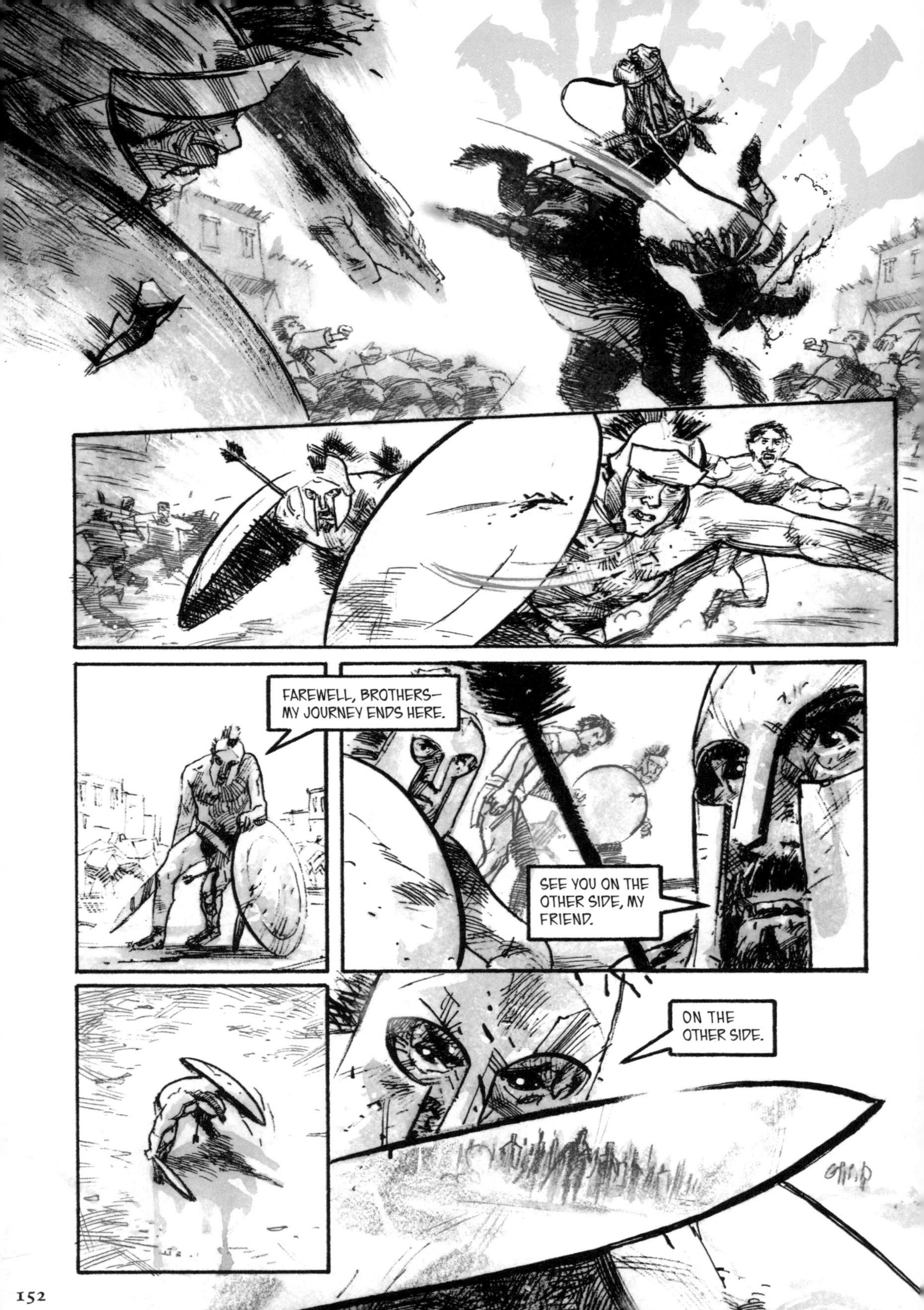
FAREWELL, BROTHERS— MY JOURNEY ENDS HERE.
SEE YOU ON THE OTHER SIDE, MY FRIEND.
ON THE OTHER SIDE.

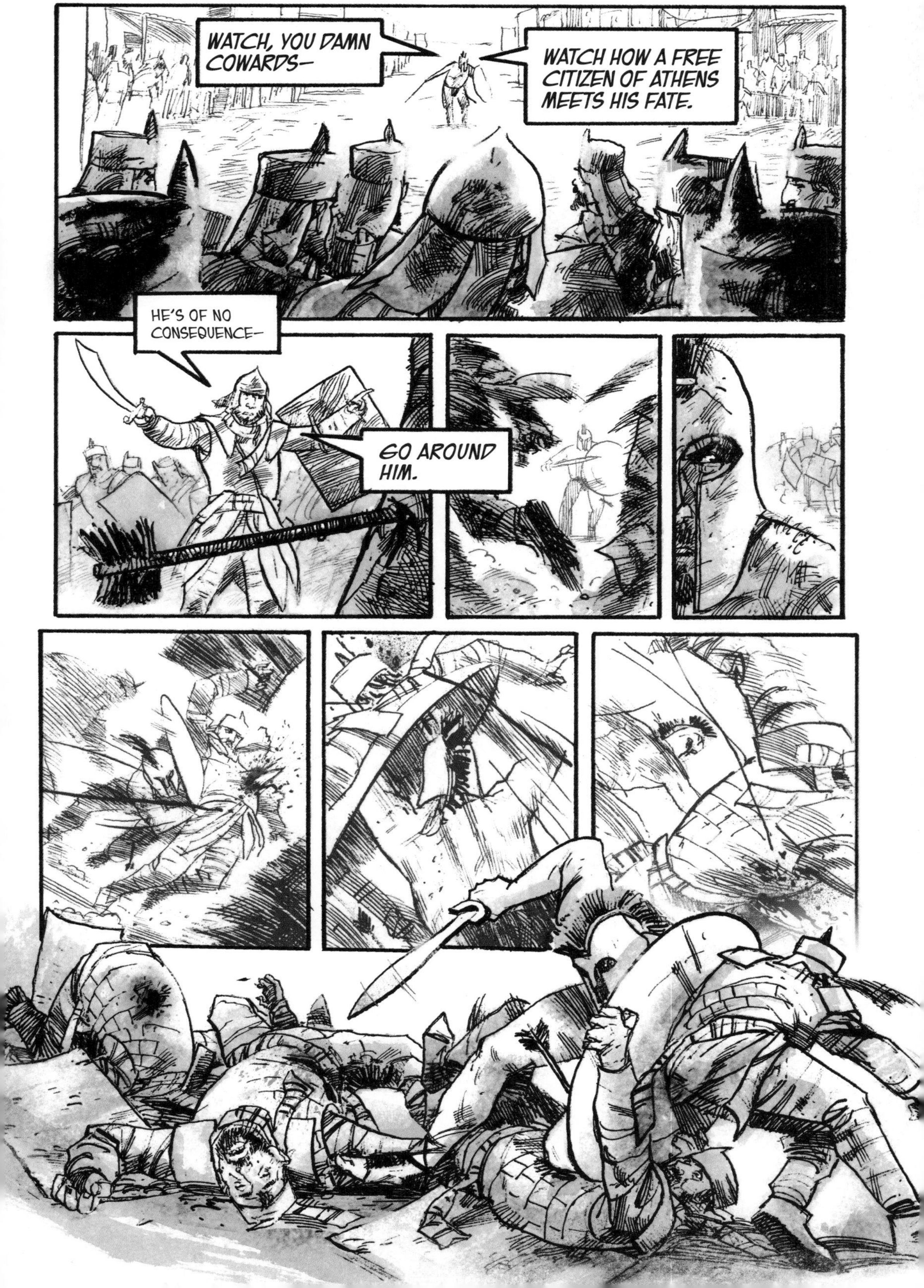
WATCH, YOU DAMN COWARDS–
WATCH HOW A FREE CITIZEN OF ATHENS MEETS HIS FATE.
HE'S OF NO CONSEQUENCE–
GO AROUND HIM.

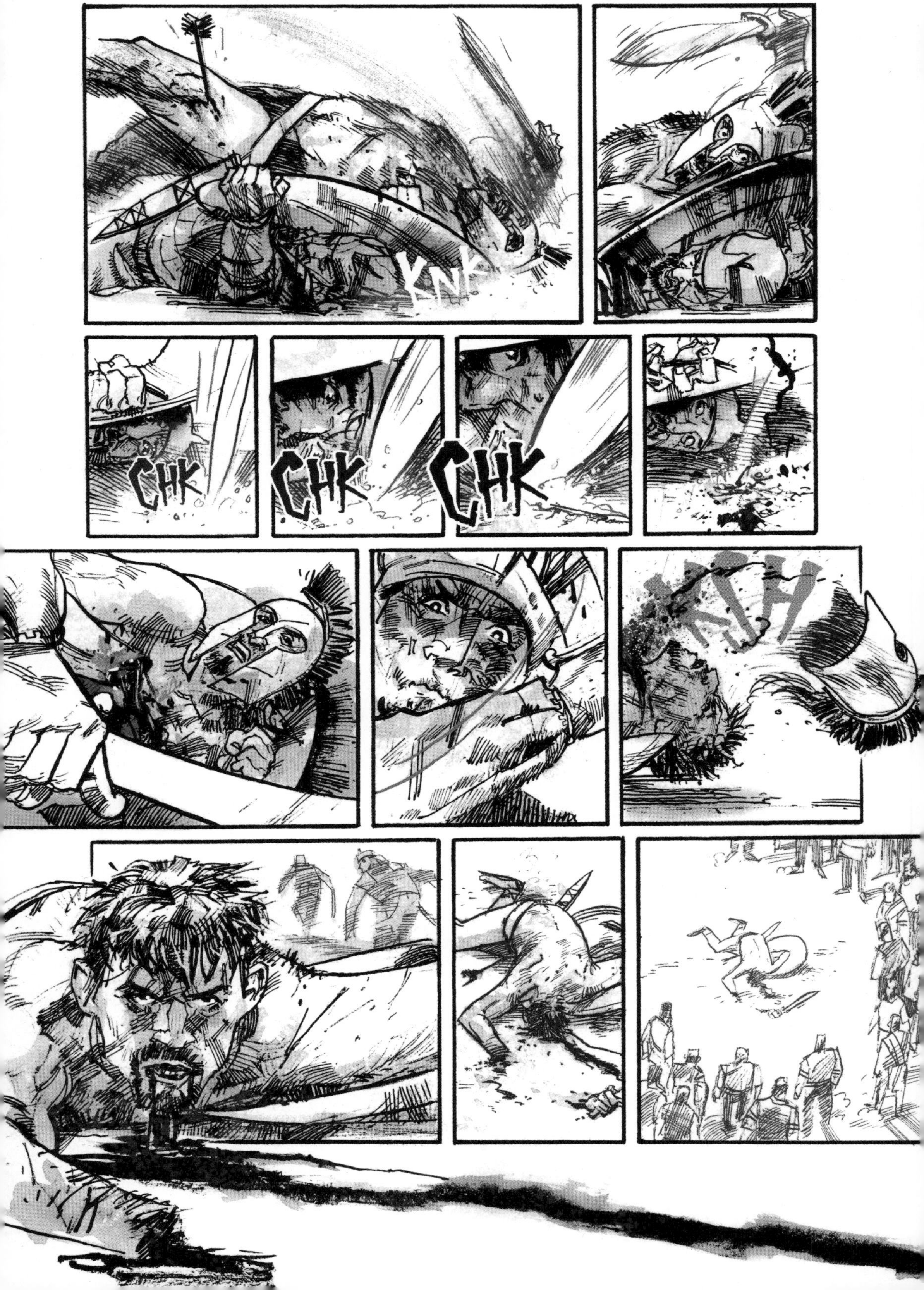
KNK
CHK
CHK
CHK

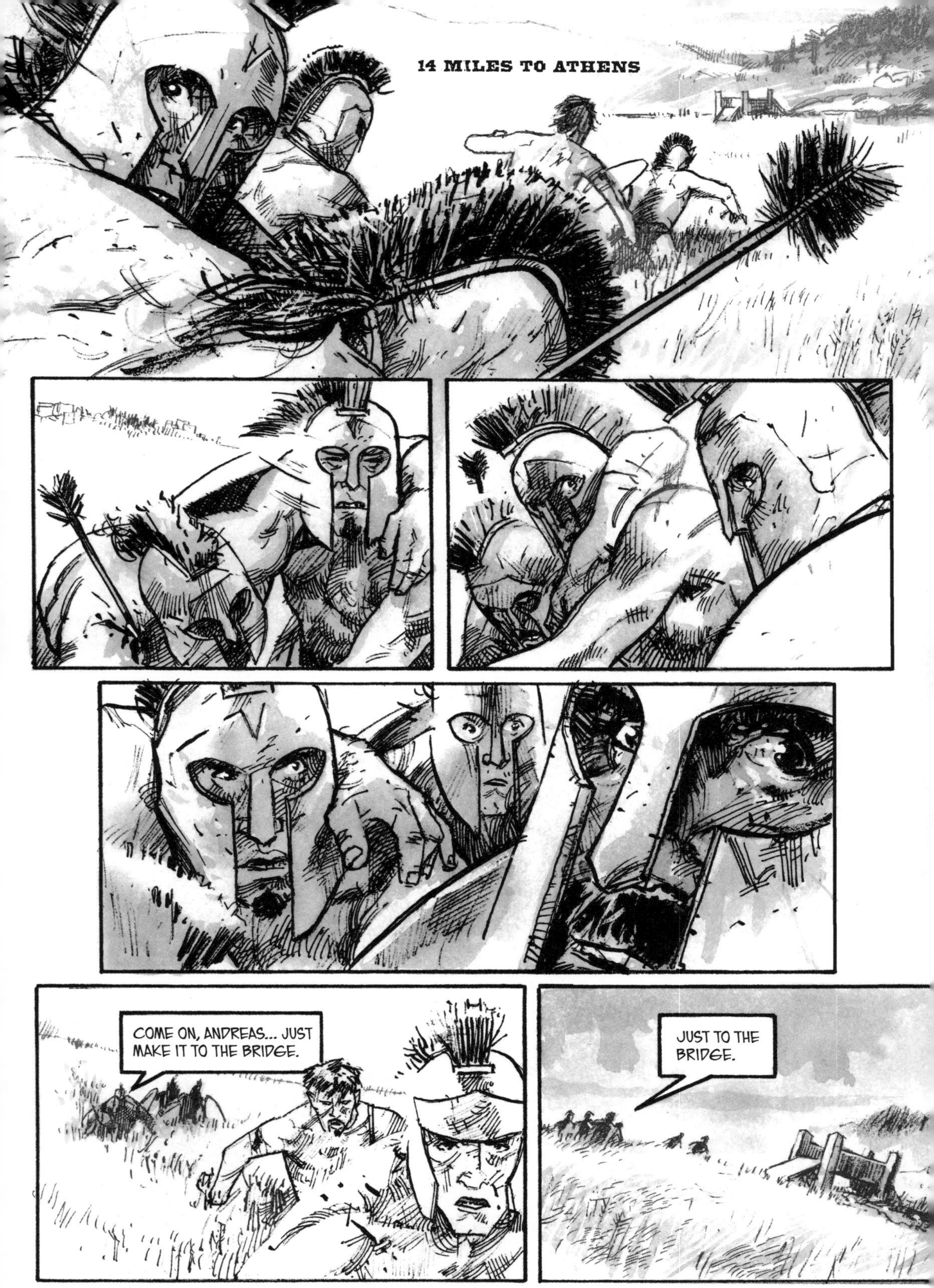
14 MILES TO ATHENS
COME ON, ANDREAS... JUST MAKE IT TO THE BRIDGE.
JUST TO THE BRIDGE.

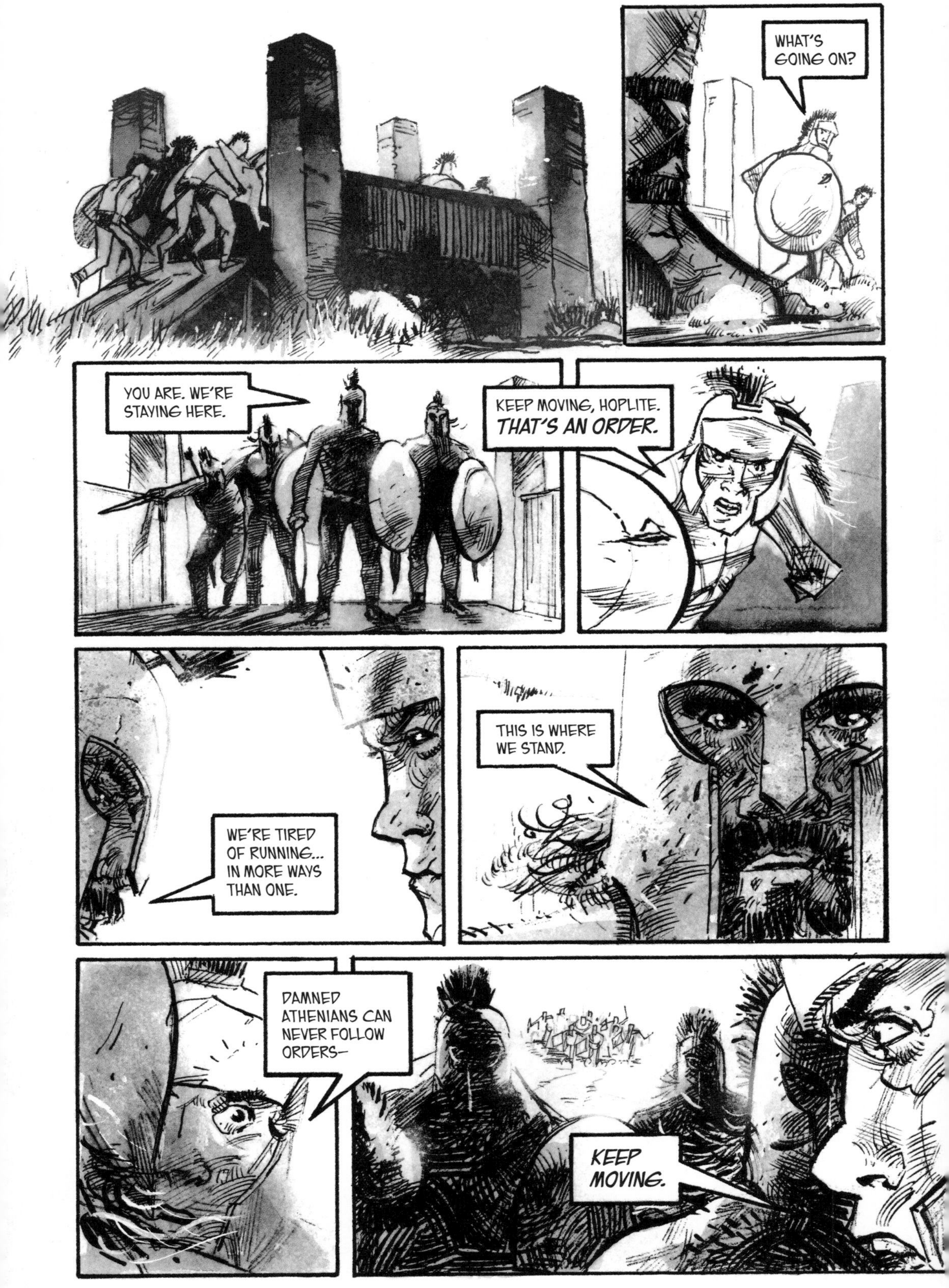
WHAT'S GOING ON?
YOU ARE. WE'RE STAYING HERE.
KEEP MOVING, HOPLITE. THAT'S AN ORDER.
WE'RE TIRED OF RUNNING... IN MORE WAYS THAN ONE.
THIS IS WHERE WE STAND.
DAMNED ATHENIANS CAN NEVER FOLLOW ORDERS–
KEEP MOVING.

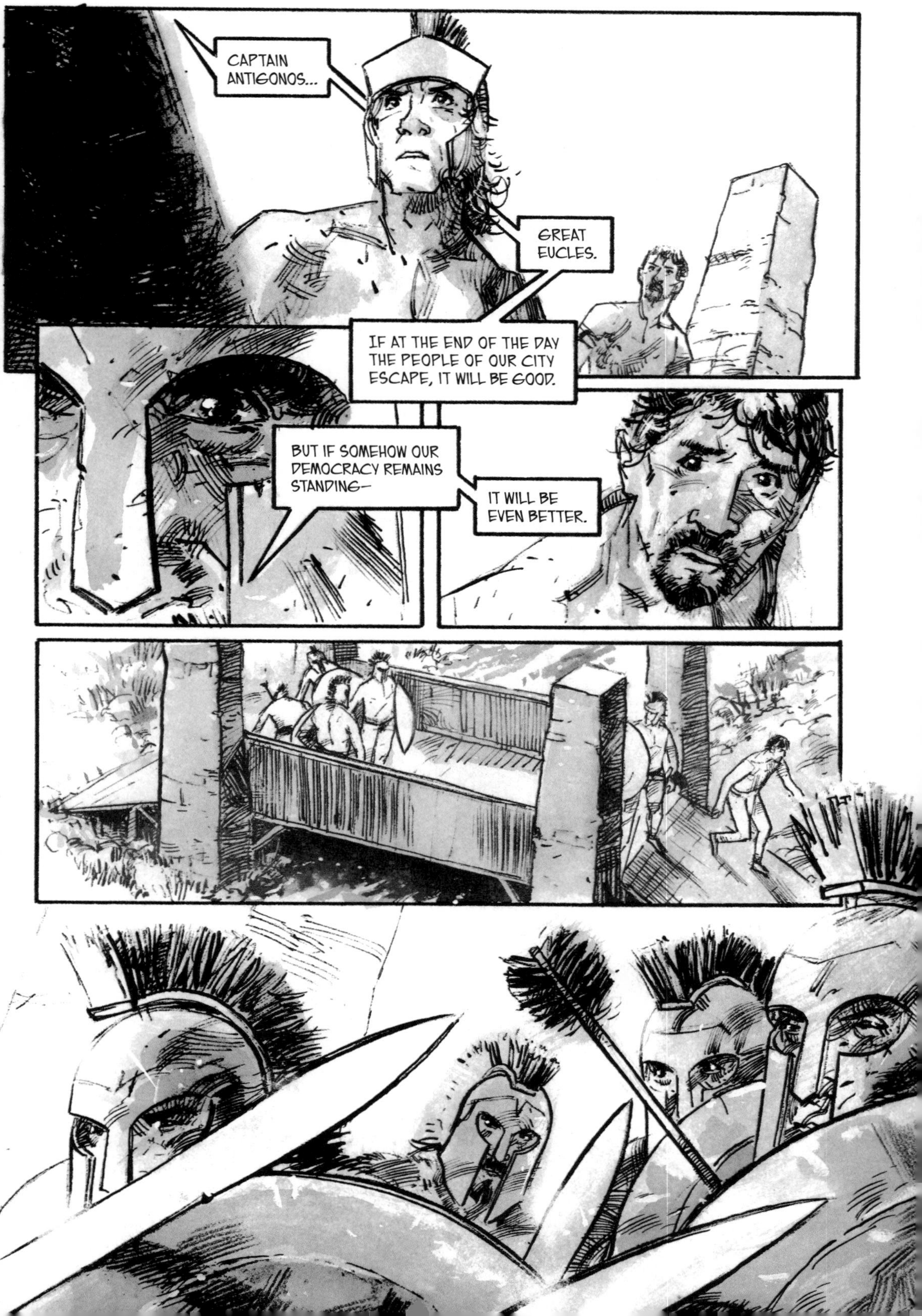
CAPTAIN ANTIGONOS...
GREAT EUCLES.
IF AT THE END OF THE DAY THE PEOPLE OF OUR CITY ESCAPE, IT WILL BE GOOD.
BUT IF SOMEHOW OUR DEMOCRACY REMAINS STANDING—
IT WILL BE EVEN BETTER.

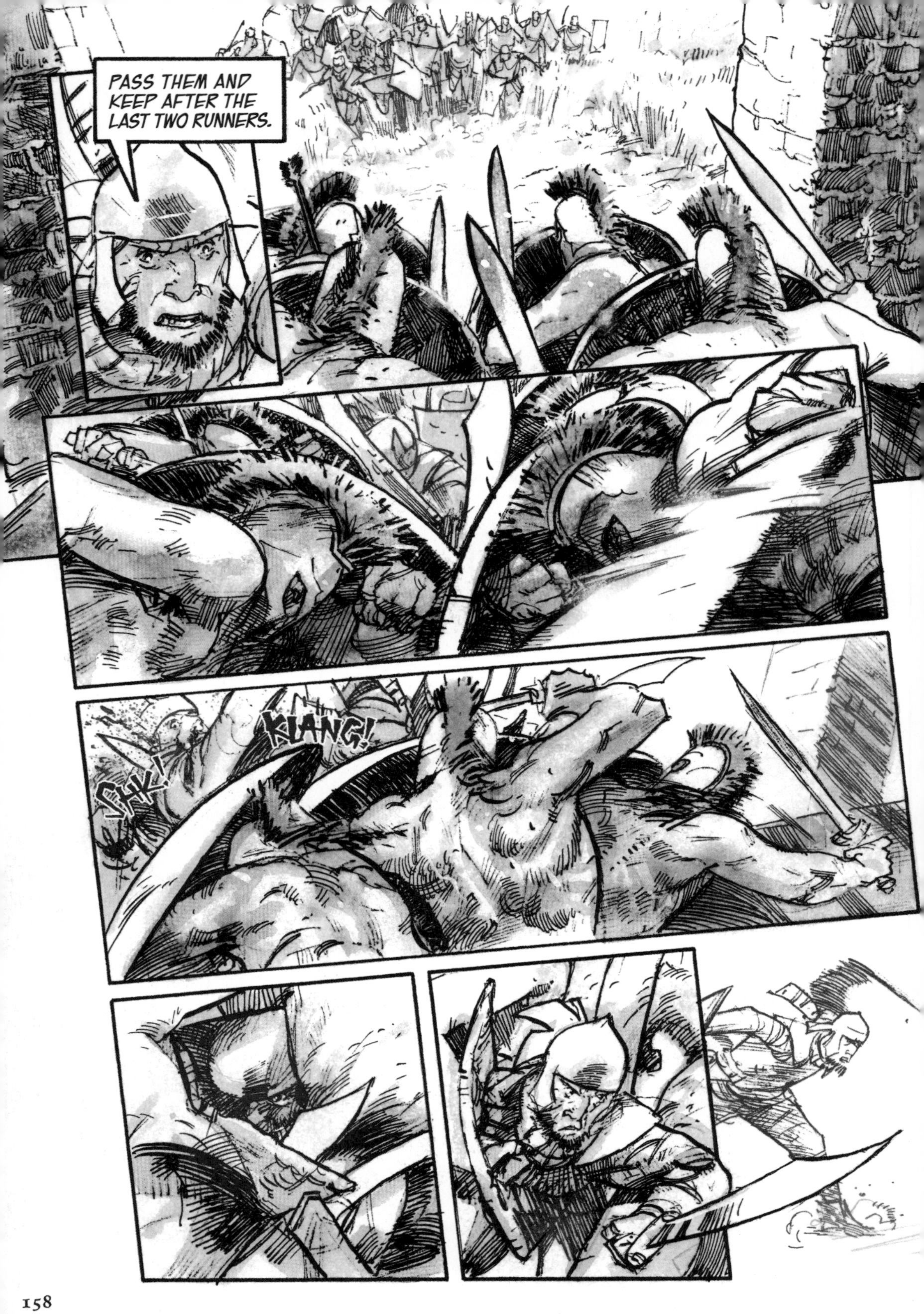
PASS THEM AND KEEP AFTER THE LAST TWO RUNNERS.
SHK!
KLANG!

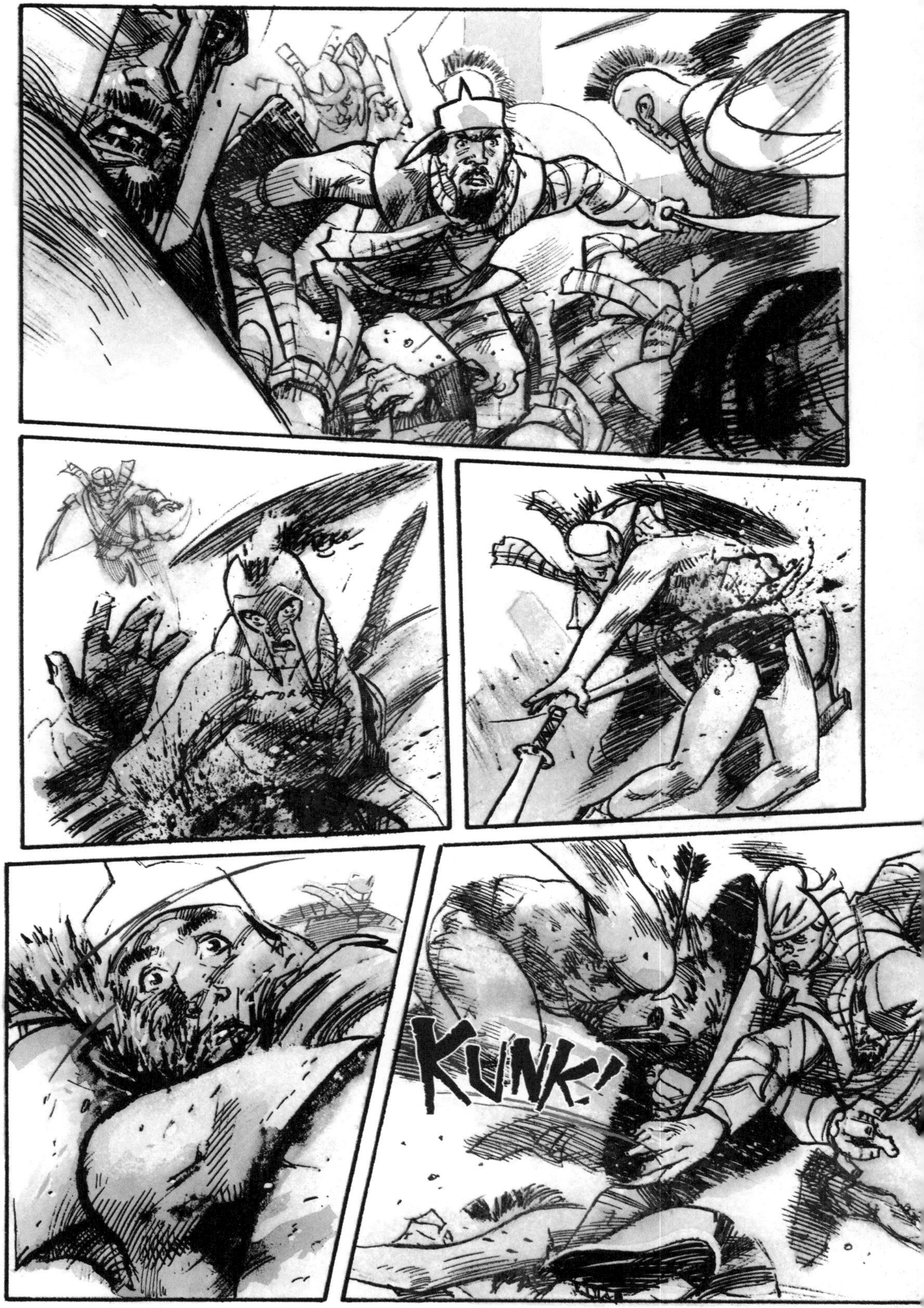
KUNK!

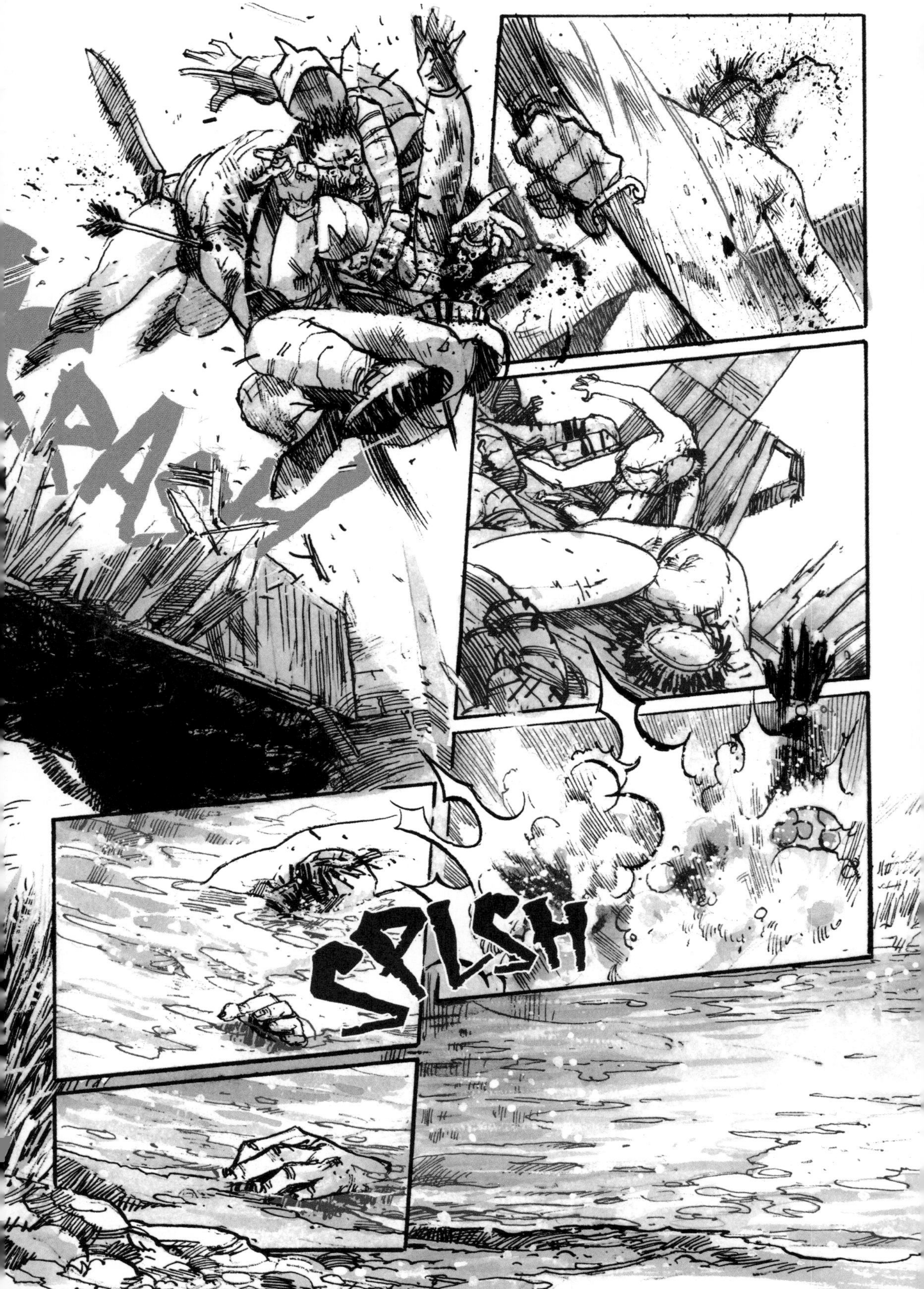
SPLSH

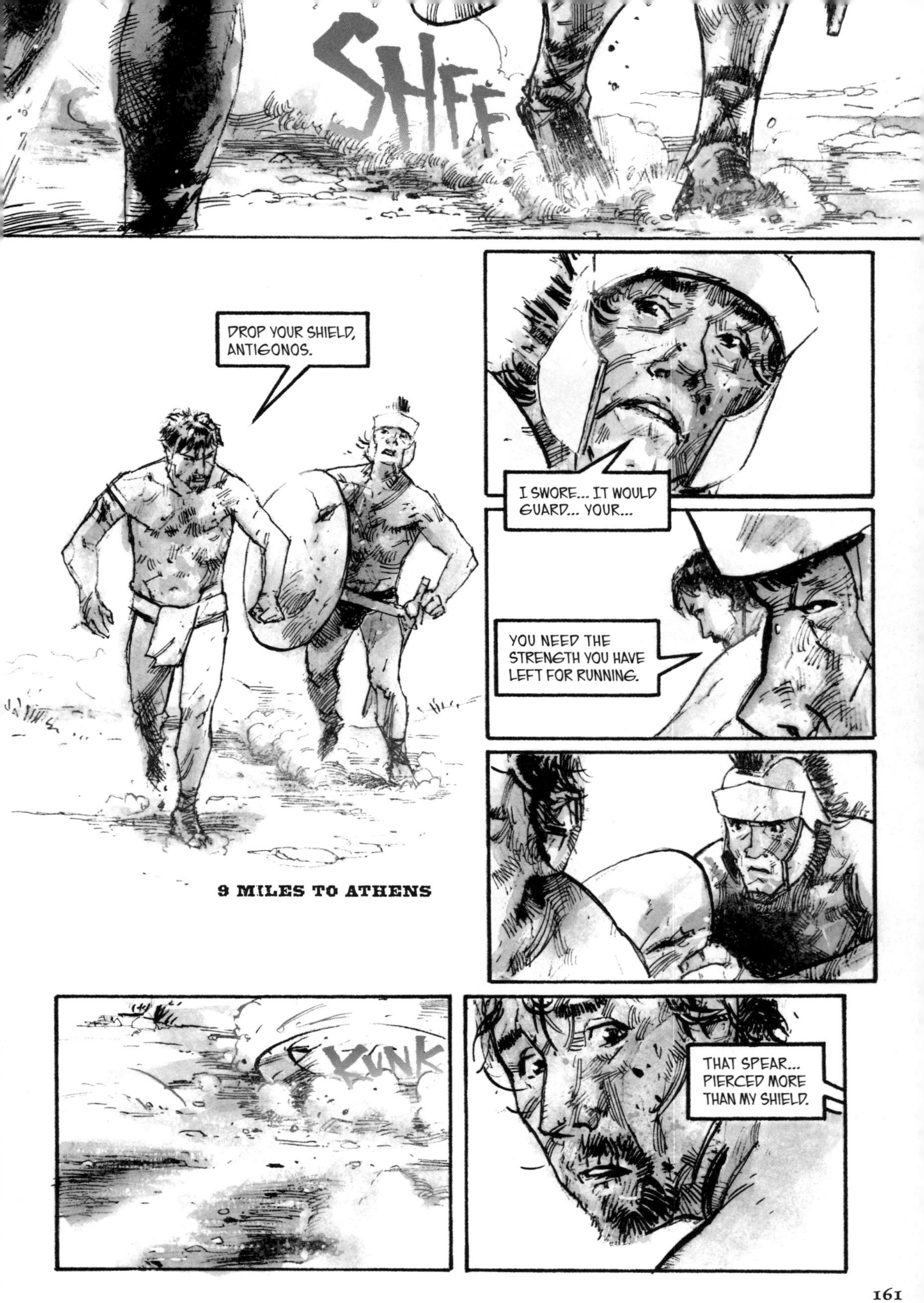
SHFF
DROP YOUR SHIELD, ANTIGONOS.
9 MILES TO ATHENS
I SWORE... IT WOULD GUARD... YOUR...
YOU NEED THE STRENGTH YOU HAVE LEFT FOR RUNNING.
KLUNK
THAT SPEAR... PIERCED MORE THAN MY SHIELD.

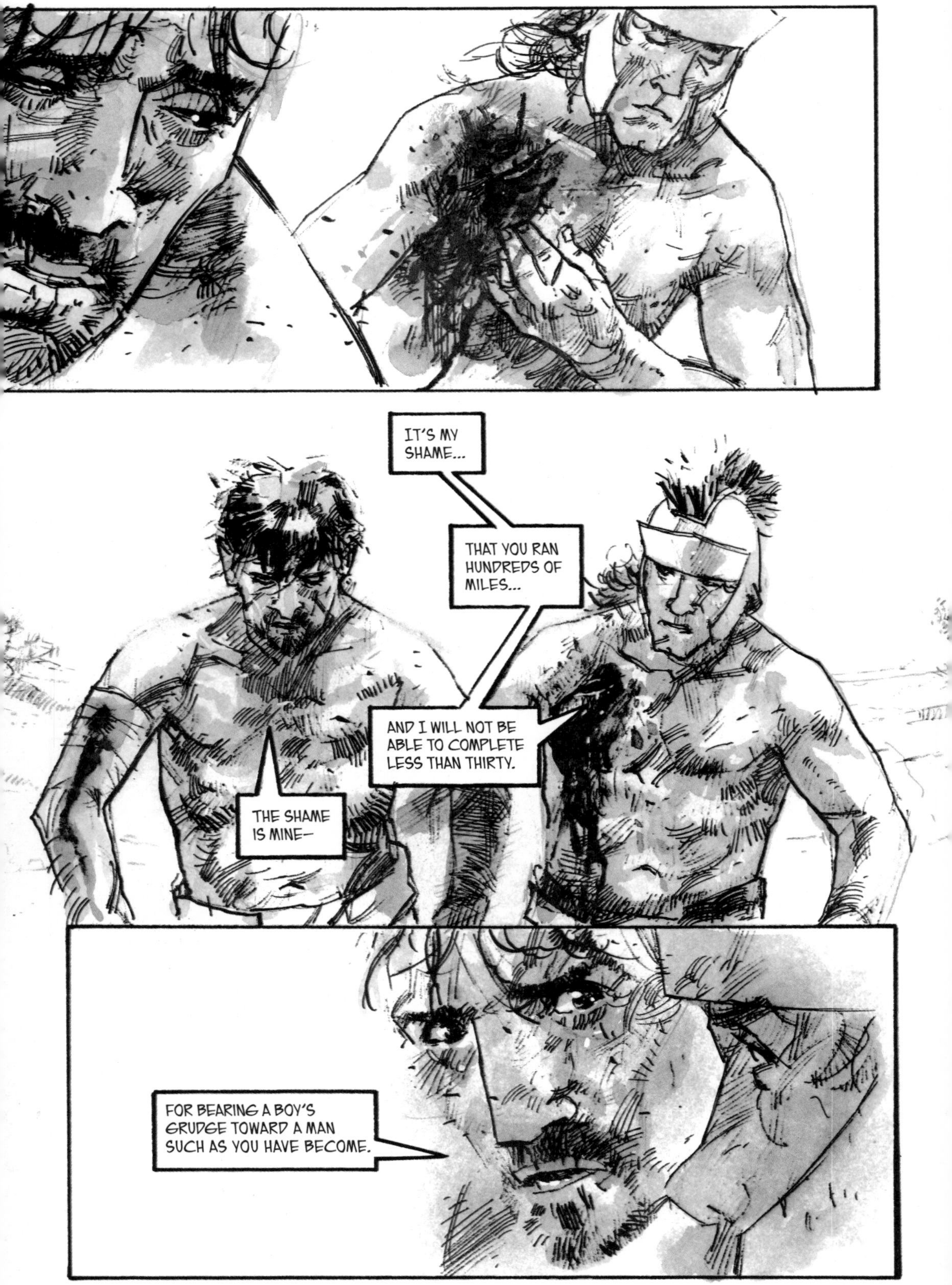

IT'S MY SHAME...
THAT YOU RAN HUNDREDS OF MILES...
AND I WILL NOT BE ABLE TO COMPLETE LESS THAN THIRTY.
THE SHAME IS MINE—
FOR BEARING A BOY'S GRUDGE TOWARD A MAN SUCH AS YOU HAVE BECOME.

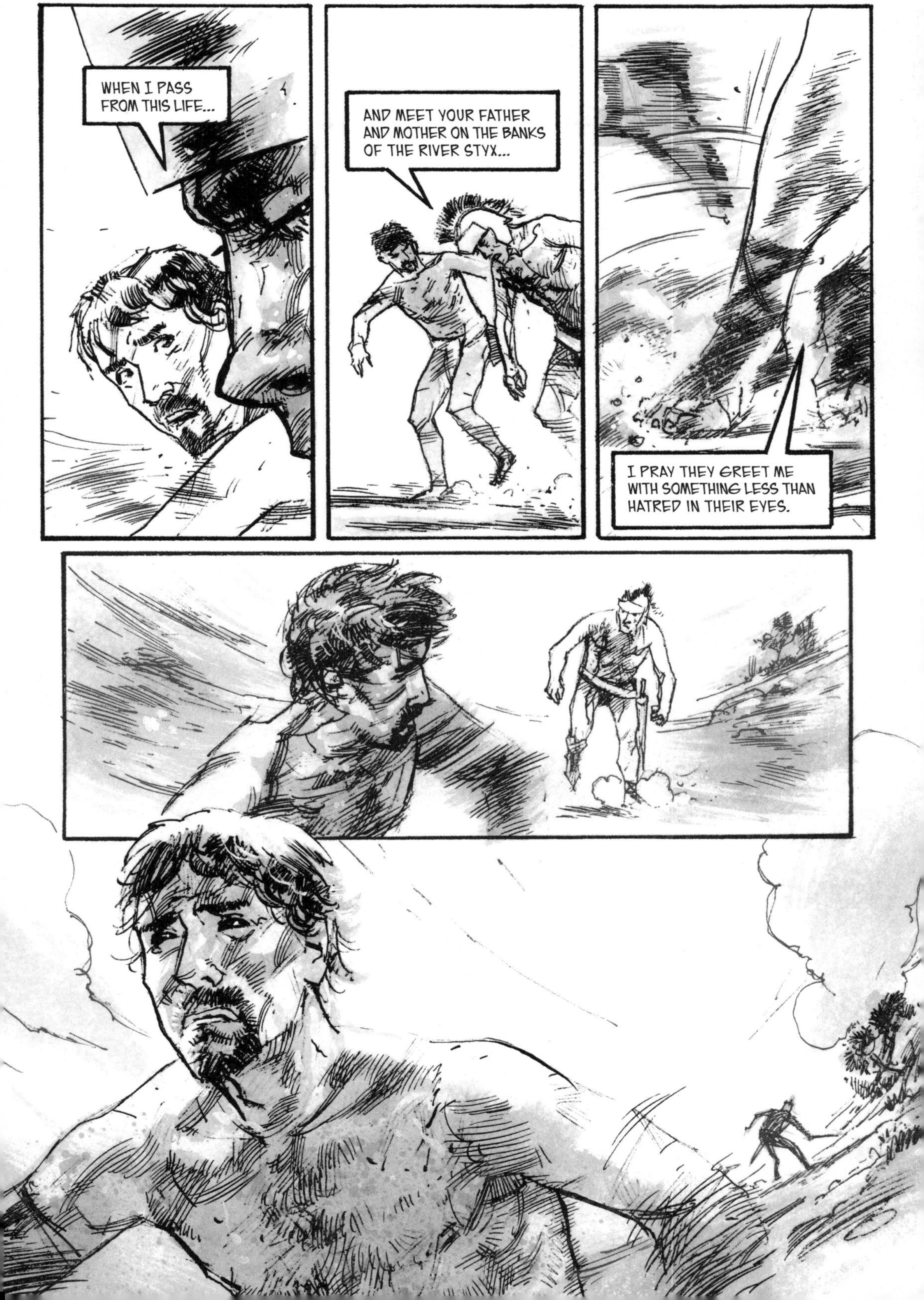
WHEN I PASS FROM THIS LIFE...
AND MEET YOUR FATHER AND MOTHER ON THE BANKS OF THE RIVER STYX...
I PRAY THEY GREET ME WITH SOMETHING LESS THAN HATRED IN THEIR EYES.

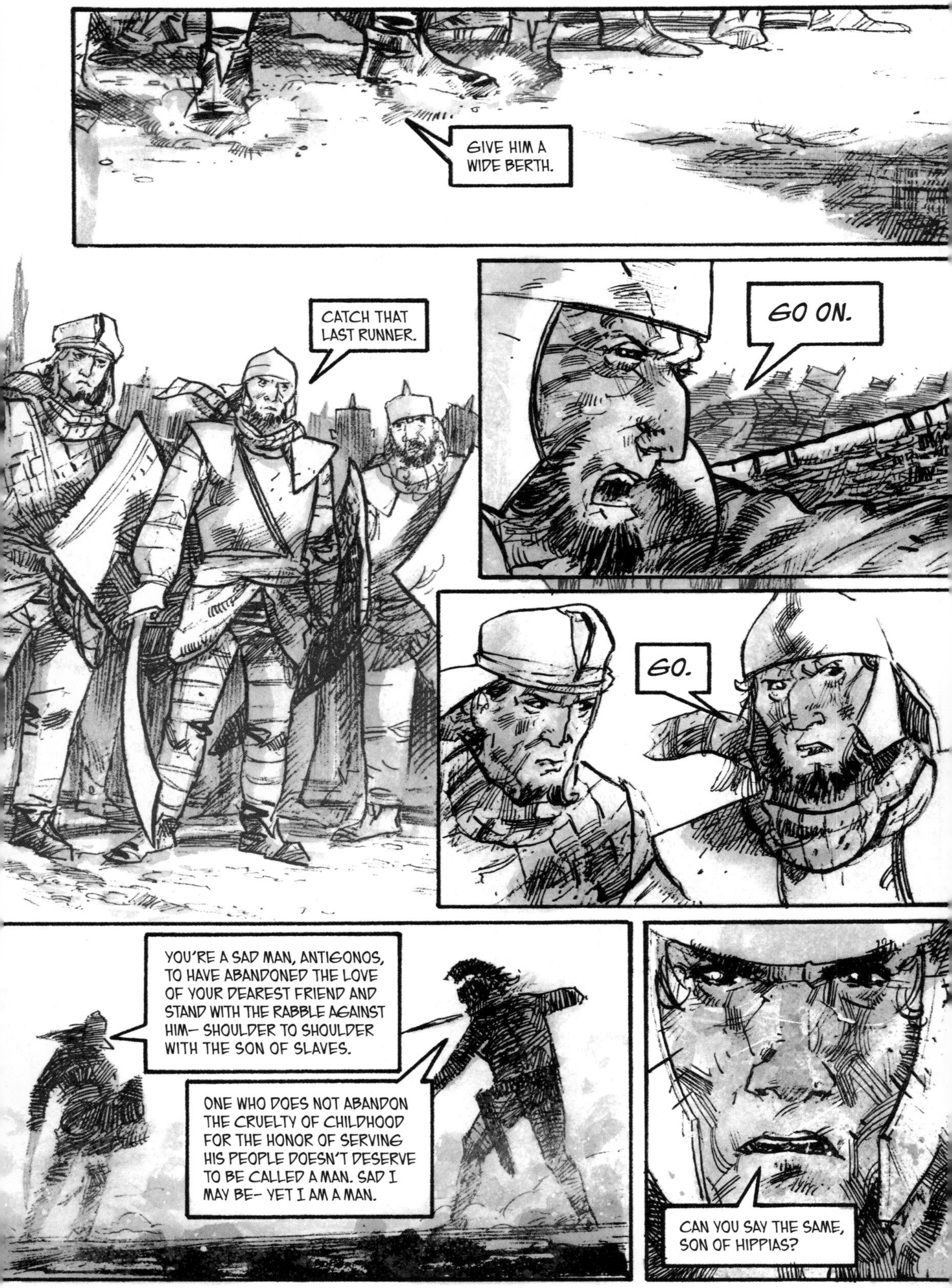
GIVE HIM A WIDE BERTH.
CATCH THAT LAST RUNNER.
GO ON.
GO.
YOU'RE A SAD MAN, ANTIGONOS, TO HAVE ABANDONED THE LOVE OF YOUR DEAREST FRIEND AND STAND WITH THE RABBLE AGAINST HIM— SHOULDER TO SHOULDER WITH THE SON OF SLAVES.
ONE WHO DOES NOT ABANDON THE CRUELTY OF CHILDHOOD FOR THE HONOR OF SERVING HIS PEOPLE DOESN'T DESERVE TO BE CALLED A MAN. SAD I MAY BE— YET I AM A MAN.
CAN YOU SAY THE SAME, SON OF HIPPIAS?

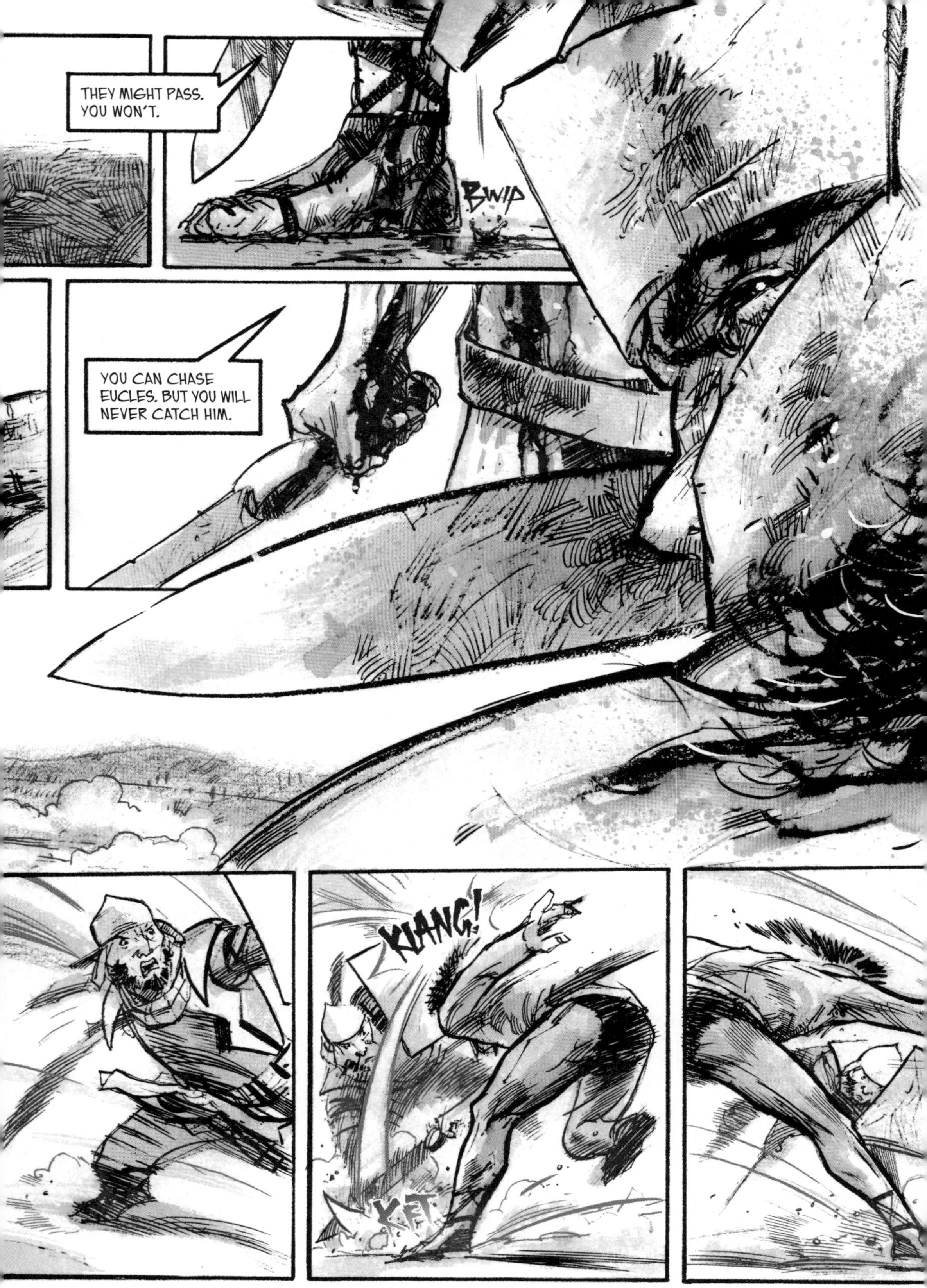
THEY MIGHT PASS. YOU WON'T.
BWIP
YOU CAN CHASE EUCLES. BUT YOU WILL NEVER CATCH HIM.
KLANG!
XFT

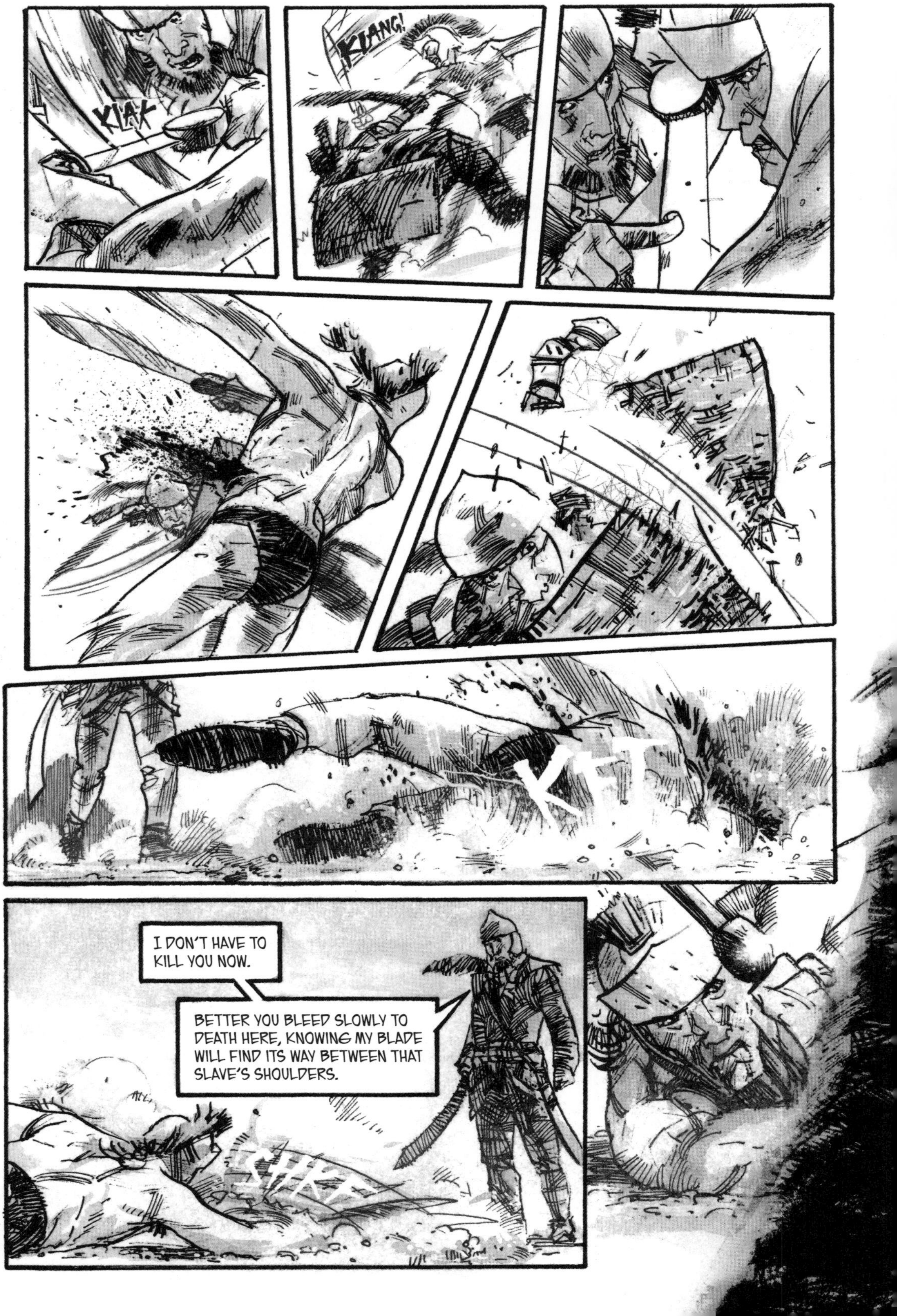
KLAK
KLANG!
KLANG
KT
I DON'T HAVE TO KILL YOU NOW.
BETTER YOU BLEED SLOWLY TO DEATH HERE, KNOWING MY BLADE WILL FIND ITS WAY BETWEEN THAT SLAVE'S SHOULDERS.
SHRT

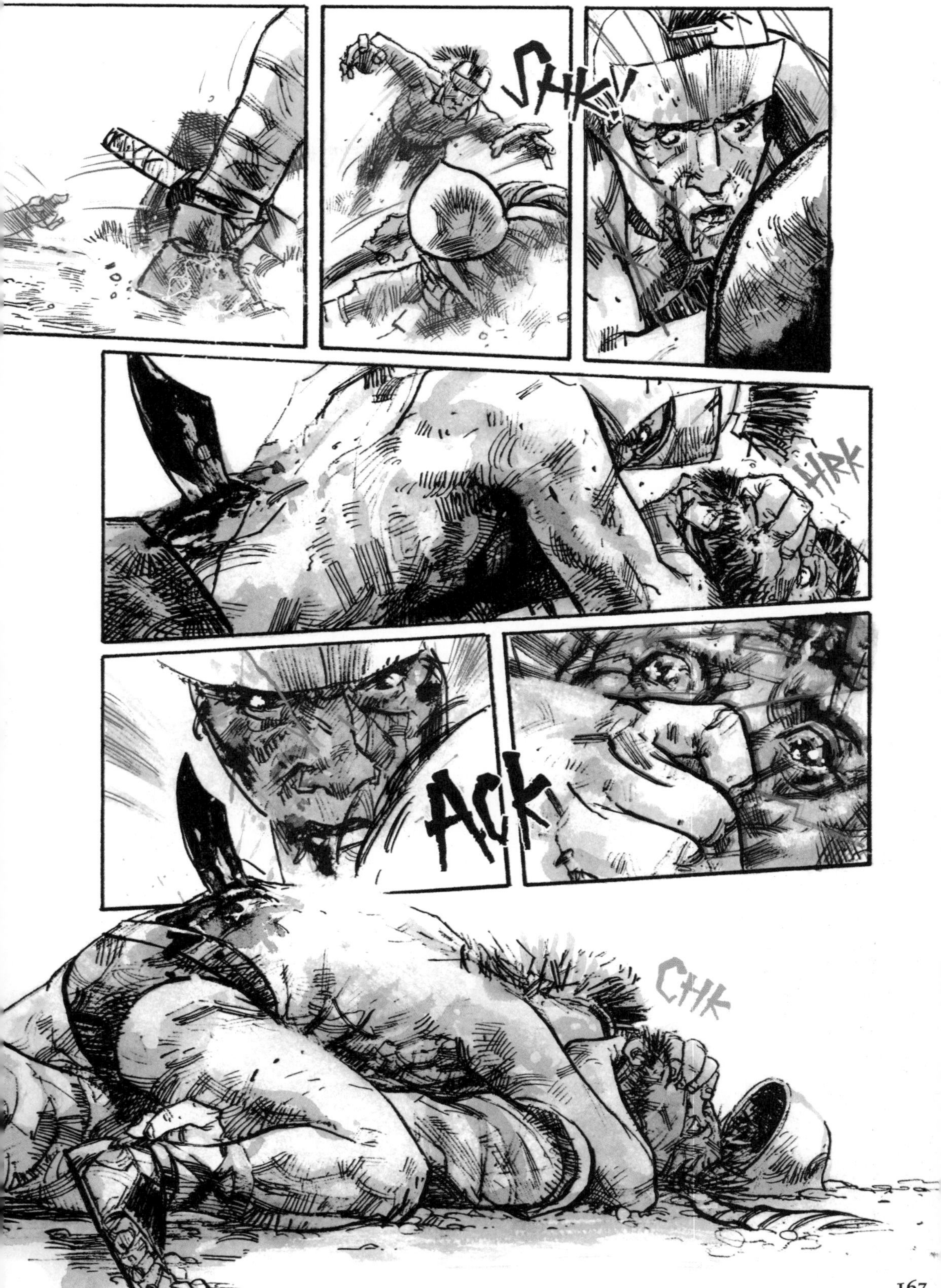
SHK!!
HRK
ACK
CHK

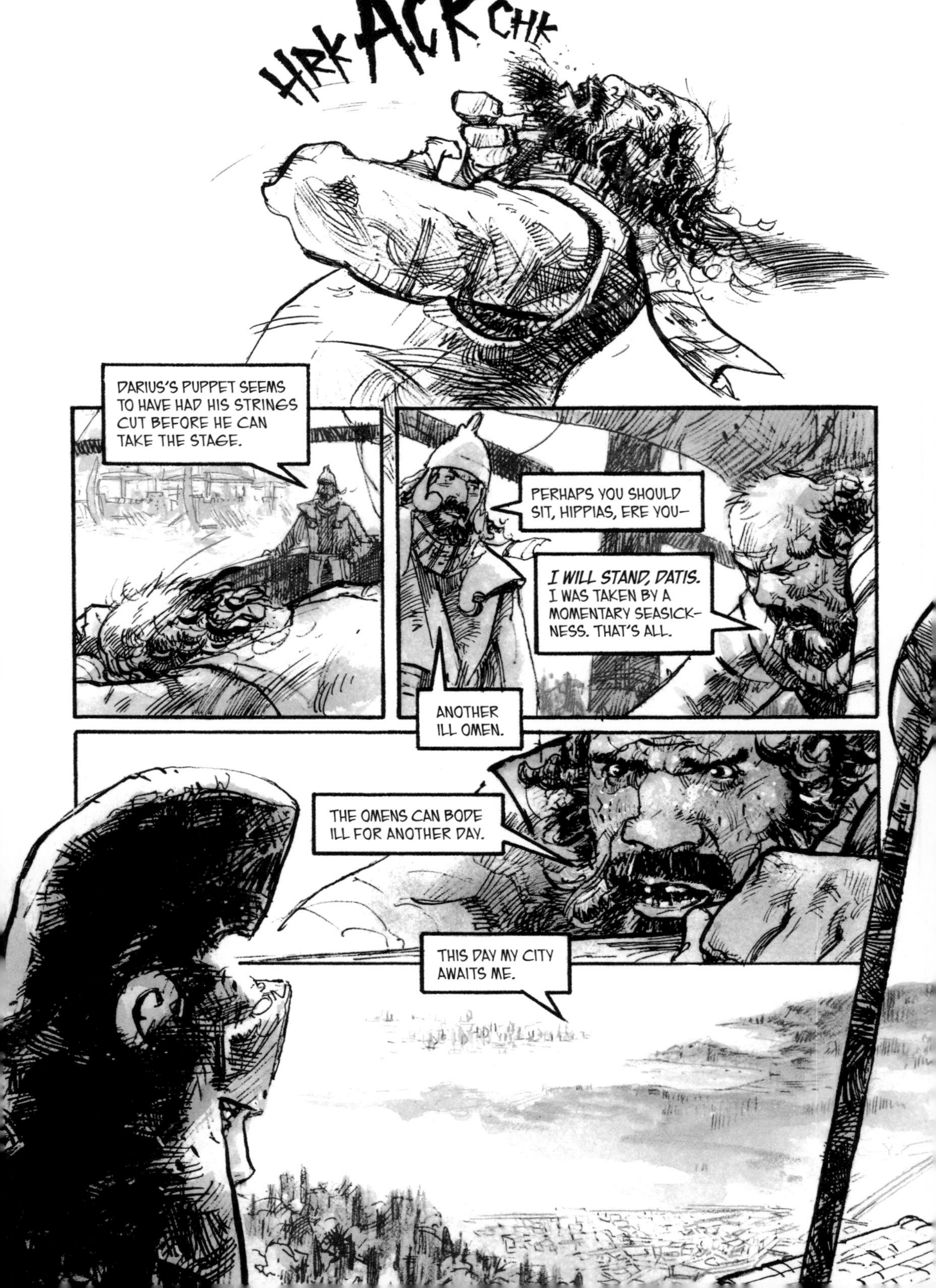
HRK ACK CHK
DARIUS'S PUPPET SEEMS TO HAVE HAD HIS STRINGS CUT BEFORE HE CAN TAKE THE STAGE.
PERHAPS YOU SHOULD SIT, HIPPIAS, ERE YOU—
I WILL STAND, DATIS. I WAS TAKEN BY A MOMENTARY SEASICKNESS. THAT'S ALL.
ANOTHER ILL OMEN.
THE OMENS CAN BODE ILL FOR ANOTHER DAY.
THIS DAY MY CITY AWAITS ME.

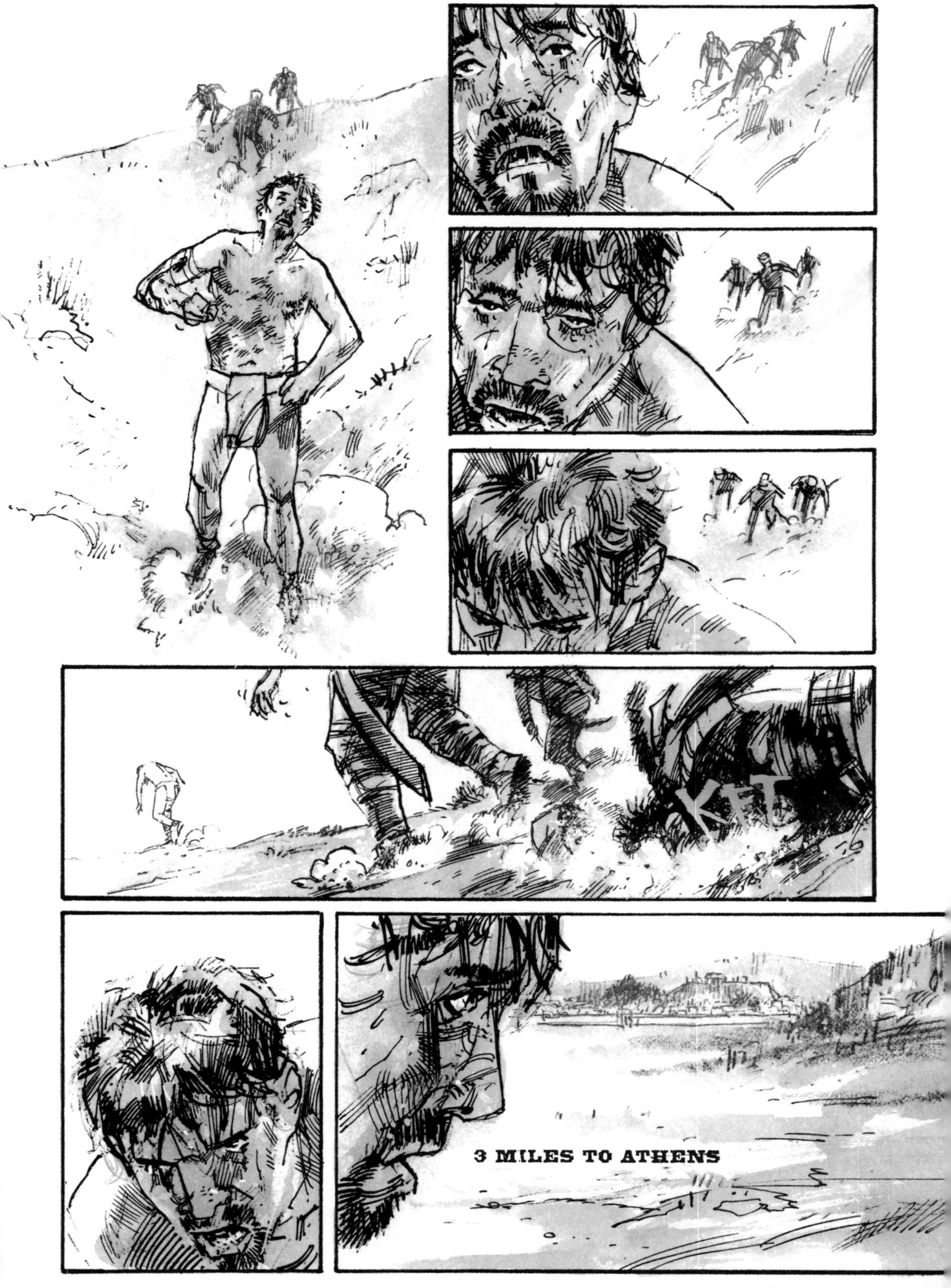
3 MILES TO ATHENS

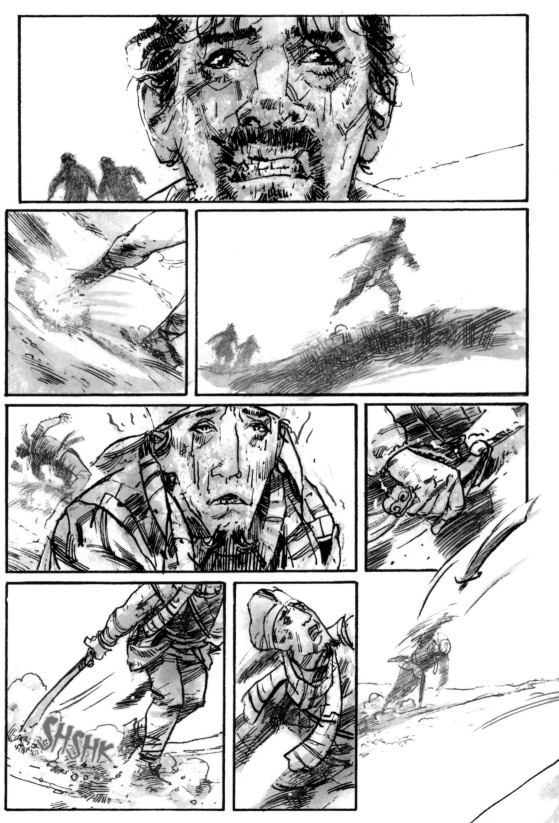

SHSHK

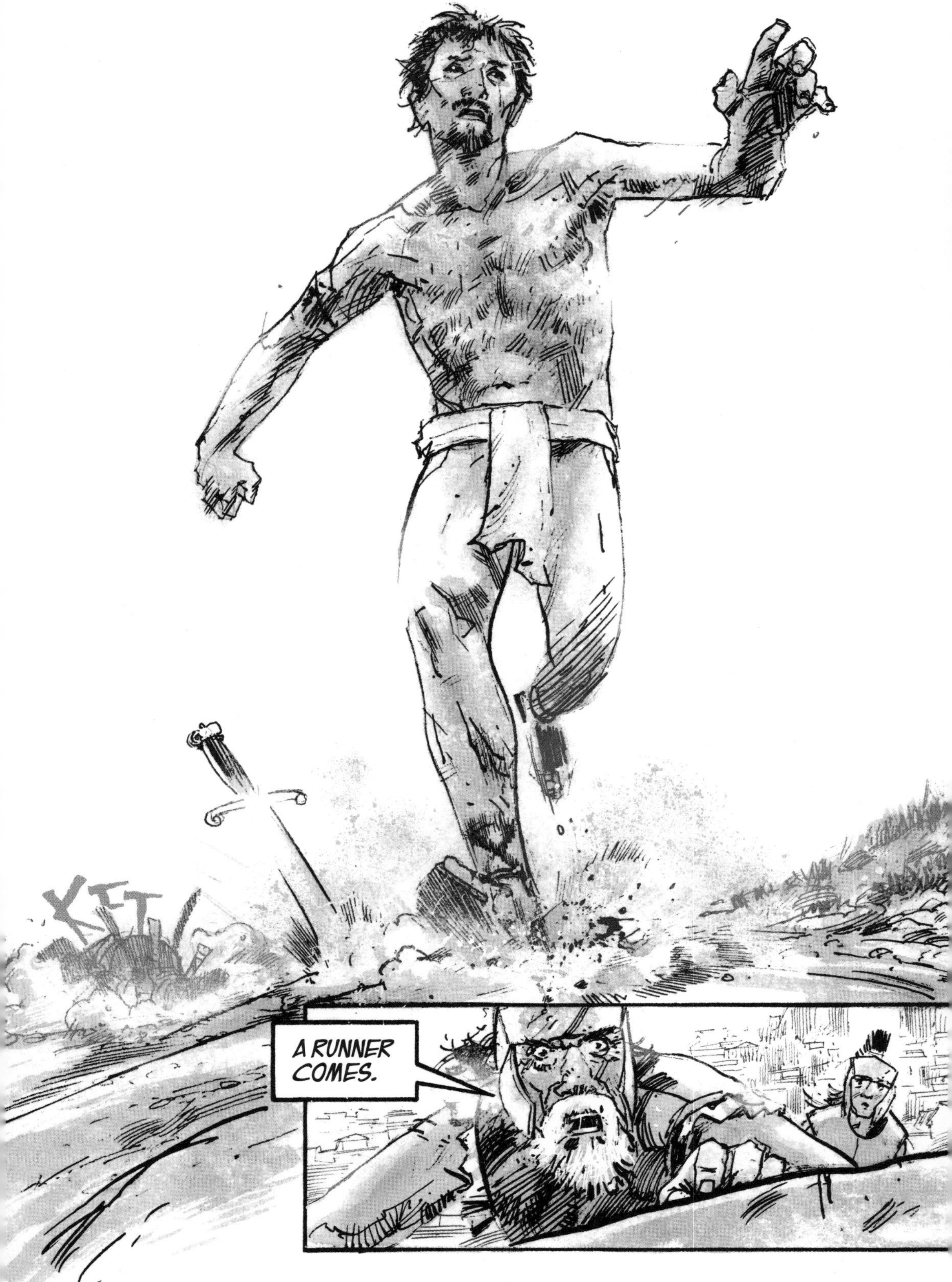
KET
A RUNNER COMES.

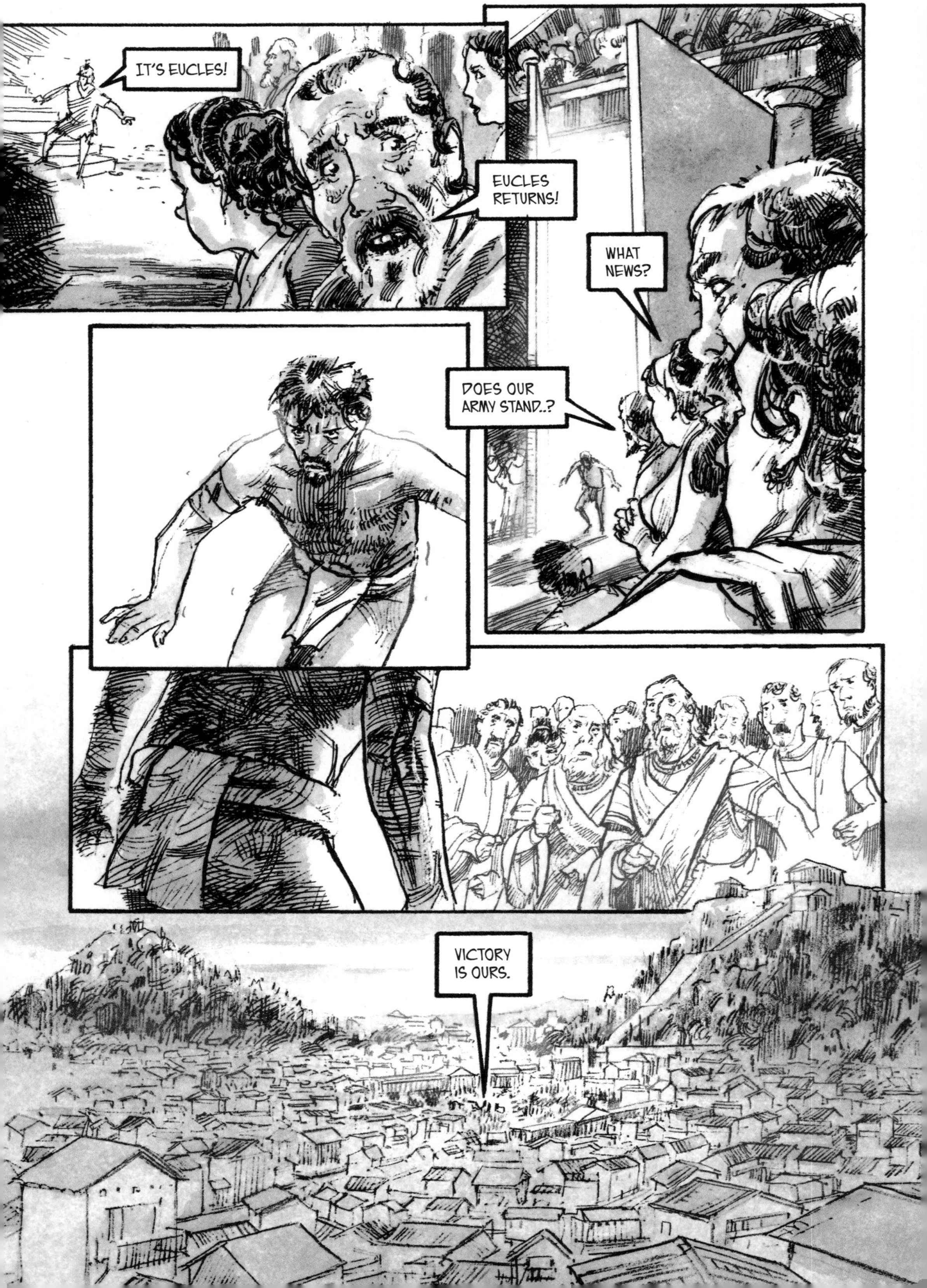
IT'S EUCLES!
EUCLES RETURNS!
WHAT NEWS?
DOES OUR ARMY STAND..?
VICTORY IS OURS.

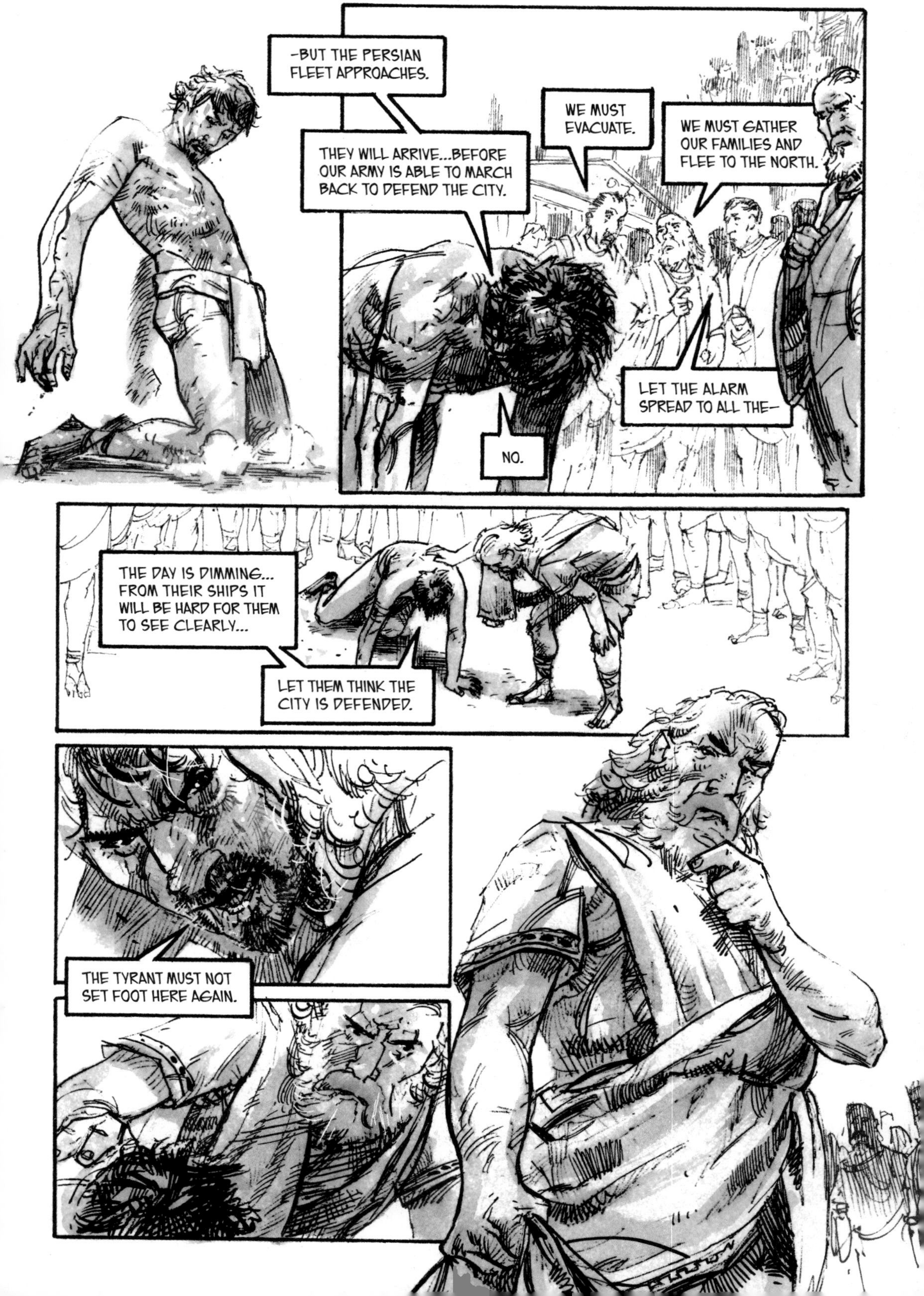
-BUT THE PERSIAN FLEET APPROACHES.
THEY WILL ARRIVE...BEFORE OUR ARMY IS ABLE TO MARCH BACK TO DEFEND THE CITY.
WE MUST EVACUATE.
WE MUST GATHER OUR FAMILIES AND FLEE TO THE NORTH.
LET THE ALARM SPREAD TO ALL THE-
NO.
THE DAY IS DIMMING... FROM THEIR SHIPS IT WILL BE HARD FOR THEM TO SEE CLEARLY...
LET THEM THINK THE CITY IS DEFENDED.
THE TYRANT MUST NOT SET FOOT HERE AGAIN.

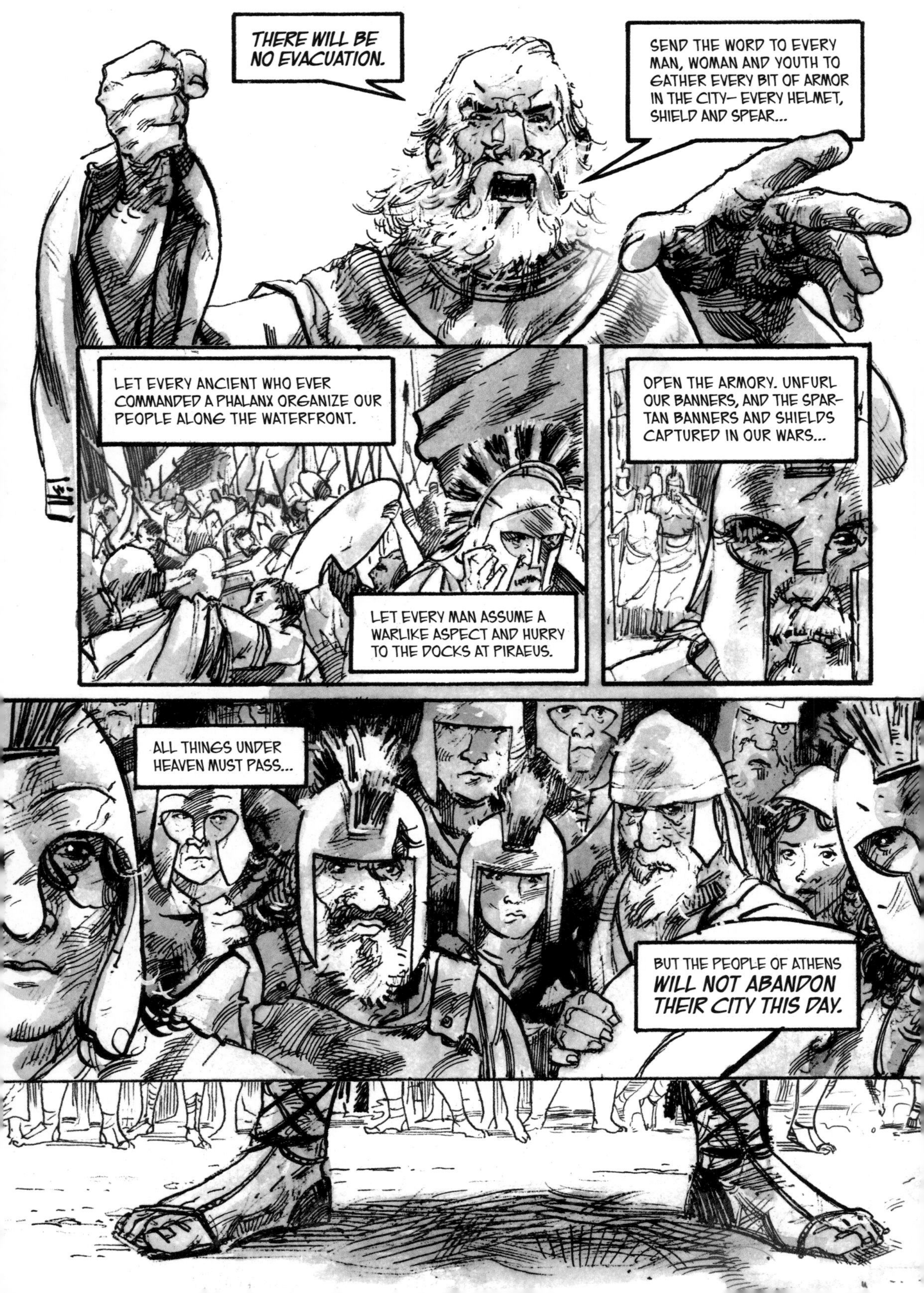
THERE WILL BE NO EVACUATION.
SEND THE WORD TO EVERY MAN, WOMAN AND YOUTH TO GATHER EVERY BIT OF ARMOR IN THE CITY– EVERY HELMET, SHIELD AND SPEAR...
LET EVERY ANCIENT WHO EVER COMMANDED A PHALANX ORGANIZE OUR PEOPLE ALONG THE WATERFRONT.
LET EVERY MAN ASSUME A WARLIKE ASPECT AND HURRY TO THE DOCKS AT PIRAEUS.
OPEN THE ARMORY. UNFURL OUR BANNERS, AND THE SPAR-TAN BANNERS AND SHIELDS CAPTURED IN OUR WARS...
ALL THINGS UNDER HEAVEN MUST PASS...
BUT THE PEOPLE OF ATHENS WILL NOT ABANDON THEIR CITY THIS DAY.

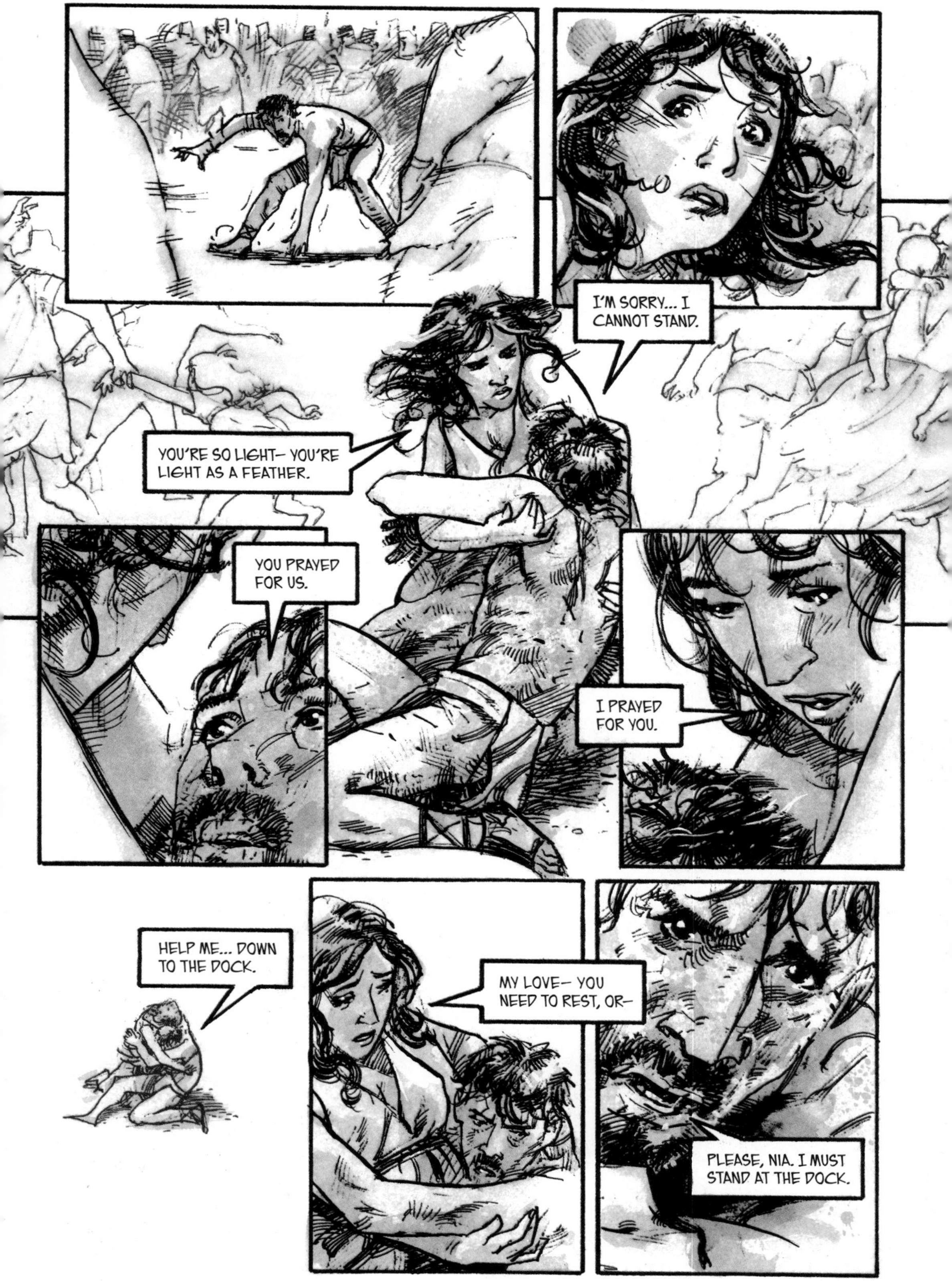
I'M SORRY... I CANNOT STAND.
YOU'RE SO LIGHT— YOU'RE LIGHT AS A FEATHER.
YOU PRAYED FOR US.
I PRAYED FOR YOU.
HELP ME... DOWN TO THE DOCK.
MY LOVE— YOU NEED TO REST, OR—
PLEASE, NIA. I MUST STAND AT THE DOCK.

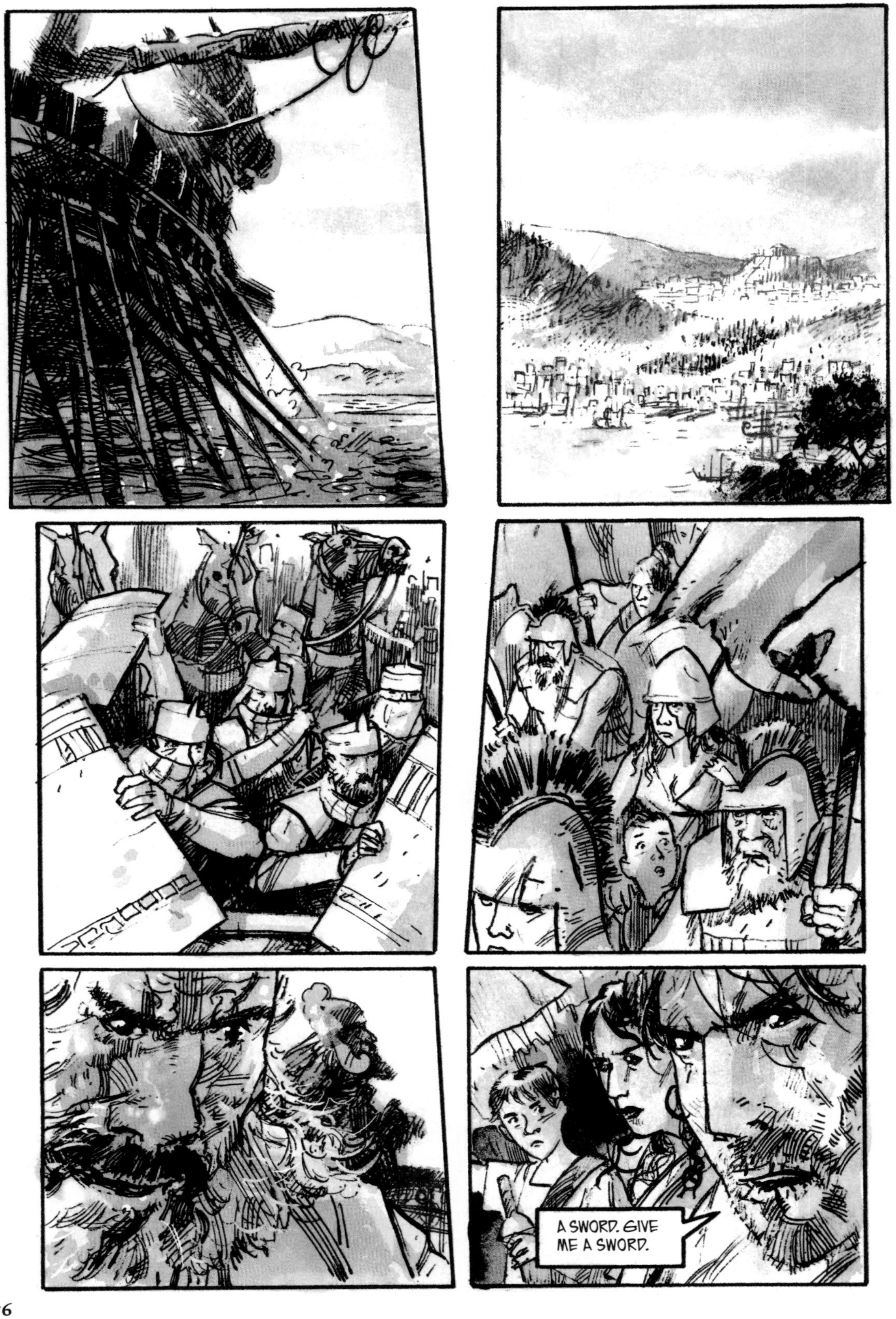
A SWORD. GIVE
ME A SWORD.

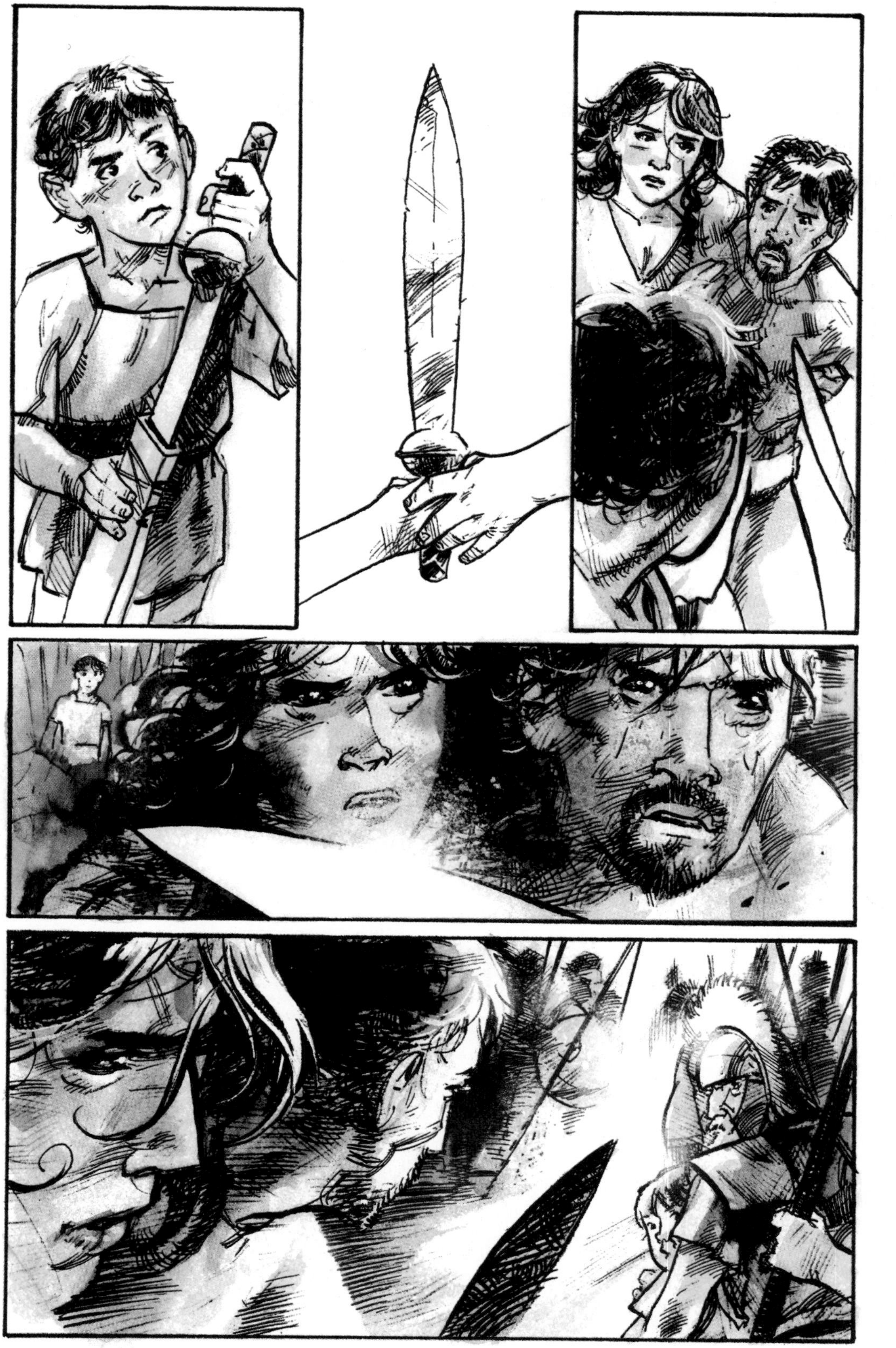

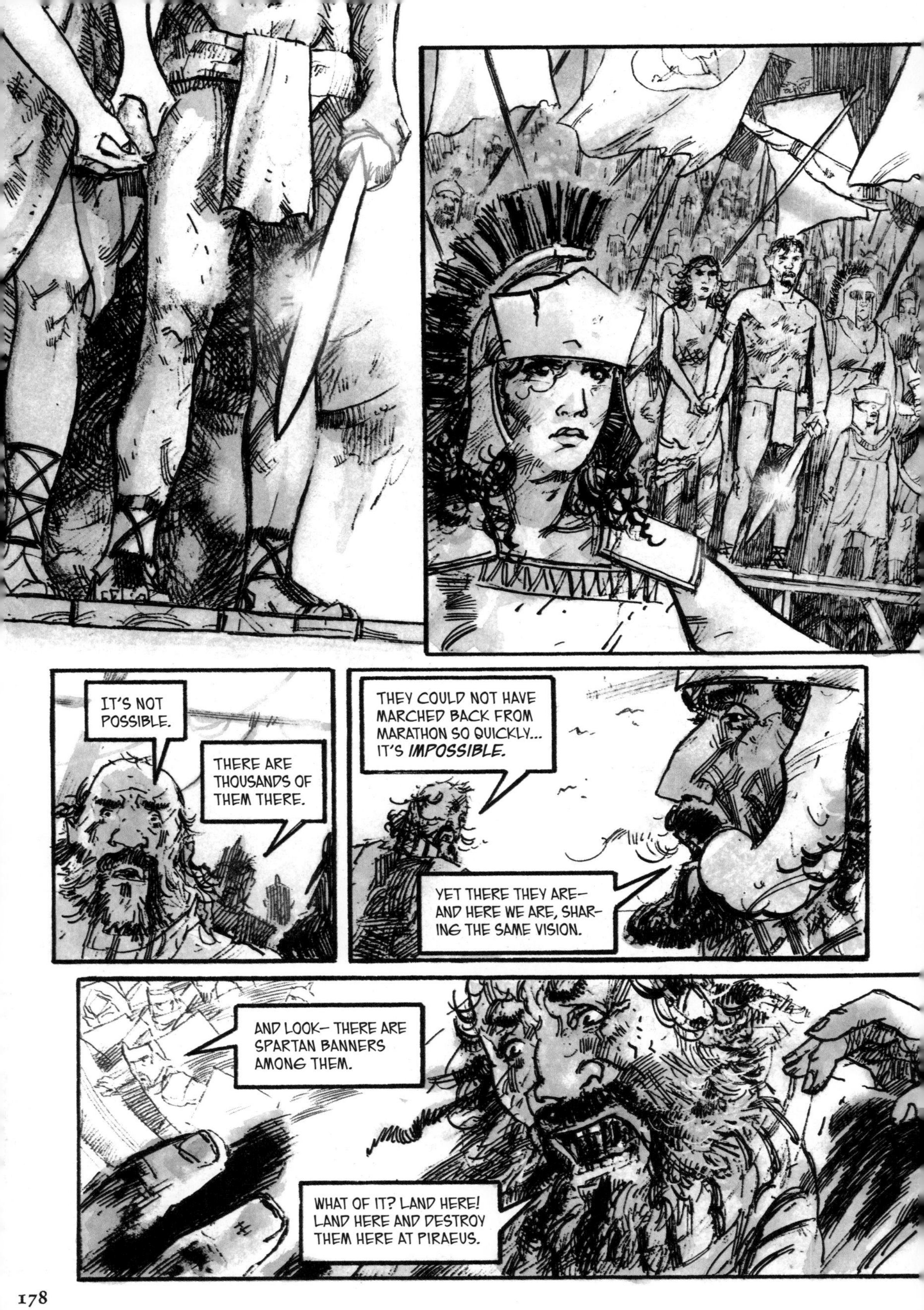
IT'S NOT POSSIBLE.
THERE ARE THOUSANDS OF THEM THERE.
THEY COULD NOT HAVE MARCHED BACK FROM MARATHON SO QUICKLY... IT'S *IMPOSSIBLE.*
YET THERE THEY ARE— AND HERE WE ARE, SHARING THE SAME VISION.
AND LOOK— THERE ARE SPARTAN BANNERS AMONG THEM.
WHAT OF IT? LAND HERE! LAND HERE AND DESTROY THEM HERE AT PIRAEUS.

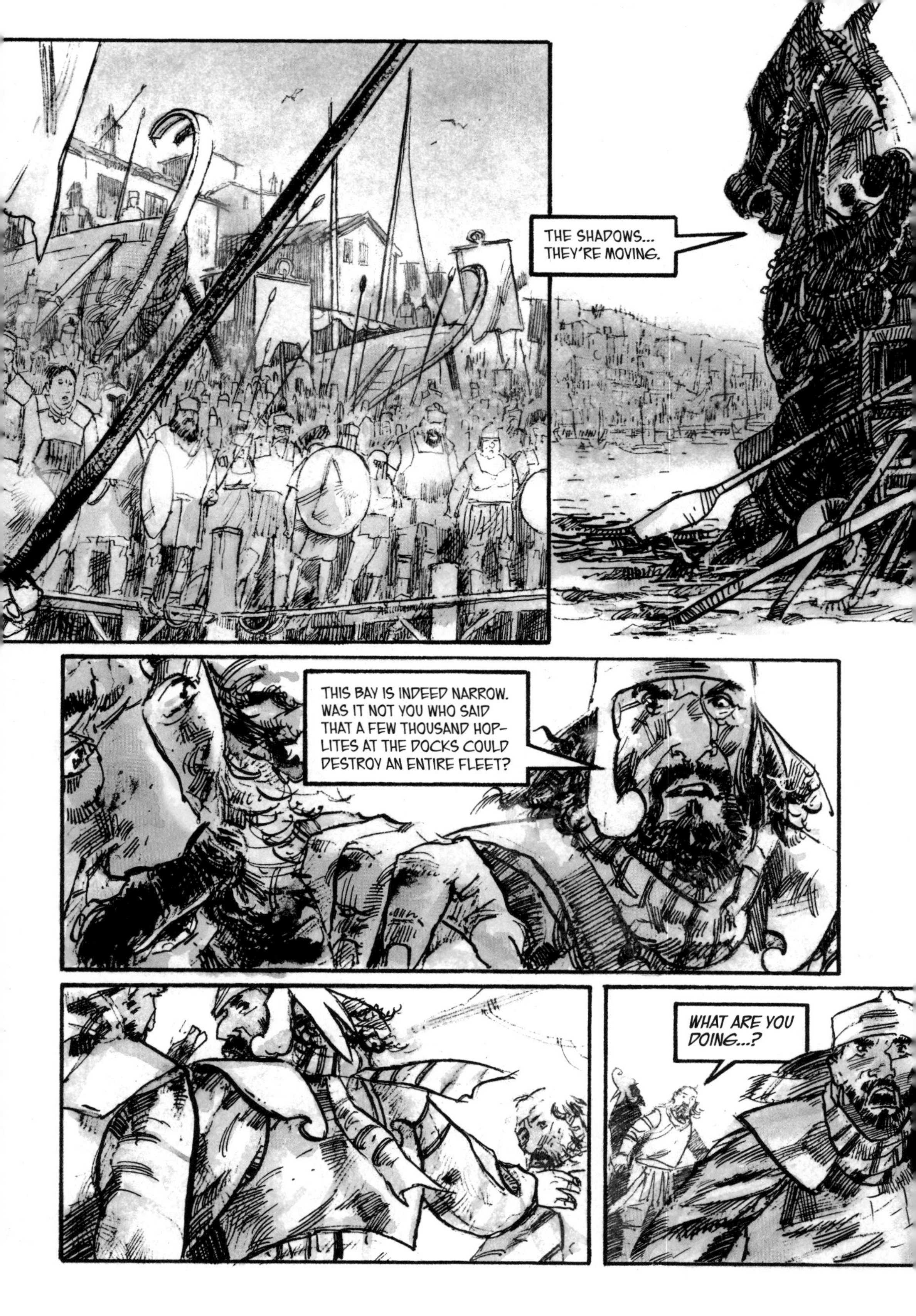
THE SHADOWS... THEY'RE MOVING.
THIS BAY IS INDEED NARROW. WAS IT NOT YOU WHO SAID THAT A FEW THOUSAND HOP-LITES AT THE DOCKS COULD DESTROY AN ENTIRE FLEET?
WHAT ARE YOU DOING...?

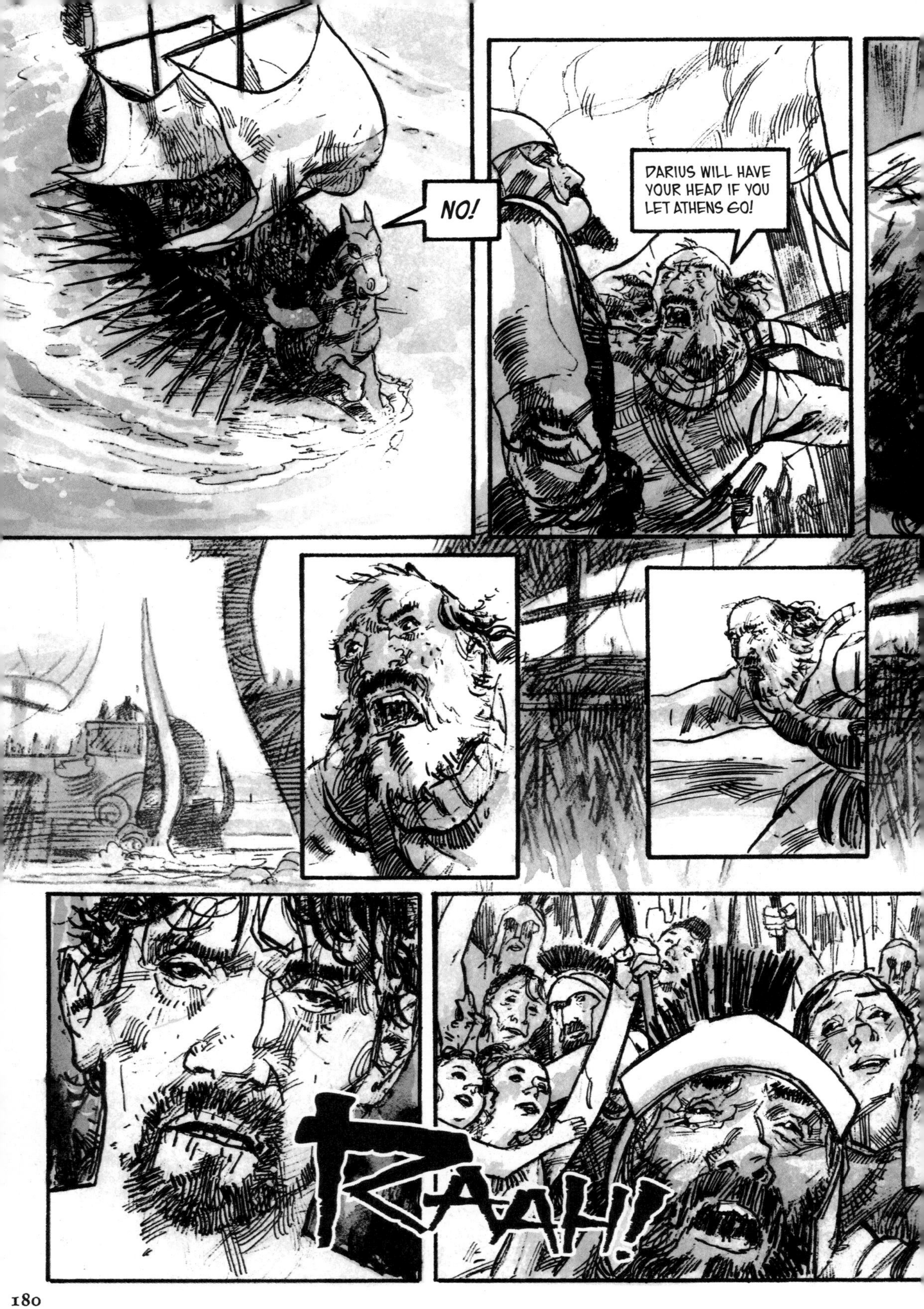
NO!
DARIUS WILL HAVE YOUR HEAD IF YOU LET ATHENS GO!
RAAAH!

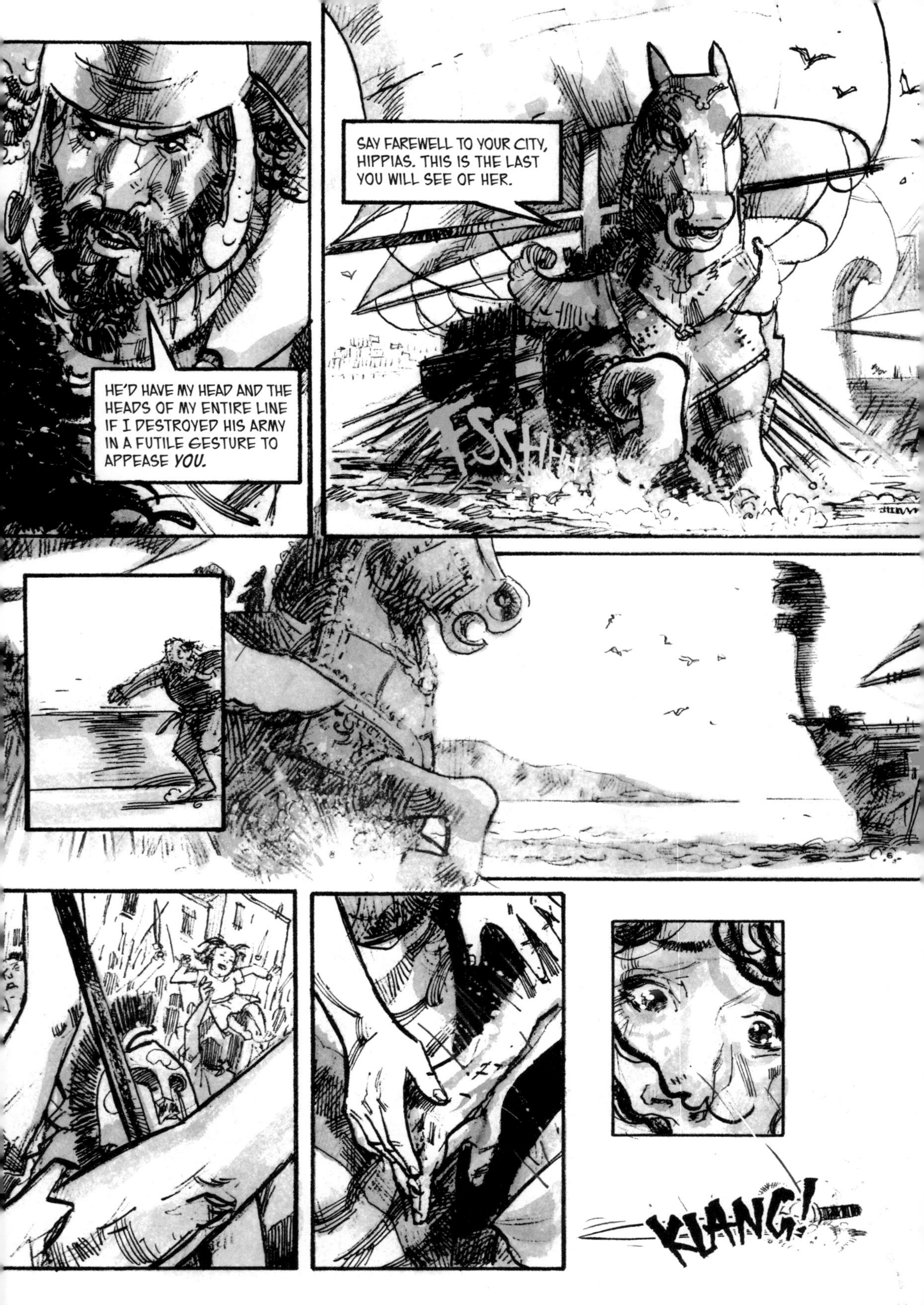
HE'D HAVE MY HEAD AND THE HEADS OF MY ENTIRE LINE IF I DESTROYED HIS ARMY IN A FUTILE GESTURE TO APPEASE *YOU.*
SAY FAREWELL TO YOUR CITY, HIPPIAS. THIS IS THE LAST YOU WILL SEE OF HER.
FSSHHH
KLANG!

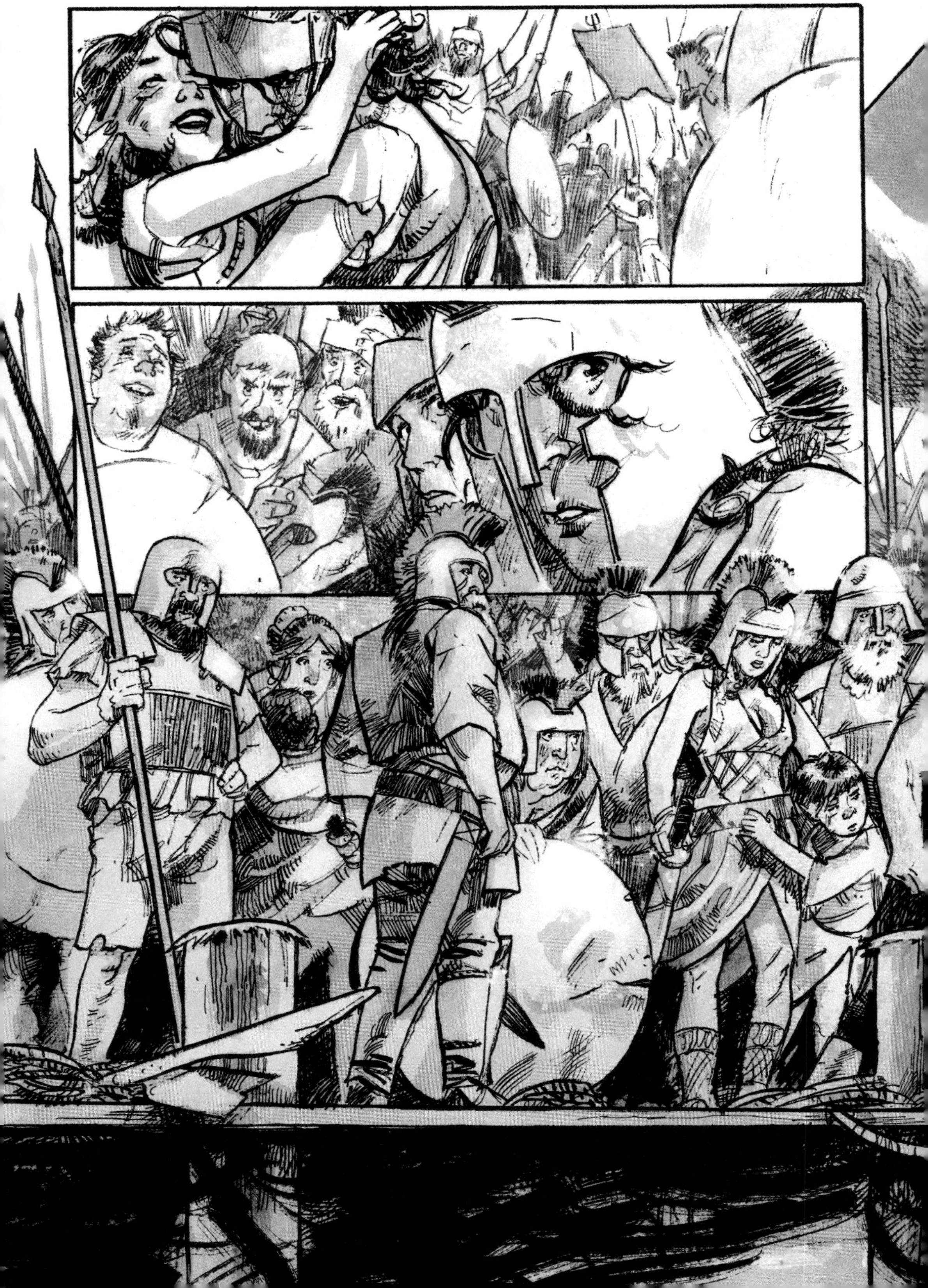

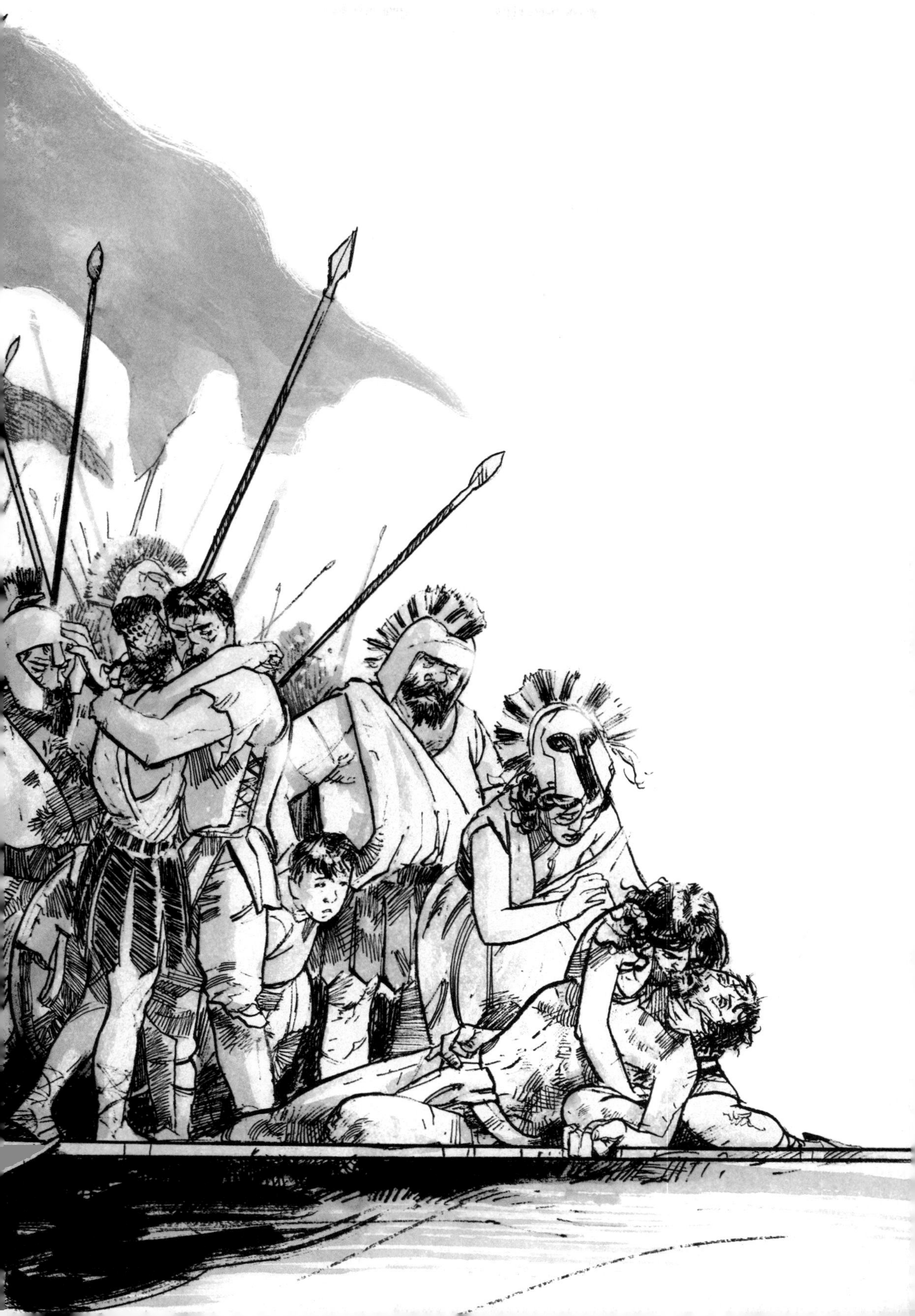

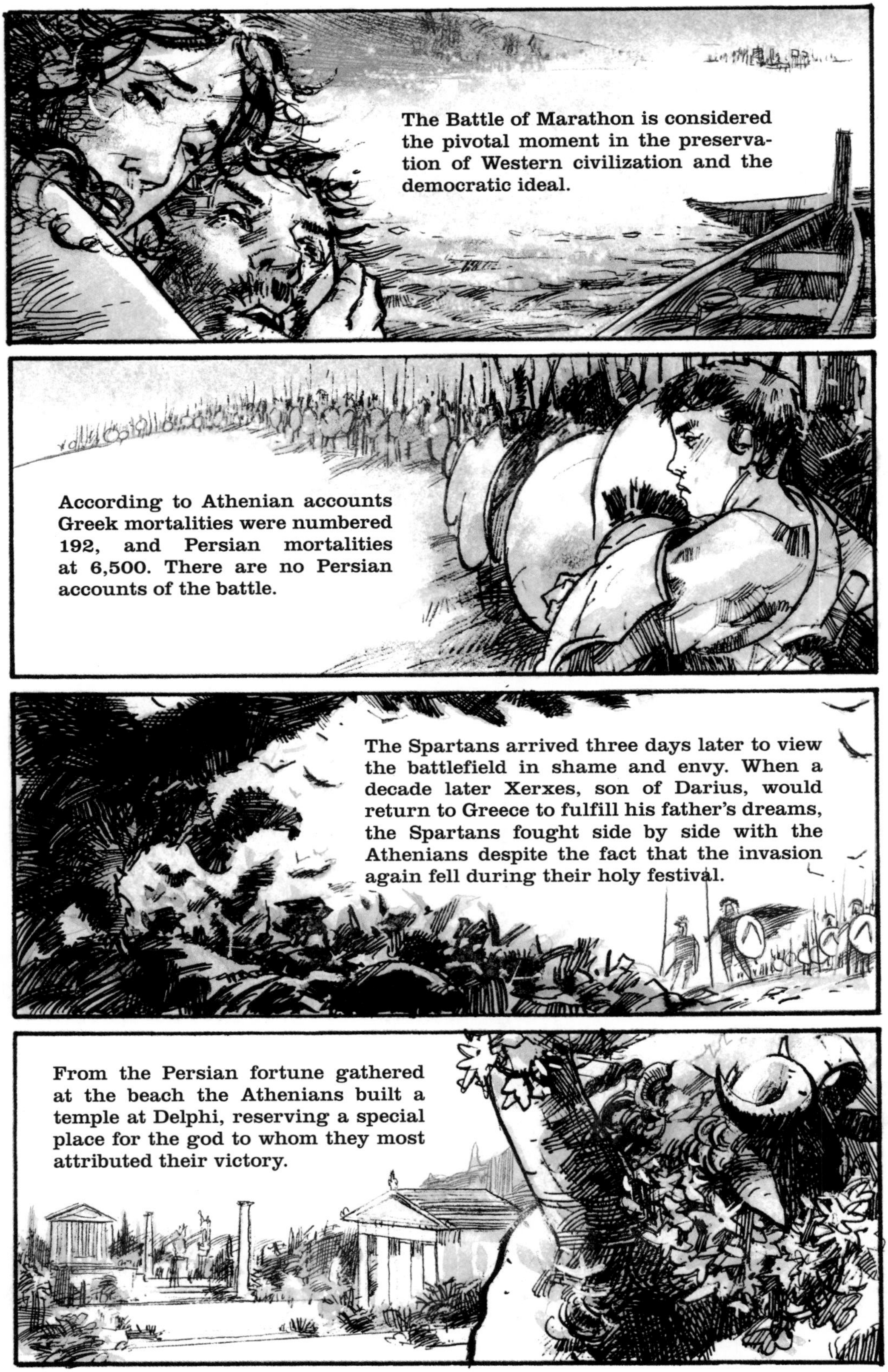
The Battle of Marathon is considered the pivotal moment in the preservation of Western civilization and the democratic ideal.
According to Athenian accounts Greek mortalities were numbered 192, and Persian mortalities at 6,500. There are no Persian accounts of the battle.
The Spartans arrived three days later to view the battlefield in shame and envy. When a decade later Xerxes, son of Darius, would return to Greece to fulfill his father's dreams, the Spartans fought side by side with the Athenians despite the fact that the invasion again fell during their holy festival.
From the Persian fortune gathered at the beach the Athenians built a temple at Delphi, reserving a special place for the god to whom they most attributed their victory.

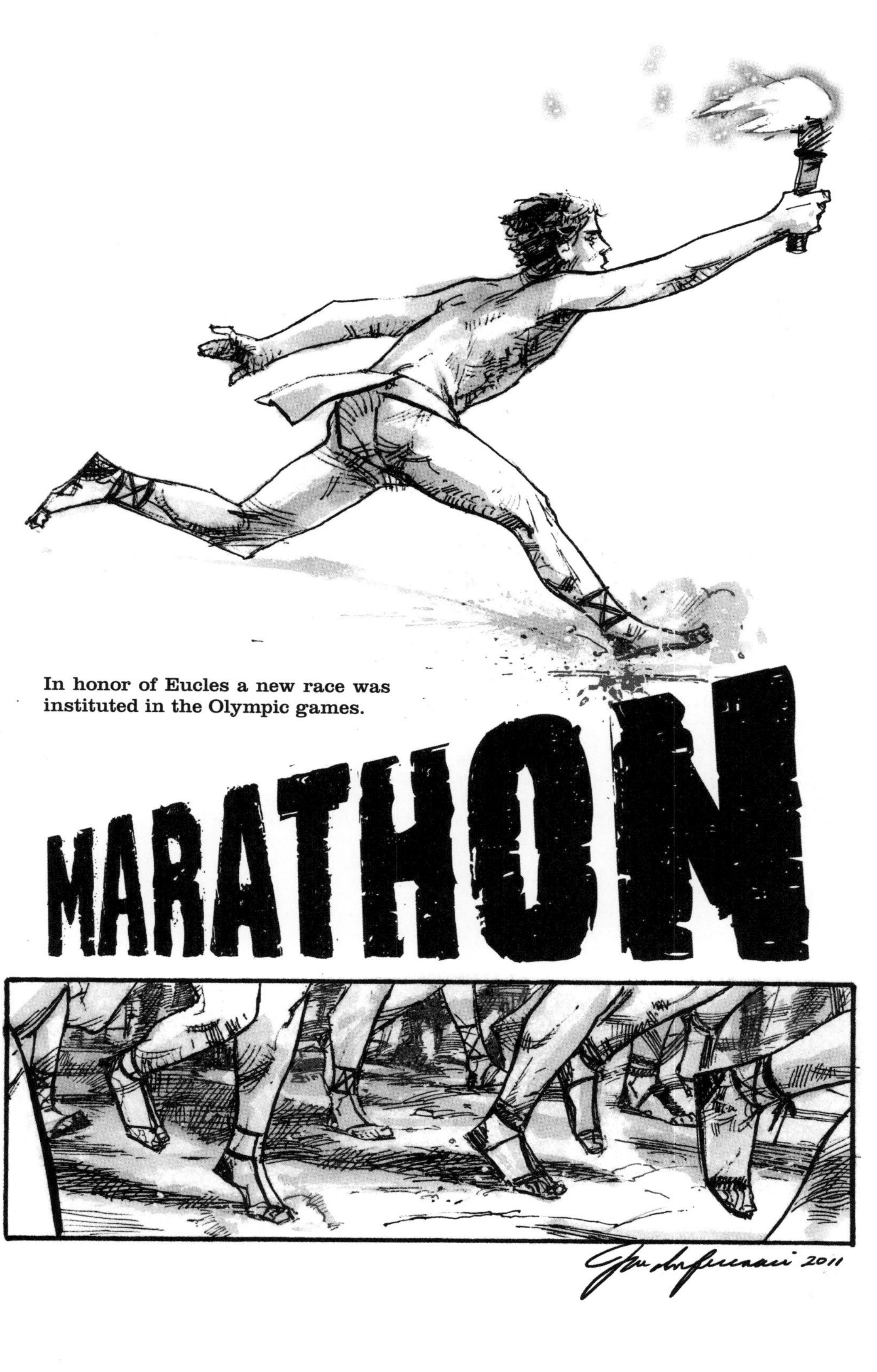
In honor of Eucles a new race was instituted in the Olympic games.
MARATHON
2011

:01

First Second

Text copyright © 2012 by Boaz Yakin
Illustrations copyright © 2012 by Joe Infurnari
Published by First Second
First Second is an imprint of Roaring Brook Press,
a division of Holtzbrinck Publishing Holdings Limited Partnership
175 Fifth Avenue, New York, New York 10010

Distributed in the United Kingdom by
Macmillan Children's Books, a division of Pan Macmillan.

Library of Congress Cataloging-in-Publication Data

Yakin, Boaz.
  Marathon / by Boaz Yakin ; [illustrations by Joe Infurnari].—1st ed.
    p. cm.
  Summary: In graphic novel form, tells the story of Eucles, the Athenian
messenger who, in 490 B.C., ran over 300 miles from Sparta to Athens,
preventing the fall of Greece to the Persian Empire.
  ISBN 978-1-59643-680-0
  1. Greece—History—Persian Wars, 500–449 B.C.—Juvenile fiction. 2.
Graphic novels. [1. Graphic novels. 2. Greece—History—Persian Wars,
500–449 B.C.—Fiction.] I. Infurnari, Joe, ill. II. Title.
  PZ7.7.Y934Mar 2012
  741.5'973–dc23

                                        2011030472

First Second books are available for special
promotions and premiums.
For details, contact: Director of Special Markets,
Holtzbrinck Publishers.

First edition 2012
Book design by Colleen AF Venable
Printed in China

10 9 8 7 6 5 4 3 2